S

The Showman of Vanity Fair

BY LIONEL STEVENSON

1902'
1973

THE SHOWMAN OF
VANITY
FAIR

THE LIFE OF

William Makepeace Thackeray

1947

CHARLES SCRIBNER'S SONS · NEW YORK

ACKNOWLEDGEMENTS

THE ILLUSTRATIONS, from sketches by Thackeray, are reproduced by the kind permission of his granddaughter, Mrs Richard Fuller.

The drawings on pages 159, 171, 172, 187, 215, 217, 224, 238, 275 and 279 appeared in the *Letters of Thackeray to Mrs Jane Octavia Brookfield and Her Husband*, published in Scribner's Magazine in 1887. Those on pages 30, 31, 43, 57, 58, 59, 63, 68, 77, 87, 147, 151, 164, 165, 171, 172, 187, 190, 223, 224, 281, 344, 345 and 383 appeared in the Kensington edition of Thackeray's works published by Charles Scribner's Sons in 1903.

The drawings on pages 32, 35, 37, 38, 47, 53, 55, 61, 103, 107, 119, 127, 130, 154, 195, 205, 327 and 355 appeared as a part of Mrs Ritchie's Introductions to the Biographical edition of Thackeray published by Harper and Brothers.

In 1875 Chatto and Windus, London, England, published a book of notes and anecdotes entitled *Thackerayana* and the drawings appearing on pages 11, 17, 41, 50, 57, 61, 211 and 258 of this book appeared in that volume.

The drawings on pages 291 and 337 were made by Thackeray for the Honorable Gerald Ponsonby.

CONTENTS

The Showman of Vanity Fair

CHAPTER 1

The Waif from India

AS THE LOFTY East-Indiaman drew away into the river, the two women standing on the *ghaut* gazed until they could no longer distinguish the couple of little boys at the rail, and then turned, blind with tears, to climb the steps that led back to the throngs and smells of Calcutta.

During the year and a half since the death of her husband, Anne Thackeray had known well enough that the inexorable code of the Anglo-Indian official caste must soon separate her from her only child. Both health and education would be ruined if a boy was not sent Home as soon as he could travel. She clung to William as long as she possibly could; but by the time he was nearing the end of his sixth year his cousin Richmond Shakespear, ten months younger, was also old enough for the journey. There was nothing for Mrs Thackeray and her sister-in-law to do but choose a trustworthy native servant to accompany their sons, and confide them to the supervision of Mr James McNab, a good-natured civilian who was homeward bound.

It was a world of generous aunts and uncles, merry cousins, and kindly dark-skinned attendants that the children were leaving behind. The birthday parties for "Billy Boy" had always been glorious foregatherings of Thackerays, Shakespears, and Bechers, all notable clans in the service of John Company. The first William Makepeace Thackeray, sixteenth child of a headmaster of Harrow and descendant of an ancient line of Yorkshire yeomen, had entered the service in the seventeen-sixties. He became a mighty hunter of tigers and elephants and an equally mighty accumulator of wealth. Two of his sisters joined him in Bengal and married there. He himself married Amelia Richmond Webb, of a family which had been distinguished in the army for generations and which proudly claimed descent from a shadowy "Roaldus de Richmond" in the days of the Norman Conquest.

Thackeray won such rapid promotion under Warren Hastings that he was able to retire in less than ten years. Six of his sons later returned to India, in civil service, army, and bar, and three of the daughters married men in the same callings. A potent interlocking dynasty was thus created.

The second of the sons, Richmond Thackeray, having distinguished himself in Arabic and Persian, rose rapidly to the rank of Secretary to the Bengal Board of Revenue, at the same time becoming popular in Calcutta society for his artistic and musical talents. In the expansive habit of the time and place he acquired a native mistress, who presented him with a dusky daughter.

3

Shortly after he received his Revenue Board appointment, a lovely girl of sixteen arrived from England and captivated the young gentlemen of Calcutta. Anne Becher's forbears had held high office under Hastings and Clive, but her childhood in India had been shadowed by scandal. When she was still an infant, her mother had deserted a civil-service husband in favor of an artillery officer, Colonel Butler, marrying him after her husband's death seven years later. At this time the little girl was sent to be brought up by her paternal grandmother in a quiet Hampshire village.

When she was fifteen Anne Becher was allowed to attend an Assembly Ball in Bath. One of her partners was a young Scotsman named Henry Carmichael-Smyth, an Ensign in the Bengal Engineers, with a ten-year record of battles and bravery in Indian campaigns. They promptly fell in love, and he followed her home for secret trysts in her grandmother's garden. When the severe old lady discovered the affair, and learned that the Ensign was a penniless younger son, she locked the girl in her room and ordered all communication to cease. Secret letters were smuggled back and forth for a while, but soon Anne ceased to receive replies; and she was then told that her lover had died of fever. In the hope that she might forget her grief, and make a more worthy match, she was shipped out to her relations in India.

Richmond Thackeray being the most eligible of her suitors, she married him after a couple of seasons as a reigning belle of Calcutta. On July 18, 1811, a son was born to them and was given the name of his grandfather. A few months later Richmond Thackeray was promoted to the desirable post of "Collector of the Twenty-four Parganas" with a handsome official residence at Alipur, just outside the city.

Among the guests that he brought home to dinner one evening was a newly-arrived Captain of Engineers whom he had met at his club, and who proved to be the long-mourned Carmichael-Smyth. As soon as they could exchange a few words in private, Mrs Thackeray learned that all his letters to her had been returned to him unopened, with a message from her grandmother that his sweetheart had repudiated him.

They both decided that it would be only honest to tell Richmond Thackeray the story; and for the remaining three years of his life there was a certain constraint in the affection that he still bestowed upon his Anne. In September, 1815, he died of fever, not yet thirty-four.

Beautiful and emotional, the young widow lavished devotion upon her son; but he spent most of his time with his *ayah*, from whom he learned a smattering of Hindustani. His mother never forgot a moment when as a tiny child, gazing at the evening star that glowed beside a crescent moon in the rich Indian twilight, he burst out with "Ecco!"—his approximation of a native exclamation meaning "Look!"

Conscious memories surviving from the first five years of life are seldom numerous or distinct. Nevertheless any violent readjustment at that age is likely to leave profound effects. Although little William Makepeace Thackeray carried away from India only a vague impression of happiness and maternal caresses and crocodiles floating on the Ganges, the necessity of facing life with sudden self-reliance, of depending on strangers for guidance and care, snapped some deeply buried strand of security, some hidden spring of confidence.

The months of the voyage to England were broken by the usual calls at the Cape and St Helena. During the latter, the native servant took Billy Boy for a long walk over the rocky hills to look into a garden where a paunchy white-faced little figure was pacing gloomily. "There he is," the man whispered; "that's Bonaparte! He eats three sheep every day, and all the children he can lay hands on!"

On arrival in England, the boy's chief task was to sort out the identity of innumerable relations that he had never seen before. The first to receive him was his father's sister Charlotte, recently married to a Scots-American business-man named John Ritchie. She proved to be very satisfactory: tall (like all the Thackerays), sweet-faced, indolent, affectionate, and quick to laughter.

From stories and pictures, Billy had formed lively expectations of the marvels of London. He made his faithful Indian take him to peep through the railings at Carlton House, and though there was nothing to stare at but the sentries, he was breathless at having seen the abode of the Prince Regent. Another thrilling moment came when he was driving through the streets with his aunt, and caught sight of a vast dome soaring above the housetops. "That's St Paul's!" he shouted triumphantly.

Mrs Ritchie marveled at his intelligence, but worried about his health. The slimness of his little body was emphasized by an enormous head. When he borrowed her husband's hat for a "dressing-up" game she was horrified to observe that it fitted him perfectly. In a flutter she whisked him off to be examined by Sir Charles Clarke. "Don't be alarmed, ma'am," was the famous physician's verdict. "He *has* a large head, but there's a great deal in it."

A whole tribe of relations was established at Hadley, near Barnet. Here his grandfather had settled after retiring from India; the old nabob had died in 1813, but his brother-in-law, Peter Moore, was Lord of the Manor, and had been appointed guardian to the fatherless grand-nephew. Mr Moore had been a friend of Sheridan and an ally of Burke in the impeachment of Warren Hastings, had promoted the Highgate Tunnel and the installation of gas-lighting, had sat with Byron on the Drury Lane Theater commission, and was later celebrated as the last gentleman in London society to wear a queue. The great man was too busy with board-meetings and parliamentary duties to take active charge of his ward, and so Billy was entrusted to a household that was to become his English home—that of his mother's grandmother at Fareham, in Hampshire.

In Fareham he stepped straight back into the eighteenth century. The little town seemed to be inhabited entirely by the widows and spinster daughters of naval officers. One of the few male residents had been at sea with Captain Cook. Its society was conducted by such precise rituals as have been chronicled by Jane Austen. Dinner was at three or four in the afternoon; home-made wine accompanied the dessert; at six, little groups of the ladies gathered at one another's houses for tea, followed by whist or quadrille; and after a ten-o'clock supper the maid servants appeared with shawls, clogs, and lanterns to escort their mistresses home. There were even a few sedan chairs for use in rainy weather. After each party the dainty old ladies would wash and polish their dainty old china tea-sets, never trusting them to the mercies of Hampshire maids.

On the walls of every house of accepted status hung portraits of gentlemen in uniform, interspersed with scenes of shipwreck and naval battles. Books were not considered suitable appurtenances for ladies' homes, but a few of the more enlightened households would club together to subscribe to a Portsmouth newspaper. Those faint echoes of the great world, however, could not compete with the gossip and rivalries of Fareham.

In this microcosm Mrs Becher was a person of prestige. At the age of eighty she was still lovely, though somewhat formidable, with a high puff of snow-white hair under her cap, black lace mittens and tiny high-heeled slippers of black velvet. She walked with a long tortoiseshell-handled cane, and wielded her snuff-box and gold tooth-pick with consummate grace. On the upbringing of children she held positive views, asserting that butter on their bread on week-days was "a pernicious luxury." She always punctiliously addressed her spinster daughter, who greatly resembled her, as "Miss Becher"; and this daughter, who had brought up her niece Nancy—teaching her at a tender age to play whist so that she could help to make up a nightly foursome—was now ready to bring up Nancy's son.

Their ancient house, in the sleepy High Street, had a steep roof, a narrow porch, a great blue china jar of pot-pourri in the corner of the staircase, and the usual array of naval and military portraits in the low-pitched parlor. Here little William entertained the old ladies with chatter about his life in India, copiously illustrated with drawings. One of them depicted his mother's house in Calcutta. "That's my pet monkey looking out of the window," he explained, "and black Betty at the top drying her towels. And there's the big room where so many people came to my birthday party." Without his comments the details might not have been recognizable, but his great-aunt was delighted with his talent, none the less.

At the time of his voyage to England he was aware that his mother intended to marry Captain Carmichael-Smyth, but the idea gave him no distress, for the tall, quiet officer had been among the kindest of his adult playmates. Shortly after his arrival, and a fortnight before his sixth birthday, his first laboriously-written letter to his mother included his love to Captain Smyth, with an added request that "he must bring you home to your affectionate little Son." The letter was adorned with a drawing of a tall gentleman on a tired-looking horse.

The affection of his English relations could not preserve him from homesickness. When his new stepfather's brother arrived from India on leave and came to inspect him, the boy was in wild spirits all day, but at bed time he broke down and cried his heart out.

"What's the matter?" asked the maid who was putting him to bed.

"I can't help it," sobbed Billy. "To see somebody that has so lately seen my dear mama and to see her picture and the dear purse she made for me!"

By this time his education had begun. The little school at the Polygon in Southampton to which he and Richmond Shakespear were consigned had been highly recommended to their parents, but for the two children the first night was a sad enlightenment. "Hard beds, hard words, strange boys bullying, and laughing, and jarring you with their hateful merriment"—these were the recollections that remained with William till the end of his life; and before long there were other abominations: "cold, chillblains, bad dinners, not enough victuals, and caning awful." The school was governed by a "horrible little tyrant" and the ideas of discipline were fantastic. One night all the small boys were aroused long after they had gone to sleep, and each was ordered to go out alone to a shed in the back garden and put his hand into a sack that he would find on a bench. Bewildered and half asleep, Thackeray stumbled out through the blackness and obeyed the instructions by the light of a flickering candle that stood beside the sack. When they all gathered in a shivering flock in the school room, each boy found his hand black with soot. After an inspection, the master sent them back to bed without a word. Later it turned out that something was missing and he was practising a theory he had picked up, that if any boy was guilty of theft he would be afraid to put his hand into the sack. Before long, William Thackeray's nightly supplication at his bedside became, "Pray God I may dream of my mother."

Fortunately Fareham was near enough for frequent visits. Old friends of his mother invited him to their homes, and with his cousin he sometimes dined with neighboring Shakespears. And in spite of hardships he made progress in his studies; three months before his seventh birthday he reported to his mother that he had been learning geography for a long while, and was beginning Latin and cyphering.

Illness later brought him escape from school, and he spent a joyous summer at Fareham, playing in the garden full of gooseberries and raspberries that sloped down to the river. His letters by this time were much more fluent: he told his

"dearest of all mamas" about the birds' nests, and his "Neptune days" when he
went bathing, and his grandmama's gooseberry pies. He was learning the "Ode to
Music" and other poems that had been his mother's favorites. He was now "a
great boy," he reported, three feet eleven and a quarter inches tall, and "strong,
saucy, and hearty." His mother's old friends pampered him with "a great many
cakes and a great many kisses," but in view of his new dignity he was not accepting
kisses from masculine relations. And from his grandmama, he added dryly, he
didn't receive many.

The greatest happiness of the summer, however, came from the decision that
he was not to be sent back to the untender mercies of Mr Arthur. Instead, he was
to be placed in a school at Chiswick, kept by Dr Turner, whose wife was an aunt
of Thackeray's mother. A special feature of the school was the Speech Day at the
end of each term; Billy Thackeray was taken up to London to hear the oratory,
and was duly inspired with ambition to become "one of those heroes."

The school was in stately old Walpole House, with a great iron gate opening
upon Chiswick Mall. Dr Turner was a tremendous personage, who read Scripture
at the school services so impressively that his wife was reminded of Mount Sinai
itself. Little Thackeray, during his first term, was not much happier than at
Southampton; once at least he reached the point of running away, and got as far
as the Hammersmith Road, but the traffic there was so terrifying that he scurried
back to the school, where his absence had not been noticed.

When he was in his ninth year his dreams came true, the reiterated request at
the end of his letters was answered—his mother came home. He was brought over
to Chatham to greet her the morning after the ship docked. Too deeply moved to
speak, he kissed her again and again and gazed at her as if he were never going to
turn to any other object. Although his eyes had grown darker, they still had the
gentle expression that she loved. He was beginning to look remarkably like his
father. As she was a deeply religious woman, her thanksgiving shaped itself in her
mind in Biblical phrase: "Lord, now lettest Thou Thy servant depart in peace."

His educational progress was equally gratifying. He stood sixth in the school,
though only four of the twenty-six boys were younger than he. During the months
that followed, the only fault that his mother could find in him was his disregard
for money; a tip of a whole guinea would disappear immediately into presents for
his friends. Under her encouragement he promised to "fag hard" in the hope of
carrying off a medal at the end of the summer term.

Quaint phrases embellished his conversation. Listening to a discussion about
some eccentric character, he remarked, "He must be a noun substantive."

"Why, my dear?" asked his mother.

"Because he stands by himself."

Still obsessed with his interest in the Prince Regent, he gave her a lively description of visiting the Royal Yacht in Southampton Water, and seeing "the bed on which His Royal Highness breathes his royal snore."

His drawings were wonderful. He was busy just then with painting the scenes of a toy theater for a young friend; and his school books and exercises were covered with soldiers and brigands, knights in armor, dragons, devils, postilions with jackets cut out of red wafers and top-boots drawn in black ink. All these romantic figures were supplied henceforth to his imagination by the books that he suddenly began to devour; during that summer he read his first novel, *The Scottish Chiefs*, lying in the summer-house at Fareham and listening to the church bells pealing for the coronation of George IV. Much though the story fascinated him, he could not read quite to the end; furtive peeps into the last pages had disclosed the death of Wallace, and as Thackeray approached that tragic scene he was too much blinded by tears to read further. From that hour he was a slave to the enchantment of fiction.

His mother attended his final Speech Day, wondering whether she would break down as she listened to "her little hero" recite Hannibal's address to his soldiers. In January of 1822 he began his residence at Charterhouse.

The famous old school in Smithfield had become very popular in those years with Anglo-Indians and others of moderate means, as the Head, Dr Russell, had lowered the fees by introducing the "Bell" or "Madras" system, which consisted in reducing the staff and putting both discipline and instruction largely in the hands of the elder boys. The school soon became seriously overcrowded, reaching a maximum of 480 boys with only eight masters; and the general result was remembered by some of the victims as "partial chaos."

Dr Russell's usual demeanor being ferocious, Thackeray's first interview was far from reassuring. "Take that boy and his box to the matron," the doctor thundered to the porter; "and make my compliments to the junior master and tell him the boy knows nothing and will just do for the lowest form."

Thackeray was assigned to board with one of the masters, the Rev Edward Penny, in Wilderness Row, Clerkenwell, where fifty boys were crammed into the house and ran back and forth to the school by a tunnel under the street. During his first winter, it was a daily ordeal for the pretty, sensitive lad to wash with the forty-nine others in a leaden trough, under a cistern, with lumps of greasy yellow soap floating about in the ice and water.

One of Russell's reforms had been the abolition of fagging, but this had merely diverted brutality into other channels. The boys recognized Thackeray as a preordained victim for bullying, not only by his gentle manners but also by his inefficiency in games, for he was extremely short sighted, and it was a handicap in hockey or cricket to be unable to see the ball.

Fights were permitted, if conducted under the supervision of the monitor of the week. One wet half-holiday afternoon a crowd of boys engineered a fight in the long-room at Penny's, between Thackeray and another urchin named George Venables. One wild blow chanced to land squarely on Thackeray's nose, which bled so profusely that the fight came to an abrupt end, and the nose was found to have been broken. The fracture was patched up, and all might have been well if a notorious bully had not struck him soon afterwards and flattened the nose beyond all hope of repair. A portrait bust of Thackeray, cast shortly before his eleventh birthday by a French sculptor named Deville, displayed the full disfigurement of the foreshortened nose, as well as the boy's spacious forehead and the comical curves that lurked around his mouth.

A year after his entrance, Thackeray had risen one form above the ignoble tenth. He vowed to his mother that he would not spend a five shilling tip she had given him unless he was promoted to the eighth. By the spring he reached the seventh. Although he advanced through the school at a good average pace, he showed little energy, and no enthusiasm for scholarship. Partly, no doubt, this was due to natural indolence; but another of his most deeply ingrained traits was pride of blood, and his aristocratic fastidiousness was outraged by the manners and methods of the masters that Dr Russell's parsimony had enlisted. In later life his recollection of them was expressed in a furious outburst: "When I saw a brute of a schoolmaster, whose mind was as coarse-grained as any ploughboy's in Christendom; whose manners were those of the most insufferable of Heaven's creatures, the English snob trying to turn gentleman; whose lips, when they were not mouthing Greek or Grammar, were yelling out the most brutal abuse of poor little cowering gentlemen standing before him: when I saw this kind of man and heard him roar out praises, and pump himself into enthusiasm for, certain Greek poetry,—I had my doubts about the genuineness of the article. . . . Fancy the brutality of a man who began a Greek grammar with 'τύπτω, I thrash'! We were all made to begin it in that way."

Nor was the conjugation an empty threat. Not a day passed that a batch of boys were not led up to the block, while an attendant stood by with a bundle of birches from which the headmaster chose his weapon; and the victims would compare notes afterwards with scientific minuteness and visual evidence.

Little wonder, then, that Thackeray's scholastic ambitions soon evaporated. "The only prize I ever remember to have got," he later declared, "was in a kind of lottery in which I was obliged to subscribe with seventeen other competitors—and of which the prize was a flogging. That I won. But I don't think I carried off any other."

He spent some of his spare time in writing letters to his mother—not to complain of his treatment, but to escape imaginatively from his surroundings. His stepfather, who had retired with the rank of Major, was for two years Governor of the East India Company's Military College at Addiscombe. As vacation drew near, time seemed to move more and more sluggishly, while young Thackeray checked off the calendar, "five weeks from the holidays . . . four weeks from the holidays . . ." until at last the rapturous day arrived.

Not that his school days were unadulterated misery. His indolent good-humor was winning friends for him, in spite of his aversion to all forms of exercise. A few older boys with literary tastes, such as Martin Tupper and John Murray (son of the publisher), began to take an interest in him. The fight with George Venables had been the prelude to a devoted friendship, and other congenial boys of his own age included Henry George Liddell, a prodigy in the classical languages, and a merry, talkative lad named Joseph Carne. On half-holidays he often went to the mellow house of his step-father's father, a prosperous old physician near Russell Square, who thrilled him by recounting personal recollections of Garrick and allowing him to sit in a chair that had been sat in by Edmund Burke. Other relations also asked him to their houses and fortified him with good dinners. His pockets were full of the miscellaneous rubbish dear to a twelve-year-old heart, including (for a

OUTSIDE CHARTERHOUSE GATES: BEADLE AND STREET URCHIN

short time) a brass-barreled pocket pistol with which he shot a button off a friend's jacket. He could find complete happiness in cramming himself with penny tarts at the pastry-cook's, often spending a whole half-crown tip on them (with the accompanying ginger beer). And at Christmas there was sure to be the supreme delight of a Pantomime. No ecstasy could possibly equal that of the moment when amid brassy orchestration the curtain rose upon a spangled chorus or a gaudily oriental panorama.

During school hours, though scarcely consciously, he was absorbing the beauty and antique dignity of the Charterhouse itself. In Chapel he was chiefly aware of the Doctor's awful eye fixed on the rows of quaking boys; the boy next to Thackeray would kick his shins during service, and the monitor would cane Thackeray afterwards for making a disturbance; and yet his mind was storing up pictures of the Founder's Tomb, with the lights and shadows bringing out its grotesque carvings, and the outstretched figure of Thomas Sutton in gown and ruff.

His attention would wander to the four-score old gentlemen-pensioners on their side of the chapel—"Codds," the boys called them—coughing feebly in the twilight. Outside the chapel was the Great Hall, with its beautiful Jacobean architecture; and the whole school was full of old staircases, old passages, old portrait-lined chambers, in which the boy felt as if he were walking in the early seventeenth century. Under the great archway he would look at the quaint square with its blackened trees and garden, and the old men creeping along in their black gowns.

The school had literary associations, too, as the place where Addison and Steele started their friendship. Not that Thackeray's delight in reading had yet matured to the point of enjoying the Augustan essayists. His preference was for any novel "without love or talking or any of that nonsense, but containing plenty of fighting, escaping, robbing, and rescuing." He shuddered over *The Mysteries of Udolpho* and *Melmoth the Wanderer*, and never tired of drawing pictures of Thaddeus of Warsaw, in a Polish cap and embroidered tights. Under the spell of these romantic heroes, he contracted a craving for a pair of Hessian boots. At last, when some generous tip brought them within his range, he ordered the most dashing pair he could find; but the authorities sent them back to the shop as unbefitting a schoolboy. The mortification of that moment stayed with him till the end of his life.

The summer of his twelfth birthday was darkened with anxiety over a debt. He had bought on credit, for three-and-sixpence, a silver pencil-case with a movable calendar attached. The contraption was soon broken; and the creditor, a large and violent boy, became nasty. "When are you going to pay me that three-and-sixpence?" he kept demanding. "What sneaks your relations must be! They come to see you. You go to them on Saturdays and Sundays, and they never give you anything! Don't tell *me*, you little humbug."

Unluckily, from May till August not a tip was forthcoming, and to save anything out of his sixpence a week of pocket money proved impossible. A gleam of hope came when he was fetched away from school to take leave of a relation who was going out to India with a good appointment; he incautiously let his creditor know that a tip was in prospect—perhaps a pound . . . why not five pounds? The relation asked him about his progress in school, heard him construe a passage of Eutropius, and dismissed him with a "God bless you." On his return the big boy took one look at his scared face and burst into ferocious threats and curses.

At last the Bartlemy-tide holidays came, and he was off to his parents, who were spending the summer at Tunbridge Wells. Mr Penny handed him his coach fare, five shillings for his incidental expenses, and twenty-five shillings to be refunded to his parents for some overpayment. In jubilant haste he paid the bully his three-and-sixpence.

Next morning he and another boy, far too excited to wait for breakfast, shared a hackney-coach to the "Bolt-in-Tun," Fleet Street, from which the mail would start. As they were an hour too early, the schoolmate marched into the coffee-room and ordered a hearty breakfast; but after the cabman had been paid and the porter tipped, Thackeray's funds were exhausted. The twenty-five shillings in his pocket was his parents' money, and not to be touched.

Unable to bear the sight of his friend tucking away, he wandered down the street and suddenly found himself reading a placard in a shop window: "Coffee, twopence. Round of buttered toast, twopence." He went in and gave his order.

All the way down in the coach, the lingering taste of the toast and coffee seemed to be choking him. When his parents met him with their carriage at the last stage, all his anticipation of their welcome was destroyed by remorse. He pulled out the twenty-four shillings and eightpence with a trembling hand.

"Here's your money," he gasped with a dry throat, "that Mr Penny owes you, all but fourpence. I owed three-and-sixpence out of my money for a pencil case, and I had none left, and I took fourpence of yours, and had some coffee in a shop."

Exalted by confession and forgiveness, he enjoyed that vacation more than he could have believed possible, though he did little except read books from the library in the Pantiles. The most thrilling moments came during a couple of days when his parents had gone to town, and he was left alone with a grim old maid-servant. He sat up late at night in the empty drawing-room and pored over *The Italian, or the Confessional of the Black Penitents*, until he was too frightened to turn round.

Though the bitterness of parting from his mother was as heartfelt as usual, he went back to Charterhouse with some degree of confidence. By virtue of his comical sketches he was acquiring a measure of celebrity among the boys, and the bullies had turned their attention to less placid victims. It was during the next year that he came on a crowd of boys initiating a tiny newcomer whom they had put upon a table and ordered to sing a song. The small boy piped up "Home, Sweet Home" so pluckily that Thackeray decided to make friends with him, in spite of six years' difference in age. He too, it appeared, loved to draw funny caricatures, and his name was John Leech.

During Thackeray's fourteenth year, several important changes affected his life. With a burst of industry he rose as high as the third form, and found himself so improved in strength and spirits that he gave a thrashing to the bully who had completed the ruination of his nose. Better still, he left the promiscuity of "Penny's House" for private lodgings with a Mrs Boyes, who lived in Charterhouse Square and took in lads belonging to both Charterhouse and Merchants Taylors. Although he occasionally quarreled with his domineering landlady, and although as a day-boy he had fewer contacts with the innermost life of the school, he was distinctly happier with the arrangement.

About the same time the guardianship of the squire of Hadley came to an end. Mr Moore, having lent his name to too many speculative enterprises, was obliged to flee to France to escape arrest. Not seeking any legal evasion of his debts, the old gentleman surrendered all his property to his creditors, and for the remaining three years of his life lived abroad in indigence.

Major Carmichael-Smyth, meanwhile, had given up his position at Addiscombe and leased a pleasant country-house at Larkbeare, in the parish of Ottery St Mary, about eleven miles from Exeter. This meant a more strenuous journey for the boy's holidays, particularly in winter—once he arrived so benumbed with cold that he had to be lifted down off the coach—but he looked forward to it with even keener pleasure than before.

When he got off the coach where the by-road to the village of Tallaton branched off the London highway, the family carriage would be waiting for him. An overhanging beech-avenue skirted a lonely, tree-fringed pond before reaching the square-faced house. The rough lawn had beds of stocks and wallflowers, a green door in the wall led to the stable-yard, and beyond was a kitchen-garden with big yellow egg-plums crowding the south wall.

For companionship there was a little orphan cousin from India, Mary Graham. The vicar, Dr Cornish, a scholar and poet who was a friend of John Keble, lent Thackeray books from his library, some of which were returned to him embellished with humorous illustrations. In fact, Thackeray sketched so lavishly that before long every drawer in his bedroom at Larkbeare was stuffed full of drawings.

He now became aware of his mother's striking beauty, and the fascination she exerted upon everyone who met her. Barely nineteen years older than her son, she was tall and graceful, with perfect features and great sweetness of expression. He never forgot an evening at a concert in Exeter, when he grew conscious that all eyes were turned toward her as she entered, splendidly dressed and bearing herself "like a duchess."

At school, as he rose to the dignity of the highest forms, he became conspicuous for his kindliness toward the smaller boys. His indolence and good nature made him substitute rewards for the customary threats and blows. He would say to little "Hooky" Carr, son of the Bishop of Bombay, "Hooky, go and fetch me a vol. of *Ivanhoe* out of my desk, there's a good fellow; in the same drawer you will perhaps find a penny, which you may take for yourself." Sometimes the penny would not be found, and the urchin would feel safe in scolding at Thackeray as "a great snob," evoking only a cheerful smile by his insults.

Scholastically, he finally reached the first form, a promotion that was supposed to depend upon three separate spells of duty as a *prepositus*, each requiring satisfactory teaching of a lower form for six weeks. Another requirement was the memorizing of all the Odes and Epodes of Horace. There is some doubt, however, as to whether Thackeray actually fulfilled these conditions. He may have been promoted abruptly in an effort to conceal ominous gaps in the highest form, for dissatisfaction with Dr Russell's regime had at last spread among the parents, and boys were being withdrawn right and left.

Dr Russell heard the lessons of the highest form himself. According to the later opinion of Venables, the doctor's character, "which was vigorous, unsympathetic, and stern, though not severe," was particularly uncongenial to Thackeray. Russell was addicted to heavy-handed sarcasm. Thackeray had the good luck to sit beside Henry Liddell, who could share in caricaturing the masters and drawing grotesque Shakespearian illustrations during class, and yet find time to help Thackeray with his Latin verses and prompt him when he was called upon to construe. This aid was not sufficient, however, to save him from frequent visitations of Dr Russell's satire. There was some touch of quizzical irony in the boy's expression, and perhaps a hint of contempt, that irritated the autocrat. With burning cheeks, thumping heart, and grimly suppressed tears, Thackeray would sit, after committing some blunder, while the doctor with clumsy witticisms held him up to the scorn of the class. He would have vastly preferred the block and the birch to the maddening torture of those jokes.

Unreformed by all assaults, however, he would pile up Latin and Greek texts on his desk, and then behind their shelter read the Waverley novels, or *Peregrine Pickle*, or preferably Pierce Egan's lively masterpiece, *Life in London, or the Day and Night Scenes of Jerry Hawthorne, Esq., and his Elegant Friend Corinthian Tom.* At times he was caught by a master, who would slip up behind him with a book in each hand, and box his ears with them. But no punishment could cure him of his addiction to *Life in London*, which seemed to him the acme of fashion, brilliance, and sophisticated grace.

Inevitably he tried his hand at authorship, until his parodies and other humorous poems began to rival his drawings in the esteem of his friends. When just fifteen, he had greeted the beginning of the summer vacation with a long *Holyday Song*, full of personal jibes about his classmates, including a quip directed towards his own puppy-love for the sister of his friend Joe Carne. Another early example of his humor was an ingenious parody of Letitia Elizabeth Landon's effusion entitled *Violets*, which he transformed into a paean of *Cabbages*. Best of all, his classmates loved one of his poems that they could recite as a luscious demonstration of Cockney diction:

> In the romantic little town of Highbury
> My father kept a circulatin' library;
> He followed in his youth that man immortal who
> Conquered the Frenchmen on the plains of Waterloo.
> Mama was an inhabitant of Drogheda,
> Very good to darn and to embroider.

In the famous Island of Jamaica
For thirty years I've been a sugar-baker;
And here I sit, the Muses' happy votary,
A-cultivatin' every kind of poetry.

But even the popularity of such compositions as these did not wholly supplant the insistent demands of, "I say, old boy, draw us Vivaldi tortured in the Inquisition," or "Draw us Don Quixote and the windmills," or some scene from the *Arabian Nights*, an inexhaustible source.

In the middle of his seventeenth year he began to look forward to release from bondage, and made a tardy attempt to improve his scholarship in order to be accepted at Cambridge; but the news of his prospective departure produced no mollification in the Head. The school had lost a hundred boys in two years, and each further withdrawal was a personal affront. Russell's sarcasm toward Thackeray changed to reproach and insult. In every letter to his mother, the boy protested the injustices that were heaped upon him, some of which in his tormented imagination became the general talk of the school. Wondering how long he could endure the daily ordeal, he felt that all his attempts to make a respectable showing as a scholar were being deliberately thwarted.

This last term at school, in the spring of 1828, he was second monitor of day-boys, and suddenly acquired much more mature tastes. With some of the other gay blades of the highest form he went as often as possible to the theater. To his dazzled eyes the actresses and ballerinas were beautiful as angels. He fell in love with Mrs Yates in *Paris and London* at the Adelphi. The latest young *prima donna* imported from the Continent was Henrietta Sontag; Thackeray worshiped her in *Otello* and *La Donna del Lago*, and was dizzy with rapture when he was admitted behind the scenes one evening between the acts, and saw her letting down her glorious hair over her lovely shoulders, preparatory to being murdered by Donzelli. He also fell under the spell of the tragic actor, Charles Mayne Young, and entertained his friends by rolling out Shakespearian passages in a fairly good imitation of Young's resonant tones.

The boys were even inspired to stage a play at the school for themselves, and selected *Bombastes Furioso*. As Thackeray was now on dignified visiting terms with the family of his old prep-school master in Chiswick, he borrowed a barrister's wig from Dr Turner, who had once been a lawyer. After the play the wig could not be found, and a long time elapsed before the embarrassed lad ventured to pay another visit to his old friends.

His literary taste was also developing beyond the level of Gothic romances. A group of the senior boys subscribed to the best literary magazines—*Blackwood*, the *London*, the *Literary Gazette*—and they would gravely discuss their opinions of the essays in each number. One of the circle was a son of Sir John Stoddard,

Hazlitt's brother-in-law, and could tell intimate anecdotes of Coleridge, Words-worth, Hazlitt, and Lamb, who were his father's friends. Through these channels Thackeray began to acquire a knowledge of contemporary literature.

As a natural consequence he helped to plan a periodical, to be called *The Carthusian*, but was not sorry when his friends dropped the notion as soon as the novelty had worn off. Debating was another popular activity, under the instigation of Joseph Carne, who was supple in oratory. The topics were apt to be portentous; one was "the expediency of a standing army," and the day before the debate Thackeray admitted that the boys had not yet decided which sides they would take.

In his new-found devotion to study, he did not read a single novel during the term except one by Thomas Henry Lister, an early exponent of the "silver-fork" school of fiction. He also took a heroic resolution for the coming summer at home "to get up at five o'clock every morning and to get four hours' sweat before breakfast." But nothing availed to protect him from Dr Russell's persecution, which ran as a *leitmotif* through his letters home. It was no longer with him a matter of counting the weeks till the holidays; now every day was important as one more link taken from his chain.

Illness released him a few weeks early on April 16. As he passed through the great archway he could scarcely believe that he would never have to re-enter it unless he chose. At the moment he felt that he never wished to see the dreary place again.

CHAPTER 2

Newton Lived Upstairs

DURING HIS last term at Charterhouse Thackeray's health was not very good. He complained of headaches, and for a while fancied he had gout, until a doctor disabused his mind of the precocious idea. Upon his return to Larkbeare he came down with a serious illness. Temporary loss of all his hair obliged him to assume a wig, and several weeks in bed stimulated a phenomenal increase in his growth. His plans for hard cramming during the summer had to be given up, and his matriculation at Cambridge was postponed for a term.

He spent the autumn quietly in Devon, studying not too strenuously. Dr Cornish helped him in classics, as well as initiating him in the mysteries of vintage port, while Major Carmichael-Smyth enjoyed the opportunity of refurbishing his own mathematics while coaching his stepson, who galloped through Euclid but found Algebra baffling.

To vary the monotony of his studies, the young man could trot on his mare into Exeter in search of such amusements as the drowsy cathedral town might offer: political meetings or an occasional melodrama by a wandering theatrical troupe. Political excitements gave a new direction to his fledgling poetic skill. When Richard Sheil, the Irish orator, failed in his attempt to make a protest at a mass meeting of opponents to Catholic Emancipation, Thackeray ridiculed him in a neat parody of *The Minstrel Boy*, which was published on November 4 in *The Western Luminary and Family Newspaper* of Exeter. Encouraged by seeing his poem in print, he followed it during the next six weeks with two further contributions, a sentimental lyric entitled *The Tear* and a translation of the First Ode of Anacreon. He also set to work upon a Greek drama, *Ariadne in Naxos*, inspired by reading some verses by Horace Smith; but in this more ambitious effort he soon lost interest.

His friend Joe Carne, who had preceded him to the university, was writing him letters full of undergraduate pranks. In January Thackeray had a preview of college life when he spent a week in Oxford on a visit to William Stoddard, who was now at St John's College. Stoddard gave two wine and supper parties for his guest, who was duly impressed by the drinking, smoking, singing, and dirty stories, indulged in by gay blades whom he had known as schoolboys six months before.

It was inevitable that Cambridge should have been chosen as his university, for Cambridge was a nest of Thackerays. The Provost of King's College was a Thackeray, and so was the Vice-Provost. Another Thackeray was a fellow of that college and his younger brother was on the verge of election to the same status. The Professor of Political Economy, George Pryme, was married to a Thackeray. A leading physician of the town was a Thackeray, whose aged mother was a sort of matriarch for the clan. In view of the oppressive concentration of Thackerays at King's College, it was a wise decision that the new freshman's college should be Trinity.

Memories of the injustices of Charterhouse had steadily faded, except for an occasional nightmare of Dr Russell looming over him with portentous frown and upraised birch. By the time he was ready to go up for his matriculation, in February of 1829, he felt mellow enough to call at the Charterhouse on his way through London, and was amazed to find that the grim doctor had shrunk to normal stature and affability. As he shook hands with the headmaster, he blushed to notice in his other hand the well-worn Latin grammar that had been so often employed to box his ears.

His stepfather solicitously accompanied him on the journey to Cambridge, and letters were addressed to his various kinsmen at the University, committing him to their charge. During their pause in London the Major and his stepson put up at Slaughter's Coffee House in St Martin's Lane, while the youth visited assorted aunts and cousins, and acquired the trousseau for his university career, including "a buckish coat of blue-black with a velvet collar."

He had sprouted up now into an amiable young giant of six feet three; but the visage that surmounted his long frame was still appealingly youthful, with its round ruddy cheeks, ready smile, and absurdly flattened button of a nose. And the personality within, for all his assumption of satiric wit and political wisdom, was as boyishly naïve as the countenance.

One of his fellow-passengers on top of the coach, as it clattered through the London streets on the way to Cambridge, called his attention to a clergyman among the passers-by. "That's Croly," he said; "everybody's talking about *Salathiel*, the book he's just written." It was Thackeray's first glimpse of an author, and as he had been entranced by the fantastic novel he craned his neck to watch the great man, until he nearly fell off the coach. The traveller who had pointed him out chuckled at such a display of enthusiasm over a mere literary man. "I see that lad is fated," was his cryptic comment.

Thackeray began his undergraduate career with good resolutions toward scholarship. The traditions of Trinity inspired him, particularly the fact that his rooms in the Great Court, opposite the Master's Lodge, were under those once occupied by Isaac Newton. His tutor, too, William Whewell, was one of the famous figures of the University, both as a scholar and as a character: radical in his enthusiasm for the natural sciences, but a militant upholder of old institutions in all other respects.

It was unfortunate for Thackeray, however, that he matriculated in the Lent term, instead of in October. His former schoolmates, though glad to welcome him, were already deep in their reading and their amusements; and it was as a solitary stranger that he had to find his place in the complex rituals of college life. On the day that Major Carmichael-Smyth left for home, Thackeray spent a rather miserable morning in his rooms, unpacking his belongings and hanging up pictures. Then he sought out a friend at Corpus, who conducted him on an exploratory walk through the fields, to get his first good views of the noble chapel of King's and the turreted magnificence of the College of the Holy and Undivided Trinity. Later in the afternoon another friend introduced him to the excitement of a boat-race; they walked a couple of miles to Chesterton and ran most of the way home along the tow-path, shouting for the Trinity crew. Following dinner in hall, he donned his spotless new surplice and mortar-board for chapel; and when the service was over, and he picked up his cap, he found that a greasy old wreck had been substituted. After bringing a couple of friends to his rooms for tea, he ended the day of initiation into the glories and trivialities of Cambridge by writing a letter to his mother, telling her all that had occurred.

The next day, Sunday, was much taken up with chapel. In the evening he went dutifully to tea with old Mrs Thackeray, who, being ninety-one, was moved to regale him with a long family history that to his youthful ears seemed to consist wholly of fevers and deaths. He was glad to meet there the Vice-Provost of King's, who made himself agreeable with a standing invitation to his lodging.

As Whewell was too great a don to afford much time to freshmen, Thackeray was to do his routine reading with a private tutor, H. E. Fawcett. By the end of his first day of study, he had almost decided to write an English Essay for a college prize, on "The Influence of the Homeric Poems on the Religion, the Politics, the Literature and Society of Greece"; but he was somewhat doubtful as to whether he would have time for the necessary reading.

His premonition was well founded. On Tuesday he walked off his dinner in a ten-mile "grind"; and was elected to the Union, where he listened to a debate on the burning Catholic question; and ended with three friends to tea. On Wednesday he received a visit from George Thackeray of King's, after which he called on the Vice-Provost, and proceeded to a wine party given by his Charterhouse comrade, Carne, until he had to go off for his hour and a half with his coach, rather glad to escape from the frequent circulation of the decanter. These engagements foreshadowed the sociable pastimes that cut into his reading time, even though he had decided that seven hours sleep a night was all that he would need.

Carne was his mentor in other new experiences, as well as wine parties. On Friday of the eventful first week, while the two friends were taking a walk toward Trumpington, they heard a sweet female voice trilling "The Light, the Light

Guitar." Exchanging a conspiratorial glance, they stole silently close below her open window, and when she reached the chorus they joined in. The next moment the house door was violently flung open. Without even waiting to see who would emerge, the culprits fled in opposite directions, and did not encounter each other again until Thackeray sought his friend's room to discover whether he had returned intact.

The next day, after lectures, he and the irrepressible Carne hired horses and rode the nine miles to Wimpole Hall. After half an hour's gallop in the Park they emerged on the wrong side, fifteen miles from Cambridge, and had a long and hasty dash for home. Though very tired, Thackeray put in his usual session with his tutor, and then read in his own rooms till nine, when he fell asleep. The next morning he was delighted to find himself feeling much better than usual, except for stiff joints, while Carne was "quite done up."

These escapades were honestly reported to Larkbeare, and Thackeray even confessed that he had kissed Carne's pretty washerwoman. "I've never been so insulted in my life!" the girl declared. Such items of news aroused Mrs Carmichael-Smyth's maternal anxiety as to the fitness of Carne as a companion; but Thackeray countered with the explanation that it was an ideal arrangement, as he was always giving Carne good advice, which was bound to be beneficial for both of them.

In the third week he discovered the library of his college, and took out five stout quartos. By this time he was confessing in his journal that his reading was proving to be "much against the grain." A few days later, flattering himself that he was beginning to get the right habit, he outlined an unimpeachable plan of study: an hour with Fawcett every other morning, followed by the mathematical lecture from nine to ten and the classical lecture for the next hour; then an hour every day of reading Greek plays with a fellow-freshman fifteen years his senior, named Badger; Euclid or algebra from twelve to half past one, and an hour in the evening on some one of the same subjects.

Resolutions of this sort were repeated often in his letters home, usually with an entirely different schedule. At one time he hoped to arrange his tutorial hour for half past four, as an excuse for refusing invitations to wine parties. Not that he had taken any Spartan vow of abstinence; he reported favorably on the college ale and waxed lyrical over the hock served by his cousin, the Vice-Provost. After a month he boasted that he was acquiring "the knack" of the wine parties, by drinking only a glass and a half at each.

His own sauterne proved so good that acquaintances were apt to drop in uninvited to share it. Sometimes Thackeray would slip away and leave them in full possession. On April 1 (when his remittance came) he paid off obligations with a wine party for nine friends, and to his relief they abstemiously drank only five bottles (twenty-seven shillings). Plans for redecorating his rooms were occupying him—thirteen pounds for painting and papering . . . a rosewood book-case at a great bargain for five pounds. When Carne had to leave suddenly because of illness, Thackeray moved into his rooms to avoid the painters, and for two weeks suffered nightly discomfort from the shortness of the bed. About the same time, he let fall a hint with studied casualness. "I should much like," he remarked in a letter home, à propos of nothing, "to take to riding." For only twenty guineas he could have the use of a horse seventy times. Before the end of April he was suggesting that it would save much postage if a sum of money were deposited for him at the Cambridge bank, instead of all bills being sent to Larkbeare.

In one burst of scholarly enthusiasm, he resolved to read his Greek play without using a word of English; and he announced that he was thus discovering unsuspected beauties, and hoped soon to reach the point of thinking in Greek. As friendships increased, however, study became harder. He soon gave up trying to read mathematics in the evening, for it seemed that he always had a man in, or went to someone else's rooms, for an hour or two of chatting. Six weeks after his arrival, his attitude was distinctly leisurely; instead of condemning himself for a rather idle day, he asserted that "a little idleness doth one good." He was falling into the way of looking for quaint old churches and suchlike pretty spots, suitable for sketching, in the otherwise ugly countryside, and he announced his intention of taking solitary walks and applying himself seriously to landscapes. Another day, when Badger came for his regular session on the Greek play, but confessed to feeling a trifle under the weather, they spent the whole morning looking over a folio of prints of statues in the Museum at Florence, which Thackeray had got out of the Trinity library in order to make copies of the hands and feet.

Even though he relaxed his strict program, however, he did not fall into the irregular habits of many of the undergraduates. More than once he was shocked, on calling on an acquaintance at one o'clock or so, to find him in bed. Each day held for Thackeray too many interests to be wasted in either wining or sleeping. As well as his drawing, he played chess, and indulged in such physical activities as his eyesight permitted. Having engaged in fencing almost every day during his first weeks at college, he liked it so well that he bought himself a set of foils and the other paraphernalia. He refused, however, to learn to row; and he professed himself bored by the horsey conversation that he heard among his cousins' friends at King's.

Political excitement was running high over the Catholic crisis, and Thackeray enthusiastically signed a petition opposing the Emancipation Bill. The Union, too, was a source of interest. Joe Carne was making a reputation there, and at one debate on Napoleon his easy fluency seduced Thackeray into catching the Speaker's eye. Although he had been regarding Carne's remarks as "all flam," Thackeray was no sooner on his legs than every idea vanished from his mind and every word

A MATHEMATICAL
LECTURER

FIRST TERM

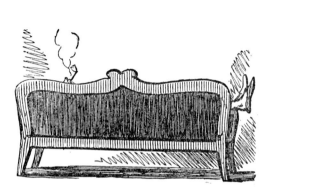

SECOND TERM

A UNIVERSITY TRADESMAN

THE COMPLETE WORKS OF OVID

from his tongue. He stood with his mouth open, and "blustered and blundered and retracted and stuttered." At last he summoned all his energy for one desperate effort, blurted out, "Napoleon as a captain, a lawgiver, and a king, merited and received the esteem and gratitude and affection of France," and sat down, determined that he would never again get up to speak in that terrifying assemblage. He imagined that the story of his disaster would be bandied throughout the University, that he had irrevocably exposed himself as a fool.

In the dingy gallery at the back of the Red Lion Inn, where the Union held its meetings, he heard some brilliant speakers and some disturbing theories. One orator was addicted to copious citation from the writings of Tom Paine. Another name that was much in the mouths of the more daring spirits was Percy Bysshe Shelley, as a debating team was preparing to defend his merits in opposition to an Oxford team supporting Byron. Thackeray got hold of *The Revolt of Islam* and became so enthusiastic over its poetic beauty that he extolled it in his next letter to his parents, promising to bring it home for inspection, even though both its plot and its republican sentiments struck him as equally absurd.

He continued to ponder the subject, with some intention of taking part in a Union debate; but his previous misadventure in that forum made him reluctant to put himself forward, and so many others spoke that the debate was finally adjourned before he got in his word. Instead he submitted his conclusions to the less exacting audience at Larkbeare: "Shelley appears to me to have been a man of very strong and perhaps good feelings, perverted by the absurd creed which he was pleased to uphold; a man of high powers, which his conceit led him to overrate, and his religion prompted him to misuse." On maturer thought, he doubted the prudence of bringing the book home to share with his parents; in spite of its high poetry, it contained "sentiments which might strongly incline one to throw it in the fire." Neither the visionary splendors of Shelley nor the eloquent radicalism rampant in the Union had quite succeeded in weaning the seventeen-year-old Thackeray from a certain innate skepticism toward all zealots.

Having found himself unequal to the rigors of Union debate, he sought a humbler substitute. Two months after his arrival he joined forces with three fellow-Carthusians to establish an Essay Club. Their intention was to increase the full membership to ten, but to admit no others from Charterhouse. It would not take up too much time, Thackeray explained, as none of them would have to provide more than three essays a year.

To catch up with his lost term's work, Whewell recommended him to remain up to read through the Easter vacation, and Fawcett volunteered to give him a fortnight's tuition during that time. Thackeray mentioned the proposal to his parents unenthusiastically, but to his disappointment they raised no objection to it.

From forming an Essay Club, and getting up subjects for Union debates, it was a short step to venturing into print. A variety of undergraduate publications were existent or projected. To compete with the established *Cambridge Magazine*, plans were afoot for a *Cambridge Gazette* and for a third magazine to be called *The Chimaera*. The last-named especially interested Thackeray, and he began to draft an essay on Shelley to be contributed when and if the magazine should ever see the light of day. Meanwhile, he took an active part in launching yet another, and less dignified, periodical.

The undergraduate sense of humor found vent in naming the paper *The Snob*—a word which in those days was solely a specimen of Cambridge slang, signifying a dweller in the town, outside the hallowed circle of University life. Its title-page mendaciously asserted that it was "a Literary and Scientific Journal, NOT 'Conducted by Members of the University.' " These disguises were for the purpose of increasing its success in heaping ridicule upon the presumed ignorance and vulgarity of all non-collegiate barbarians. The first number appeared on April 9. To the surprise of the editors, it was warmly received and survived successfully for ten weeks, until the coming of the summer vacation. Thackeray was deep in conspiracy with its editor, W. G. Lettsom. One Monday evening when the two of them sat down at nine o'clock to write the next Thursday's *Snob*, Thackeray laughed so much at some of their efforts that on going to bed at two he was uncomfortably ill. His attack lasted for ten days, and he called in his cousin, the physician, who prescribed leeches and low diet, and refused to accept a fee. "What!" snapped Dr Thackeray; "do you think me a cannibal?"

As might be expected, the exquisite humor of *The Snob* was more irresistible to its own concocters than to the outsider. Thackeray was responsible for two or three comic poems and several pieces of prose, under the pseudonyms of Frederick Tudge and Dorothea Julia Ramsbottom. The latter character was plagiarized entire from Theodore Hook's popular series then running in *John Bull*, and Thackeray had no trouble in imitating the outrageous malapropisms that were Mrs Ramsbottom's chief merit.

One contribution, however, attracted wider notice. For the Chancellor's Prize Poem that year, the assigned subject was "Timbuctoo." As there was an exceptional number of ambitious young poets just then in college, the competition was keen. The medal was awarded to Alfred Tennyson for a poem that had more merit than the others for the simple reason that he had previously written it on "Armageddon," and added only a few lines to make it appear relevant. The absurdity of the topic moved Thackeray to produce a burlesque, which was printed in *The Snob*, fully equipped with self-laudatory footnotes. When he dropped in to a friend's wine party that evening, he found his poem being enthusiastically praised. None of those present knew who had written it, and as he "eagerly sucked in" the commendation, he was amused to realize how much it delighted him.

These varied activities, all crowded into the first two months of his college life, evoked warnings from those who were responsible for his academic progress. In view of his mid-winter matriculation, he ought to have been reading almost twice as much as his friends, if he wished to overtake them by the end of the year. His tutor tried to frighten him with a lurid description of the May examination, lasting for a week of eight-hour days, but Thackeray's easy-going disposition was only moderately disturbed. His estimate of his competitors was that if he were lucky he might have about as many below him as above him. He assured his mother that he was determined to do his best, and could do no more.

His cousin the Vice-Provost advised him to "keep Non-ens"—i. e., to abstain from sitting for the May examination; but as this would lengthen his college residence by a year, he did not look favorably on the scheme. Instead, he resolved to grapple with the examination, and perhaps, if he had luck, he would confound his pessimistic advisers. For several weeks he really worked hard. Fawcett's patient efforts to elucidate trigonometry, however, only succeeded in making the student utterly confused about matters that he previously thought he understood. Then came his ten days' illness, at the most critical time; he was sure that it would lower him two classes in the examination. As the fatal week approached, he predicted gloomily that he would be lucky to get a fifth class. As it turned out, he managed to get a fourth, a status usually regarded as indicating a man who had some brains but had neglected his reading.

In July he went to Paris in company with one William Williams, who had just taken his degree at Cambridge and who was to coach him in mathematics during the vacation. Their first boarding house proved to be so inhabited by English people that Thackeray had no opportunity to improve his French, and after a few days they took a suite of rooms at 54 Rue Neuve St Augustin. Occasionally lonely and homesick, Thackeray was not much impressed with Paris. He found Notre Dame shabby and the Tivoli inferior to Vauxhall. The pictures at the Luxembourg and Versailles were mostly bad—there was too much of the school of David. Even French cooking seemed to him inferior to English. He did approve of the theaters, however; he admired Taglioni's dancing at the Opéra, and Mlle. Mars's acting at the Comédie Française, and he was enchanted by Leontine Fay, comedienne at the Théâtre de Madame. To his mother's objections he explained that the theaters provided his best opportunity for learning good French.

In addition to desultory struggles with algebra and trigonometry, Thackeray took French and German lessons from a Napoleonic veteran with whom he had fierce arguments over the battles of the war. With Williams and another Cambridge man he also undertook a course of dancing lessons from Coulon, an old instructor at the Opéra. When the three Englishmen stood up, coatless, in front of mirrors and began to dance solemnly while the tiny teacher sawed away on his kit, the absurdity of the scene struck Thackeray so strongly that he halted his posturing to roar with laughter. Coulon's dignity was so insulted that he refused to let the big English lad continue as his pupil.

The most disturbing new experience was with the gambling tables. An evening with three friends at Frascati's introduced him to the fascination of rouge-et-noir. Thackeray began by winning two hundred francs, then lost it all, and would have staked more if he had not previously lent the rest of his money to his companions. The game haunted his dreams that night, and for the next few days he was in a state of excitement that warned him of how dangerous the temptation was. Upon hearing of it, his mother wrote to him in terms of such reproach that he defended himself in an indignant letter, adorned with Scriptural quotations. He promised her, however, that he would stay away from the gaming rooms thereafter.

He found time for rides in the Bois de Boulogne, and for some reading of novels. Bulwer's *Devereux* spurred him to confess that he was thinking of trying his hand at fiction himself. At the end of his three months in Paris he came home with a bundle of prints, spent a few days in London—where he enjoyed seeing Fanny Kemble in *Romeo and Juliet*—and reached Cambridge in time for the beginning of Michaelmas term.

None of his intercourse, for so far, had been with the amazing group of young geniuses who in those very years were preparing for careers that were to bring glory to the University as a whole, and to Thackeray's own college in particular. The "Cambridge Conversazione Society," better known by its nickname of "The Apostles" because it was limited to twelve gifted and ambitious undergraduates, had been in existence for eight or nine years, and its members had been so preponderantly Trinity men that it held all its meetings in that college. Some of its earlier notables, such as Charles Buller and John Sterling, had left before Thackeray came up; but among those who remained were Alfred and Charles Tennyson, Arthur Henry Hallam, Richard Monckton Milnes, and Richard Chenevix Trench. Also at Trinity, though not an Apostle, was Edward FitzGerald. During Thackeray's first year he was as oblivious of the existence of these paladins as they were of his. He attracted no notice by achievements in scholarship or debate, and his literary output was of a frivolous nature that did not impress them.

When he returned for his second year he began to overcome the handicap of his obscure arrival. Two of his Charterhouse friends, Henry Lushington and George Venables, now came up as freshmen, and as brilliant scholars were received into the Apostles' set. Another Trinity freshman who made an immediate impression, being a couple of years older than the average and conspicuous for charm and good looks, was William Henry Brookfield. He had a talent for inspired nonsense and comic mimicry, and with him Thackeray soon struck up a friendship. Quizzical Edward FitzGerald, also, who had been drifting comfortably toward his degree for three years, began to realize that the towering young fellow with the monocle and the humorous glance was a kindred spirit, and before long he and Thackeray were exchanging comical notes and sketches.

The success of *The Snob* had fired Thackeray with journalistic zeal. The plans for *The Chimaera*, for which he had worked on his Shelley essay while in Paris, did not mature; a sequel to *The Snob* was undertaken instead. The humor of that title having worn off, the new series bore the more appropriate name of *The Gownsman*. Partly edited by Thackeray, it ran from November 5, 1829, to February 25, 1830, a total of seventeen numbers. Of his contributions, the most characteristic was a parody of Thomas Haynes Bayly's popular song, "I'd be a Butterfly, Born in a Bower." He had written it two or three years before, while at Charterhouse, but he still felt the contempt for facile sentimentality that had prompted his outrageous burlesque:

> I'd be a tadpole, born in a puddle,
>   Where dead cats, and drains, and water-rats meet;
> Then under a stone I so snugly would cuddle
>   With some other tad that was pretty and sweet
> I'd never seek my poor brains for to muddle
>   With thinking why I had no toes to my feet. . . .

His satiric touch was undeniably strong rather than subtle.

The Essay Club of the previous term was replaced by a small debating society. It never achieved the dignity of a name, although one of the members proposed calling it "the Covey," because "they made such a noise when they got up" (to speak). Of its seven members, the majority were destined to win moderate distinction; but unlike those of its model, the Apostles, who rose to fame chiefly by political and literary achievements, these found their niches in the Church and the University. Even in this small group Thackeray took an inconspicuous part; he was remembered chiefly for reading a paper on dueling that provoked argument, and for his enthusiasm on behalf of the old English novelists, particularly Fielding.

The general opinion of him was later summed up by one of his companions in "the Covey," William Hepworth Thompson, who ultimately became Master of Trinity: "He led a somewhat lazy but pleasant and 'gentlemanlike' life. . . . He had always a flow of humour and pleasantry, and was made much of by his friends. At supper-parties, though not talkative—rather observant—he enjoyed the humours of the hour, and sang one or two old songs with great applause. 'Old King Cole' I well remember to have heard from him at the supper I gave to celebrate my election as a scholar. It made me laugh excessively, not from the novelty of the song, but from the humour with which it was given."

Thackeray's most devoted friend in "the Covey" was John Allen, a dark, unkempt, earnest young man who was sadly concerned over Thackeray's religious laxity. By reading the gospel of Matthew to Thackeray he removed certain doubts as to whether Christ was equal with God; and on another occasion his "serious conversation" reduced Thackeray to tears and to a vow of immediately beginning a new life.

For the Easter vacation Thackeray planned to go for a lark to Paris, where FitzGerald was staying. Having scraped up twenty pounds, he did not risk telling his parents of the scheme, and blandly informed Whewell that he was going to stay with a college friend in Huntingdonshire. As FitzGerald had spent some of his boyhood in Paris, Thackeray had an experienced guide. He started the return journey with dangerously depleted funds and a deepening attack of conscience. The four hours' journey to Calais was darkened by guilty thoughts; by the time he reached Dover and paid for his place to London, he had only twelve shillings left. In a reaction from anxiety to bravado he went into the Ship Hotel and ordered a large dinner—whiting, beefsteak, and a glass of negus—which left him but half-a-crown for tipping the guard and coachman, and deposited him in London without a penny. Fortunately he had loyal friends there, and no word of the escapade ever penetrated as far as Larkbeare.

The adventure was symptomatic of a growing restlessness, a desire to try his wings. He had begun to ask himself, in his graver moments, why he was at Cambridge and toward what end he ought to be directing his studies. For none of the learned professions did he feel any vocation; and his self-consciousness at the Union debates, in the midst of so much epigram and eloquence, was sufficient proof that he was not cut out for a political career. Taking the undergraduates as a whole, those who were definitely not "reading men" were usually wealthy and extravagant, sons of landed noblemen or plutocratic bankers and manufacturers; with this group Thackeray had neither the means nor the tastes to become closely associated. With him it was a noteworthy occasion when he had half-a-dozen friends to dinner. He lovingly recorded the menu: soup, smelts, soles, boiled turkey, saddle of mutton, wild ducks, creams, jellies, and sauterne. Such prodigality as this could not be too frequently enjoyed by one whose income, though comfortable, was distinctly limited. The fortune which had been left by his father, and was being administered by Major Carmichael-Smyth as trustee, brought in something like five hundred a year, and the household at Larkbeare could not afford to add much to this to cover his expenses at the University. Now that his friendships and amusements were expanding, he was already drifting beyond his depth by indulging certain natural impulses toward smart clothes, good wine, and card playing; not indeed to anything like the extent of the "swell" set, but sufficiently to confront him, at the end of the year, with a surprising total of unpaid bills. Probably some inquiries from home emphasized the question of what ultimate advantage he had in view.

His hobby of sketching had never been taken seriously enough to impel him to make any thorough study of technique or anatomy; it remained nothing more than an enjoyable way of entertaining himself and his friends by capturing on

A LITTLE DINNER

paper the quaint or ludicrous aspects of themselves and the life around them. His writing, similarly, was purely dilettante, arising from his onlooker's amusement at the minor drolleries and pretensions of humanity. College life was undeniably agreeable: it brought him congenial friendships and widened his perception of character; but he was intelligent enough to realize that if human nature was to be his study, it could be observed in all its variety far more richly anywhere else than within college walls. Of the chief subjects which would have to be pursued if he sought a degree, his interest in Greek was but tepid and his grasp of mathematics seemed to grow steadily weaker. The only series of lectures which perceptibly appealed to him was that in Political Economy; but his interest was probably sharpened by the fact that the Professor was the husband of one of his many

A FEW LITTLE BILLS

cousins. Since all his efforts in his first year had gained him nothing better than a fourth class, he faced the prospect of a longer and duller grind if he expected to take a degree with any sort of distinction; otherwise he might easily suffer the indignity of being plucked.

With these divers considerations in mind, he decided that completion of his University course would not repay the time and effort required. Cambridge had already given him all that was relevant to the existence of elegant leisure and amusement that he contemplated. On completion of his year as a "junior Soph," he put his books and furnishings into storage (in case he should ever decide to return and take his degree), fixed his monocle more firmly in his eye, and strolled out of Cambridge to confer his amused inspection upon a wider world.

CHAPTER 3

From Grand Duchy to Law Office

IN SPITE of all the mutual affection between Thackeray and his mother and step-father, he could not feel thoroughly at home under their roof. Between the ages of five and ten he had never seen them; and thereafter till he was seventeen the few weeks of vacation every year were too much like blissful dreams to establish any normal habits of companionship. Now that he was grown up, his love for them was tempered with good-natured amusements at their foibles—his mother's impracticality and Major Carmichael-Smyth's interminable stories of military life in India. At rare moments there was even a vague twinge of jealousy at the thought that the worthy major had so completely supplanted in his mother's heart the handsome young father whom he could not remember but to whom, by contagion from all the family-proud Thackerays, he was unspokenly loyal.

On leaving Cambridge without either qualification or apparent preference for a career, he would undoubtedly have been welcome to settle down in the rural placidity of Larkbeare; but he was eager for more amusing experiences. In his first term at the University he had pointedly quoted in a home letter a remark by his cousin the Vice-Provost, "that he thought every young man should go abroad after he had taken his degree." Now that the tedious ritual of taking a degree had been dispensed with, the visit abroad need no longer be delayed. After a course of German lessons in London from a Herr Troppenheger, he set out upon what was in those days the inevitable pilgrimage of English devotees of the picturesque—the Rhine.

At the end of July, 1830, he was in Coblentz, and his report to his mother, illustrated with sketches, dealt with the usual scenes—various styles of churches, the "Castled Crag of Drachenfels," and striking figures of fellow-travelers on the steamer. He described the Rhine as "almost equal to the Thames," and extolled the beauties of Prussian military music.

Thence he traveled to Godesberg, a tiny spa four miles from Bonn, where he stayed for a while and improved his acquaintance with German life by watching the duels of Bonn University students and attending one of their "wine, tobacco, and song" parties, at which he patriotically performed "God Save the King." The sour wine disagreed with him, however, after Cambridge port and punch, and the fleas at his lodging tormented him. He made progress with his German, bought an eighteen-volume set of Schiller, and put the legend of the Drachenfels into sprightly verse.

When the impulse stirred him, he wandered on to Cologne, and thence moved deeper into Germany through Elberfeld, Cassel, and Gotha. At the end of September he reached Weimar. By this time, beginning to tire of inns, he felt ready to settle down for a longer stay in one place. His college friend Lettsom, fellow-author of *The Snob*, who was domiciled in Weimar with a German family, assured him that the drowsy little Saxon city would suit him exactly. Something like a score of well-connected young Englishmen were living there, either to study German or to enjoy the hunts and *battues* of the vicinity. An Anglophile tradition had been established at the court of Saxe-Weimar-Eisenach by the late Grand Duke, whose successor retained three or four Englishmen in his entourage and welcomed others of the breed to attend his receptions. Lettsom arranged for Thackeray to study German with his tutor, Dr Weissenborn. Hoping for better luck than at Paris, he enrolled for a course of lessons in the waltz and the gallopade.

Pleasant rooms were found for him in a home overlooking the sunny *Platz*. He had the privilege of using the town's good library, and for a shilling a night he could see excellent plays. In addition to the usual amenities of a little grand-ducal capital there was the literary aura of its most celebrated resident, Goethe. The young stranger soon met Frau Ottilie von Goethe, who promised to introduce him to her great father-in-law.

Meanwhile, presentation at the Grand Duke's Court was imperative. Thackeray hastily had to have a pair of trousers cut down into breeches for the ceremony, and obtained a cocked hat; but in the midst of all the gorgeous uniforms he felt in his all-black outfit like "a cross between a footman and a Methodist parson." Knowing that he would have to make further appearances, he sent an urgent appeal to his parents to obtain for him a cornetcy in Sir John Kennaway's yeomanry. He confessed that it was "a very absurd favour" and rather lamely explained that of course he could get along with his makeshift costume in Weimar, but if he were to be presented at other Courts in any part of Europe he would need a more suitable outfit, and a yeomanry uniform "is always a handsome and respectable one."

Never before had he felt so self-confident as in this miniature state, with its childish make-believe dignity that appealed to both his sense of humor and his youthful love of display. This was just what he had come abroad for: to find out whether he could establish his own place in a social group, alone and unsponsored. Weimar was an intimate stage that did not dwarf him to insignificance.

Though he admitted that the Court was absurdly ceremonious, he thought that it would "rub off a little of the rust" that he had derived from school and college. As everybody talked French, he had more practice for his French than for his German. Court was held twice a week from seven to half past nine; tea was served, and the older members of society played cards, while the gentlemen of the assemblage stood about uncomfortably for the two and a half hours. Half past nine was bed-time.

The place was so small that everybody knew everybody else. Living was remarkably cheap. At the Court balls and assemblies one could arrive without discredit on foot; or if the weather was snowy one ran to the old-fashioned luxury of a sedan chair and a pair of sturdy bearers. Even important officials of the state had to be very frugal in the matter of invitations to dinner; but on evenings when

DUEL AT GODESBERG

there was no Court function, innumerable tea parties were given in cozy homes. Both at the Court and the private parties, conversation was agreeably adorned with allusions to art and letters: the Grand Duchess graciously questioned the young English guests about their literary tastes and pursuits, borrowed books from them, and even lent them volumes from her own shelves. When Thackeray had been in Weimar a couple of months, he wrote home to say that he would greatly like to be appointed an *attaché* and make a career for himself in the diplomatic service.

The arrival of the gaudy yeomanry uniform increased his self-confidence. Much to his delight, he was able to buy a sword that had once belonged to Schiller; thus he not only completed his Court regalia but also symbolically affiliated himself with a poet to whose works he had become deeply attached.

Good music and drama were almost as much of a novelty to him as was Grand Ducal ceremonial. He pasted all the playbills in a scrap-book, and made endless sketches of the performers. The Court Theater retained much of the distinction that it had won during the years of Goethe's directorship. On the two or three nights a week when there were performances, the whole society of Weimar assembled in the mood of a vast family party. In addition to the excellent resident company, leading actors and singers from all parts of Germany felt honored to appear as guest stars. Operas were performed frequently, the orchestra being conducted by the noted composer and pianist, Johann Nepomuk Hummel. Plays ranged from Shakespeare through Schiller to a translation of *Hernani*, the latest romantic storm-center in Paris.

In particular, Thackeray fell under the spell of the great actor Ludwig Devrient. The first time he saw him, a special trip had to be made to Erfurt, for the play was *Die Räuber*, which was "a little too patriotic and free" for the Court Theater. One of the Weimar actors accompanied Thackeray and took him backstage to meet the star and see all the mysteries of the green-room and the fly-loft. Devrient's performance of Franz Moor was the most terrific experience that Thackeray had ever been through. Franz's prayer while his castle was being attacked—"I am no common murderer, mein Herr Gott"—made such an impression on Thackeray that for days afterwards he could do nothing but try to make an adequate drawing of his face in that awful scene. Before the season was over he saw Devrient in Shylock, Hamlet, and Falstaff, and admired also his beautiful wife, Wilhelmine Schroeder, in *Fidelio*, but it was Franz Moor that remained burned into his memory.

His enthusiasm for Schiller was thereby strengthened. He was reading Shakespeare in German, and began to entertain ambitious visions of translating Schiller into English. "I should be proud of having conferred a benefit on my country," he wrote home, with unwonted earnestness; "I do believe him to be, after Shakespeare, The Poet." He was young enough to be more deeply stirred by the energy and rebelliousness of Schiller than by the less flamboyant genius of Goethe, even though that old sage was still dominating Weimar in the flesh.

Inevitably, the atmosphere of romantic *Empfindsamkeit* conquered an impressionable youth who had previously divided all his time between the monastic masculinity of Charterhouse and Cambridge and the social barrenness of a Devonshire village. The pretty, playful Saxon girls could talk English, their mothers could not, and the tall young Englishman had plenty of time on his hands for drawing quaint pictures in plush-bound albums and practicing the art of flirtation. The Hof-Marschall of the court, Baron von Spiegel, had a beautiful daughter Melanie, with whom Thackeray immediately fell in love. Having made good progress with his dancing lessons, he got up courage to waltz with her at a Court Ball; but the floor was as slippery as ice, his long legs were under uncertain control, and the outcome was a disastrous spill.

Perhaps as a result of this mishap, his ardor for Fraülein von Spiegel waned, and he became infatuated with another of the young maids of honor, who was not quite so pretty as Melanie but was more intellectual and vivacious. This was Jenny von Pappenheim, an illegitimate daughter of Jerome Bonaparte, one-time King of Westphalia. In approved fashion, he stood in the dark street to gaze at her window and watch for her shadow on the blind until the light went out. One

SCENE FROM "DIE FREISCHÜTZ"

evening he was on the verge of going on his knees and making an eloquent proposal, but did not quite manage it; and after three weeks of adoration he was cut out by a newly-arrived young ex-Guardsman with flowing moustachios, a variety of gorgeous waistcoats, and ten thousand pounds a year.

The rejected admirer was soon able to joke about both his love affairs in his letters to his mother, burlesquing the passionate lyrics he had written, and illustrating them with his usual caricatures. He admitted that a single souvenir—a little glove—was still hidden in his drawer, and that he had controlled an impulse to make it into a pipe-cover. When the Baroness von Gustedt (née von Pappenheim) wrote her memoirs half a century afterwards, she spoke kindly of Thackeray's "apt humor, his tender heart," the amusing sketches he could draw in one minute, his "beautiful eyes and thick curly hair."

One of the most hospitable of the tea-tables was that of Ottilie von Goethe, where Thackeray and his young compatriots spent many a delightful evening in

THE BEAUTY AND HER VICTIM

talk and music, reading novels and poems in French, German, and English. The enthusiastic Ottilie ("the crazy angel," as her father-in-law called her) was at that time conducting a little privately-circulated magazine named *Chaos*, consisting of contributions in several languages by the frequenters of her drawing-room. Thackeray's friend Lettsom was one of the circle, and Thackeray probably also wrote for it, although the identity of the individual contributors was not revealed. Among the papers left by Ottilie are two manuscript poems by Thackeray—a rollicking drinking song and a translation of the "Flea" passage from *Faust*—but neither of these was printed in the magazine.

He seldom left Madame von Goethe's house without drawing a caricature for the children; and he had a thrill of pride on being told that some of these found their way into the private apartments of the great poet, for though the old man received only a few privileged visitors, he was keenly interested in the characters and doings of the strangers outside.

Thackeray had been several weeks in Weimar before his promised presentation to Goethe took place. When he was formally notified that the Herr Geheimrath would see him on the morning of October twentieth, the suspense produced a ridiculous perturbation. A trifle shaky at the knees, feeling (as he afterwards said) as if he were paying a visit to the dentist, he made his way to the little antechamber of the poet's private suite. There, surrounded by antique casts and bas-reliefs, stood the great man, clad in a long gray coat, his hands clasped behind him, just as in a familiar statuette. When he turned his dark and piercing eyes on Thackeray, the young man's nervousness grew almost to panic. Into his mind had suddenly come a vivid recollection of the uncanny hero of *Melmoth the Wanderer*, one of the tales of terror which had fascinated him ten years before. For a moment he was no longer a sophisticated young traveler, but a trembling schoolboy, crouching over a book and scared to look behind. Then Goethe addressed him, in a rich, sweet voice; and Thackeray's self-possession came back to him with a rush when he noticed that the great man spoke French with a thick German accent.

Goethe questioned him about himself in a kindly way, and showed that he already knew a good deal about the young artist; Thackeray answered as best he could, meanwhile storing up a vivid portrait of the old man in his memory. A clear and rosy complexion, a majestic air, and the penetrating eyes—these were the chief details that he carried away, to be reinforced by a couple of later glimpses of the poet, once walking in his garden, and again starting off for a carriage drive on a sunny day, wearing a cap and a cloak with a red collar, and accompanied by a little golden-haired granddaughter.

The one conversation had been enough to give Thackeray the feeling that he was admitted to the poet's circle of friendship, and for the rest of his stay he used to send any new books or magazines from England, for Goethe to look at. The recently-founded and lively *Fraser's Magazine* proved to be his favorite, because it was publishing a series of drawings by Maclise, depicting the leading authors of the time. In December, as Thackeray reported with awe in his letter home, the old man burst a blood vessel and yet in spite of his eighty-one years was within a few days writing and drinking as hard as ever.

Thackeray's delight in every moment of his sojourn in Weimar was heightened by a growing realization that it was an island in time—an idyllic interlude, like a fairy tale miraculously come true, in which he played a rôle unrelated to the real world that must reassert itself when the spell should break. Though his assured income might have maintained him in that thrifty duchy as a gentleman of leisure, the idea of becoming a permanent resident never seriously occupied his mind. He was uncomfortably aware that his mother had been distressed by his withdrawal from Cambridge and that she was eager for him to adopt a profession. This spectre of the inevitable awakening colored his perception of everything around him with a half-melancholy, half-humorous affection and a total disregard of the less enchanting elements. Other visitors to the little Grand-ducal capitals became conscious of narrow and provincial standards, of gossip and backbiting, of artificiality and pomposity. To Thackeray, Weimar's smallness and its elaborate ceremonials made it a sort of humanized puppet-show; and his naïve appreciation served to call forth all the kindliness of those who met him. He amused them, and they amused him; what happier relationship could be conceived?

As the winter wore on, he began to mention plans for a walking tour over the Hartz Mountains, or perhaps through Saxon Switzerland, with vaguer allusions to an eventual exploration of all the less familiar parts of the country, with sketch-book and note-book, and "I fear, still a dictionary," collecting material for a volume. His own interest in learning about so many things in Germany, such as customs, folk-songs, legends, local costumes, made him realize how little was known in England on the subject. In further satisfying his own curiosity, he might also enlighten the "British Public."

More ominous was his mention of taking "a little recreation in the fields of Civil Law." He was not amused by Justinian, but he persisted. If he were to adopt the Law as a career, it would not be with any illusions about enjoying it, but as a "noble and tangible object, an honorable profession, and I trust in God a certain fame." He added whimsically that his way of winning the fame, for so far, was to lie on the sofa and read novels—and think about it. He solemnly affirmed that he was not actuated by "merely an appetite for novelty"; he was nearly twenty years old, and at that age his father had already been for five years in a profession. "I am fully aware how difficult and disagreeable my task must be for the first four years, but I have an end in view and an independence to gain; and if I can steadily keep this before me, I shall not, I trust, flinch from the pursuit of them."

Sustained by these admirable sentiments, he came home from his wanderings to find his mother and stepfather both ill and promptly to fall ill himself. As soon as he recovered he went up to London, took chambers at 5 Essex Court, Middle Temple, and with the help of a lawyer friend from Devon arranged to read with a special pleader and conveyancer, William Taprell, of Number 1, Hare Court. As only ten days of the Trinity term remained after his admission, he soon returned to the country and spent the summer at Larkbeare and neighboring houses. He tried to work upon a translation of Konrad Mannert's History of Germany, but found rural life sadly dull after the amenities of Weimar. In a nostalgic letter to Ottilie von Goethe he declared that even the London theaters had bored him, though he had been looking forward to them so eagerly. "How I long for the dear little Weimar Theatre where one could sit quiet and cozy in the parquet, neither

A STUDENT

A STUDENT IN UNIFORM

GOETHE

squeezed, smothered, or pelted." He admitted that "the Theatre is still my rage (don't think me conceited or say anything about it); I intend fully to try my hand at farce, tragedy, or comedy—which I cannot say yet—all three perhaps. . . Now for the next thirty years I shall be in London eight months of the twelve. At the end of thirty years I shall be most likely Lord Chancellor (at least my Mother believes so)." With this letter he enclosed a graceful little lyric, *The Stars*, which Ottilie duly printed in her *Chaos*.

Throughout the summer he carried on an emotional correspondence with FitzGerald, to whom on his twentieth birthday he gloomily dilated upon his idleness and dissipation, his wasted life and his determination not to pursue the profession of law. In another letter to Fitz he proposed a grand scheme for an adventurous walking tour of Italy and Spain next year; but in more immediate prospect were the amusements of London. He was starving for the theater. "Really," he declared, "London is to me only the place where the theatres are."

The Middle Temple's chief appeal to him was in its literary traditions. He conjured up glimpses of Sir Roger de Coverley strolling in the Gardens, of Henry Fielding grinding out his articles for the *Covent-Garden Journal*, of Johnson lumbering up to Goldsmith's chambers in Brick Court, and Burke and Reynolds joining in the brilliant talk. The rooms were dark and draughty and smelled of ancient dust, but every sag in the passage floors and every creak in the staircase was another reminder of the crowding generations that had laughed and argued and written within those crumbling walls.

Life in London offered all the merriment that he had looked forward to. The theater, of course, ranked first: *The Judgment of Paris, The Barber of Seville*, Braham in *Fra Diavolo*, Macready in *The Merchant of London*, the incomparable Madame Vestris in burlesques and extravaganzas at the Olympic—these and many others provided all the tinsel and bombast that he loved beyond the footlights. Notions of realism were never more remote from the stage than then, and Thackeray reveled in its blithe flouting of plausibility.

Before long he became irregular in his attendance at Mr Taprell's. There were new novels to read, and there were headaches after late nights, and there were sessions at the gambling hells in Regent's Quadrant. He lost as much as eight or nine pounds in an evening, and occasionally won four or five.

There was no danger of his being lonely, what with Ritchie and Shakespear kinsfolk of all ages, and in particular an uncle, the Rev Francis Thackeray, author of dull historical works, who was a trustee of his estate and who invited him to dinner two or three times a week, until the young man was hard put to find excuses in order to have time free for seeing something of younger and gayer friends.

Several of the most congenial of his contemporaries at Trinity were now established in London. Among them were Henry and John Mitchell Kemble, of the famous theatrical family. John Kemble was the wittiest of all the Apostles, and yet one of the most erudite. After taking his degree he had gone to Göttingen to study philology under the Grimms, and Thackeray found his conversation some-

A GAMBLING HELL

what too scholarly except when it was varied with exciting tales of his recent adventures while taking part in the Torrijos insurrection in Spain. Their sister Fanny was at the height of her fame as an actress, drawing crowds to Covent Garden. Thackeray seldom saw her when he visited her brothers at the family home in Great Russell Street, but he had some glimpses of the younger sister, Adelaide.

The first time he saw seventeen-year-old "Totty" (as the family called her), she was playing a guitar and he was greatly struck by her charm and grace.

Another pair of brothers were Charles and Arthur Buller. Charles had shared with "Jacky" Kemble the distinction of being the chief purveyor of wit and sparkle in the debates of the Apostles, and was now already a rising young Radical M.P. He and Thackeray had much in common, not only birth in Calcutta but also an astonishing physical resemblance, with broken noses and towering stature. Alfred and Frederick Tennyson and their friend Arthur Hallam also appeared sometimes at the convivial evenings; Tennyson's poems were read aloud with rapture, and the critical assaults on his recently published volume were hotly discussed.

In November FitzGerald came to London to stay with his friend. The intimacy between him and Thackeray had now become deeply affectionate, as indicated by a long poem that Fitz wrote at this time:

> ... The thought of my Willy is always a cheerer,
> The wine has new flavour, the fire burns clearer,
> The sun ever shines, I am pleased with all things,
> And the crazy old world seems to go with new springs ...
>
> And when we're together—oh, soon may it be—
> The world may go kissing of comets for me;
> The chair that Will sat in I sit in the best,
> The tobacco is sweetest which Willy hath blessed;
> And I never found out that my wine tasted ill
> When a tear would drop in it for thinking of Will.
> And now on my windows October blows chilly,
> But I laugh at blue devils and think of my Willy,
> And think that our friendship will not drop away
> Like the leaves from the trees, or our locks when they're gray;
> And I think that old age shall not freeze us until
> He creeps with Death's warrant to me and my Will ...

"What *passions* our friendships were!" wrote Thackeray in later years, looking back to this golden time.

In December he paid a visit to Cambridge, on the pretext of seeing whether his belongings were safe. During his four days he was treated to such a round of meals that he grew amazed at the gormandizing; he did his best to keep up, but found himself to be a delicate eater in comparison with his friends. He came away with a determination to return sometime and keep another term.

By this time his theatrical debauch had worn itself out. He seldom went more than once a week; fortunately there were long runs at all the theaters and he had decided that none of the current productions was worth seeing more than twice. He began to find Shakespeare tedious, except occasionally one of the tragedies with

Miss Fanny Kemble. More to his taste was *The Beggars' Opera*, which he saw in company with Jacky Kemble, and described as "the pleasantest play in our language." Best of all, "in a few days come the Pantomimes! Huzza!"

He now found himself free to translate into action the "Life in London" that had captivated his schoolboy mind in the pages of Pierce Egan. After an evening at the theater, it was his delight to adjourn with a few of his friends for welsh-rabbit and glee-singing at the Spotted Dog or the Eagle Tavern, the Cider-Cellar, or the Coal-Hole, or the Widow's in St Martin's Lane. These "musical clubs" were smoke-filled caverns, where young bloods rubbed elbows with a raffish crowd of reporters and hack-writers, and shabby hangers-on of questionable repute. The young gentlemen felt that they were devilish men of the world when they drank their stout or their brandy-and-water in such a haunt, and stood treat to the glee-singers or exchanged chaff with the autocratic "President" of the meeting.

Here Thackeray rapidly grew acquainted with the profession of letters on its seamiest side. London had a large contingent of clever and penniless men, chiefly Scottish and Irish, who had come there dreaming of fame and fortune through the pen and had remained to scrape a precarious living by journalism, while they drank hard and exhausted their credit and became bitterly cynical of all that was prosperous or platitudinous. London newspapers were at a low ebb in those days, limited in circulation, burdened by the exorbitant stamp tax, scurrilous in dispute. New ones were spawning and old ones decaying, in a ruthless struggle for the overcrowded market. The hard-bitten scribblers, free of any sense of personal responsibility, reveled in the opportunity to show their brilliance in personal invective. Though their earnings were pitiful, they felt a keen aesthetic pleasure in the satires and slanders that they could toss off with half-tipsy fluency.

Acknowledged overlord of this journalistic Bohemia was William Maginn, precocious LL.D. of Dublin and prodigy in languages. Maginn was incredibly facile as a writer and exasperatingly impractical in worldly affairs. Thackeray fell promptly under the spell of "the Doctor"—his kindly, boyish face crowned with a mop of gray hair, his stammering gentle voice that flowed on through wit and erudition and ribaldry, his air of omniscience and his pitiless scorn of pretension. Maginn had an enviable position in the journalistic world, as editor of *The Standard*, which was at the moment the leading Tory paper; and he was also *de facto* editor of *Fraser's Magazine*, the most sparkling and audacious among the monthlies. From these he drew a comfortable income, but his generosity and carelessness kept him always in debt.

Thackeray was charmed to be initiated by Maginn into the secrets of journalism. The Doctor took him to the office of *The Standard* to show him "the mysteries of printing and writing leading articles." Two days later Maginn had the novice to dine at the King's Head tavern, but Thackeray described the company cavalierly in his diary as "a dull party of low literary men." More satisfactory was a meeting with Stanley Lees Giffard, editor-in-chief of *The Standard*, "a very learned and pleasant man."

The Doctor fascinated Thackeray still more, however, by displaying the riches of his scholarship. When Maginn spent a whole morning reading Homer to him, with comments that mingled wit, learning, and deep poetic feeling, Thackeray felt that these hours were among the pleasantest he had ever passed. He had never admired Homer so deeply before, and he even took a vow, under Maginn's urging, to read some Homer every day, which vow, he confessed in his diary, "I don't know whether I shall keep."

Two months after their first meeting, Thackeray was so touched by Maginn's accounts of his financial woes that he volunteered to lend him money. The next week Maginn attended to another phase of his young friend's education by taking him one night to a brothel, at which Thackeray left him and went home in sickened disgust.

About this time Thackeray started a negotiation for investing in a newspaper; but the transaction fell through when he was unable to raise cash for his down payment, and later he found out that he had been cheated by the man he had dealt with. In the same ambitious mood he made arrangements for a printseller to market some of his caricatures. He also sent a couple of poems to the editor of *Fraser's Magazine*, only to have them rejected. The idea of writing fiction lingered in the back of his mind. When he read Bulwer's *Eugene Aram* he felt sure that he would be able to produce a better novel. In fact, every time he heard praise for Bulwer's talent he was stirred with a sense of rivalry.

For the present, however, any such undertaking would be too energetic. Again and again, in his diary and letters, he accused himself of idleness and absence of mind. Within a few months, when he should reach the age of twenty-one and come into control of his inheritance, he might be able to buy a newspaper and become a useful patron to Maginn and his clever, jolly friends.

There was another reason for his concern about his approaching financial freedom. As well as the devil-may-care crowd of reporters, he had made acquaintance with certain gentry of a different stamp—quiet of voice, smooth of manner, chilly of eye—who invited the neophyte to their rooms (which happened, by amazing coincidence, to be directly across the street from his own), where champagne, *pâté de foie gras*, and other delicacies abounded. A friendly game of écarté was proposed. For a while Thackeray won from his affable hosts; then imperceptibly the stakes grew larger and the luck began to run all the other way. The sequel was a gloomy drive into the City in the smart cabriolet of one of the imperturbable gentlemen, and a conference with a broker to raise fifteen hundred pounds on the future inheritance.

In contrast with amusements and disasters such as these, his hours on a high stool in Mr Taprell's dingy office were tedious enough. Soon after starting his work he began to drop hints that he found lawyers too formal. The work was "really very pleasant," he declared, without enthusiasm; "one's day is agreeably occupied; there is a newspaper and a fire and just enough to do." One day he was occupied with "a long-winded Declaration about a mortgage"; another time it was

LEGAL AMBITIONS

"a long pedigree case." He admitted that "it is difficult to read dry law-books and to attend to them. I have to lay out nearly £5 today for these same ugly books." He planned to brighten the atmosphere by having his friend Kemble appointed as an extra assistant to Mr Taprell. Then in another letter he lashed out rebelliously: "This lawyer's preparatory education is certainly one of the most cold-blooded, prejudiced pieces of invention that ever a man was slave to. . . A fellow should properly do and think of nothing else than L A W. Never mind. I begin to find out that people are much wiser than I am (which is a rare piece of modesty in me), and that old heads do better than young ones—that is, in their generation, for I am sure that a young man's ideas, however absurd and rhapsodical they are, though they mayn't smack so much of experience as those of these old cold calculating codgers, contain a great deal more nature and virtue."

With the coming of spring his unrest was heightened by the political crisis over the Reform Bill. His friends the Bullers were deep in the agitation, as was the Hon Richard Curzon, a former schoolfellow at Charterhouse. On April 29, after dining with Arthur Buller and Alexander Kinglake (another Trinity friend), he went out ironically canvassing for "Percy and Reform" (Percy being a vociferous Tory). "It was a silly prank," he noted in his diary, "but has shown me how easy it is to talk men over." A few days later, by virtue of an admission-order from Curzon, he listened to a debate in the House of Commons. "It will soon, I suppose, be a house of deputies," he remarked. "Bought a big stick wherewith to resist all parties in case of attack."

His political ideas were in a state of change. Three years before, during the almost equally bitter crisis over Catholic Emancipation, he had parroted the prejudices of his caste. Now, however, the enthusiasm of Buller and the general idealism and humanitarianism among the radicals won him over. He felt a trifle embarrassed in adopting a cause for which people were struggling with quite ungentlemanly fervency; but so long as he could label his adherence a "prank" or mask it with an epigram, his growing sympathy could be allowed to prevail.

His thrilling sense of national peril and impending revolution made the pleader's office duller than ever. "The sun won't shine into Taprell's chambers," he wrote home on May 22, "and the high stools don't blossom and bring forth buds. . . I do so long for fresh air—and fresh butter I would say only it isn't romantic." He sought solace in a long walk to Kensington Gardens and a stroll on the green banks of the Serpentine.

An opportunity for escaping from his high stool soon occurred. On June 19, while he was breakfasting with Charles Buller, a letter arrived from Buller's constituents in Liskeard, Cornwall, begging him to come down at once and begin canvassing for the approaching election. As Buller was feeling too ill for the journey, he asked his brother Arthur and Thackeray to go as his deputies. In high excitement, they set off on that same night's mail coach as outside passengers, reached Plymouth the next morning, and with scarcely a pause pushed on to Liskeard, where they went into immediate consultation with attorneys and campaign agents. By these authorities, the campaign address which had been written by Charles Buller was pronounced unsatisfactory. A new one was drawn up by Arthur, with Thackeray's aid. Then late at night, in pouring rain, they went on to the home of the Bullers at West Looe.

After a long night's sleep, Thackeray awoke to find himself in a lovely old West-Country mansion. The servants all mistook him for Master Charles. Mr and Mrs Buller proved to be of the truest vintage of hospitable county families, and Mrs Buller, he learned, had once been a flame of his father's in Calcutta. He soon made friends with the jolly neighbors who were constantly coming and going.

For the next couple of weeks his life was a delightful round of walks, and rides, and conversation, and making sketches of the pretty countryside, and even a mild flirtation or two. He did not neglect his duty, however, but rode out on canvassing expeditions; one day he spent twelve hours in the saddle, and was distinctly stiff on the morrow. Keeping his pose that it was all a quaint caprice, he wrote to FitzGerald describing how they pledged Buller "to reforms in politics and religion, of which we knew nothing ourselves; but, nevertheless, the farmers were highly impressed with our sagacity and eloquence." In his diary he was more sober, and remarked that he "found much more good feeling and intelligence among the farmers than I had expected."

When he had been there a week, he wrote to tell his mother all his adventures. "I have been lying awake this morning," he added, "meditating the wise and proper manner I shall employ my vast fortune when I come of age, which, if I live so long, will take place in three weeks. First, I do not intend to quit my little chambers in the Temple, then I will take a regular monthly income which I will never exceed. . . ."

This was all very well for a dreamy summer's morning, with the birds singing outside the window, and a pleasant realization that he had slept off the fatigue of his first over-strenuous canvassing. But if his mother read the letter with acumen, she must have smiled to find him, a few sentences later, begging permission to stay on at Polwellan long enough to take part in Charles Buller's triumphal arrival. To return from the clamor of the hustings to the sound of pen-scratching in Hare Court would need heroic will-power. And ten days later he was writing to Fitz-Gerald proposing a walk in Normandy, to be followed by a month in Paris. "I have a strange idea that I shall be in Italy before the autumn is over, and if my dear old Teddibus would but come with me, we will be happy in a paradise of pictures."

The arrival of the candidate had all the fanfare that Thackeray loved. Liskeard was alive with flags, bands, and triumphal arches. The devoted pair of canvassers rode out to meet the approaching hero, and had the honor of being with him in his carriage when the horses were taken out and it was dragged through the town by cheering constituents. Three days later the whole performance was repeated: after a Presbyterian minister had addressed the crowd in approval of Buller's moral principles, the candidate made a speech, and the electors sat down to a free *al fresco* dinner in a downpour of rain. Thackeray was mightily gratified on three separate occasions to hear the crowd singing a particularly ribald song that he had written to ridicule the political agent of the Tory candidate. He confessed to his diary that he was developing "Parliamentary visions" on his own account, and he outlined a platform of romantic and patriotic Toryism that strangely foreshadowed the revivification of that party which was later achieved by Disraeli.

As the campaign advanced to its climax, Thackeray's personal climax also approached. He made plans for donating some fraction of his income to his Eurasian half-sister, who had married in India and was living in poverty. On July 18 he wrote in his diary, "Here is the day for which I have been panting for so long." Not many days later a new assistant was clearing out the desk in Hare Court, and turning over huge stacks of sketches and caricatures to Mr Taprell. Mr Thackeray had gone to France.

LEGAL TERM ILLUSTRATED:
"POSSESSION"

CHAPTER 4

The Way the Money Goes

APART FROM the urgent need to escape as far as possible from the dingy purlieus of the Temple and never venture near it again, Thackeray's motive in going to France was nothing more than a general scheme of improving his knowledge of French language and literature. After a week in Havre he made his way to Paris by way of Rouen, sketching as he went.

Paris was in the midst of the romantic upheaval. He read the latest outpourings of Hugo and Balzac with enjoyment, but with a derisive eye for their extravagances and bombast, and he thought vaguely about writing a magazine article on modern French literature. He even dreamed of writing a witty novel, though he had not yet invented a plot for it. As usual, he haunted the theaters, and somewhat less often the Bibliothéque Royale, where he copied engravings. Having subscribed to a quiet reading room in the Palais Royal, he was briefly fascinated with the psychological writings of Victor Cousin. For the month of September he took a room in Choisy-le-roi, but as it was only a few miles from Paris he came into the city fairly often.

Gambling continued to occupy many of his evenings. A solemn vow to resist the temptation was broken the very next day after too many glasses of wine at dinner at the Trois Frères. In this idle life with a few boon companions a twenty-pound note melted away every week with ominous regularity.

Among new acquaintances was the English farce writer, J. R. Planché, who was on a visit to Paris. "He was at that time a slim young man," Planché says, "rather taciturn, and not displaying any particular love or talent for literature. Drawing appeared to be his favorite amusement; and he often sat by my side while I was reading or writing, covering any scrap of paper lying about with the most spirited sketches and amusing caricatures."

When he went back to London at the end of November, he was made so welcome by the Bullers and a crowd of other friends that the sensitive FitzGerald complained pathetically about being allowed so little of his time. More serious concerns were also occupying him, for he was becoming anxious about his finances. He tried to recoup some of his losses by lending his money through a bill-discounting firm in Birchin Lane. Occasionally he marketed a caricature; the day after seeing the sensational American Negro actor, Ira Aldridge, in *Othello*, he walked into a lithograph shop, made a sketch of the actor from memory, and sold it then and there.

A more important undertaking was the purchase of a weekly newspaper. Sonorously entitled *The National Standard and Journal of Literature, Science, Music, Theatricals, and the Fine Arts*, it had begun publication in January, 1833. The first editor was a young hack writer, Frederick William Naylor Bayley, known as "Alphabet Bayley" to distinguish him from "Butterfly Bayly," the drawing-room poet; but the issue of May 11 announced a change in ownership and editorship. Full of enthusiasm over this opportunity to improve the public taste, to publish his own writings, and to grow rich in the process, Thackeray promised his readers that he would have "the assistance of a host of literary talent."

One of the quaintest characters who had struck up a friendship with him was Francis Mahony, a priest from the County Cork whose convivial habits had brought him into disfavor with his superiors. After wide wandering on the Continent, Mahony had come to London and attached himself to the Irish journalistic brigade that was led by his fellow-townsman, Dr Maginn; and he asserted, twenty years later, that he helped Thackeray to obtain the services of Maginn in editing *The National Standard*. Although the tale shows certain discrepancies with known facts, it is circumstantial and probably true in the main, for while the Padre never hesitated to make a good story better he was too loyal a friend of Thackeray to lie about him.

The gist of the story is that Thackeray asked Mahony to recommend an editor, and Mahony nominated Maginn. With customary effrontery, Maginn demanded an advance payment of five hundred pounds, "for deck clearing." Although protesting, Thackeray finally consented, and handed over the first hundred, whereupon Mahony arranged a meeting between the two at the Crown Tavern, Vinegar Yard, Drury Lane, at which plans for the paper were discussed.

To magnify his own share in the transaction, Mahony asserted that this was the first meeting between Thackeray and Maginn, whereas in fact they had become acquainted a year before, while Mahony was living abroad. Thackeray did indeed advance five hundred pounds to Maginn about this time, but it was regarded as a loan to rescue him from the debtors' prison, rather than as a retaining fee. On the other hand, even such an open-handed patron as Thackeray would hardly have advanced so large a sum to so notoriously irresponsible a borrower without some *quid pro quo*. Thackeray certainly needed someone of experience to guide his first editorial toddling; and Maginn, with several other and more important irons in the fire, must have been glad to pick up some easy money in his spare time, without allowing his connection to be publicly announced. The existence of an editorial "ghost" is indicated by the fact that as soon as Thackeray tired of his new toy he was able to go abroad and apparently to handle it by remote control.

At first, however, he plunged into the new task with his usual enthusiasm. Although his mother was staying in Bayswater, he sent the office-boy to her with a note to say he was far too busy to come and see her. For six weeks he worked diligently, turning out reviews of books and plays, interspersed with pretty shabby lampoons in verse and prose at the expense of current notables, illustrated with woodcuts by the author. Then he suddenly decided that it would "look well" for the paper to have a Parisian correspondent, and so he rushed back to France.

He told his mother that he expected to be able to collect enough material in a month to last for nearly a year; but in the very next sentence he confessed that

he was thinking seriously of turning artist. He regarded drawing as his best talent, and he certainly liked it better than any other work; and he insisted that in Paris a painter had greater prestige than a lawyer or a clergyman. The only obstacle would be the three years of study that he deemed necessary.

His four despatches as Paris correspondent were largely devoted to assailing the extravagance and morbidity of the young romantics:

AN ARTISTIC FRENCH FAMILY

. . . . Faublas is an absolute Joseph compared to the Satanico-Byronico heroes of the present school of romance. As for murders, etc., mere Newgate Calendar crimes, they are absolutely drugs in the literary market . . . To satisfy La Jeune France, you must accurately represent all the anatomical peculiarities attending the murder, or crime in question; you must dilate on the clotted blood, rejoice over the scattered brains, particularize the sores and bruises, the quivering muscles and the gaping wounds.

He summarized a popular volume of tales by making a statistical table of the murders, rapes, executions, adulteries, and suicides; and in his next letter he sardonically recounted the actual suicides of several of the Byronic young gentlemen of the Boulevards.

Repelling the seductions of art study, he was soon back at his desk in St Paul's Churchyard. In spite of frequent editorials that boasted of growing circulation and influence, the paper was putting up a losing fight against such powerful rivals as the *Literary Gazette* and the *Athenaeum*. According to Mahony's account, its ill success led to quarrels and mutual recrimination between Thackeray and Maginn.

Thackeray had an idea of selling the journal, but Maginn put in a preposterous claim that he was a part owner and would have to be consulted. Mahony, again serving as peacemaker, arranged another meeting at the Crown Tavern; Maginn flew into a towering rage, and put on such a dramatic performance that Thackeray, half amused and half alarmed, gave up trying to assert his perfectly valid authority.

This episode is perhaps connected with Thackeray's remark to his mother in September that he had received an offer of a partner, and thought he would accept it, but that the matter could not be settled for a week or ten days. Maginn's tantrum may have been the reason why the projected partnership was never mentioned again.

The sales of the paper had increased by about twenty during the past month, Thackeray reported in November. "At this rate I shall be ruined before it succeeds." Not unnaturally he gave way to depression and a growing weariness of "this dismal city." He found even his favorite resort, the theater, "tedious beyond bearing, and a solitary evening in chambers more dismal still." He complained of the cold weather, and of the bad effect of journalism on his style, causing him even in friendly letters to try to end every sentence with "a pert, critical point."

His one place of refuge was the Garrick Club, which had recently been founded as a gathering place for literary and theatrical men. Thackeray had taken the lead in demanding the inclusion of a smoking room, and he soon formed a regular habit of dropping in to read the latest reviews and smoke and chat with the agreeable coterie. He told his mother that it was the only spot where he could mingle with "gentlemen who drop their absurd English aristocratical notions. You see by this what I am thinking of—I wish we were all in a snug apartment in the Rue de Provence."

His longing for Paris seems too intense to be inspired wholly by intellectual affinities. More than once in his letters of this time, masked with his customary jesting tone, there are allusions to marriage. In the letter just quoted, he contrasts London with Paris "where one makes friends; here, though for the last three years I have lived, I have not positively a single female acquaintance. I shall go back to Paris, I think, and marry somebody." And a month later, when he had returned to Paris, he remarked again: "I want now to settle, to marry, and then to live in the little house in Albion Street, going to church regularly, rising early, and walking in the Park with Mrs T." This was accompanied by a sketch showing him as a plump and pompous husband, escorting a parasolled wife and four remarkably plain children.

Although still ostensibly managing the *National Standard* and writing his share of its contents, he now applied himself seriously to his training in art. He worked from morning to night at Le Poittevin's *atelier*, and began to think that within a year he might be able to paint something worth looking at. As usual, however, his interest in people conflicted with his persistence in work: his fellow-students delighted him with their merriment and their Bohemian ways, their poverty and their racy *argot*. Most of them, in his opinion, showed more skill in fencing than in drawing. He described a typical breakfast for five, "consisting of five sausages, three loaves, and a bottle of wine, for fifteen sous. Afterwards pipes succeeded, and then songs, imitations of all the singers in Paris." This scarcely

DREAMS OF MATRIMONY

sounds like the training of an Academician, any more than the snug suppers at Trinity had laid a sound foundation for scholarship or the bar.

For several months he traveled back and forth between the two cities, living a double life as journalist and art student; but the paper had little chance to gain strength under absentee management. In December he was too busy to accept an invitation to Christmas dinner, as he was very anxious to make a good showing with the first number of the new year; he was changing the title of the paper and raising the price to threepence. In spite of this display of courage, no profits materialized; and at the end of January, nine months after Thackeray had gaily assumed the editorship, the *National Standard* was silently furled.

One reason for this sudden change of tactics was the utter loss of his remaining capital. He had probably spent almost half of the twenty thousand pounds that his father had left, and the rest vanished with the failure of a Calcutta bank in 1833. Much of his stepfather's funds having been lost in the same crash, the Car-michael-Smythes took a small house in London and prepared to give up their country estate. Thackeray, trying to face disaster manfully, said, "I ought to thank Heaven for making me poor—it has made me much happier than I should have been with the money."

Relieved of all other responsibilities, he went back to the *Pays Latin* with fresh vigor. He worked under several masters, including Antoine-Jean Gros, who only a few years before had been created a Baron for his huge heroic compositions, but who was now so badgered and ridiculed by the romantics that while Thackeray was in Paris he drowned himself. Among the English artists, Thackeray's chief associates were two, both older than himself, William Darley and John Brine. Darley, a brother of George Darley, the poet, was a shy hypochondriac who wore thick carpet slippers over his shoes in a vain effort to keep warm. Brine was a Scotsman who aspired to paint vast gloomy landscapes in the manner of Salvator Rosa, but who changed his mind so often that all his ambitious works were in a constant state of being repainted.

The bearded, lounging, smoking, quarreling, starving, insouciant life of studio and garret, a by-product of the turmoil of romanticism, was later to be sentimentalized by half a century of authors from Murger to Du Maurier; but when Thackeray knew it, it was still unchronicled. To him, its childlike naïveté and disregard for the concerns of the practical world were pleasantly reminiscent of the life in the little German court as he had enjoyed it four years before. The antics of a young model who was too vivacious to pose, but sang songs and cut capers all around the studio; the grotesque scurrilities uttered by the dignified-looking *maître*, who outside of painting hours was a worthy family man and wearer of a *cordon d'honneur*: glimpses such as these were lovingly recorded in his notebook, beside the sober entries of the paintings he copied in the Louvre, and his considered judgment that Lucas van Leyden was a better draughtsman than Dürer. Once, when he was challenged by a custodian in the Louvre for sketching a painting without a student's permit, he answered in a grotesque jargon of Anglicized French and persuaded the man that he was ignorant of the French language.

Writing a little later about the cheapness and thoroughness of the Parisian art schools, he declared: "Here, a young man, for his ten pounds [a year], has all sorts of accessory instruction, models, etc.; and has, further, and for nothing, numberless incitements to study his profession which are not to be found in England—the streets are filled with picture-shops, the people themselves are pictures walking about; the churches, theatres, eating houses, concert rooms are covered with pictures; Nature herself is inclined more kindly to him, for the sky is a thousand times more bright and beautiful, and the sun shines for the greater part of the year."

Adelaide Kemble was in Paris, studying singing, and Thackeray sometimes visited her in the Rue de Clichy, where she lodged with a Miss Foster. His warmest friendships, however, centered in the home of Eyre Evans Crowe, the Paris cor-

TYPES OF THE LATIN QUARTER

respondent of the *Morning Chronicle*. In their apartment *au cinquième*, in the Rue 29 Juillet, Mrs Crowe kept open house every Saturday night with Irish hospitality, to a motley crowd of artists and writers, French, German, and British. She would rattle off Irish jigs and Scottish reels, or bring the whole company around the piano to shout German *studentenlieder*; but always (as one of the sons later stated) "the supreme enjoyment" was a song by Thackeray.

AN ENGLISH FAMILY IN THE TUILERIES

He was the favored guest, with a chair reserved for him every Saturday at dinner. Arriving an hour before the meal, he could scarcely enter the drawing room before the children pounced on him with demands that he draw pictures for them. He produced a series of grotesque illustrations of Byron, and others to accompany cautionary nursery rhymes, such as:

> Little Miss Perkins she loved pickled gherkins;
>   She went to the cupboard and stole some;
> But she found her mistake when her stomach did ache,
>   They were so shocking unwholesome.

His masterpiece, however, was an illustrated record of the imaginary adventures of their friend Brine in Spain. The painter had gone to Madrid in the hope of finding commissions for portraits, and Thackeray made up an outrageously comic legend of his romantic career there. In a kindly, laughter-loving, child-infested home, such as the Crowes', Thackeray always found his fullest happiness.

Outside of the British circle, he made few friends. In spite of his fluency in French conversation, he was inclined to regard the natives as amusing—and sometimes exasperating—puppets rather than as human beings. He did become accepted in the coterie of Roger de Beauvoir, a young man who had acquired notoriety not only by his romantic novels but also by his prodigality and his amatory adventures. Another writer of romances, the Comtesse Dash, who met Thackeray at Beau-

THE GALLERY AT DEBUREAU'S THEATRE

voir's, described him in her Memoirs as "rather a whimsical young man, full of wit and humor; he talked by fits and starts, but, when he was in the mood, he ran off witticisms that were quite French in style, and said them with all the calm impassiveness of his nature."

Even in Paris he was not free from the ramifications of his clan. His maternal grandmother, Mrs Butler, was in residence there, and for some time he made his home with her, enduring with wry good-humor her sarcasm, tea-parties, gossip, and hypochondria. As 1834 wore on he began to realize that he was not likely to become a competent painter in a year, as he had anticipated—or even in the three years of his earlier estimate. His own particular style of quick caricaturing had become too deep a habit to be set aside in favor of serious and thorough workmanship. His months in the *ateliers* had little if any perceptible effect upon his invincibly amateurish type of sketch—the lumpy, short-necked figures, the sawdust-doll attitudes, and the hearty drollery that survived all technical defects. He began to consider the advisability of making new plans for a career.

His alternative would have to be literature. Sometime during 1834 he was definitely adopted as a contributor to *Fraser's Magazine*. Maginn is said to have specially insisted upon his acceptance into the group, as a consequence of their recent association in *The National Standard*. The off-hand manner in which material from many sources went into a common pot and was stewed into a spicy ragout, with Maginn as chef, makes the identifying of individual work amazingly difficult. Thackeray's only unquestioned contribution in 1834 was an adaptation of Béranger's "Roi d'Yvetot." Perhaps he also wrote *Hints for a History of Highwaymen*, which was a satire on Harrison Ainsworth's sensational stories of criminals. He may have supplied short reviews of poetry and novels, incorporated into articles by Maginn. At any rate, by the end of the year he was regarded as one of the editor's coterie, and his portrait was included in a group picture of the contributors, drawn by Maclise, in the issue of January, 1835.

The identification of Thackeray's work is rendered baffling by the intentional uniformity of style cultivated by the staff. Maginn's brilliant informal manner set the pattern, and the others willingly echoed it. Thackeray had not as yet developed any literary technique of his own. In the days of *The Snob*, he had been content to imitate such popular humorists as Theodore Hook, and his later contact with Maginn had only encouraged him in the same vein. The ease, gaiety, and headstrong assertiveness of Maginn's writing were altogether to his taste. His first work for *Fraser's*, then, however much or little it may have been, was important in shaping him as an author. The magazine offered not only a vehicle for publication but a compulsive model to be imitated, and Thackeray had no scruples of self-conceit to prevent his compliance.

The year 1835 is practically a void in his career. He rebelled at last against his grandmother's scoldings and established himself in a "little den" in the Rue des Beaux Arts, where, as usual, he made an optimistic vow to work hard and "lead a most pious, sober, and godly life." Among his friends was Henry Reeve, a rather priggish young scion of the Norwich Unitarian circle, who was wintering in Paris to study the prison system. In a letter to his mother Reeve tells that after attending the opera he and Thackeray "took tea and had a long talk of the doings of French artists. He complains of the impurity of their ideas, and of the jargon of a corrupt life which they so unwisely admit into their painting rooms. Thackeray's drawing—if I may judge by his note-book—is as pure and accurate as any I have seen. He is a man whom I would willingly set to copy a picture of Raphael's, as far at least as the drawing goes; but he does not seem likely to get into a system of massive colouring, if I may judge by what he said."

News of the doings of his friends in England was brought by the indefatigable gossip Mahony, who was by this time better known by the pseudonym of "Father Prout" under which he contributed to *Fraser's Magazine*. When Prout reported triumphs achieved by the young painters, Frank Stone and Daniel Maclise, Thack-

A PARK SCENE

THACKERAY AND A FRIEND

eray fell into despondency. The sum total of his two years in Paris was "an awful collection" of costume studies and "some infamous water colour copies perpetrated at the Louvre." "I have got enough torn-up pictures to roast an ox by," he wrote gloomily to Stone. "The sun riseth upon my efforts and goeth down on my failures, and I have become latterly so disgusted with myself and art and everything belonging to it, that for a month past I have been lying on sofas reading novels, and never touching a pencil. .. O God, when will Thy light enable my fingers to work, and my colours to shine? If in another six months I can do no better, I will arise and go out and hang myself."

He made friends at this time with a triumvirate of clever young Englishmen who helped to turn his attention from painting to letters. Occupying lodgings in the Rue d'Amboise was John Barnett, the composer of a recent operatic success, *The Mountain Sylph*. With Barnett lived Henry Mayhew, who had fled from the solicitor's office of his father to see life and learn to be an author. These two had encountered Douglas Jerrold, who, though already famous for *Black Eyed Susan* and other plays, was temporarily taking refuge in Paris from the consequences of an incautiously endorsed bill. Thackeray usually made a fourth in a nightly rendezvous for "coffee and caporal" at Barnett's rooms. Interspersed with nonsense and chaff, the conversation often developed into arguments over the old problem of aesthetics,—"which is the highest art, music, painting, or drama?"—with Barnett championing the musicians, Thackeray sticking up for the painters, and Jerrold usually winning the debate with magniloquent citations from Shakespeare to prove the preeminence of the playwrights.

Tom Trollope was visiting Paris that spring at the apron strings of his mother while she wrote one of her sprightly travel books. To enjoy the early June sunshine, a large picnic party, with several nationalities represented, spent a merry day in the woods of Montmorenci. Half a dozen of the young men, including Trollope and Thackeray, hired some donkeys and tried to rouse them to racing speed. Amidst various ludicrous episodes, Thackeray's mount bucked its long-legged rider over its ears and into a heap of sharp stones. The fall was so heavy that the party were alarmed for a few minutes, and indeed the victim was left with a scar added to his already disfigured countenance.

With no more serious occupations than these, Thackeray was restless. He planned to go to Germany for the summer and Italy in the autumn, but when he heard that his parents were intending to come to Paris for a month he changed his mind and decided that he could profit by further tedious days of copying in the Louvre. Then his friend Curzon happened to mention to him that a château in Normandy, with an excellent garden and a wilderness, was available at an annual rent of sixteen pounds. Thackeray wrote ecstatically to FitzGerald, suggesting that they take it and withdraw from the world for a year. "We would fit it up in the old style, and live in it after the manner of Orestes and Pylades."

He applied to the *Morning Chronicle*, presumably on the strength of his friendship with Crowe, to be appointed correspondent in Constantinople, thinking that thus he could earn a good salary for a year and at the same time fill his sketch-book with picturesque scenes. Three months later, although the hope of the appointment had faded, the scheme of a Mediterranean tour was still alive. He intended to travel from Munich to Venice by the most scenic route, and then cross over to Turkey for a week or so, "just to be able to say in a book that I have been there"; after which he would make a thorough tour of Italy. Upon taking the manuscript to England he would get three hundred guineas for it; "then I will exhibit at the Water-colour Society, and sell my ten drawings forthwith."

In spite of these rosy dreams, he did little except drift rather aimlessly about the studios of the Latin Quarter. In January, 1836, however, his friend Reeve reported that "the excellent and facetious being is at the present moment editing an English paper here, in opposition to Galignani's." It was a venture sponsored by G. W. M. Reynolds, an enterprising young Englishman, who had his headquarters at a bookshop in the Rue St Augustin. Many years later, Thackeray told James Payn that the first publisher who ever paid him for something he had written was Reynolds. He did not hold the position long; in the spring Reynolds was advertising for a new editor who would be willing to invest two hundred pounds.

In thus taking a salaried position, Thackeray abruptly emerged from his dilettante existence in a lather of energy and ambition. While dining with a friend at a boarding-house he had met a gentle, red-haired Irish girl of seventeen, Isabella Getkin Creagh Shawe. Her late father, Colonel Matthew Shawe, of Doneraile in the County Cork, had been military secretary to the Marquess of Wellesley when he was Viceroy, and had known some of the Thackeray and Becher connection in his old Indian days. Mrs Shawe, who had been a Miss Creagh, also of a Cork family, belonged to that tribe of matchmaking mammas who lived on the Continent because of the limited income of officers' widows, and scanned prospective suitors of their marriageable daughters with the intensity of a hawk.

Thackeray heard Miss Shawe sing in a sweet little voice, and was captivated. In the diary of the supercilious Reeve, the news was chronicled: "Thackeray . . . has fallen in love, and talks of being married in less than twenty years. What is there so affecting as matrimony? I dined yesterday with his object, who is a nice, simple, girlish girl; a niece of old Colonel Shawe, whom one always meets at the Sterlings'."

Realizing how completely he had lapsed into indolence within the ever-narrowing confines of his allowance from home, Thackeray bestirred himself to the unprecedented task of earning his own living. He wrote an article for *Fraser's* on

"Paris and the Parisians in 1835" (a review of Mrs Trollope's book). He sought commissions as an illustrator, but destroyed his own trial drawings in disgust. And he produced his first independent publication, a little brochure of eight lithographs entitled *Flore et Zéphyr*, repeating in visual form a burlesque of that classical ballet that he had written for *The National Standard* three years earlier. His drawings show a very muscular and hard-featured pair of performers in six of the conventional postures theoretically symbolic of profound emotions; the two final pictures of the series are Hogarthian glimpses of the hero and heroine in their private haunts. The booklet appeared simultaneously in London and Paris; the titles of the drawings were in French, and the artist assumed the name of "Théophile Wagstaffe," thus accounting for the monogram of "W. T." which appeared in the corner of each picture.

None of these undertakings promised to yield profits sufficient for setting up housekeeping, but a more hopeful vista was about to open. Undeterred by the fate of *The National Standard*, Major Carmichael-Smyth was preparing to speculate in journalism on a much more imposing scale. A group of the radical politicians of the day, including Joseph Hume, George Grote, Sir William Molesworth, J. A. Roebuck, and Thackeray's friend Charles Buller, were anxious to promote the founding of a daily newspaper that would voice their doctrines of religious and civil equality, universal ballot, and triennial parliaments. Presumably Buller consulted Thackeray, who in turn introduced his stepfather. The Metropolitan Newspaper Company was formed, with a capital of £60,000, and with Major Carmichael-Smyth as chairman. Thackeray put in recommendations on behalf of his friends in the literary profession, with the result that Laman Blanchard was engaged as editor and Douglas Jerrold as dramatic critic, while Thackeray himself was promised the post of Paris correspondent. A small and moribund paper, *The Public Ledger*, was purchased, and plans were laid to rename it *The Constitutional* and to begin publication as soon as a reduction in the stamp duty, which had just passed parliament, would enable the paper to sell at a lower price.

These plans did not immediately wean Thackeray away from his previous intentions. While he was in London at an early stage of the negotiations, he talked to William Macready at the Garrick Club, and the actor noted the encounter in his diary thus: "Met Thackeray, who has spent all his fortune, and is now about to settle in Paris, I believe as an artist." And just at the same time he made his most positive bid for employment as an illustrator.

The firm of Chapman & Hall, he learned, was in a quandary over one of their publications. Having engaged a promising young journalist named Charles Dickens to provide letterpress for a series of comic engravings by Robert Seymour, they had no sooner launched *The Posthumous Papers of the Pickwick Club* in monthly parts than Seymour inconsiderately shot himself, and the venture was in imminent danger of ruin. Thackeray promptly picked up a few specimens of his sketches and sought out Dickens at his chambers in Furnival's Inn, to offer himself as artist for the continuation of the serial.

As he climbed the shadowy staircase and sniffed the musty odors of cobwebs and legal documents, he must have been reminded of his own recent and unlamented sojourn in the Middle Temple. This interview assumed in his mind the significance of an augury. If his drawings were accepted, he would be permanently launched on the profession of illustrating; if they were not, he would feel that fate meant him for other things. He looked with interest at the smallish young man with the dark curls and flashing eyes, in whose slightly theatrical voice and distinctly gaudy clothes he intuitively recognized what he and his friends summed up in the Cambridge slang word "snob." Half a year younger than Thackeray, Dickens had already won some repute for his magazine and newspaper sketches under the name of "Boz"; self-confidence and energy radiated from him; no one could fail to share his own certainty that he was on his way.

Boz looked without enthusiasm at the drawings—grotesque little figures with arms like flippers and a persistent tendency to squint. From the paper he glanced up at his visitor, with his Cambridge drawl and his monocle, and the somewhat patronizing manner that masked his diffidence. Dickens felt vaguely discontented in the presence of anyone so outrageously tall. There was satisfaction, however, in the fact that this supercilious young giant was applying to him for employment. Politely but firmly, he stated that the drawings did not satisfy him; he didn't think that his sense of humor and Mr Thackeray's would be likely to harmonize. As the rejected artist groped his short-sighted way down the stairs again, he knew that he would accept the proffered engagement as Paris correspondent for the future *Constitutional*.

A few weeks later, as it happened, after he had returned to France, he received overtures for his services as illustrator to another popular novelist. The next book by Harrison Ainsworth, *Crichton*, was to be laid largely in Paris; and Father Prout, who was helping Ainsworth with the details of local color, recommended his friend Thackeray as being well qualified to make the drawings. Ainsworth sent suggestions to Thackeray, and the publisher, Macrone, forwarded the proof sheets of the book; but the drawings were not forthcoming.

Thackeray was probably not too eager to be associated with the chief novelist of the "Newgate Calendar" school, which he despised. By the beginning of July Ainsworth made up his mind that he would rather have the book illustrated by Daniel Maclise. Consequently Father Prout was placed in an awkward position. "As to any fear of compromising me," he wrote to Ainsworth, "don't let that annoy you—my cloth protects me from pistol shots; besides it is I who ought to call out Thackeray. It would be more business-like were you to write *in propia persona* both to Maclise and Thackeray. I fear the latter at least may have thought so and have disdained to answer *me*. Painters and poets are all crank people apt to take umbrage at imaginary offenses."

A week later Ainsworth wrote to his publisher to say: "I saw the 'Father' this morning. He has heard nothing from Thackeray, and expects to hear nothing. I am not displeased with this, as I am sure Maclise will make admirable illustrations."

Thackeray's failure to provide the drawings was probably caused chiefly by mental disturbance over his love affair. Not at all favorably disposed toward her daughter's penniless and unemployed lover, Mrs Shawe was doing everything she could to break up their engagement. When Thackeray had to be absent in London, the few brief letters that he received from Isabella were full of doubts, and after he returned to Paris her mother ordered her to see him less often. Early in July Isabella took offence because Thackeray gave her too much good advice. In one quarrel he accused her of frivolity, and in a more serious one she declared that his love was not "pure" enough for her. A brief separation ensued.

Thackeray was not unaware that his beloved was indolent and immature, and he heartily disliked her mother; but his love was made all the more tender by an element of protectiveness, and he trusted that her character would develop under his guidance. His appeals brought a reconciliation, and on August 20 they were married at the British Embassy in Paris by its chaplain, Bishop Luscombe. The bride's mother promised an allowance of fifty pounds a year for pin money, to eke out the eight guineas a week that Thackeray was to receive as soon as his work for *The Constitutional* should commence.

The young couple established themselves in apartments at 15 *bis*, Rue Neuve St Augustin. They slept late in the mornings, and Thackeray could smoke his cigars in the drawing-room unreproved, and for dinner with Bohemian friends it was only a few steps to Terré's restaurant, famous for its Spanish dishes, bouillabaisse, and good claret. "I am sure," Thackeray wrote to his mother, "I love you better since I was married than before; perhaps it is because, being so happy, I am grown a little more *good*."

The appearance of *The Constitutional* had been delayed from month to month, as government red-tape delayed the reduction in the stamp-tax; and several of its original proponents lost heart during the interval. At last, four weeks after Thackeray's wedding, the first number came out; and for the next five months Thackeray's Paris despatches, signed "T. T.," appeared fairly regularly, two or three times a week. The responsibility of keeping them up, and earning a salary thereby, was a heavy drag on him. "I have become a woeful bad scribe since I have begun to sell my pen at so much a line," he wrote ruefully to FitzGerald, excusing himself for the infrequence of his letters.

The interests of his paper were boresomely political. In consequence, his despatches were dull, laborious, and impersonal, with little of the sparkle that had enlivened his four Paris reports for *The National Standard*. He hammered monotonously on his profound contempt for Louis Philippe. To Thackeray, the Government of July was the acme of reaction and despotism, with the full blame resting on the futility and moral cowardice of the King, "the old humbug," whose defection from his early preachment of liberalism rendered him all the more contemptible. Such digressions as Thackeray allowed himself from this theme usually uttered equally somber views on the degrading social influence of capital punishment, or the French hatred of England's foreign policy for its intrigues and meddling.

The writing of the despatches, however, did not absorb all his time. He found employment on *Galignani's Messenger*, the leading English journal in Paris, at wages of ten francs a day; but as the paper consisted almost wholly of personal gossip transcribed from English newspapers, his work must have been unutterably dull. In December he heard a rumor that another evening paper was being planned in London, and sent an eager request to his friend John Kemble begging for his recommendation as Paris correspondent. The fact that he was serving a rival paper did not disturb him. "I have plenty of time for another similar duty, and plenty of employment for the additional weekly guineas it might bring. . . I have an alarming prospect before me of many additions to the race of Roaldus de Richmond. . . I am grown strangely fat, and am the happiest man in the neighborhood; I have a good wife, good dinners, plenty of work, and good pay—Can a man want more?"

The rumored newspaper did not materialize, but another suggestion in the same letter may have borne some fruit. Kemble was editor of a new quarterly, *The British and Foreign Review*, and Thackeray proposed sending an article for it, on the ground that "we want lightness, to my thinking." The extent of his contributions has not been determined, but there is little doubt that Kemble accepted contributions from his friend.

Nor had Thackeray given up his ambitions to be an artist. In January the proposal to illustrate *Crichton* was suddenly renewed—Maclise to provide frontispieces and Thackeray the rest of the illustrations. He promised to work better and more speedily than four months before. The arrangement fell through, however, because Ainsworth changed his publisher. Thackeray next sent a batch of drawings to London to be submitted with an application for membership in the Water Colour Society, and begged his friends Frank Stone and George Cattermole to use their influence in his behalf. Though far from confident of acceptance, he promised that "I will work hard and, please God, improve. Perhaps also the waggish line which I have adopted in the drawings may render them acceptable for variety's sake." There is no indication, however, that the committee of the Society was amenable to waggishness.

The Constitutional was suffering heavy weather. In the first number of the new year, it printed a solemn pledge from its distinguished Radical supporters that they would subscribe to it for the twelvemonth, and hoped that their followers would do likewise; but by the middle of February a crisis was imminent. The editor, with a wife and five children, had not been paid for months; the correspondent in Lisbon sent word that he was destitute. The shareholders were called upon to subscribe an extra pound per share. The size of the paper, which had been enlarged by a column a page, was reduced to its former dimensions. The staff was drastically cut. And Thackeray was brought home from Paris to earn his salary by serving as managing director.

FANNY ON CANE-BOTTOMED CHAIR

These agreeable essayists and playwrights were clearly incapable of managing a daily paper. The scanty available cash was being foolishly applied. More and more of the preliminary patrons were withdrawing their support. The question in Thackeray's mind became: Which would occur first, the suspension of the paper or the birth of his child? On his eight guineas a week, he had actually been able to save money during the first six months of his married life; but now doctor's bills had to be prepared for. His mother-in-law failed to pay the third quarterly instalment on the dowry of fifty pounds a year, and thereafter, except for one payment of ten pounds "on account," never supplied a single *sou*. For the time being, Thackeray and his wife were staying with the Carmichael-Smyths; but if the paper failed, the last vestige of their wealth would go too, and the Thackerays would be not only penniless but literally homeless.

On June 9, a daughter was born to the Thackerays at the Carmichael-Smyth's house, 18, Albion Street, Hyde Park. Three weeks later, Laman Blanchard had to pawn his watch to help to pay for the last number of *The Constitutional*, which, in a heavy mourning frame, simultaneously announced the death of King William IV and its own demise.

Major and Mrs Carmichael-Smyth withdrew to Paris, the haven of bankrupt

Englishmen. Unlike most of those refugees, the Major retained a hope of paying off his debts, and Thackeray promised to contribute his share. For the moment, however, neither of them had anything but promises to offer.

The Thackerays and their infant daughter, Anne Isabella, took a house at No. 13, Great Coram Street, near Brunswick Square, in the quiet confines of Bloomsbury. A devoted retainer, "old John," remained with them as the sole survivor of the household at Larkbeare. On the same day that the slim and shy young Princess Victoria found herself called to ascend a throne, William Makepeace Thackeray had found himself unwillingly compelled to become a professional author.

CHAPTER 5

Learning the Trade

AS HE FACED his uncertain future and weighed the prospects, Thackeray was sober but not appalled. He was not without advantages. He was young, he had influential friends, already he had won a little reputation by his newspaper work. Besides, he had an alternative talent to fall back upon: he was still inclined to think that his true profession might be drawing. His efforts to illustrate *Crichton* having shown his inability to make copper-plates, he cultivated the friendship of George Cruikshank, and practiced etching under the guidance of that master, so that he might be better prepared in the techniques of illustrating books. Commissions, however, were slow in coming. An old friend of his Charterhouse days, John Barrow, engaged him to draw three illustrations for a one-act play, *King Glumpus*; but as only one hundred copies were issued, for private circulation, it brought the artist little in either cash or professional fame.

Whether he was to live by the pencil or by the pen, he still asserted some freedom of choice as to the road he would follow. He declined the first definite offer he received, the editorship of the *Carlisle Patriot*, on the ground that the paper was "too Tory for him." Politics in Cumberland were dominated by the powerful Lonsdale interests, and Thackeray had no desire to be the controlled spokesman of a great county family. Nor could he face the prospect of drawing a safe but tedious salary in a small town on the Scottish border. He would take the risk of surviving as a free lance in the metropolis, where things were happening.

Luckily for him, English journalism was assuming a cast which suited his talents to the full. Both the magazines and the newspapers gave far more scope for a lively, witty, imaginative writer than they had given even ten years before. The heavy old quarterlies, with their long, erudite, anonymous articles, were being rivaled by sprightly magazines that spiced their reviews with humor and were increasing their proportion of fiction. *The New Monthly, Bentley's Miscellany, Fraser's Magazine*—all were hospitable to bright young men with ideas. Newspapers, too, were going through a revolution. Previously they had been either stodgy digests of official records or else scurrilous compilations of scandal and political invective. Now several were acquiring energy, independence, and literary distinction, and of these the most successful was *The Times*, under the editorship of Thomas Barnes.

Thackeray had more than one channel of approach to that paper. The leading editorial writer was Captain Edward Sterling, whose son John had been one of the founders of the Apostles at Cambridge. Having left the University before Thackeray went up, John Sterling had not become one of his intimates; but the Kembles, the Bullers, and others, admirers of both men, formed a link between them. A closer link with the family, however, was provided by Thackeray's wife. The Shawes and Sterlings had been friends for many years, and in her girlhood Isabella Shawe had lived for long periods, almost as a daughter, in Captain Sterling's home. Naturally she brought her husband to the house of these old friends in South Place; and when this led to his being introduced to Thomas Barnes and finding employment with *The Times*, she boasted with laughing pride that she was launching him on the way to fortune.

One of the features in which *The Times* excelled most of the other papers was its book reviews, and in this department Thackeray was engaged. The first book sent to him for review was Thomas Carlyle's massive work, *The French Revolution*, and his problem in dealing with it was rendered delicate by more than its peculiarities and his inexperience. Carlyle was the devoted friend of John Sterling, and had been the tutor of the Bullers. He and Thackeray, however, had not struck up any great intimacy. Both of them were active members of the Fraserian circle, and both were friends of the Goethe household—Carlyle, like Thackeray, had been contributing to Ottilie's *Chaos*. These common interests supplied a basis for conversation, but the craggy Scotsman did not quite know what to make of the quizzical gleam in the young artist's eye.

Considering the hazards, Thackeray's review of *The French Revolution*, which appeared on August 3, must be set down as a competent piece of work. Apart from uttering a warning of the stylistic oddities, he praised it generously and with critical acumen. Fortunately, it reached Carlyle under favorable circumstances. For more than a week the family at Scotsbrig had been waiting impatiently for news of the book's reception, and the author and his two brothers happened to be strolling over Potter Knowe, on a sunny morning, when the postgirl met them and handed them the newspapers. Not too unwillingly, Carlyle consented to sit down in the shade of the hedge, rip open *The Times*, and read the review aloud then and there, "amid considerable laughter and applause."

Through his Sterling connection, Carlyle knew positively who had written it. "The writer is one Thackeray," he informed his brother, "a half-monstrous Cornish-giant kind of painter, Cambridge man, and Paris newspaper correspondent, who is now writing for his life in London. His article is rather like him, and I suppose calculated to do the book good." In another letter, his comment was, "One is obliged to men in these circumstances, who say even with bluster and platitude greater than Thackeray's, 'Behold this man is not an ass.' "

Grudging though these acknowledgments sound, they were as near as Carlyle could come to purring with gratification. To John Stuart Mill he actually admitted that the critique was "a friendly, helpful sort of thing." In fact, so firmly did he establish "that dog Thackeray" in his mind as an admirer that he attributed to him (sometimes erroneously) every favorable allusion that appeared in *The Times* for many months afterwards. Twelve years later, talking to Duffy, he named Thackeray with Mill and Sterling as the men who "had written of his work in various quarters with appreciation and more than sufficient applause."

Thus safely launched as a contributor to *The Times*, Thackeray was soon a familiar denizen of the newspaper quarter. He often dropped in at *The Morning Chronicle*, hoping that he might be eventually appointed to the staff. He did some political reporting for *The Globe*, and was willing to supply society gossip for his friend Laman Blanchard, who had become editor of *The Court Journal*. When Blanchard came into his office one day, accompanied by Richard Hengist Horne, he found Thackeray seated at the editorial desk. "Oh, thank you!" exclaimed Blanchard; "what are you writing there?"

"I don't call it writing," replied Thackeray, without looking up, "so much as squirting a little warm water down a page of your journal."

The London and Westminster Review, edited by John Stuart Mill, was owned by Sir William Molesworth, who had been one of the guarantors of *The Constitutional*. For it Thackeray wrote a review of the second series of *Sketches by Boz*.

By this time, Thackeray and Dickens were becoming better acquainted. The meteoric success of *Pickwick* had carried Dickens into a social circle where Thackeray was already welcome for other reasons. In the same month that his review of *Sketches by Boz* appeared, Thackeray and Dickens were both at an evening party of Mrs Buller's, the other guests including James and Harriet Martineau, John Stuart Mill, Macready, and several Radical politicians. "About Mr Thackeray," reported the redoubtable Miss Martineau, "I had no clear notion in any way, except that he seemed cynical." Dickens had recently become editor of a new magazine, *Bentley's Miscellany*, which was going further than its competitors in printing fiction and other light entertainment as its principal contents. Dickens was on the look-out for promising contributors; Thackeray was eager to find markets for his wares. In the September number of *Bentley's*—just two months after Thackeray's review of Dickens's book in *The London and Westminster*—appeared the first original work of fiction by Thackeray to achieve the glory of print.

His contribution might easily have passed for another of the *Sketches by Boz*. Entitled *The Professor*, it had all the mannerisms of the early stories of Dickens, such as his invincible jocosity and jauntiness and his accurate use of detail in depicting lower middle-class London. The action of the story was divided between a young ladies' school in Hackney and an oyster-shop in Cheapside. As compared with the Dickens sketches, however, it showed many traces of the amateur, in its lame explanations, jerky movement, and sudden accessions of flagrant burlesque.

The pen-name that was signed to this tale was "Goliah Gahagan." The periodical literature of the time was much addicted to pseudonyms, as a transition from the anonymity of the older reviews. Popularized by *Blackwood's Magazine* and carried further by *Fraser's*, the device of giving the contributors not only fanciful names but fictitious characters and careers had several advantages: it established in the readers a sense of intimacy and continuing interest which sometimes tided over thin spots and repetitions; it provided the writers with a ready-made jumping-off place when they approached each new topic; and it sometimes served as a useful defence against libel actions and horsewhippings.

Dickens himself had first appeared under the name of "Boz"; but he had made no effort to create a fictitious personality, and he soon dropped the nickname as his fame increased. With Thackeray, however, the case was different: the use of a definite *alter ego,* such as he had grown accustomed to among his friends on the staff of *Fraser's,* was a real and welcome protection. Subconsciously, perhaps, he was influenced by the old prejudice that authorship was not a gentleman's game— just as Walter Scott had doggedly clung to the legend of "the great unknown"; but a more potent incentive was his sincere humility. He had no thought of gaining personal renown by his writings; they were the only way by which he could earn a living for his little family, and he asked nothing more than to be left alone and unrecognized among his congenial friends.

The first assignment which came to him from *Fraser's,* after his definite adoption of a literary career, gave a perfect opportunity for inventing such a disguise. The volume to be reviewed was *My Book; or, The Anatomy of Conduct,* by John Henry Skelton. Its author was a once-prosperous West-End woolen-draper who had acquired a monomania that he was the successor of Beau Brummell and the destined arbitrer of every point of etiquette. Having spent all his money in giving dinners and receptions to such members of "smart society" as would attend—and most of them went in order to enjoy the fun of ridiculing their host thereafter—he led a threadbare existence in dyed whiskers, varnished boots, and a Regency cravat, while he wrote the book that would—in his opinion—establish the science of etiquette forever. Discreet silence would have been the kindest reception for the book; but kindness was never a distinguishing trait of *Fraser's Magazine,* and Maginn and his friends pounced on Skelton as a heaven-sent butt.

Thackeray's treatment of the book, however, was not determined wholly by this irrepressible sense of the ludicrous. The venom of his attack sprang from a graver source. To him, Skelton was a symptom of the infection which he despised most deeply in the society of his day—the outburst of pretension and social "climbing." All his training had conditioned him to believe in the inviolability of caste: his army and country-squire and imperialist ancestry, his Anglo-Indian childhood, his public-school and university friendships. In his view, the smug vulgarity of the newly-rich generation of tradesmen, thrown up by the tides of the factory system and the Napoleonic wars, represented a fatal menace to all culture and good taste. He had already been pillorying their attempts at gentility ever since his schooldays: in his Cockney rhyme about "the romantic little town of Highbury," in his "Ramsbottom" papers for *The Snob*, in his short story for *Bentley's Miscellany* only two months ago. In Skelton he saw such an egregious specimen of the tribe that he set out to demolish it once and for all.

Intending to burlesque Skelton's pose of dignity, he wrote the review in the character of that embodiment of upholstered self-importance, a London footman. Charles Jeames Yellowplush, in his monumental conceit and his idolatry of "fashion," undeniably fulfilled his mission of exposing "Skeltonism" to pitiless mirth. But Thackeray found that he had achieved far more than that: with his flowery speech, misused and misspelled in the manner that had first been practiced in the Ramsbottom papers, and with his knowing comments on society from the vantage-point of below-stairs, the pompous footman became an irresistible comic character in his own right. So prompt was the favorable response of the reading public that the editors of *Fraser's* encouraged Thackeray to delineate him at greater length.

Beginning in January, 1838, therefore, and continuing for eight months, "The Memoirs of Mr C. J. Yellowplush" exploited the phonetic spelling and sophisticated wisdom of that worthy. The series had no coherent structure: against a background of Mr Yellowplush's life and engagements, Thackeray offered a diversity of material. There were three short stories, two of them concerned with an unprincipled gambler, the Hon. Algernon Percy Deuceace, modeled upon the sharper who had fleeced Thackeray in his first London days. Interspersed among these were two further assaults upon current literature, one being a blast against the gossip-mongering of Lady Charlotte Bury's *Diary Illustrative of the Times of George IV*, while the other opened a withering fire upon the most popular "fashionable novelist" of the day, Edward Lytton Bulwer.

Before the "Yellowplush Memoirs" began their run, the unfortunate Dr Maginn, although still nominally the editor of *Fraser's*, had taken refuge in France from the debts which had already occasioned him a sojourn in the sponging-house. Thackeray naturally was disturbed over the five hundred pounds that Maginn had borrowed five years before. When he went over to Paris in February to review the *Salon* for *The Times* and to collect material for other literary projects, he took the opportunity of interviewing the fugitive in Boulogne. Maginn agreed to a firm demand that all the proceeds of his writings for *Fraser's* should be turned over directly to Thackeray by the publisher. Thackeray wrote immediately to Fraser, asking that Maginn's earnings for the past two months be paid to Mrs Thackeray.

The interview had a further result. Revealing to Thackeray that other contributors to the magazine were paid at a higher rate, Maginn incited him to try to profit by his new success. The letter to Fraser therefore included an ultimatum that the Yellowplush papers would not continue unless the payment was increased to twelve guineas a sheet, plus two guineas for an illustration with each instalment.

Thackeray did his best to make the threat effective. He told Fraser that he was in the midst of writing Mr Yellowplush's next adventures, and would "send them to you or not as you like, but in common regard for myself, I won't work under price." He also mentioned that he had discussed another contribution with Maginn, and expected to write most of it in the *diligence* the next day, on his way to Paris.

The severity of the demands, however, was weakened by his obvious discomfort in making them. It was the first time he had ever bargained over his services, and he felt humiliated. At intervals in the letter, the bluntness of the trader lapsed into the apologetic tone of the gentleman: "Pray do not be angry at this decision on my part: it is simply a bargain, which it is my duty to make. Bad as he is Mr Yellowplush is the most popular contributor to your magazine, and ought to be paid accordingly. If he does not deserve more than the Monthly Nurse or the Blue Friars, I am a Dutchman. . .Well, I dare say you will be very indignant, and swear I am the most mercenary of individuals. Not so. But I am a better workman than most in your crew and deserve a better price. You must not, I repeat, be angry, or because we differ as tradesmen, break off our connection as friends. Believe me, that whether I write for you or not, I shall always be glad of your friendship and anxious to have your good opinion." And there is even a hint of panic in the postscript: "Write me a line at Meurice's, Rue de Rivoli. I can send off Yellowplush twenty-four hours after I get yours, drawing and all."

It was a manful effort to adopt a professional attitude toward his work. The positive arrangement with Maginn, to be sure, did not last long—only twenty pounds of the five hundred was ever salvaged. But Thackeray had gained enough confidence in his own value to assert it in terms of cold cash.

The visit to France brought him face to face with another decision. One of the English correspondents in Paris was dying, and Thackeray was certain he could obtain the appointment. The salary was £350, and he would be living once more in the city he loved best. The temptation was strong, but he withstood it. "Then I throw away a very good position in London, where I can make as much, and a little fame into the bargain," he wrote to his wife. "My game, as far as I see it, is to stick to the *Times*."

Either as a cause or a result of this resolution, as well as because he was lonely without his "Toby," he found Paris less enticing than usual. He had always been impatient with the Gothic excesses of the French romantics, and the latest example, Victor Hugo's tragedy of *Marion Delorme*, was the worst of all. After seeing it he felt "sickened and disgusted with the horrid piece. . . . The last act ends with an execution, and you are kept a long hour listening to the agonies of parting lovers and grim speculations about head-chopping, dead bodies, coffins, and what not—I am as sick as if I had taken an emetic." His feelings were too naïvely responsive to suffering to let him enjoy orgies of anguish.

On this visit other features of French culture were also beginning to pall on him. He went to a benefit performance at the Opera, consisting of short turns from all the theaters, and found "everything intolerably tedious" except an act from Gluck's *Orpheus*. And a day at Versailles produced the verdict that the gallery was "a humbug—a hundred gilded rooms with looking-glasses and carved ceilings, and two thousand bad pictures to ornament them."

The short sojourn in Paris marked a definite end to six years in which he had regarded that city as his principal home. When he returned to London this time, it was with a sigh of relief and a clear recognition that the literary profession there, overworked and underpaid and embittered with jealousy though it was, had enlisted him for good. Even the possibility of owning a journal was luring him again, in spite of his two disasters. He wrote to William Jerdan, whose *Literary Gazette* was beginning to slip from the pre-eminence that it had enjoyed for twenty years: "Is it fair to ask whether the *Literary Gazette* is for sale? I should like to treat, and thought it best to apply to the fountain head." But as Jerdan had no intention of parting with his paper, Thackeray's hankering to be a proprietor had to remain unsatisfied.

Competition in the businesses of writing and publishing had risen to cutthroat intensity. In particular, the rival firms of Colburn and Bentley waged war to the knife. Colburn had been for twenty years the most enterprising publisher in England, ready to pay unheard-of prices to successful authors, prompt to capitalize on the name of any person of title or notoriety, no matter how low the literary quality of the resulting works might be. He had been the first to employ large-scale advertising, and had brazenly subsidized critics to "puff" his books. His *New Monthly Magazine* had taken the lead in displacing the stodginess of the older periodicals. Richard Bentley, beginning as his partner, had recently set up in business for himself, and was challenging Colburn's supremacy by using the methods which he had learned in Colburn's own counting house. Naturally, their former friendship was changed to bitter animosity; and the authors profited by the war.

When Bentley, at the beginning of 1837, launched his *Miscellany* amid vast fanfare as a predominantly humorous magazine, with Dickens as editor and a galaxy of other wits to contribute, Colburn made a convulsive effort to revamp his *New Monthly* in response. It had long been his policy to hire some celebrated author as nominal editor, while an underpaid hack did all the work. He now installed the aging Theodore Hook in the seat of honor, and set aside the front section of each month's issue with a separate title as "The Humorist." Naturally,

1. ANCIENT CARLIST 2. BONAPARTIST 3. PARIS ARTIST (CENTER). LOUIS-PHILIPPE GUARDED BY LOYAL GRO- CER AND SERGEANT OF POLICE 4. THE PEOPLE IN A PASSION 5. GENTLEMAN OF FASHION 6. A PRIEST OF PIOUS MIEN

too, he tried to seduce his rival's contributors. And of these, one of the most sus- ceptible proved to be Thackeray. Perhaps Dickens rejected his further offerings;

perhaps Thackeray fancied he would be happier in dealing with another editor; or perhaps simply Colburn offered higher terms. Whatever the reason, his initial story in *Bentley's* had no successor, and five months later he started a series in the *New Monthly* under the same pseudonym.

When signed to *The Professor*, "Goliah Gahagan" had been merely a funny-sounding name, without further identification; but now its bearer emerged in a full-length portrait, not at all consistent with the sort of person who could have been imagined as writing the previous story. Gahagan, it appeared, was a retired officer of the Indian Army, red-whiskered, Irish, and a ferocious fire-eater. His adventures, as recounted in the *New Monthly* during 1838, would have aroused envy in Munchausen. Again Thackeray had discovered an easy formula of entertainment: the tall tales of an unblushing boaster could be spun out as indefinitely and as laughably as the misspelled aphorisms of the footman. For the local color of the exploits in India, Thackeray drew on a vast fund of family traditions; and for the characterization of the impecunious Major he found models in scores of half-pay officers, nearly all Irish and debt-ridden, who haunted the French watering-places.

The two series, running concurrently in *Fraser's* and the *New Monthly*, formed the bulk of his original work during 1838. And in the middle of them he created for himself a third fictitious personality. For the June number of *Fraser's* he wrote a review of the Royal Academy exhibition, and cast it in the form of a letter to an imaginary French painter from an English *confrère* by the name of Michael Angelo Titmarsh. The criticism was frank and amusingly informal; and the characterization of the critic was more subtle than that of Yellowplush or Gahagan for the simple reason that Mr Titmarsh was in all essentials Mr Thackeray. Even the *prénom* of "Michael Angelo" was selected in allusion to the broken nose of that master. Titmarsh, fresh from studying in the Paris *ateliers* and still proud of his own paintings, was Thackeray under the thinnest of disguises, which was yet sufficient to let him feel free to asperse or praise the exhibitors without restraint.

In the course of the year he eked out his literary earnings with some illustrating. As his letter to Fraser indicated, he was able to use the success of his stories to enforce the acceptance of pictures that he drew for them. He also received two outside commissions of some consequence. For his friend Douglas Jerrold's three-volume work entitled *Men of Character* he made twelve full-page illustrations, which were bluntly described by *The Athenaeum* as "only remarkable for the badness of the drawing, and the total absence of humour." This was a publication of Colburn, and just at the same time he was working on a more ambitious undertaking for the rival house. Bentley had offered him twenty pounds to make eighteen colored plates for a travel book, *Damascus and Palmyra*, by Charles G. Addison. The fact that his only knowledge of the Near East was derived from *The*

Arabian Nights was no deterrent to Thackeray; he must have smiled to think of this as the fulfilment of his scheme of three years before to visit Turkey and return with a bulging sketch-book.

All this work combined with his friendships and his domestic happiness to keep him cheerful and confident. He became a member of the Shakespeare Club, which was not so academic as its name suggested but held convivial dinners enlivened with much oratory and argument. The leading participants included Dickens, Jerrold, Blanchard, Macready, T. N. Talfourd, John Forster, Barry Cornwall, and several of Thackeray's painter comrades. His intercourse with a different circle was maintained by his acceptance into the Sterling Club, recently formed by John Sterling to meet once a month at Wills' Coffee House for a cheap dinner and brilliant conversation—"the members chosen unanimously," as the secretary, James Spedding, explained, "from the witty, the worthy, the wise, and the inspired." It included almost all the old "Apostles" group from Cambridge, with the addition of a few gifted writers, painters, publicists, and clerics. At such gatherings Thackeray could sharpen his wits on others that were worthy whetstones.

At home he was devoted to his pretty wife and baby. In July of 1838 a second daughter was born. In spite of his narrow income and his uncertain prospects, Thackeray had been able to write to his wife, during his trip to Paris, in all sincerity: "Here have we been nearly two years married and not a single unhappy day. Oh, I do bless God for all this happiness which He has given us. It is so great that I almost tremble for the future, except that I humbly hope (for what man is certain about his own weakness and wickedness) our love is strong enough to withstand any pressure from without, and as it is a gift greater than any fortune, is likewise one superior to poverty or sickness, or any other worldly evil with which Providence may visit us. . . I think happiness is as good as prayers, and I feel in my heart a kind of overflowing thanksgiving which is quite too great to describe in writing."

As a matter of fact, the only serious threat to his happiness, at the moment, inhered in Thackeray's own temperament and professional conduct. He did not realize that he had picked up his tactics of controversy in a moribund school. The habit of violent invective and personal insult, which Maginn and his friends had practiced for twenty years in *Blackwood's* and *Fraser's*, was going down to defeat before the more responsible and courteous spirit of the new generation. Not only was Thackeray belated in becoming addicted to the bludgeon, but also he learned it as an amateur, and had not been taught by hard experience to beware of its perils.

His first encounters were trivial enough. In a review of a batch of novels he upbraided Mrs Trollope for her narrow religious intolerance. "Oh, that ladies would make puddings and mend stockings! that they would not meddle with religion (what is styled religion we mean) except to pray to God, live quietly among their families, and move lovingly among their neighbours! Mrs Trollope, for instance, who sees so keenly the follies of the other party, cannot see that there is any hypocrisy or bigotry on her part. . . Always bitter against the Pharisees, she does as the Pharisees do. . . Is Mrs Trollope serving God, in making abusive and licentious pictures of those who serve Him in a different way?" And he went on to give a lively picture of Mrs Trollope among the persecutors of the woman taken in adultery. Shortly afterwards, a friend invited him to a party and mentioned that Mrs Trollope would be present. "Oh, by Jove," exclaimed Thackeray, in dismay, "I can't come! I've just cut up her *Vicar of Wrexhill* in a review. I think she tells lies."

In the same article in *Fraser's*, and also in a review in *The Times*, he was equally mordant toward Bulwer's *Ernest Maltravers*, denouncing the author for having his hero seduce an innocent girl. In *The Times*, however, the editorial hand sometimes interfered with Thackeray's copy. His assignments included some dramatic criticism, and he was thereby brought into an embarrassing position with his friend Macready, who was managing Covent Garden Theater with an ambitious program of reviving the glories of the national drama by presenting a Shakespearian repertory interspersed with new plays by English authors of literary distinction. Morbidly suspicious of offence, Macready was convinced that the press had conspired to ruin him, and that *The Times* was the ringleader. The production of Bulwer's *Lady of Lyons*, in February, 1838, was a case in point: the first night was reviewed caustically enough, but when Bulwer's authorship of the play was avowed, a week later, another article appeared in *The Times* and was described by Macready as "vulgar, virulent, and impotent from its display of malice—such an article as I could *wish* my enemy to write against me." Thackeray, meanwhile, had been indicating his personal interest in the Covent Garden venture; on encountering Macready in the Garrick Club, looking up costumes for King Lear, he had gone out of his way to lend him a book on the subject. His conscience, however, cannot have been clear, for in April he called on the actor at the theater and told him "that he had written the criticism on Macbeth in *The Times*, but that much of it had been cut out—that in what he wrote of Bulwer every word of praise was omitted." Macready might have been dubious about the assurance, had he not learned a little later, through an independent source, that John Oxenford, the chief dramatic critic of *The Times*, also admitted to editorial control of his comments on the Macready productions.

Not always, however, could Thackeray thus disavow the blame for his diatribes. In spite of his good-humor in everyday life, he was apt to fall into a blind ideological rage whenever one of his prejudices was inflamed. Nor were these prejudices consistent with each other. The only person whom he despised more than a vulgarian and a *nouveau-riche* climber was the one man among his professional rivals who was definitely better born than himself—Edward Lytton Bulwer. His ostensible reason for attacking Bulwer was his hatred of the "Newgate Calendar" type of fiction, in which, in his opinion, Bulwer and Ainsworth were catering to a debased element in the public and encouraging an appetite for cheap sensationalism. In this he was largely echoing his mentors of *Fraser's*, who had adopted Bulwer as their victim from the very outset of his career. Such a motive, however, is insufficient to justify the malice of his attacks. Thackeray was actuated by personal antipathy far more than by aesthetic theory. Even though he met Bulwer only once, at the home of Ainsworth, the sartorial elegance and mannered pose of the author of *Pelham* infuriated him beyond all reason.

Bulwer was frankly an ambitious young man who had taken to authorship as the readiest way to get wealth and public favor. He was ready to exploit any fad, personal or literary, that would conduce to that end. He exasperated most of his fellow-writers by maintaining a pose of aristocratic superiority while at the same time he made a lot more money than his hard-working competitors. In short, they were envious, and only envy can account for such an unpardonable travesty as Thackeray (himself an invader of authorship from the leisure class) uttered through the mask of Yellowplush:

> ... slim with a hook nose, a pail fase, a small waist, a pare of falling shoulders, a tight coat, and a catarack of black satting tumbling out of his busm, and falling into a gilt velvet weskit ... He fluffed the dust of his shoos, looked at his wiskers in a little pockit-glas, settled his cravatt ... and when I asked him his name, said, in a thick gobbling kind of voice—
> "Sawedwadgeorgeearllittnbulwig."
> "Sir what?" says I, quite aghast at the name.
> "Sawedwad—no, I mean Mistawedwad Lyttn Bulwig."
> My neas trembled under me, my i's fild with tiers, my voice shook, as I past up the venrabble name to the other footman, and saw this fust of English writers go up to the drawing-room ...

The sketch contained long burlesques of Bulwer's high-flown rhetoric and ridicule of his self-praise, including jibes at his expectations of a baronetcy.

It did not take long for the author of such a caricature as this to make enemies, and to be regarded with suspicion as a dangerous man. His relations with his colleagues were being affected in some way by John Forster, whose bulky figure and domineering manners loom large in the literary landscape of the time. Although the devoted admirer of Dickens, Forster was also the confidential editorial adviser of Colburn, and was credited with having been instrumental in luring Thackeray away from *Bentley's* to contribute to the *New Monthly*. He was a bosom companion of Ainsworth, and became a sort of father-confessor to Bulwer. And yet he seldom moves across the scene unaccompanied by an aura of jealousy and suspicion. During the summer of this year he and Thackeray spent many pleasant hours together at the villa which Dickens had rented at Twickenham. In November, however, Macready noted in his diary that Forster called "and showed me a very kind letter from Bulwer to him; asked my advice as to his proper course of conduct with Thackeray, who he said had disclaimed acts of treachery, of which he, Forster, was well assured (on confidential statements) he had been guilty. I told him his only course was to be passive." Whatever the "acts of treachery" may have been, this distant rumble of discord might well grow into a tempest.

Most of Thackeray's readers, being free of personal concern, enjoyed his outbursts of spite as lending piquancy to his work. His unsigned reviews in *The Times* continued to provide a steady income; during 1838 his receipts from this source sometimes exceeded twenty guineas a month. Incidental commissions came his way. In April, 1839, he had articles in two of the serious reviews, the *British and Foreign* and the *London and Westminster*. His loyal friend Barrow had him supply four illustrations for another privately printed play, *The Exquisites*. A further promising idea in that direction, however, met with disappointment. Dickens had picked up a luscious version of the old folk ballad of *Lord Bateman*, and was singing it to all his friends in the Cockneyest of tones. Thackeray decided that it ought to be published with suitable illustrations; he made a set of designs, sold them to a publisher, and was beginning to transfer them to copper when he learned that Cruikshank was in the midst of an identical undertaking. As Cruikshank's greater fame would blanket his publication, he canceled the whole affair. The momentary and accidental rivalry caused no ill-will between the two men; the issues of Cruikshank's *Comic Almanack* for 1839 and 1840 contained stories by Thackeray with Cruikshank's illustrations, although Thackeray was annoyed by the sketchiness of the drawings and generally shoddy effect of the publication.

None of this, however, meant any increase in general fame. At one of the Shakespeare Club dinners, Dickens was in the chair, Forster made a speech, and various other celebrities took part; but Thackeray was hidden among the rank and file of members, and Charles Knight—who, as a publisher, knew the literary world intimately—spoke of being "at a side table with a remarkable-looking young man opposite to me, who I was told was the Michael Angelo Titmarsh of *Fraser's Magazine*." The very thought of being asked to make a speech at such an affair would have been agony to Thackeray, who had never recovered from his breakdown at the Cambridge Union; but there was little danger that he would be asked to make one.

During the early months of 1839 he started work on a longer piece of fiction. His loathing for the Newgate-Calendar school had by now almost reached the stage of fascination. The former success of Bulwer's *Paul Clifford* and *Eugene Aram*, and of Ainsworth's *Rookwood*, had been eclipsed by Dickens's venture into the underworld, *Oliver Twist;* and in January, 1839, a new serial by Ainsworth, *Jack Sheppard*, aroused a wilder excitement than any of them. Thackeray decided that the best way of making the reading public ashamed of itself was to write a crime-story of his own that should carry the gruesome horrors to their logical extreme of nausea. Digging into the inexhaustible Newgate Calendar, he encountered one Catherine Hayes, a particularly callous murderess of the same epoch as Jack Sheppard; and in the May number of *Fraser's* appeared the first instalment of *Catherine*. As a suitable pseudonym that should not suggest any of his other disguises, he borrowed the name of a notorious Fagin-like rascal, and called himself "Ikey Solomons, Junior."

Before the story was well launched, sorrow invaded Thackeray's domestic circle. His second daughter died just as she was beginning to display premature intelligence and sweetness of nature. Both the young parents were heartbroken, and Thackeray adopted a stoical tone. "I would not ask," he wrote to his mother, "to have the dear little Jane back again and subject her to the degradation of life and pain."

In this time of misery, he was surprised and touched by the loyal friendship of his old Cambridge companion, John Allen, who was living across the street from him as a hard-working curate, with children of the right age to be playmates with his two-year-old Annie. Allen had been one of the least conspicuous members of their undergraduate "Covey," but now his unselfishness came opportunely at a moment when Thackeray was growing cynical about his fellow beings. "The man is just a perfect saint, nor more nor less," he wrote in amazement to his mother; "and not the least dogmatical or presumptuous." This discovery of a really good man left a lasting impression on his mind.

The necessities of earning a living made it impossible for the Thackerays to go away somewhere long enough to recover from their loss. A jaunt to Gravesend was a memorable event. Longing to go over to Paris, Thackeray knew he must stay in London ready for any opportunity that might turn up. Written in these circumstances, *Catherine* was bound to be a depressing work. Furthermore, it was fundamentally unsound, because Thackeray had not made up his mind as to what sort of effect he intended. It was not a burlesque, aiming at cheerful absurdity. It was meant to be a purgative satire, and yet to be a considerable work of art. In stripping away the aura of bombastic sentiment that made heroes of highwaymen and murderers in the novels of Bulwer and Ainsworth, he adopted the unsparing realism of Defoe; but the more fully he achieved that end, the less valid became its critical function of satire. The fact was, just as Fielding had found with *Joseph Andrews*, that a parody in such an extended scale was bound to take hold of the author's imagination and develop into an independent creation. Never since *The Beggars' Opera* had a gang of scoundrels been so ruthlessly paraded, but Thackeray's tale had none of the urbane liveliness that makes Gay's extravaganza endurable.

The public was merely repelled by the savagery of *Catherine*, and Thackeray was inclined to share their feeling. "Carlyle says it is wonderful," he informed his mother (as one would expect that perverse misanthrope to say), "and many more laud it highly, but it is a disgusting subject and no mistake. I wish I had taken a pleasanter one." After four instalments had appeared in *Fraser's* there was a lapse of three months, while the Thackeray family took a vacation in Paris; the serial was resumed in November, and then another month was missed before the two final instalments came out. Whether these breaks were due to objections from the editor or hesitation in the author, they hint at the unsatisfactory nature of the tale. It was "a mistake all through," Thackeray concluded sourly; "it was not made disgusting enough. . . The triumph of it would have been to make readers so horribly horrified as to cause them to give up or rather throw up the book and all its kind; whereas you see the author had a sneaking kindness for his heroine, and did not like to make her quite worthless." It was never published in volume form during his lifetime.

Meanwhile, in quest of new markets for his miscellaneous wares, he enlisted the aid of his friends. One of them, the Rev James White, a prolific contributor to *Blackwood's Magazine*, wrote to Robert Blackwood: "By the by, there is a friend of mine that I promised to introduce to you. He is the cleverest of all the London writers, I think—his name is Thackeray; a gentleman, a Cambridge man. I told him he had better not waste his time with the inferior magazines when he writes the best things (he is the Yellowplush of *Fraser* and the Major Gahagan of the *New Monthly*), but go at once to you. He is shy, I suppose, for he said he wished you would *invite* him to contribute. If you will let me know whether you wish to hear from him I will communicate your reply."

This letter seems to have been written as early as the spring of 1838, and some sort of negotiations finally developed between Thackeray and the Edinburgh firm, but apparently a year or more had elapsed, and the details are not clear. A letter from Alexander Blackwood speaks of sending back a bundle of prose and verse mixed, which had been submitted by Thackeray, but this material has not been further identified.

In the summer of 1839 he had slightly better success with another personal recommendation. Henry Cole, a young civil servant with a hand in many schemes for social improvement, the most lasting of which was the invention of the Christmas card, was associated with Richard Cobden in the recently-founded Anti-Corn-Law League, and saw a chance of getting his friend a commission to draw cartoons for the *Anti-Corn-Law Circular*. Thackeray, somewhat suspicious that he might be expected to contribute his services for the good of the cause, replied pointedly, "I shall be glad to do a single drawing, series, or what you will, for *money.*"

Cobden, as master-mind of the whole movement, had definite ideas about the contents of the *Circular*. He sent elaborate descriptions of the cartoons he had in mind, accompanied by crude sketches. When Cole transmitted these, Thackeray firmly protested: they contained far too much detail to be reproduced on the small scale that was required, and the allegories would be over the heads of the general public. Thackeray therefore submitted a few sketches embodying his own ideas: in place of Cobden's vague suggestion of "a demon" keeping out Polish corn, he drew the familiar symbol of authority, an English soldier with fixed bayonet; and another of his proposals was "a howling group with this motto, 'GIVE US OUR DAILY BREAD'—the words are startling."

Cole was now in a position that tested his powers of diplomacy. Anxious to help Thackeray, he had to mollify Cobden and make him believe that the Thackeray drawings had really been inspired by the Cobden suggestions, even though they looked quite different. To make matters worse, Thackeray had just been approached by one Schönberg, inventor of a new process of engraving, who persuaded him that it would exactly suit the cartoons for the *Circular*. Three drawings were handed over, and Schönberg had to confess complete failure with all three. Thackeray therefore reverted to his customary wood blocks.

In breaking to Cobden the news of the delay and extra expense, Cole waxed dithyrambic in praise of his friend:

> The artist is a genius, both with his pencil and pen. His vocation is literary. He is full of humour and feeling. Hitherto he has not had occasion to think much on the subject of Corn Laws, and therefore wants the stuff to work upon. He would like to combine both writing and drawing when sufficiently primed, and then he would write and illustrate ballads, or tales, or anything. I think you would find him a most effective auxiliary, and perhaps the best way to fill him with matter for illustrations would be to invite him to see the weavers, their mills, shuttles, et cetera . . .

Thackeray was probably not attracted by such a strenuous industrial tour as Cole proposed. Two drawings by him have been identified in the *Circular*; he may have contributed others, and prose or verse as well, but the lack of accord between his notions and Cobden's prevented his becoming the "effective auxiliary" that Cole hoped for.

By this time, his writings had attracted notice across the Atlantic. *The Yellowplush Correspondence* was issued in a volume by Messrs Carey & Hart, of Philadelphia. Of course, the custom of literary piracy rendered it unnecessary for the American firm to pay the author anything, or even find out his identity; but their considering the stuff worth stealing was a testimony to its success. And this early transatlantic appreciation is particularly notable because the comic devices used in *Yellowplush*—monstrous misspelling, malapropism, and plebeian sententiousness—were those which later came to be considered typical of "American" humor, in the work of such buffoons as Artemus Ward.

In the summer of 1839 the irrepressible American traveler and interviewer, Nathaniel Parker Willis, first of the roving correspondents, was paying one of his visits to England, sending back gossip to a New York weekly which he had recently founded with the romantic name of *The Corsair*, and also picking up contributors for it. In a letter to his partner, Dr T. O. Porter, he gleefully announced his latest catch: "Who do you think? The author of 'Yellowplush' and 'Major Gahagan.' I have mentioned it in my jottings, that our readers may know all about it. He has gone to Paris, and will write letters from there, and afterwards from London, for a guinea a *close column* of the *Corsair*—cheaper than I ever did anything in my life. I will see that he is paid for a while to see how you like him. For myself, I think him the very best periodical writer alive. He is a royal, daring, fine creature, too."

The accompanying paragraph in Willis's "Jottings" is of particular interest. It is typical of Willis in its superlatives and inaccuracies—he adds seven years to Thackeray's age and attaches him to the staff of *Blackwood's*. But it is the first description of Thackeray to appear anywhere in print, and the first equating of his work with that of Dickens:

I have been delighted to find that the authors of the two best periodical series of papers that have appeared for twenty years are one and the same person. One of my first inquiries in London was touching the authorship of *The Yellowplush Papers* and the *Reminiscences of Major Gahagan*,—the only things in periodical literature, except the *Pickwick Papers*, for which I looked with any interest or eagerness. The author, Mr. Thackeray, breakfasted with me yesterday, and the *Corsair* will be delighted, I am sure, to hear that I have engaged this cleverest and most gifted of the magazine writers of London to become a *regular correspondent of the Corsair*. He left London for Paris the day after, and having resided in that city for many years, his letters thence will be pictures of life in France, done with a bolder and more trenchant pen than has yet attempted the subject. He will present a long letter every week, and you will agree with me that he is no common acquisition. Thackeray is a tall, athletic man of about thirty-five, with a look of talent that could never be mistaken. He has taken to literature after having spent a very large inheritance; but in throwing away the gifts of fortune, he has cultivated his natural talents very highly, and is one of the most accomplished draftsmen in England, as well as the cleverest and most brilliant of periodical writers. He has been the principal critic for the *Times*, and writes for *Fraser* and *Blackwood*. You will hear from him by the first steamer after his arrival in Paris, and thenceforward regularly.

Thackeray went to work on the assignment with a will. The same number of *The Corsair* that contained Willis's introduction of him also printed the first of his

Letters from London, Paris, Pekin, Petersburgh, &c. It was signed with "T.T." (for "Timothy Titcomb"), and ended with a modest little expression of his delight "in finding good friends and listeners among strangers far, far away—in receiving from beyond seas kind crumbs of comfort for our hungry vanities." For two months his letters appeared almost every week; then, as *The Corsair* sank into financial difficulties, they became intermittent, and the last one was printed in March, 1840, just before the paper ceased publication. Most of them did double duty, by being sold also to *Fraser's* or elsewhere.

By the end of 1839, then, Thackeray could regard himself as successfully established in his profession. He had sought no personal recognition, but he was making a sufficient income, his work was being published steadily in a wide variety of forms, and people on the inside of the literary market were speaking of him unequivocally as the cleverest of the periodical writers in London. To be sure, he was not such a hard bargainer as he might have been—witness Willis's good-humored contempt for his low fee—but this was the natural result of modesty and a gentlemanly horror of haggling. Everything pointed to happiness and moderate prosperity in a vocation that pleased him well.

CHAPTER 6

Disaster

AFTER THREE years of copious and varied professional writing, Thackeray had not yet found his métier. In spite of having learned much by painful trial and error, he was stranded midway between criticism and fiction. As a critic, his judgment was impaired by elements of impulse and emotion that bespoke the imaginative creator; as a story-teller, he was hampered by the critic's tendency to digress into commentary. His criticisms, whether of pictures or of literature, were indeed based on two or three recurrent axioms; but those axioms happened to be contradictory of one another.

He loathed the bombast, sentiment, and morbidity that marked the decadent romanticism of his time, whether in French drama or English fiction. Even for the great progenitor of the cult, Byron, he had no tolerance:

> Give me a fresh, dewy, healthy rose out of Somersetshire; not one of those superb, tawdry, unwholesome exotics, which are only good to make poems about. Lord Byron wrote more cant of this sort than any poet I know of. Think of "the peasant girls with dark blue eyes" of the Rhine—the brown-faced, flat-nosed, thick-lipped, dirty wenches! Think of "filling high a cup of Samian wine"; small beer is nectar compared to it, and Byron himself always drank gin. That man *never* wrote from his heart. He got up rapture and enthusiasm with an eye to the public . . .

In this "romantiphobia" Thackeray harked back to the eighteenth century, a belated disciple of the healthy realism of Fielding and the blunt common sense of Johnson. This was the side of his nature that made him relish the bawdy jests of the Montmartre studios and the salty conversation of the Garrick Club smoking-room.

On the other hand, there was an equally strong strain of prudery in his disposition. Partly it may have been due to conventional Protestant moralizing by his childhood mentors, partly to an instinctive recognition that a new era of public squeamishness had set in and that a writer who had to earn his living had better cater to the demand; but chiefly it was due to an admixture of almost feminine sensibility in his own nature. The cruelty of some of his sneers at namby-pamby sentimentalism was almost masochistic; he was lacerating a shrinking victim within himself, which had been driven into hiding on his earliest school-day at Southampton and terrified beyond recovery by the crassness of Charterhouse. The only outlet for this suppressed and distorted softness was in sudden flashes of austere moralistic disapproval.

These two incompatible prejudices gave rise to most of the conflicts in his critical views. They were responsible, too, for his bursts of temper. When he blackguarded an artist or a dramatist, his rage was actually aroused by his own inward confusion. Tormented by the effort to believe two mutually exclusive ideas at the same time, he avenged his agony on the nearest target.

As a matter of fact, his criticism was usually sound in ultimate verdicts. In both painting and writing England was at a low ebb during the late thirties, and most of the stuff that came under Thackeray's lash merited condemnation on so many counts that he was bound to put his finger on some of them. One of his first long reviews for *Fraser's* was on the "Annuals" of Christmas, 1837, and the next year he returned to the attack. These satin-bound monstrosities were the best-selling publications of the decade, and a shameless disclosure of its lack of taste. Silly, conventional engravings formed their mainstay; the contributors were hired to write poems or tales with some sort of relevance to the pictures, and likely to be as silly and conventional in their turn. Because of the high prices that the publishers could pay, the leading painters and writers were glad to accept the commissions, and therefore Thackeray was attacking the work of many of his friends; but he tried to make clear that his disgust was for the public taste and the venal publishers who demanded verses of "sham sentiment" and "these eternal fancy portraits of ladies in voluptuous attitudes and various stages of dishabille, to awaken the dormant sensibilities of misses in their teens, or tickle the worn-out palates of rakes and roués." The silver-fork novels that he reviewed in batches, the Academy exhibitions that he visited in the person of Titmarsh, were of a piece with these fine flowers of sensibility.

He entered the year 1840 in high good-humor and confidence. His more raffish tastes were remarkably chastened by domesticity. In a pleasant social round, Mr and Mrs Thackeray visited the artist Cattermole and his bride in Clapham, and the Carlyles in Chelsea. Mrs Thackeray and FitzGerald were with the Kembles in their private box at Covent Garden to see Leigh Hunt's play, *A Legend of Florence*, while her husband stopped at home and worked. When Planché's masque of *The Fortunate Isles*, in honor of the Queen's marriage, was to be favored by the presence of the royal bride and groom, Thackeray sent a note to Planché, requesting a permit to come back stage, on the pretext that his wife was "mad to see the sight." The note was illustrated with a caricature of the royal couple in their box; and Charles Mathews, the lessee of the theater, sent the desired pass on condition that he should receive a duplicate of the drawing. The Thackerays were therefore in the privileged throng on the stage who viewed the packed house as the curtain rose to the National Anthem.

In spite of many such concessions to Isabella's entertainment, Thackeray could not entirely give up his clubs and his evenings of cigars and conversation with such old Cambridge friends as FitzGerald and Saville Morton—the latter a brilliant and somewhat dissolute journalist. Mrs Thackeray sometimes showed a hint of jealousy toward them; but her husband felt that after a long day of strenuous writing he deserved some "jollification." Besides, if he was to give best expression to his opinions on pictures and books he had to discuss them with others who shared his interests. When he was nominated to the Reform Club, where the Radical politicians foregathered, the twenty-guinea admission fee was a serious obstacle; but the tribute to his increasing reputation was too flattering to be rejected. His wife begged him anxiously not be to carried away by compliments.

For any sudden additional expenditure like this, he had to borrow money. Otherwise, he was just able to pay his way with his earnings, though usually each month's compensation had been spent several weeks before the publishers got around to remitting it to him.

His prospects, however, were becoming more and more encouraging. He had begun the year by reviving Yellowplush for another "thundering article against Bulwer," this time on the subject of his new play, *The Sea-Captain*. A sour little story of Thackeray's, *The Bedford-Row Conspiracy*, was running serially in *The New Monthly*; it was chiefly marked by the self-seeking and insignificance of its characters and the dubious ethics of its climax, and it did not even have the merit of originality, being adapted from a French novel by Charles de Barnard. A better augury for his career was an agreement with John Macrone, the publisher who had launched Dickens, for the assembling of his Parisian articles and stories in two volumes, with his own illustrations. He had first proposed it to Macrone three years earlier, when they were negotiating over the *Crichton* drawings.

Some of his friends were concocting an ambitious scheme. It originated in the studio of Orrin Smith, an engraver, where a group of struggling young artists and writers were in the habit of meeting. One of the productions of the group was a periodical series entitled *Heads of the People*, edited by Douglas Jerrold, with essays by various contributors to accompany drawings by Kenny Meadows. Three of the essays were supplied by Thackeray, two signed with his own name and one by "Titmarsh." The same engraver, publisher, printers, and writers became enthusiastic over the idea of launching a satirical weekly modeled upon the successful Parisian *Charivari*. Jerrold and Thackeray took an active part in the arrangements; Thackeray was confident that he could get contributions from John Poole, a famous old wit and a pillar of the Garrick Club, and he also brought in the friend of his school days, John Leech, who was beginning to win fame as a caricaturist.

The financing was to be co-operative, the various writers and artists owning the paper jointly. The project is said to have reached the point at which the first material was set up in type, when Thackeray raised an unexpected objection. Probably remembering his difficulties with Maginn over *The National Standard*, he declared that each of the partners might automatically become liable for the private debts of the others. None of them having enough knowledge of business to fathom this mystery, and all of them perhaps feeling that they were undertaking an enterprise beyond their resources, they abandoned the whole affair, not without regretful visions of what fun it would have been.

Thackeray, at any rate, was no more deterred than by his previous misadventures in journalism. By the middle of April, 1840, he was deep in plans for a weekly to consist entirely of his own skits and comic pictures. The title was to be "The Foolscap Library," and the first number was to contain "The Veracious History of Dionysius Diddler," lampooning Bulwer and Dr Lardner, a compiler of cheap encyclopedias. Mrs Thackeray tried vainly to curb her husband's wild enthusiasm, beseeching him to assume no financial risks and to be content with half of the profits, if any profits should accrue. "He says I am a *coward*," she reported to Mrs Carmichael-Smyth, "but I think we are properly balanced. . . It is a kind of pastime for William for you know it gives him no trouble to sketch."

A letter of his own to his mother, ten days later, showed what little effect his wife's warnings had produced. He breathlessly summarized his "ceaseless whirl and whizz from morning to night." He was preparing *The Paris Sketch Book* for publication, making the drawings for *Dionysius Diddler*, writing articles for *The Times, Fraser's*, and other journals. He had just completed a "huge article on George Cruikshank for *The London and Westminster Review*. "The days pass away to me like half-hours." He then went on to boast of his pet project. He intended to strive for popularity by curbing his tendency toward bitterness: "You will see in the Cruikshank article some remarks against myself; I fail by sneering too much; but I think *Foolscap* will succeed." If he could keep the enterprise entirely in his own hands he would not have to share his enormous profits with any publisher or bookseller. He admitted that he might have to ask his stepfather for a small loan: "The thing is a fortune, but wants about £30 to start it." According to his calculations, he would make eight pounds on every thousand copies; his mind soared off to a circulation of ten thousand copies a week, four thousand pounds a year, of which he would be able to save at least three thousand. . .

Such optimism ought to have swept away the most cautious of wives; but Isabella was expecting another baby, and her nerves became more and more overstrained. Unluckily an officious friend of Thackeray's mother came over from Paris on a visit, and took the opportunity of lecturing Isabella upon the duties of a good wife, with implications that Mrs Carmichael-Smyth sometimes expressed doubts of her daughter-in-law's competence. Poor Isabella was overcome with a sense of guilt.

In May Thackeray felt so much need of a holiday from the crowded little house and the obstetrical preparations that he went for a few days to Warwickshire and enjoyed the placid rural atmosphere in spite of anxiety lest the confinement might occur while he was away. He returned to London in time for the birth of a daughter on May 28. Three days later he managed to finish the last page of *The Paris Sketch Book*.

At the same time he was starting a new serial, *A Shabby Genteel Story*, in *Fraser's*. An almost brutally sarcastic narrative of vulgar, sordid characters, it promised to be more nearly a novel of contemporary life than anything he had yet attempted.

Finding that this work was not enough to fill his time, he tried another appeal to the House of Blackwood. He proposed supplying *Blackwood's Magazine* with a series of monthly papers on current matters, "no politics, as much fun and satire as I can muster, literary talk and criticism of a spicy nature, and general gossip." At the Reform Club and the Garrick he would be able to pick up "plenty of rambling stuff." He suggested a dazzling list of topics for the first month. The sensation of the hour was the trial and conviction of a valet named Courvoisier for the murder of his master, Lord John Russell. The counsel for the defence was considered to have used methods that violated legal ethics. Thackeray promised to attend Courvoisier's hanging and describe it in his article, as well as discussing the barrister's censured speech to the court. He would also deal with the London Library, a squabble between Carlyle and *The Times*, the newly-published autobiography of the pompous theatrical manager Alfred Bunn who was a butt of all the wits, and finally Thackeray's erstwhile American patron, N. P. Willis, who had irritated the English with his impudent gossip. This latter subject, Thackeray promised, "may be racy enough." He appealed to the Blackwoods for an immediate opinion of the project: "I can't afford to begin and send the mss. in advance, for if you shouldn't approve the design my labour would be wasted, as the article would be written for your special readers, and no good next month."

The Blackwoods remained deaf to his blandishments. The only result of the idea was that he did go to witness the execution of Courvoisier. Thackeray's Cambridge friend, Monckton Milnes, now a noted Member of Parliament, was agitating for the abolition of capital punishment, and intended to be present at the execution in order to study its effect upon the public mind. His invitation to share the experience was accepted by Thackeray.

As the adventure neared he felt some qualms. He rejected Milnes's scheme to sit up all night and go straight from the Club to Snow Hill in time for a point of vantage in the crowd. Suggesting that Milnes would be welcome to a sofa at Coram Street, he added, "I most strongly recommend sleep as a preparative to the day's pleasures."

In spite of this resolution, he lay awake all night, listening to the clocks and picturing with his novelist's imagination the last hours of the doomed man. When

Milnes arrived at three o'clock for breakfast, full of witticisms about murder that he had heard during his late sitting at the Club, Thackeray was definitely shaky. A pick-me-up of sherry and soda did little good; his nerves cried out for a cigar, and to avoid shedding ashes on the new silk linings of his friend's elegant carriage, he sat on the box with the coachman and breathed in the unwonted freshness of a London summer dawn as they drove to Newgate.

Three hours in the crowd around the scaffold, observing the commonplace behavior and remarks of forty thousand people from every walk of society, increased his horror for the blood-lust that brought them all there. When the final moment came, and the victim was blindfolded, Thackeray closed his eyes till all was over; but for weeks afterwards he was haunted by the scene, and he wrote a full account of it for *Fraser's*, a piece of work which, for sincerity, restraint, and power, was the best that he had yet produced. His comments upon the experience were an earnest plea against the death penalty. "I fully confess that I came away down Snow Hill that morning with a disgust for murder, but it was for the *murder I saw done*. . . I feel myself ashamed and degraded at the brutal curiosity which took me to that brutal sight; and I pray to Almighty God to cause this disgraceful sin to pass from among us, and to cleanse our land of blood."

This solemnity was not altogether the result of a single shocking experience. It was merely one element in a growth of political and social conscience. The high spirits and love of excitement that had led him into Charles Buller's election campaign eight years before were now replaced by personal conviction. His membership in the Reform Club, his studying of material for the *Anti-Corn-Law Circular*, his friendships with assorted radicals from Buller and Molesworth to Dickens and Jerrold had more than counteracted the rabid Toryism of *Fraser's Magazine*.

Those were the days of the great Chartist uprising, and Thackeray took up a line that was more extreme than that of his own radical friends. His letters to his mother became full of revolt. "Priests and aristocracy have killed the spirit of Christianity, I think—the one by inventing curses, the other honour." Again, "I am quite certain that a certain part of us are going to the deuce, and that a tremendous revolution is preparing. There will be no end to it when it comes, and you will have barricading again in Paris, and there will be similar work all through Europe. . . Had it not been for a rainy night and the cowardice of that scoundrel Frost [leader of the abortive Chartist rebellion in Wales] we might have been now the British Republic for what I know, and Queen Victoria in her uncle's dominions of Hanover. Thank God that the Chartists have not a man of courage at their head who might set the kingdom in a blaze. With their views about property— robbery, in fact,—of course a revolution effected by them could not last long."

Six months later, when his views had crystalized further, he declared *à propos* of "the rascally Whigs and Tories": "When is the day to come when those two humbugs are to disappear from among us? Don't be astonished. I'm not a Chartist, only a Republican. I would like to see all men equal, and this bloated aristocracy blasted to the wings of all the winds. It has been good and useful up to the present time,—nay, for a little time longer perhaps—just up to the minute when the great lion shall shake his mane and scatter all these absurd insects out of it. What stuff to write, to be sure. But I see how in every point of morals the aristocracy is cursing the country."

In July, 1840, *The Paris Sketch Book* was published. As it was the first sizable book of Thackeray's to be issued in England, he used all his personal influence to get it recognized. With the review copies he sent appeals to his friends. "I do solemnly and pathetically adjure you," he wrote to James Wilson, editor of the *Anti-Corn-Law Circular*, "to give poor Titmarsh a puff, for surely no man ever wanted one more than he." One of the chief reviewers of *The Athenaeum*, Henry Fothergill Chorley, was now the house-mate of Thackeray's old companion Henry Reeve; when Chorley gave the book a kindly notice, the author thanked him effusively: "Name anything you wish as a proof of my gratitude. . . Never was such a good-natured puff." Most of the notices were favorable; but the book—a rather flimsy assemblage of reviews, personal experiences, and somewhat mannered short stories—lacked general appeal.

Meanwhile, his essay on Cruikshank had been considered good enough for re-issue as a separate brochure. On hearing about it, he wrote eagerly to Henry Cole, who had obtained the commission for him, suggesting that "the author, who was paid ½ price in the first instance, should be paid something for his name and his permission to use his writing." As a matter of fact, the little book did not mention his name, and so he presumably received no payment.

All this concern over money contrasts pathetically with his former lordly nonchalance; but necessity was driving him hard. His projected weekly had now been renamed *The Whitey-Brown Paper Magazine*, and the first number was actually in proof, but he was not yet able to finance its issue. His ambitions, however, were shifting in a new direction. The success of *The Paris Sketch Book* attracted the interest of several publishers, and Thackeray suddenly began to see a real hope of escape from the soul-killing strain of writing for newspapers and magazines. The firm of Chapman & Hall, which was making its own fortune along with that of Dickens, was especially favorable, and to them Thackeray proposed a two-volume work of travel sketches, to be called *Titmarsh in Ireland*. They also offered an immediate contract for a short guide-book on Belgium and the Rhine, for which they would pay seventy pounds.

As the redoubtable old Mrs Butler had come over from Paris to look after Mrs Thackeray, he felt justified in making a fortnight's tour of Belgium to collect the necessary material. He was somewhat disturbed, however, by her hysterical laughter when he was saying good-bye to her; and when he got back from the tour he found her much depressed by the old lady's bullying. Upon their doctor's advice he took her to Margate for change of air. There he had to pay a high rate for a three-room lodging; and the cramped quarters, as well as Isabella's need of his attention, played such havoc with his work that the next installment of *A Shabby Genteel Story* was not ready in time for inclusion in the magazine. His current assignment for *The Times* was a review of Fielding's works, which would normally have been a congenial task; but in order to work upon it he had to walk three miles to a little bowling green at which there was an arbor where he could write undisturbed. When he stayed in the house his wife's vague, pathetic gaze made him feel helpless and miserable.

After a couple of weeks she seemed much better, but as soon as they returned to London the cloud closed down upon her again. At this moment he signed his agreement with Chapman & Hall for the book of Irish travels, for which they paid down an advance royalty of £120. Troubled over this commitment for work that was not even begun, he wrote to the only solvent member of the family—his cousin Mary Graham, who still made her home with the Carmichael-Smyths,— asking her to guarantee repayment in case of his failure to carry out his share of the contract. Before her reply arrived, he found another solution by depositing the family chest of silver plate with Chapman & Hall as a hostage. This glimpse of financial instability made him resolve that as soon as he could afford treatments to cure a stricture of the urethra that sometimes gave him pain, he would insure his life.

As the contract called for delivery of the completed manuscript in less than four months, and as he had never set eyes on Ireland in his life, an immediate visit to that country was imperative. Mrs Shawe and her unmarried daughter Jane were now living in the old family home at Cork. He therefore decided to take Isabella over with him, in the hope that childhood associations would restore her spirits. The house in Coram Street was left in the charge of the old Devon butler, John Goldsworthy, who was slowly dying, and the Thackerays took with them a devoted Scottish maid to look after the children.

The three-day voyage to Cork was started hopefully enough; but before the first day was over, Mrs Thackeray climbed through a porthole and plunged into the sea. After a twenty-minute search she was found, paddling with her hands to keep afloat. When brought aboard she proved to be suffering no physical injury, but Thackeray could no longer shut his eyes to the fact that she was insane. The next day she made a second attempt at suicide, and for the rest of the nightmare journey he did not dare to let her out of his sight.

For a month of misery they remained in Cork. Local doctors encouraged him to hope for his wife's recovery, and some days she seemed more coherent; but always the melancholia would return, and she remained apathetic toward her children. Fearing further efforts to take her own life, Thackeray tied her wrist to his with a ribbon every night before going to sleep.

The visit resulted chiefly in intensifying his dislike for his mother-in-law to hatred. She let it be seen that she suspected him of having ill-used his wife. He became certain that she too was mentally unbalanced, though in a more belligerent form. Unable to make his intended tour in search of material for the book, he stayed close to his wife and tried incongruously to write a comedy, which Matthews had promised to consider for production at Covent Garden. He grew half-frenzied as he thought of the opportunities he was losing, at the very moment when fortune had been turning in his favor.

After suffering his mother-in-law's insults as patiently as he could for four weeks, he decided that he must take Isabella and the children to France to be looked after by his relations. The journey was made in easy stages, with a pause in London to try to put his affairs into order. The crisis had obliterated his sources of income. The plans for the gay little *Whitey-Brown Paper Magazine* were discarded forever. The *Shabby Genteel Story*, begun in happier times, he had no heart to continue, and it was terminated perfunctorily in one further instalment. With no prospect of the Irish book being written, his plate-chest gathered dust in the vault of Messrs Chapman & Hall. And in spite of favorable reviews, he learned that *The Paris Sketch Book* had sold scarcely any copies.

He was reduced to making humiliating appeals to his employers, and even these were fruitless. *The Times* refused his request for an increase in the five guineas he was paid for each week's reviews, and the editor of *Fraser's*, though owing him £13 10s, would not advance him fifteen pounds. The career that had begun in the light-hearted speculations of a wealthy young amateur in journalism, and had later been established in all the confidence of a prolific and accepted professional, had crashed in ruins before he reached the age of thirty.

His elder girl was a precocious three-year-old, and one of her earliest recollections was of their journey to Paris. As the *diligence* creaked through the gathering darkness, she grew frightened of a cross-looking man in the other corner, and began to whimper that she wanted to get out and walk. Her harried father tried to amuse her by lighting a toy lantern, but she only cried the louder. The baby in the nurse's arms woke and joined the chorus, and Thackeray grimly blew out the little light. Incredulous, Annie screamed in the darkness for it to be lighted, but her father refused. Such discipline had never been inflicted upon her before, and she sobbed herself to sleep on her father's knee. Through the long night, as he sat holding the child in the rattling coach, and listening to the other man muttering over and over, "J'ai la fièvre, mon Dieu, j'ai la fièvre," he had ample time to plumb the depths of his despair.

His parents gave them a loving welcome in Paris; but they too, living meagerly on two hundred pounds a year, could not be expected to offer permanent sanctuary to two infants and a nurse. Mrs Thackeray was placed in what was probably the best mental hospital in Europe—and proportionately expensive. After six weeks of treatment the proprietor held out some hopes of her recovery. Meanwhile, the Carmichael-Smyths had to leave for Italy for the wedding of Mary Graham to an elderly brother of the Major's. The care of Thackeray and his daughters therefore devolved upon Mrs Butler, who was somewhat more prosperous but distinctly less amiable to babies.

By the end of the year he was getting back into harness. His friend Milnes, visiting Paris in November, accompanied him to see the state funeral of Napoleon, whose body had been brought from its former tomb in St Helena. More than seven years before, in one of his despatches to *The National Standard*, Thackeray had ridiculed the attempt of Louis Philippe to show respect for Napoleon by erecting the column in the Place Vendôme; and now all the pomp and extravagance of the funeral ceremony inspired him to write a report that mingled graphic description with an undercurrent of satire. His recollection of seeing the Little Corporal in his lonely exile added a further strain of irony and pathos to his mood. He wrote the essay in four days, and as it was too long for an ordinary magazine article he sent it to Hugh Cunningham, who had just taken over Macrone's business. If it could be published promptly in booklet form, it might exploit the public interest in the event.

As the Napoleonic theme was still working strongly in him, he decided to write a ballad recounting the glories of French arms, to complement the prose report. It was his first serious venture into poetry, and to his surprise it proved much harder work than the burlesque rhymes that he had always enjoyed tossing off. "Never was an unfortunate fellow so plagued," he lamented to his friend Mrs Procter, the wife of Barry Cornwall. "For a whole week you would have fancied me a real poet, having all the exterior marks of one—with a week's beard, a great odour of tobacco, a scowling, ferocious, thoughtful appearance. I used to sit all day meditating, nail-biting, and laboriously producing about twenty lines in twelve hours. Are all poets in this way?"

The little half-crown volume, containing *The Second Funeral of Napoleon* and *The Chronicle of the Drum*, under the now customary name of M. A. Titmarsh, was rushed through the press by Cunningham, and the author's admirers made a noble effort to ensure its success. FitzGerald wrote to a friend, "Have you read Thackeray's little book? If not, pray do; and buy it, and ask others to buy it, as each copy sold put $7\frac{1}{2}$d in T's pocket, which is very empty just now, I take it. I think this book is the best thing he has done." To Mrs Procter, who was also going to a lot of trouble on behalf of it, Thackeray sent a comical calculation of how his sevenpence-halfpenny royalties, on a sale of a hundred thousand copies, would amount to £3125; but he added drily, "One hundred copies have already been sold, so that you see my fortune is very clear."

To his annoyance, *The Athenaeum* despised it, and Forster in *The Examiner* accused him of "John Bullish Franco-mania." *The Times*, in a generally favorable review, called him flippant and egotistic for refusing to be impressed by the ceremonials, and Thackeray retorted lengthily in his next article for *Fraser's*: "Oh, you thundering old *Times!* Napoleon's funeral was a humbug, and your constant reader said so. . . There may be irreverence in this, but surely there is no conceit. The shamming of modesty is the most pert conceit of all, the *précieuse* affectation of deference when you don't feel it, the sneaking acquiescence in lies. It is very hard that a man may not tell the truth as he fancies it, without being accused of conceit." After pinning the charge of "humbug" on *The Times* itself in a pair of burlesque sonnets, he went on: "Well, then, the Funeral of Napoleon was a humbug, as Titmarsh wrote, and a still better proof that it was a humbug was this, that nobody bought Titmarsh's book, and of the 10,000 copies made ready by the publishers, not above 3000 went off."

This and other sneers indicate that the disappointment had cut him deeply. Great though his need of money was at this juncture, his need of encouragement and sympathy was greater. His anxiety and loneliness could not be endured without the aid of someone to confide in. Of all his old comrades, FitzGerald was the only one who could be trusted to listen with patience and understanding; he had abundant leisure and kindliness, with no ambitions of his own to intrude between him and his friend. To "old Fitz," therefore, Thackeray poured out his troubles in frequent letters; and when business called him at intervals to London, where he retained the Coram Street house in the merest shadow of a hope that his family might be reunited, Fitz dragged himself away from the comfort of Suffolk as often as possible to stay with him and try to enliven the dim desolate rooms with cigar smoke and laughter and chat.

But even FitzGerald's warm-hearted affection could not supply the sort of consolation that Thackeray needed most—the admiring sympathy that had been lavished on him by his submissive little wife. Mrs Procter's regard, therefore, became precious to him, and with many apologies—for he knew she was having worry and grief of her own—he wrote to her repeatedly and unburdened his soul. After admitting that he had just torn up a letter he had written to her, on realizing that it was "only a long selfish account of my own particular sorrows," he added frankly, "Don't be angry if I tell you that on reading your letter I felt glad that somebody else was miserable and lonely." A famous hostess and conversationalist, Mrs Procter usually displayed such a caustic wit that her nickname was "Our

Lady of Bitterness"; but toward Thackeray in his despair she was unremittingly patient and comprehending.

A welcome appointment came to him in February when he was asked to contribute regularly to *Britannia*, a weekly paper edited by Samuel Carter Hall, a ubiquitous journalistic hack who had previously been sub-editor of the *New Monthly*. By this time Thackeray also felt equal to the strain of writing a long story again, and asked advice of his friends. One of them, the Reverend Richard Harris Barham, whose *Ingoldsby Legends* were popularizing a quaint type of burlesque mediaevalism, reported to his publisher, Bentley: "Thackeray called here yesterday; wants to be busy, so I recommended him to treat with you for a three vol. historical novel, which he is very well inclined to do. From his reading I think he would succeed, especially if, as I suggested, it were of the *Queen-Hoo Hall* style, illustrated by his own woodcuts of costume, caricature, &c., in the livelier parts."

It was becoming vaguely known that Mr Thackeray was writing some sort of books, though the secret of his pen-names was not yet generally pierced. Henry Reeve reported to him that everyone in London thought he had written *Cecil*, a new book published anonymously by Mrs Gore, one of the society novelists he made fun of. "O just punishment of vanity!" he wrote to Mrs Procter in wry amusement. "How I wish I had written it, not for the book's sake, but for the filthy money, which I love better than fame. The fact is, I am about a wonderful romance, and I long for the day when the three volumes shall be completed." He apologized again for the letter he had written her some weeks before. He had then been unaccustomed to misery, he explained; he "is not a whit happier now, only he bears his griefs more composedly."

The historical romance, which was somebody else's idea, after all, was not congenial to him. Entitled *The Knights of Borsellen*, it was full of the mediaeval trappings that were the heritage of *Ivanhoe*; and the narrative moved as heavily as its armor-sheathed characters. Thackeray's restiveness was betrayed in a remark to his mother: "I am getting dreadfully bitten with my old painting mania, and as soon as I have written that famous book you know of, and made a few hundred pounds, make a vow to the great gods that I will try the thing once more." Very soon the story creaked to a permanent standstill.

The failure of *The Second Funeral of Napoleon* did not wholly discourage the publisher. It is true that he discarded a plan of following it with another small book by the same author, *Dinner Reminiscences, or, The Young Gormandizer's Guide to Paris*. Although this had been announced in the end-paper of *The Second Funeral* as "preparing for immediate publication," it was transformed by Thackeray into an article for *Fraser's Magazine*. The stories and sketches which had already won a reputation were another matter, however, and Cunningham was willing to bring out a collection of them in two volumes, similar to the *Paris*

Sketch Book of the year before. Thackeray was beginning to realize the disadvantages in his habit of scattering his work under many pseudonyms; he was not ready to emerge in his own proper person, but he was more and more at home in the disguise of Michael Angelo Titmarsh, and it was under that name that the collection was "edited," although it was made up largely of the works of Yellowplush and Major Gahagan.

These *Comic Tales and Sketches*, published in May, 1841, were little more successful than the two previous ventures. Just as with *The Paris Sketch Book,* the material was too varied, and much of it too topical, to attract the novel-reading public. Those who could appreciate its wit had already grown familiar with the sketches in the magazines and saw no need of buying them in volume form. The proprietor of *Fraser's* had given him permission to reprint the *Yellowplush Papers* "with a smile" (as he afterwards described it)—"almost an ironical one, as much as to say, 'Much good may you get out of them.' " Not yet was he on the road to fortune.

No wonder his next letter to Mrs Procter was a long rambling screed of self-satirizing irony. "Please when you write not to give me any account whatever of any gaieties in which you indulge, or any sort of happiness falling to the share of you or anybody else. . . Despair, madam, is the word. Byronish, I hate mankind, and wear my shirt-collars turned down."

By now the experts of the *maison de santé* had decided that they could do nothing for Mrs Thackeray, and so he took her back into his own charge, hiring a woman to look after her during the day while he had to work. He read novels aloud to her, and took her out walking whenever the weather was fine. But to write in such depressing conditions was almost impossible. After describing to Mrs Procter the tiny table cluttered with all his writing and drawing impedimenta, he added: "I have not the courage to clear the table, nor indeed to do anything else, and truth to tell, am quite beaten down. I don't know when I shall come round again; not until I get a holiday, and that mayn't be for months to come."

To a man once so fond of good conversation and smart dress and all the petty luxuries as Thackeray had been, this drab indigence was deadlier than positive suffering could be. During these same months his old friend Maginn, ten years ago the heartiest spirit among the London writers, was dying miserably of tuberculosis in the Fleet prison, and Thackeray sometimes in his black moments must have wondered if he were drifting to a similar doom.

The wished-for holiday came unexpectedly soon. One of his friends in Paris was John Bowes, a Member of Parliament for the southern division of County Durham; a general election was to occur in July, and Bowes asked Thackeray to visit his constituency and help with the campaign. This was a tactful pretext for giving him the holiday he could not afford otherwise to take. The visit to the pleasant north-country estate did wonders for his spirits, and in spite of his gruff allusions to "the cursed racket of this infernal election," it helped to restore his interest in the human comedy.

Although his conscience was driving him to hurry back to Paris, he succumbed to the persuasions of Monckton Milnes to stay for a few days at his father's magnificent country-house at Fryston, one of the show-places of Yorkshire. Pemberton Milnes, who had been a noted political figure in his younger days, received his guest with old-fashioned courtesy. "You may smoke anywhere in the house— in your bedroom, if you want to," he said. "Mrs Milnes doesn't mind it in her drawing room. Only you mustn't smoke in Richard's room, for he doesn't like it."

Turning to his friend, Thackeray exclaimed, "What a father is thrown away upon you!" And when he was leaving at the end of his visit he told Mr Milnes gratefully that "your house combines the freedom of the tavern with the elegance of the château."

His impressions of the election were written for *Fraser's* in a burlesque upon the inaccurate reporting of his American one-time patron, Willis. During his visit with Bowes he also picked up a dramatic episode in the eighteenth-century annals of the family, wherein a Countess of Strathmore married a rascally Irish adventurer. To Fraser he suggested writing a story on the subject, to be serialized in the magazine and simultaneously brought out in separate monthly parts, as Charles Lever was doing with his novels in Dublin.

Meanwhile, he was contriving to get another work of fiction into shape. Its differences from his previous stories were the measure of what he had suffered. Entitled *The History of Samuel Titmarsh and the Great Hoggarty Diamond*, it conformed to his favorite whim by being supposedly related by a cousin of Michael Angelo Titmarsh, who figured incidentally in the narrative. For the first time in Thackeray's stories, good and gentle people are portrayed, even though they are victimized by the hypocrites and bullies who bulk sufficiently large. He had felt the pinch of poverty sharply enough to learn the pathetic anxiety overshadowing those who have no assured income. The hero is contemptible, to be sure, with his conceit and his dependence upon his unselfish wife; but the wife and mother are sweet, sincere women, and the scene of the child's death has a note of true pathos lingering from Thackeray's own bereavement of two years before. With a kind of boyish awkwardness, he was trying to write tenderly without falling into the mawkish sentimentality that he always castigated.

The story assumed a special place in his own esteem. Some years later, when it came to be republished in book form, he remarked that "it was written at a time of great affliction, when my heart was very soft and humble." He offered it first to the Blackwoods, and when they turned it down he was more distressed than by their previous rejections. "They refused the best story I ever wrote," he declared, six years afterwards. His old stand-by, *Fraser's*, was more hospitable, and it appeared in the last four numbers of the year; but the author was required to reduce its length, perhaps—as one of his acquaintances states—because readers complained of it after the first instalments appeared.

A few, of course, admired it. John Sterling, in particular, was moved to extravagant praise. After reading the first two parts, he burst out: "What is there better in Fielding or Goldsmith? The man is a true genius; and, with quiet and comfort, might produce masterpieces that would last as long as any we have, and delight millions of unborn readers. There is more truth and nature in one of these papers than in all [Dickens's] novels together."

As a matter of fact, the characters were still as badly articulated as those in Thackeray's drawings, the digressions satirizing social pretensions were tedious, and the plot had a loose construction that cannot be attributed solely to the enforced compression. But to a friend like Sterling, anxiously aware of the author's personal tragedy, the evidence of a mellower sympathy toward human frailty was an encouraging hint of regeneration.

This mood of the book clearly reproduced his own feelings. His mother's boundless affection during his troubles, and the unselfishness with which even obscure servant women looked after his wife and children, gave him a new respect for feminine character. He was embarrassed, sometimes, to find himself in tears when he thought about these kindnesses. In his gloomiest moments he blamed himself for his misfortunes, and prayed for strength to control his impulses of lust and sloth. The discovery in his portfolio of an article he had written two months before, and totally forgotten, frightened him into deep vows to become systematic and conquer his muddle-headed confusion.

While *The Great Hoggarty Diamond* was appearing in *Fraser's*, its author was making another effort for his wife's recovery. His parents, who had repeatedly been converted to new theories of health, after a long period of devotion to homeopathy had just found out about hydropathic treatments. They insisted upon going with Thackeray and his wife to Marienberg, on the Rhine, where a medicinal bathing establishment was becoming famous. His cousin Mary and her new husband joined them for a while, and solved his immediate financial problems with a loan of five hundred pounds. At the same time he heard that his half-sister had died in India, with the probability that a few hundred pounds more would come to him in consequence.

Three months of strenuous sweating, soaking, and cold showers produced definite improvement in the patient. For most of the time Thackeray remained faithful to his task of supervising her baths and her walks; but in October he was so worn out that he had to escape for a few days of peace at Heidelberg, where he was too lonely to derive any benefit from the change. He did some sketching, and wrote the first act of a tragedy in blank verse, hoping that it might be suitable for Macready.

In November, after their return to Paris, the family circle was enlarged by the arrival from London of his favorite aunt, Mrs Ritchie, and her husband, who had now followed the example of his kinsmen by losing his money in the failure of a bank of which he was a director.

Thackeray had not yet gone far in re-establishing his market. During the year he had gradually stopped reviewing regularly for *The Times*. His work for the insignificant weekly *Britannia* brought small profits. In October he had a story, and in December a long ballad, in George Cruikshank's *Omnibus*, but when his total payment for the two contributions proved to be a single sovereign he vowed that even his friendship with Cruikshank would not induce him to do any more work for the artist's periodicals. Had it not been for the loyalty of *Fraser's*, he would have been without visible means of support.

By the end of 1841, nevertheless, the crisis of his career was past. He had grappled with his disaster and conquered it, had schooled himself to endure poverty, loneliness, hope deferred. The baby daughters whom he idolized were allowed to visit him at his lodgings, to watch him shaving in the morning, or writing, or drawing. If he were not busy with writing, he would amuse by tearing a sheet of paper into a procession of little pigs. Although his wife showed no real sign of improvement, she was usually sweet and gentle and happy to see him. Out of his months of anguish had come fortitude and a tolerant understanding of his fellow-men such as he had never learned before. He was ready to undertake new ventures, to achieve maturer artistry.

CHAPTER 7

The Most Distressful Country

IN FEBRUARY, 1842, Thackeray gave up the effort to take care of his wife, and committed her permanently to a private hospital at Chaillot, near enough to Paris for him to visit her frequently. Literary engagements were requiring him to spend more time in London, and there he found a new friendship that helped to restore his spirits. His old college companion, William Henry Brookfield, now a popular clergyman, had recently married Jane Octavia Elton, daughter of Sir Charles Elton of Clevedon Court, niece of Henry Hallam the historian, and since childhood a friend of the "Apostles" circle.

The first time Brookfield encountered Thackeray after the event, he carried him proudly home to have dinner at their lodgings in Jermyn Street, and meet the bride. Thackeray was enchanted by the tall, beautiful young woman, who was five feet nine, with expressive blue-gray eyes and an exceptionally graceful carriage; but she was sadly embarrassed by the plainness of the family dinner, and hastily sent the maid to the nearest pastry-cook's for a dish of tartlets. When this rather obvious makeshift was produced at the end of the meal, Mrs Brookfield timidly offered him a small one, saying, "Will you have a tartlet, Mr Thackeray?"

"I will, but I'll have a twopenny one, if you please," he answered, with a grin; and simple though the joke was, it dissipated all their constraint in a burst of laughter. Before the evening was out, Thackeray felt sure that another had been added to the small total of homes in which he could find a sincere welcome and tactful sympathy that helped him to escape his solitude.

The Brookfields were devoted friends of Alfred Tennyson, who was now at length establishing a wide poetic fame. Whenever Tennyson stayed in London he would visit Thackeray, whom he often described as "a lovable man." They both enjoyed dining at various taverns where they could indulge in beefsteak, cheese, good port, and copious tobacco smoke. One such dinner, given by Thackeray, was apparently intended to promote Tennyson's reputation by introducing him to some members of circles that he did not frequent. The guests were James Emerson Tennent, M. P., John Forster, Daniel Maclise, Evans Crowe, and Saville Morton. At the beginning Samuel Lover, the Irish song writer, came in and amused the company by coolly expressing to Tennyson his delight in meeting "a brother poet."

Another time, Tennyson went with Thackeray and FitzGerald to dine at the home of Charles Dickens. The evening was occupied with a round game of cards and mulled claret. Dickens played the host gracefully, striking FitzGerald as being "quite unaffected, and seeming to wish anyone to show off rather than himself."

Although Thackeray reciprocated Tennyson's regard, he could not share the solemn devotion with which the ex-Apostles listened to him chanting his own poetry or proclaiming his verdicts on the classics. Thackeray's schoolboy dislike of Greek was as strong as ever; and besides, there remained in him an adolescent impulse to jeer when anyone revealed strong emotion about such matters as love and beauty.

He therefore used to describe scoffingly, in later years, how Tennyson gloried in his *Ulysses*, and especially in the line "And see the great Achilles, whom we knew." "He went through the streets," Thackeray would say, "screaming about his great Achilles, whom we knew, as if we had all made the acquaintance of that gentleman, and were very proud of it."

On another occasion, when Tennyson had pontifically recited two passages to exemplify the "tenderness" of Catullus, Thackeray remarked brusquely, "I do not rate him highly. I could do better myself." Tennyson serenely refused to be annoyed, but at two o'clock in the morning Thackeray woke in a state of horror at his own arrogance, and as soon as he got up he wrote a contrite apology: "When I have dined, sometimes I believe myself to be equal to the greatest painters and poets. The delusion goes off; and then I know what a small fiddle mine is and what small tunes I play upon it. It was very generous of you to give me an opportunity of recalling a silly speech; but at the time I thought I was making a perfectly simple and satisfactory observation. . . Why should I be so uneasy at having made a conceited speech? It is conceited not to wish to seem conceited." Tennyson admired the "generous spirit" of this letter, saying that "no one but a noble-hearted man" could have written it.

On other matters their taste was better in accord. Saville Morton describes calling on Tennyson one day and finding Thackeray there, and "a stack of shag tobacco with Homer and Miss Barrett on the table." In the ensuing conversation, the two authors vied in praising Miss Barrett's poetry. On another occasion, with his typical assumption of bluntness, Thackeray burst into a Tennysonian disquisition with the remark, "My dear Alfred, you do talk damned well!"

With Thomas Carlyle, too, an intimacy was growing. John Sterling's diary records a "pleasant evening" in Cheyne Row, when Thackeray made a "first-rate pen sketch of Carlyle sitting on a tub and smoking—only to be paralleled by the Prophets of Angelo—I never laughed more heartily at anything."

Opportunities were coming to Thackeray in a profusion almost magical after the leanness of the preceding year. His friend Ainsworth set the pace. Too amiable either to feel or to incur the jealousies that prevailed among many of his colleagues, Ainsworth had a suburban villa where he entertained his friends in a simple domestic style. It was a meeting ground for writers whose orbits seldom otherwise crossed, and although Thackeray continued to ridicule Ainsworth's books from time to time, he was always a welcome guest.

Having gained some experience in editing through being Dickens's successor in charge of *Bentley's Miscellany*, Ainsworth decided to set up a monthly of his own, and the first number of *Ainsworth's Magazine* appeared in February, 1842. A brilliant group of his friends was represented, Thackeray's contribution being a fable in *Arabian Nights* style, entitled *Sultan Stork* and supposedly "translated from the Persian" by Major Gahagan. This appeared in two instalments, and was followed by one of his "Titmarsh" reviews of the current art exhibitions.

For *Fraser's* he wrote an essay on *Dickens in France* which gave him the double opportunity of praising Boz and of taunting the critical arrogance of Jules Janin, with many incidental sneers at the general French ignorance of everything English. A new market was also open to him, whenever he chose to deal with it. The project of a "London Charivari" had been revived some months before, and carried to fulfilment under the title *Punch*. This time the moving spirit was Henry Mayhew, who had remained a friend of Thackeray since their old Paris days. He and Douglas Jerrold were its principal writers, and their first cartoonist was John Brine, Thackeray's one-time comrade of the *ateliers*. Although he was implored to participate, Thackeray hesitated: the paper was staggering along with very little money, and some of his friends advised him against appearing in this undignified vehicle of a shabby Fleet-Street coterie.

He was sharing the house in Coram Street with the former Polly Graham and her husband, Colonel Carmichael, who at this time dropped the "Smyth" from his name. Though Thackeray still felt grateful for the financial aid that his cousin had supplied in various emergencies, he found that at close quarters she was uncomfortably jealous and peremptory, as well as being fussy over her infant son. Partly for this reason, perhaps, he decided to clear his conscience of Chapman & Hall's £120 and redeem his plate-chest by making the tour of Ireland that had been planned two years before.

Nevertheless, he did not want to let it interfere with any chance of more permanent employment. In the middle of March, when he learned that Chapman & Hall had just assumed ownership of the *Foreign Quarterly Review*, he applied for the post of editor. "Unless you have a great man like Mr Carlyle at the head of your undertaking, please to think of your humble servant, who is very anxious to have a calling and regular occupation of some kind, and could really, I think, do your duty very well. I know a couple of languages, French and German, and could know Italian in another month, having already a smattering; and if your intention is not to have a pompous review, but a smart and lively one, I believe I should make as good an editor as another." He added that he would have no hesitation in giving up the Irish tour in favor of the appointment, or even for a temporary mission abroad—perhaps to Germany—on behalf of the *Review*.

The publishers apparently did intend it to be pompous rather than smart and lively, as they gave the editorship to John Forster; but Thackeray was enlisted among the regular contributors, and immediately supplied his first review, on Hugo's *Le Rhin*.

Before launching out on the risks of the Irish campaign, he also started a series of sketches for *Fraser's*; and to give some coherence to what threatened to be a rather miscellaneous collection he invented a new personage as the narrator. These were to be the confessions of George Savage FitzBoodle, Esq., a typical London clubman, younger son of an aristocratic family, a sportsman who never reads a book and heartily despises "scribblers," but who has decided to write his recollections as a solace to boredom after being "cleaned out" at whist. This might sound like an opening for another of Thackeray's slashing caricatures; but as a matter of fact FitzBoodle is rather sympathetically portrayed, and Thackeray succeeds in the difficult task of showing that a gentleman can be likable even if he is stupid. Indeed, there is a good deal of autobiography in the

SKETCHES EN ROUTE TO IRELAND

sketches: FitzBoodle, like Thackeray, was educated at "Slaughterhouse" School, and a number of his experiences in Germany are modeled upon Thackeray's during his season at Weimar, which figures in FitzBoodle's memoirs as Kalbsbraten-Pumpernickel. His work for the *Foreign Quarterly* was turning his thoughts back to those months in Saxony with considerable feeling.

In the same month when the first "FitzBoodle" came out in *Fraser's*, he also acceded to Mayhew's persuasions and began to write for *Punch*. As late as May 22, FitzGerald was asking a friend to advise Thackeray "not to go into *Punch* yet," but just four weeks later his first contribution appeared. A pseudo-Arabian apologue, reminiscent of his recent *Sultan Stork*, it made good-natured fun of the metaphysical poetry of John Abraham Heraud, one of his old Fraserian comrades. This was followed by a series called *Miss Tickletoby's Lectures on English History*, an easy burlesque device that would carry itself without much strain on his inventive powers.

Having erected several safe financial defences in his rear, he set out on his travels. He followed a leisurely itinerary through Bristol, Wales, Shrewsbury, Chester, and Liverpool, writing comical inscriptions in the visitors' books along the way; and on July 4 he arrived in Dublin. It was the first time he had had a predetermined scheme to be carried out, the first time he had entered a strange scene with the credentials of a professional writer. He brought with him letters of introduction that opened friendly doors and won aid for his inquiries. All this was balm to the bruises inflicted by two years of neglect and disappointment.

All his urbane irony was needed to preserve his balance amid the contradictory impressions and emotions that surged over him. Almost simultaneously he was moved to laughter, pity, and exasperation, as he encountered the dirt and sloppiness of his hotel in the nation's capital, the humor and generosity and improvidence that he found in people of all ranks, the unutterable destitution of the poor, the violent political antipathies. His book would not be easy to write.

One introduction was to Charles Lever, who was riding the wave of his success as a humorous novelist and lifting the *Dublin University Magazine* to international renown under his editorship. Lever invited the English visitor to dinner to meet two military men, Captain Siborne, author of a history of the campaign of 1815, and Major Frank Dwyer of the Austrian service, who kept a full and somewhat naïve record of the occasion.

Having been invited to meet a humorist, Dwyer was disappointed to find Thackeray "at first reserved, earnest, and quiet; what was most observable seemed to be that he was himself carefully observing, and desirous of not being drawn out, at least not prematurely." There were reasons for the constraint: the Irishmen were trying to discover their guest's political color. At last, "Thackeray praised some *fricandeau de veau*, a thing rarely seen on Irish tables, which led to mention being made of the artistical arrangements of the kitchen at the Reform Club. That was just what we wanted—we then knew of course what Thackeray's politics were.

"As dinner proceeded, and after the ladies had retired, the two protagonists began to skirmish, endeavouring to draw each other out. Neither knew much of the other, beyond what could be gleaned from their published works. The conversation had been led by Lever to the subject of the battle of Waterloo. . . Thackeray soon joined in; he did not pretend to know anything about the great battle, but he evidently wished to spur on Lever to identify himself with Charles O'Malley. He seemed always to wish to betray every Irishman he met into boasting in some shape or on some subject. . . Quickly perceiving his antagonist's game, [Lever] met his feints with very quiet, but perfectly efficacious parries. It was not a little amusing to observe how these two men played each a part seemingly belonging to the other, Thackeray assuming what he judged to be a style of conversation suitable for Lever, whilst the latter responded in the sarcastic and sceptical tone proper to an English tourist in Ireland.

"French and German literature next came on the tapis, Thackeray expressing a preference for German books. . . Thackeray paid Lever the very handsome compliment of saying that he would rather have written Lorrequer's English version of the student song, *The Pope he leads a Happy Life*, than anything he had himself hitherto done in literature. Lever could scarcely give credence to this strong piece of flattery; it was quite evident, however, that he was very much pleased, and also finally convinced that Thackeray really meant what he said. . . From that moment they became much more cordial to each other, and the conversation ran smoother and with less restraint than it had previously done.

"In the brilliant conversational encounter that ensued, the two principals exerted themselves to the utmost to please each other. Perhaps neither ever showed to greater advantage than when contrasted with the other. Thackeray's conversation flowed more evenly on the whole, like the deeper current of a river meandering through a cultivated country, and only occasionally quickening its pace and gathering force to dash over some well-selected point; Lever's, on the contrary, resembled a mountain torrent leaping over rocks and precipices, from pool to pool, in clouds of sparkling spray."

By this time Thackeray was thoroughly at ease. He "criticized the French theatre very sharply, and came out with a strong bit of humorous representation which convulsed us with laughter. It had reference to some opera in which the principal male character comes on the stage with a pirouette, and waving his hand in a majestic manner to a chorus, representing Jews in exile in Babylon, says, 'Chantez-nous une chanson de Jérusalem.' Thackeray rose from his seat and did the thing, pirouette and all, most inimitably. He was fond of exhibiting his French pronunciation, also of caricaturing very cleverly that of his own countrymen, the English."

The next day Thackeray accompanied Lever and Dwyer to see a grand review in the Phoenix Park. When Lever happened to become separated from the other two, Thackeray saw a good chance to pull the leg of his military-minded companion. At the beginning of a cavalry charge, he pretended to be terrified of their being ridden down, and begged the Major to run to safety; the approach of a dragoon officer was taken as a threat to expel them from the field. Aghast at such ignorance, the Major felt incumbent upon him "the duty of pointing out the general object and nature of the movements that were being carried out;" but after Thackeray had listened politely for some time, he "begged of me not to take any more trouble on the subject, as he felt that he should never understand the least about these matters," and added that he would much prefer to review the ladies.

After Lever had driven off to his villa, Thackeray and the Major walked into Dublin together, still discussing military topics. "Thackeray remarked that a great amount of interest still attached to everything connected with Waterloo, the British public seeming never to tire of it; he had been thinking since we met at dinner of writing something on the subject himself, but he did not see his way clearly. Lever's treatment of it in *O'Malley* seemed to him much too imaginative and high-flown, in fact audacious and regardless of all probability."

The imperfect sympathy between the worthy Major and the literary man was revealed again on their next expedition together, when Lever took them both to Maynooth, the site of the new Roman Catholic college. Observing Thackeray's "sardonic smile of utter derision and contempt" as he looked at the squalid place, Dwyer commented that "Maynooth certainly is most desolate looking;" but his feelings were sadly hurt when "Thackeray shut me up by replying that Trinity College was not a whit better in respect of cleanliness." Being a loyal son of T. C. D., the Major immediately concluded that Thackeray was actuated by "dislike of Protestant ascendancy and Saxon supremacy in Ireland."

Thackeray was anxious to complete his long expeditions before the autumn should set in, leaving the details of Dublin for the end of his stay. The first stage of his travels was arranged by Peter Purcell, an uncle of Edward FitzGerald and a leader in schemes for scientific agriculture and other welfare projects. A visit of a day or two in the rambling, easy-going country-house at Halverstown, County Kildare, was sufficient to captivate Thackeray completely with the warm affection and inexhaustible laughter of the numerous Purcell family, most of whom then escorted him as far as Cork—a two-day journey—in the family carriage. While in Cork he was rather bored by an agricultural show that was Mr Purcell's pet project of the moment. He was more interested in making the acquaintance of Father Mathew, leader of a gigantic temperance campaign. He also suffered himself to be conducted nervously and sentimentally through an Ursuline convent.

Upon leaving his friends in Cork, he plunged into the unknown. By jaunting car and "Bianconi van," or in ramshackle mail-coaches, staying at over-crowded lodging-houses and slovenly hotels, soaked by downpours of rain and baked by sudden intervals of sunshine, he scoured the South and West as far as Galway, and pushed into Connemara to be the guest of Richard Martin, M. P., equally famous as the last great Irish duelist and the founder of the Society for the Prevention of Cruelty to Animals. At Martin's estate, Ballinahinch, which was the largest in Ireland, Thackeray could observe the best surviving example of feudal paternalism.

From the remote West he went straight across the midriff of the country to Dublin, made a perfunctory round of the beauty-spots in Wicklow, and then gratefully settled down for a few more days with the merry Purcells.

At this juncture, disquieting news reached him from London. Delay in the arrival of his payments from *Punch* had made him wonder whether his friends had been right in their warnings against the paper; but now when a remittance of twenty-five pounds reached him, it was accompanied by the humiliating statement that the editors were not satisfied with his series of skits.

Miss Tickletoby's Lectures were undeniably rather forced in their humor, which consisted of persistent naïveté, commonplace puns, and an occasional touch of vulgarity—as in the slang phrase that constituted the schoolmistress's name. Thackeray replied to the editor, more in sorrow than in anger, protesting that he had done his best, "just as much as if I had been writing for any more dignified periodical." After expressing the hope that the series could be replaced with "some more amusing and lively correspondent," he said that he would be spending the winter either in Paris or in London, "where, very probably, I may find some other matter more suitable to the paper, in which case I shall make another attempt upon *Punch*." His comic survey of English history accordingly stopped short with Edward III.

This news, reaching him when he was on the eve of starting the second major portion of his tour, distinctly affected his spirits. Even through the discomforts and tedious spells of his travels in the South and West, he had been sustained by a mood of adventure and kindliness, but now his hopes for a successful career seemed to be dashed once more. Gloomily he moved northward to make the acquaintance of a distant cousin, the Reverend Elias Thackeray, who was vicar of Dundalk and Louth; and he found only a melancholy gratification in the benevolence with which his cousin used almost all his large income for schools, hospitals, and the poor. Thackeray was touched almost to tears by the sight of the well-scrubbed children in the Dundalk institutions.

To leave the charitable atmosphere of his cousin's home and face strangers required courage. It was now October, and the weather was growing steadily worse. As he advanced into Ulster he was repelled by the grim, unfriendly manner of the Northerners. In Belfast, an introduction from Lever to a wealthy manufacturer was a slight alleviation, but by this time he was longing for the whole affair to be ended. Writing to his mother about how much he enjoyed the scenic drive from Belfast along the coast, he added, "but I think I shall enjoy a visit to St Germain still more. Meanwhile I dream of you and the little ones every night, which, to be sure, is not much comfort."

The climax of his misery came with a visit to a famous resort of tourists, the Giant's Causeway. The austere scenery, the vile weather, and the loneliness combined to prey upon him; his mind was growing incoherent from solitude. When he was taken out in a boat for a better view of the cliffs he was horribly seasick, and upon going ashore he slipped on the wet rocks and fell sprawling. Eating dinner at the huge gloomy hotel he found himself the only customer, "the last company being a corpse which had just gone. I think the ghost was there still, and I got out of the place in a panic." As a pilgrim of the picturesque, Thackeray was a rank failure.

To get from Coleraine to Londonderry he had a solitary car-drive of many miles across bleak peat-bogs. Physical and spiritual exhaustion alike beset him. Then in the little town of Limavady he received a bright smile and a friendly word from a pretty waiting-maid at the inn. The mishap of his spilling a glass of beer on his trousers gave them the pretext for a laugh together; and so touched was he by this glimpse of simple human kindness that he expressed his captivation with the girl in a poem, whimsical and yet more than a little sincere in its half-hysterical gratitude for restoration to faith and cordiality.

From Londonderry he hastened southward through sleet and mud, seeing no more of the scenery than was visible through the bespattered windows of the mail-coach. For the next few weeks, while putting his notes into shape, he luxuriated in the sociability of Dublin, and now the friendship of Lever proved its full worth. In his published narrative, Thackeray estimated at fifty the number of dinner-parties that Lever gave for him at "his mansion of Templeogue;" and in the same mood of hyperbole he told Lever that "he had met no such collective agreeability anywhere." The Dublin literary men were a witty and convivial crew, with Lever their unflagging instigator.

"Thackeray was on a visit with me while I was writing *Tom Burke*," he recollected long afterwards. "I believe, though we discussed every other book and book writer, neither of us ever by a chance alluded to what the other was employed on. Nay, I am wrong. Thackeray once referred to his Irish book. It was in the drawing-room after dinner, when I had some twelve or fourteen friends anxious to meet him. 'Can any of your friends here,' whispered he, 'cram me on the subject of the Irish corporation?'—it was the time of O'Connell's mayoralty—'I must give them a page or two.'

" 'There's your man,' said I, leading him to Isaac Butt. 'He is an alderman, and in a question of cram equal to anything—from the siege of Troy to Donnybrook Fair.'

"My friend Butt did not discredit the reputation I gave him. He invited us both to breakfast for the following Monday; and for Thackeray's entertainment and amusement, he got up a debate, which incidentally opened up the question of Repeal of the Union, and called up the Liberator himself to speak with an amount of temper and passion, that showed he had detected the spirit of the discussion, and knew it to be merely a 'field day,' got up to amuse the stranger."

In return for so much help, Thackeray took it upon himself to give Lever advice on the profession of authorship. He assumed that Lever must have quarreled with the English publishers, as there was no visible reason for his having settled in Dublin instead of London, and he offered assistance, with either cash or intercession. To his surprise, Lever insisted that he preferred to remain in Ireland.

"Look around you," Thackeray expostulated. "You are surrounded by a lot of third-rate men. Able Irish writers are numerous, but they have gone to London, where alone their talents are rewarded. None remain at home except a few that look for advancement in the professions or from the sham court. In Ireland there is no public opinion; Dublin is split up into factions, coteries, and classes, jealous of each other, and engaged in miserable squabbles. Though you are just now popular, you will some day, perhaps, inadvertently tread on some Irishman's corns—and Irishmen's feet are all corns—and then your worshipers will treat you as the Chinese do their gods when they disappoint them—chop off their heads. Of every pound that goes into your pocket, nineteen shillings is English money, and but a single shilling Irish money."

Five years older than Thackeray, and vastly more famous and prosperous, Lever regarded such counsel as a trifle presumptuous. "Thackeray is the most good-natured man alive," he told a confidant, "but help from him would be worse than no help at all. He is like a man struggling to keep his head above water, and who offers to teach his friend to swim. He would write for anything, and about anything, and his status in London is not good."

This unvarnished verdict was painfully near the truth. The winter months, while he was waiting for *The Irish Sketch Book* to be published, were again a time of discouragement. As often before, his current series in *Fraser's* was his only regular means of support, eked out with articles in *The Foreign Quarterly Review*. In the opening months of 1843 he was still beset with anxieties. His loneliness in Coram Street was mitigated by the presence of FitzGerald, one of the few friends whose companionship never palled upon him, chiefly because Fitz did not intrude himself too much, but went his own way and foregathered with his host only at breakfast and over a cigar at night for half an hour of cheerful nonsense. In spite of Thackeray's enjoyment of social gatherings, he could seldom endure patiently the day-by-day intimacy even of people whom he loved and admired. His mother's worrying over his health and habits, his stepfather's crotchety opinions, his cousin Mary's possessive attitude, all wearied him at close quarters; he could appreciate their virtues better when he visited them only at intervals.

As his lease at Coram Street was about to run out, much of his spare time was spent in house-hunting. Optimistic ideas of his wife's recovery encouraged him to look for a home in which she and the children could join him; but any house with enough rooms and a patch of garden was far too dear for his overstrained pocket-book. One of the creditors of *The Constitutional* instituted a long-threatened action for payment, and Thackeray was faced with the alternative of making a compromise settlement or declaring himself a bankrupt.

He suffered more and more frequent discomfort from his urethral stricture, a condition that was probably aggravated by his nightly potations of wine. To his mother's protests about his dining out too often and drinking too much, he replied rather impatiently that he not only wrote more upon such a regimen but also felt much better.

In the early spring he became London correspondent of *The Calcutta Star*, and also undertook to write book reviews and art criticism for a new illustrated weekly, *The Pictorial Times*. "So satisfied was he," says the founder of the paper, a young man named Henry Vizetelly, "with the three guineas offered him for a couple of columns weekly, that he jocularly expressed himself as willing to sign an agreement for life upon these terms."

The first number of the new paper appeared in March, and a few weeks later his Irish travels were published in two volumes. As he had depicted himself in the guise of an unsophisticated English sightseer, he intended to name it *The Cockney in Ireland*, but "the pathetic remonstrances of the publishers" induced him to adopt the more conventional title of *The Irish Sketch Book*. Although the title-page bore the familiar pseudonym of "Mr M. A. Titmarsh", for the first time the real name of the author appeared, appended to the dedication, which was a warm expression of gratitude to Lever.

The book was favorably reviewed by the London papers, but in Ireland it created a furore. As Thackeray had sagely remarked to Lever, Irishmen's feet are all corns; and at a time of intense bitterness the almost contemptuous irony of his report enraged both parties. He ridiculed the frenetic oratory of the Repealers, but he was not much more respectful to the complacency of the ascendancy party. He saw much that was good in the ministrations of the Roman Catholic Church, but sneered at the pomp and pretentious titles of its hierarchy, while the narrow dogmatism of the Protestants also came under fire. But beyond all factional disputes, he outraged every patriotic Irishman by saying little about the country's lovely scenery and glorious legends, and reverting tirelessly to the filth, the laziness, the foul climate, the cringing beggars, the hordes of ragged children. The genteel class was insulted by his allusions to their brogue and their toadying to aristocracy; the proponents of local industries complained because he implied that most of these were impractical or already abandoned. All his favorable allusions to the politeness and cheerfulness of the masses, to the efficiency of certain charitable organizations, were obliterated by the verdict that it was "another insult to Ireland." Even the unoffending Lever lost much popularity in the country through being blamed for supplying Thackeray with data.

The most violently anti-English journal in Dublin was *The Nation*, a weekly edited by a young enthusiast named Charles Gavan Duffy. At the very moment when Thackeray's book was being scourged by the outraged Irish, and by *The Nation* most loudly of all, Duffy was astounded to receive a batch of contributions from Michael Angelo Titmarsh. It happened that Peter Purcell, among his humanitarian causes, had come into violent conflict with the government over a mailcoach monopoly that was causing unemployment among the Irish coachmakers. Out of gratitude to Purcell, and genuine sympathy with the victims, Thackeray sent two drawings and a poem, full of indignant satire. Duffy was glad enough to use such effective missiles, whatever the source; but only the first picture and the poem were published, as the authorities suddenly gave way before there was time for the second picture to come out.

In letting his true name appear in *The Irish Sketch Book* even as inconspicuously as he did, Thackeray was making a reluctant concession to public curiosity. In the very same month he had a taste of how galling that intrusiveness could be. An article in *Fraser's*, with the title *Illustrations of Discount*, went out of its way to include a verbal caricature of "Bill Crackaway," represented as an habitué of the "Grubwell Club" and

> . . . one whom we have always looked upon as a bird of ill omen. His long ungainly person is crowned with a face which Dame Nature must have fashioned just after making a bad debt, and therefore in the worst of tempers. A countenance of preternatural longitude is imperfectly relieved by a nose on which the partial hand of Nature has lavished every bounty—length, breadth, thickness, all but a—bridge; a mouth that seemed suddenly arrested in the act of whistling, and, from its conformation, could only eliminate [sic] a sinister sneer, but was physically incapable of the candour of an honest laugh, which, with a most inhuman squint, gave a rare finish to the *os frontis* of this Corinthian capital of our club.

The anecdote went on to depict him as speaking "lispingly" and using the sporting slang of the day; and the writer asserted that "Crackaway" was not only the editor of a "a pseudo-philosophical magazine" but also in business as a bill-broker in the City.

Thackeray was certain that the author of this gratuitous affront was a certain David Deady Keane, a lawyer and journalist. They had been contemporaries at Cambridge and were friendly during Thackeray's early years in London. In fact, they had Christmas dinner together in 1833, the year in which Thackeray was dabbling in the discounting business in Birchin Lane. After ten years he did not enjoy being reminded of such indiscretions; and he was all the more infuriated by the article because he had no reason to regard Keane as anything but a friend; they had chatted and shaken hands at the club only a few days before the magazine came out. To let his rage cool, he waited for a week before taking any action, and was relieved that no one he met seemed to have identified him as the target of the libel. Needless to say, he did not call anybody's attention to it. But at the end of the week he wrote a letter of cold fury to Nickisson, the publisher of the magazine: "As, in a private house or an Inn, if any person with no other provocation but that of drunkenness or natural malice should take a fancy to call me by foul names, I should have a right to appeal to the host and request him to have the individual so offending put out of doors—I may similarly complain to you that I have been grossly insulted in your magazine. . . If Mr Deady Keane continues his contributions in any form, mine must cease. I am one of the oldest and I believe one of the best of your contributors. . . I make this demand not in the least as an act of retaliation against Mr Keane, but as an act of justice I owe to myself and which is forced upon me. At the present at least it cannot be said that my anger is very revengeful or that his attack has rendered me particularly vindictive. . ."

Such a protest came somewhat strangely from one who had not scrupled to publish highly personal lampoons against Bulwer, Lardner, and other authors. The present situation was somewhat different, to be sure, in that the victim had never sought publicity, whereas those others had courted the limelight. Moreover, this attack carried a flavor of treachery by being admitted into a periodical of which Thackeray was almost a staff member.

But his indignation sprang from a deeper source. The abnormal sensitiveness that drove him to avoid public recognition and seek refuge in fictitious personalities was an inevitable result of his disfigurement. From boyhood he had learned that strangers were bound to be amused at his flattened nose; and by the time his full growth had made him even more conspicuous, the ill effects of the injury had extended to the whole expression of his face. Prone to imagine covert ridicule of his looks even when none existed, he erected a defence of sardonic wit which made fun of himself to forestall others, and made fun of everyone else's foibles to ensure that nobody should remain superior and self-satisfied. Hence came the sneering manner—for which his face was all too well adapted; hence came his agony if obliged to make a public speech; hence came the almost terrifying outburst of rage and shame whenever he was unkindly described. And as the obverse of the trait, he was pathetically grateful to anyone who showed no hint of considering him peculiar, especially when the person was a pretty woman, whether the baronet's daughter, Jane Brookfield, or the humble tavern-maid, Peg of Limavady.

He rationalized his use of pen-names by arguing that a hard-working professional author would lose the public's respect if he were recognized as producing too many different types of work and appearing in publications of varying prestige at the same time. During 1843, therefore, he retained his latest disguise of George FitzBoodle for his stories in *Fraser's* even though it was no longer plausible, as he had finished the "Confessions" of that easy-going man-about-town and was now writing a series of quite different tales entitled *Men's Wives*. The longest of these, *The Ravenswing*, reverted to the back-streets setting, the unscrupulous husband, the exploited wife, of *A Shabby Genteel Story* and *The Great Hoggarty Diamond*. Two of the shorter stories achieved a level of grimness that Thackeray had never sought before.

In May he moved out of the Coram Street house, spent a few days in Brighton, and then took a room at a London hotel and spent his days at the Reform Club and the Garrick. His intimacy with Dickens and his circle was increasing: Thackeray was one of the hosts at a dinner at Greenwich given for the retiring editor of *The Morning Chronicle* by a group that included Dickens, Forster, and Albany Fonblanque of *The Examiner*.

Still planning the book on the Low Countries that he had promised to write for Chapman & Hall three years before, he spent August in Belgium and Holland with an artist friend, but the venture proved disastrous. He began by losing his wallet containing twenty pounds. During the rest of the trip his friend Stevens generously paid most of the expenses, but clung so persistently to Thackeray that no sketching, writing, or thoughtful observation was possible. After finally parting from his companion, Thackeray ran out of cash in Lille and had to wait more than a week before funds reached him from his grandmother. Inflammation of the eyes increased his misery. When he arrived in Paris he was again so destitute that his angry cabman had to be paid on the doorstep by the Carmichael-Smyth's cook.

At this time he made a determined effort to start writing a novel. Ever since his visit to John Bowes at Streatlam Castle two years before, he had kept in mind the idea of using the character of the Irish adventurer, Stoney, with whom Bowes's grandmother, Lady Strathmore, had eloped in 1777. His experience with *Catherine*, too, had left him with a subconscious wish to wipe out the failure by producing a serious story dealing with the same period and the same types. The eighteenth century appealed to him on several counts. His ancestors had distinguished themselves then in many directions, from the Rev Thomas Thackeray's headmastership of Harrow to General John Webb's heroism at the battle of Wynendael and Colonel Richmond Webb's service at Culloden. His innate patrician sympathy was drawn to a time free of the bourgeois vulgarities of his own era. The rationalism and the satiric acerbity of its thinking, too, had early won his favor in the novelists and essayists. It was altogether natural that for his first planned and ambitious work of fiction he should select that epoch for his scene.

The demands of historical accuracy required harder work than any of his previous writings. In September and October, when his daughters were staying in the country at Montmorency, he spent only a day once or twice a week with them and the rest of his time in the Carmichael-Smyth's house in Paris, "working, or pretending to work." November found him in London again "to have his eyes doctored;" he rented lodgings over a shop at No. 27 Jermyn Street, and Fitz-Gerald, as usual, came up from the country and stayed with him for ten days.

At this time he became officially a member of the staff of *Punch*. During the year he had contributed occasionally; and the paper, having forged ahead in popularity, had been taken over by a prosperous publishing firm, so that on both sides there was now a willingness to co-operate. The regular contributors had worked out an agreeable system of editorial conference, in which they met for dinner once a week to discuss the next issue and in particular to decide on an idea for its political cartoon. Thackeray joined the group in the seat previously occupied by Albert Smith, whose witticisms had proved too labored for permanent consumption. Thackeray's first contribution under the new contract appeared on December 16, and thereafter he was represented almost every week.

His high spirits at this juncture were displayed on an occasion that was chronicled by Jane Welsh Carlyle. The birthday of Macready's little daughter occurred at Christmas, and as the tragedian was away on an American tour, his friends decided to console the lonely wife and family with a party. The absence of the austere head of the house had a miraculous effect on the affair; Mrs Carlyle described it as "the *very* most agreeable party that ever I was at in London." The fact that she, too, was a grass-widow for the moment may have been partly responsible for her enjoyment. Dickens occupied a whole hour with his best conjuring tricks, aided by Forster. Then dancing began: "old Major Burns with his one eye, old Jerdan of the *Literary Gazette* (escaped out of the rules of the Queen's Bench for the great occasion!), the gigantic Thackeray, etc., all capering like *Maenades*." Refusing to waltz, Mrs Carlyle devoted herself to "talking the maddest nonsense" with Dickens, Forster, Maclise, and Thackeray. At supper there was pulling of crackers, drinking of champagne, and making of speeches, after which came a riotous country dance. "In fact," says the delighted Jane Welsh, "the thing was rising into something not unlike the *rape of the Sabines*" before midnight caused dispersal. "Dickens took home Thackeray and Forster with him and his wife '*to finish the night there*,'" Mrs Carlyle adds, "and a royal night they would have of it, I fancy! ending perhaps with a visit to the watch-house."

Another ridiculous episode occurred about the same time. Among the Carlyle circle was a young Scot named John Robertson, who served as Mill's sub-editor of *The Westminster Review*, "and who took absurdish airs on that dignity," as Carlyle remarked. In Mrs Macready's drawing-room Thackeray informed Dickens and Mrs Carlyle, in the hearing of several other people, that he had just encountered Robertson "in the last extremity of fate," and had slipped five shillings into his hand. Astounded at the story, Mrs Carlyle soon afterwards heard the other side of it from Robertson, who was still totally unaware of what had been in

Thackeray's mind. Thus she learned "the real facts of how the money was put into Robertson's hands with certain mysterious words—and how Robertson stared after 'the odd mortal' as he ran away, in total bewilderment as to what Thackeray designed him *to do* with the said shillings! and how he called next day to return them and ask the meaning—and found him 'out'—and on the next day again and found him 'gone to Paris.' "

Mrs Carlyle hastened to inform Dickens of the true state of the case, and he replied that he had already suspected the accuracy of Thackeray's story, "and consequently I did not back up a vague suggestion thrown out by Titmarsh, touching a Subscription List in behalf of its unfortunate subject." Dickens added, however, that Thackeray's mistake had been justified by Robertson's "meek face" and "the gasp and struggle which precedes all his cod-fish-like attempts at speech. . . I had picked him up one day in Bond Street, not long before; and such a watery, washed-out, vapid old rag of humanity never presented itself before my mental vision."

The whole occurrence was characteristic of Thackeray—the absent-minded blundering that caused the mistake, the immediate generosity that prompted both the five shillings and the projected subscription, and the tactlessness that blazoned the story abroad. At the same moment he was in a scrape with *Fraser's Magazine* over a similar effort. One of his oldest boon-companions in Paris, an erratic Irishman named O'Donnell, came with one of his periodical requests for the loan of a sovereign; and being short of cash Thackeray offered instead to place an article he had written with the magazine. He even withheld his own contribution that month in order to make way for his friend. No sooner was it published than Nickisson discovered it to be a verbatim plagiarism of an article in another periodical. Thackeray felt that he was really learning something about the Irish character when he went furiously to berate the offender, only to be greeted with howls of laughter. O'Donnell regarded the matter as a rich joke.

As episodes like these got into circulation, Thackeray was well on his way toward being one of the noted anecdote-provoking "characters" of literary London.

CHAPTER 8

He Sails Before the Wind

THACKERAY'S novel, *The Luck of Barry Lyndon*, began to come out in *Fraser's* in January, 1844, again with the absurd attribution to "FitzBoodle," even though the story was written in the first person as the memoirs of the swaggering rogue whose name it bore. Although Thackeray had been planning it and making notes for several months, he had written only enough for the first instalment, and throughout the year he was perpetually harassed by the demands of the editor. Living from hand to mouth, sometimes in London, sometimes in Paris, he could not afford the time to complete the novel before it began to bring in returns. The necessity of producing each section by a fixed date was also a valuable discipline to prevent him from putting off the hard work of creation. A diary that he kept at the time contains a monotonous refrain of weariness. On January 11 he wrote till five o'clock, and then went to the theater, "quite tired and weary with writing, which the evening's amusement did not cure." A week later he admitted that he was "beginning to flag." During the next week he "got through the fag-end of Chap. iv with a great deal of dulness, unwillingness, and labour." In the middle of February it was, "Passed the whole of these days reading for *Barry Lyndon*, and writing, with extreme difficulty, a sheet." Then, a few days later, "Wrote all day *Barry Lyndon*, at 5 went out very tired, and came back still more tired at $9\frac{1}{2}$. . . . Continual labour annoys and excites me too much."

The work had to be interspersed with journalistic tasks. An egregious publicity-monger in New York, Henry Wikoff, had started a newspaper named *The Republic*, and hired Thackeray as Paris correspondent with promises of liberal payment. In spite of his previous experience with Willis, Thackeray accepted the offer, and during January and February took days out of his work on *Barry Lyndon* to compose three "American letters." At the beginning of March, however, he went back to London, and apparently a disagreement over methods of payment put an end to his despatches for *The Republic*.

In the same weeks he had undertaken an English translation of *Les Mystères de Paris*, by Eugène Sue, to be published in monthly parts by Chapman & Hall. He handed over the first pages of his manuscript to the French agent with the stipulation that it must not be sent to press unless he received his payment. When the proofs were submitted to him without the remittance, he sent them back uncorrected, with a stiff letter, and the translation was then assigned to another writer.

His work for *Punch* obliged him to accept whatever topics might be chosen by the editorial conclave. Jerrold was conducting a persistent campaign against the *Morning Post* for its grandiloquent airs and its toadying of the aristocracy. He had invented the character of "Mr Jenkins" as the sycophantic reporter of Court functions. Leech made Jenkins equally ludicrous in his drawings, and during 1844 several of Thackeray's skits dealt with Jenkins's bad French and ignorance of etiquette. The crusade had no effect upon the "Court and Society" columns of the *Post*, but it aroused natural resentment in Mr Rumsey Forster, the reporter who handled that assignment.

During the spring Thackeray's most important *Punch* contribution, which ran for nine weeks, was *The History of the Next French Revolution*, a clever piece of mock-history, recording a musical-comedy affair in which all the political parties and assorted Pretenders of France led revolutions at the same time. Searching for additional tasks, he proposed to the publishers of *Punch* that he should edit a new weekly paper "which should have a decided air of white kid gloves." His idea was to use signed literary articles by his most distinguished friends, such as Carlyle, Milnes, John Forster, and Charles Buller. Thackeray himself would deal with "the fine arts, light literature and the theatre." As he admitted that the circulation would be "gentlemanlike" rather than large, he aroused no enthusiasm either in Bradbury & Evans or in Chapman & Hall, whom he also importuned with the scheme. Nor did Bradbury & Evans respond to his hint that "an enterprising publisher" might bring out a new collection of his stories and literary articles, reprinted from the magazines, "as I have got a public now."

With all these irons in the fire he came back from Paris to his Jermyn Street quarters at the beginning of March and plunged immediately into a round of dinner parties. He saw a good deal of Brookfield, who would drop in frequently and persuade him to come out for a long walk, and who enjoyed the sense of escape from his clerical dignity whenever Thackeray asked him to dinner with a Bohemian group at some tavern. In April FitzGerald came up to London to see his friend, but reported crossly that he "went off to Brighton the night after I arrived, and has not reappeared." Six weeks later Fitz informed Frederick Tennyson that Thackeray was "in full vigour play and pay in London, writing in a dozen reviews, and a score of newspapers; and while health lasts he sails before the wind."

Several of his friends succeeded in getting him appointed to *The Morning Chronicle*. He was supposed to earn forty pounds a month for book reviews and political articles, but soon found the latter so boring that he preferred to confine himself to the reviews, for half the salary. He also started writing a biography of Talleyrand, having met the great statesman's private secretary, Colmache, whose wife was a friend of his mother's. He promised to have it ready for Chapman &

Hall by December 1, and they accordingly advertised it as the first of a series of biographies.

He became optimistic enough to plan for his wife to come over and live in a private home in Twickenham, where he could spend two or three days with her every week. His mother and the little girls went to Chaudfontaine, near Liège, for the summer; but he was too busy to join them, and was receiving, he told his mother, "a great deal of small flattery at tea and dinner parties."

Barry Lyndon was probably the reason for the "flattery." With great skill he was telling a lively picaresque tale and yet subtly revealing depths of depravity and sadism through the boastful narrative of the egotistical hero. It was a masterpiece of sustained irony.

The only complaints about it came from Ireland. Thackeray's assumption that bragging was a typical Irish trait, which had already annoyed Major Dwyer, colored the characterization of Barry. Charles Lever was smarting under the attacks he had suffered as proxy for the author of *The Irish Sketch Book*, and at this juncture Thackeray reviewed his new novel, *Tom Burke of "Our's."* Though Thackeray innocently regarded his article as very favorable, Lever took offense at some frank comments, and wrote angrily to Ainsworth about "Thackeray's rascality." Some compensation for this break with a cherished friend was supplied by the effusive gratitude expressed by Dickens for Thackeray's praise of *A Christmas Carol*, in the same article.

Later in the summer Thackeray was able to run over to Belgium for a visit with his family. He took seven-year-old Annie out for walks among the neat Walloon trees and hills. But he could not remain long away from London. One day he left Chaudfontaine intending to spend a short time in Brussels finding data for the biography of Talleyrand and the current chapter of *Barry Lyndon*. Just when he was expected back his mother received a letter with an Ostend postmark, explaining that he had not found even a History of England in Brussels, and was hurrying back to the British Museum. When his train passed Malines, where he would have changed to go back to Chaudfontaine, he felt as in his boyhood days at the end of a vacation at Larkbeare, "with the dreadful *Defiance* coach coming over the hill."

Nevertheless, his days in London were pleasant enough, with a widening circle of party-giving friends. One evening he dined at Disraeli's—a significant occasion in view of the fact that only three months previously he had reviewed *Coningsby* in *The Pictorial Times* and *The Morning Chronicle* with his customary irony, plainly branding its author a coxcomb. His work for Vizetelly's paper, undertaken with such gratitude the year before, was discontinued about this time. After a four-year interval, he had resumed writing for the *New Monthly*; the numbers for May, June, and July contained work of his, signed with the name "Lancelot

Wagstaff," a reminiscence of the one he had used for *Flore et Zephyr*.

Barry Lyndon did not become any easier to write. "At home all day drawing and dawdling," his diary reports in the middle of August, "with *B. L.* lying like a nightmare on my mind." The only effective antidote for this boredom would be complete change to new scenes; and a few days later a prospect of such an adventure was eagerly seized upon. He was dining at the Reform Club with an artist friend, Samuel Bevan, and at the same time a farewell dinner was being held for James Emerson Tennent, a well-known politician and writer of travel books, who was on the eve of starting with his family upon a ten-weeks tour of the Near East. In the course of the evening Tennent suggested that Thackeray should accompany the party.

In spite of many practical obstacles, Thackeray could not resist the idea. Nourished by his youthful love of *The Arabian Nights*, his interest in the Levant had long ago found expression in his visionary schemes to be a newspaper correspondent in Constantinople or to make a sketching pilgrimage through the Eastern Mediterranean. After lying dormant for ten years, his Oriental enthusiasm had recently wakened again; several of his lighter sketches of the previous year had been in the Arabian manner.

Although he was up to the eyes in literary tasks, and the voyage was to begin in three days, he fell an easy victim to Tennent's persuasion. "In all your life," urged the friendly M. P., "you will never probably have a chance again to see so much in so short a time. Consider—it is as easy as a journey to Paris or Baden." Thackeray tried hard to weigh the problem judicially, but, as he afterwards confessed, "with every glass of claret the enthusiasm somehow rose, and the difficulties vanished." His last scruple was overcome when Tennent promised to use his influence with the directors of the Peninsular and Oriental Steam Navigation Company, organizers of the tour, to obtain a free passage for him.

When he awoke the next morning and realized that he had committed himself to the venture, there was nothing for it but to make the best arrangements he could. His first interview was with Chapman & Hall, who agreed to postpone his obligation for the life of Talleyrand and pay him two hundred pounds instead for a book of his eastern impressions. Next the editors of *Punch* were consulted, and they too proved willing to accept travel sketches, in a more frivolous vein. When the complimentary ticket from the steamship company was duly forthcoming, he found no pretext for reconsidering the plan; but at a dinner party that night, in spite of exceptional brilliance on the part of FitzGerald, he was, he admitted, "too much flustered thinking about the great voyage to enjoy the fun much." The next day was spent in buying eighteen shirts and "a sea-stock of Russia ducks," in cancelling accepted invitations and in writing to his mother, rather ruefully breaking the news: "My heart fails me as I send it, and I wish it weren't true."

The morning of the 22nd found him on board the paddle-wheel steamer *Lady Mary Wood*, pulling out of Southampton, still scarcely able to believe that he was actually there.

After two days of miserable sea-sickness in the Bay of Biscay, he had his first brief shore-visit at Vigo, and thereafter was able to take an interest in his fellow-travelers. At Gibraltar, which he found "the most unromantic, uncomfortable, and prosaic of towns," the party changed to another steamer. All this while, he had *Barry Lyndon* "hanging round his neck," as he put it; in every spare hour he toiled over the story, with intervals devoted to writing skits and drawing pictures for *Punch.* For three days out of Gibraltar, the voracious bugs in his berth were the only drawback to enjoyment; the weather was fair, and Tennent had solemnly sworn that the Mediterranean was never rough. Then they ran into a head wind, and his diary recorded once more, "Basins in requisition." When too sick to write or draw, he still stuck to duty by reading books that prepared him for his future explorations—Morier's *Hajji Baba* and the newly published *Eothen* of his college friend Kinglake.

At Malta, where he impressed his fellow-travelers by serving as interpreter on the strength of Italian phrases derived from operas, he found Valetta as charming and picturesque as Gibraltar had been the reverse. But of Greece his impressions were the most unfavorable of all. The ship spent only one day in the harbor of Piraeus, and the party made a quick expedition to Athens in ramshackle carriages. Thackeray frankly admitted that he was hopelessly prejudiced by the "ten years' banishment of infernal misery, tyranny, annoyance" when he was supposed to be obtaining a classical education, so that "I have the same recollection of Greek in youth that I have of castor oil." When, in addition to this antipathy, he was abominably overcharged at the inn and bitten by bugs even more ferociously than elsewhere in the journey, he had no eyes for the beauty of the Acropolis, but lavished all his eloquence on the ragamuffin soldiers and on the "gobemouche of a Bavarian" who had become King Otto only to suffer from "the bother of perpetual revolutions" in his "huge plaster-of-Paris palace." His opinion was summed up in the statement that "the shabbiness of this place actually beats Ireland, and that is a strong word."

After being soothed by two days of cool calm weather while the ship cruised among the lovely Greek islands, he found in Smyrna all the enchantment he had been seeking. Minarets, kiosks, camels, date-palms, veiled women—it was the veritable land of Haroun al Raschid that he had dreamed of so long; when he wandered through the bazaar he felt entirely at home, and loved all the friendly-looking Moslems as much as he had despised the Greeks. Undoubtedly he was controlled by half-remembered emotions of his infancy in India. The smells and colors and noises of Asia—all those elements that probe the memory more searchingly than rational facts can do—had suddenly transported him to that far-off time and place, the only period of his life when he had been completely happy, before his banishment into self-reliance.

The mood of irrational amiability persisted as they sailed past the plains of Troy and reached Constantinople. It dictated his description of the first view of the city, as disclosed by the rising of the morning mist; he turned to the other ecstasy of his boyhood, the Drury Lane Pantomimes, and compared the scene to one of Stanfield's dioramas, "seen at the best period of youth, when the sound of the bugles and fiddles, as the scene unrolled, and the gorgeous procession meandered triumphantly through it, caused a thrill of pleasure and awakened an innocent fulness of sensual enjoyment that is only given to boys."

During his week's stay in Constantinople the spell was unbroken. He put up at Misseri's Hotel at Pera, and divided his days religiously between sightseeing and writing his despatches for *Punch*, so that by the middle of the week he had completed four of the "Letters from the Fat Contributor"—for such was the latest of his Protean disguises. He spent so much time gazing fascinated at the activities of the Bosphorus that he did not have time to visit some of the prescribed sights of the region; but those which he did inspect were recorded vividly. His description of a Turkish bath is a masterpiece; he went through the slave market, was rowed on the Golden Horn, got into the Seraglio gardens and started to make a sketch of the Sublime Porte itself, but was driven away by the eunuchs on duty, when a crowd gathered to look on. As the fast of Ramazan was in progress, many of the usual activities were suspended and such tourist haunts as the mosque of Saint Sophia were closed to visitors; but he had a good view of the Sultan going to worship at the mosque of Tophana amid petitions for justice from the crowd, and felt very sorry for the Commander of the Faithful for his "seedy" looks and oppressive ceremonials.

For the next stage of the journey to the Holy Land, he boarded another steamer, the *Iberia*, upon which he found an amazing assortment of races, with nothing in common but their filth and stench: Turks of all ages, a Greek priest making the pilgrimage to the Sepulchre, a Greek nun who combed nits out of her hair with her fingers, a large party of Jewish refugees from Poland, seeking a new home in the land of their ancestors and performing all the rituals of their faith with great formality. In the midst of this distraction he had to resume the inevitable writing of *Barry Lyndon*, and by desperate effort was able to complete twelve pages in time to send them off by a ship that was about to sail from Smyrna as they called in there. His manuscript arrived too late, however, for the October number of *Fraser's*.

A visit to Rhodes filled him with regret for the wretchedness of "the noble desolate old town," a regret compounded of characteristically mixed emotions—

admiration for the courage and splendor of Crusaders and Saracens alike, and realistic acknowledgment that the world is much more comfortable now when "the grocer governs" than in those days of barbaric violence. The following morning at dawn the ship ran into a sudden "white squall" that inspired him to describe it in a lively poem. At Beyrout he admired the prettiness of the girls; and the waggish officers of an English man-of-war that was in port passed him off as an equerry of the Prince Consort, in order to impose upon a shopkeeper of the town who had once been received at Windsor on the pretext that he was a Syrian prince.

At Jaffa the party disembarked, and through a misunderstanding about obtaining horses had to spend a flea-bitten night at the British consul's there before making an early-morning start by moonlight for Jerusalem. To alleviate the uncomfortable and dangerous sensations of riding in a high Turkish saddle, Thackeray found that he could wedge himself in place by sticking his umbrella across the saddle-peak, and thus he took his place in a very pantomime-like caravan across the Plain of Sharon. The fourteen-hour journey was broken by a meal with the American consul at Ramleh, and another pause for refreshment at a pleasant village which they vacated hastily on discovering that its Sheikh was a notorious bandit.

A week was spent at Jerusalem, divided between work and exploration as before. He took walks to Olivet and Bethany, and rode to Bethlehem and Siloam, sketching much and acquiring a deep horror for the bleak, savage landscapes, which seemed to symbolize all the cruel events that had occurred there from the days of the Pentateuch to the present. The commercialization, the impostures, and the sectarian quarrels infesting the Holy Places disgusted him, and it was with deep relief that he set out on the return to Jaffa—relief intensified by the fact that he had obtained an English saddle for the journey.

His two weeks in Egypt proved rather an anticlimax. He was not much impressed by the desert and the pyramids, he was embarrassed by riding on donkeyback, and he found Alexandria and Cairo remarkable chiefly for being so like French or English cities. An invitation to an execution was firmly declined. "Seeing one man hanged is quite enough in the course of a life," he said. "*J'y ai été*, as the Frenchman said of hunting."

In the last week of October the party got back to Malta, and were promptly clapped into quarantine. The prospect of seventeen days in the grim lazaretto was not cheering, and the death and funeral of one of the party made Thackeray gloomier than ever. *Barry Lyndon* was brought to an end "after great throes" late at night on the seventh day of his captivity. Appropriately enough, the hero of the novel was shown as ending his career in prison.

With ten days still to put in, Thackeray set to work on his next story, a somewhat Dickensian piece to be entitled *Mrs Perkins's Ball*. A vague intention of

INTERLUDES OF SIGHTSEEING

spending the winter in Malta having been dispelled by the misery of the quarantine, and a winter crossing of the Bay of Biscay being unthinkable, he fled to Naples and then Rome. His painter friend Bevan, who was in Rome for the winter, and who wrote his own book of experiences a few years later, says that, "installed in a quiet bedroom at Franz's, on the Condotti, he appeared to amuse himself with peering into the studios of his countrymen, and while he rummaged over their dusty portfolios, or critically scanned the pictures on the wall, would unconsciously read their secret thoughts, as it were the arcana of their pockets, without allowing them for a moment to imagine that he intended aught save a friendly visit. Many, however, were the poor devils who managed to push through the winter on the strength of the timely fillip administered by Titmarsh." The memory of his own recent struggles must have prompted these tactful donations; and his feeling free to dispense them is evidence of his greater sense of security.

Bevan describes his being voted into the chair at a dinner held by the artists to discuss a dispute among factions of the English Academy. "A considerable portion of the evening was consumed in long-winded speeches, and had it not been for a proposal on the part of our friend Beardman 'to take the basso part in a glee,' a harmonious feeling would hardly have been arrived at. His instigation was succeeded by a call for a song from the chair, amid a vociferous shout of 'Viva Titmarsh!' and a deafening clatter of dessert furniture. Our great friend assured us that he was unable to sing, but would endeavour to make amends by a recitation, if some one in the meantime would make a beginning. Whilst a few were tantalizing the company by a tortured version of one of Calcott's glees, Titmarsh, busy with his tablets, produced the affecting narrative of the Three Sailors [better known as *Little Billee*], of which he soon after delivered himself in a fittingly lugubrious tone of voice."

After six weeks in Rome and two in Florence, he came home by way of Leghorn and Marseilles. When he arrived in Paris to see his family, his younger daughter failed to recognize him because of his new moustache, and cried in terror; and so when he reappeared the next morning the moustache had vanished. He could spare them only a few days before hurrying over to London, to pick up the threads of his neglected work.

The professional outlook was by no means rosy. At that moment the world of Fleet Street was horrified when Laman Blanchard, driven to distraction by the anxieties of supporting his family, committed suicide. In this tragedy of a hardworking former colleague and congenial friend, Thackeray read a grim warning of perils that might still beset him. He had not yet risen above the humiliating necessity of beseeching and threatening certain publishers for the money he earned. *The Pictorial Times* had never paid him for his last contribution, and he sent a note of comic despair to Vizetelly, declaring that the firm that printed it ought to have been posted as a defaulter "at the top of Cheops' pyramid for the information of future gadders about."

Two of his most influential literary friends, Albany Fonblanque and John Forster, were editor and literary editor, respectively, of *The Examiner*, and in March Thackeray accepted an appointment as a sort of sub-editor, writing a few minor book reviews but spending much of his time with scissors and paste pot, summarizing political speeches. He tried to reconcile himself to the tedious job with the reflection that it provided him with ideas for his *Punch* skits and his monthly letter for *The Calcutta Star*; but he was aware that his spasmodic, absent-minded habits made him rather incompetent for this sort of routine work. After four months he was glad to be replaced by some methodical nonentity. The loss of four guineas a week was compensated by his sense of release from galling shackles.

Meanwhile he had taken lodgings at 88 St James's Street, within comfortable reach of the Brookfields, who were living in Great Pulteney street. He had a standing invitation to breakfast with them every Saturday, as well as coming to frequent dinners or dropping in for a late smoke. Sometimes the breakfasts included other members of their pleasant, cultivated circle—"The Set," as Thackeray called it—Buller or Spedding, Aubrey de Vere or Stephen Spring-Rice. On Mrs Brookfield's birthday, Thackeray gave her a Turkish shawl—a trophy of his tour—and was the only outsider invited to dinner with the family party. Even to people who did not know Mrs Brookfield he insisted on singing her praises, and he tried hard to persuade Dickens and Forster to make her acquaintance by coming with him to drink tea at her house.

His friendships were not all, however, on this polite level. The questionable resorts that had amused him during his first days in London reasserted their hold. A convivial dinner at a tavern was a relief after a day of grinding work, even if it meant a headache and soda-water the next morning. He had an insatiable appetite for the primitive quartets and impersonators that provided nightly entertainment at the "poor man's clubs." The most notorious was the Cyder Cellar in Maiden Lane, conveniently near the stage door of the Adelphi Theater. Here Thackeray could usually find some newspaper men and actors to share his amusement at the performance, and as an habitué of so many years's standing he had a prestige in the eyes of newer recruits, who listened respectfully to his reminiscences of carousers and comedians already growing legendary.

Several of his *Punch* colleagues shared these raffish tastes, and one survivor of the Fraserians was also much in evidence. The gnomish Frank Mahony, "Father Prout," having been one of Thackeray's first admirers, now constituted himself a sort of familiar spirit. The slovenly little figure of the priest was equally well known in London, Paris, and Rome, picking up a living as a newspaper writer and drifting about the purlieus so mysteriously that he was reputed to dabble in name-less intrigues. His polyglot learning and ribald anecdotes made his company ac-ceptable not only to Thackeray but to as many other literary men as could toler-

TAVERN MUSICIANS

ate his habits. Thackeray enjoyed bringing young writers and artists to meet him at a favorite haunt of theirs, the Deanery Club in Dean Street.

Mahony was also addicted to quarreling. For several years he had been pour-ing invective upon his one-time patron, Ainsworth, and on Ainsworth's friend and illustrator, Cruikshank. Nor was he the only trouble-stirrer among Thackeray's friends. The chief personage at the *Punch* round-table, the dwarfish Douglas Jerrold, was notorious for his hasty temper and whip-lash tongue. In view of these associations, the most remarkable trait of Thackeray was his ability to remain on friendly terms with most of the antagonists, and to keep his own satirical jibes relatively inoffensive.

His former employer, Vizetelly, gives testimony to his congenial manner. "He never appeared to me to shine in conversation, and he most certainly made no kind of effort to do so—never in fact talked for effect, and, indeed, never usurped any large share of the conversation. Ordinarily, he would interpose occasional quaint humorous comments, and would show himself far more tolerant than men of his capacity usually are of bores. Whenever the talk grew dull and wearying, he would content himself by filliping it up with some witty or shrewd satirical remark, and turn it into a new channel. At this period of his career his placid temper and pleasant courtesy, in spite of the mild sarcasms in which he indulged, charmed all who came in contact with him."

He was making slow headway with his book. He had given up the plan of writing the life of Talleyrand, and his publishers had released him from the contract; but other tasks were in hand or in prospect. Thomas Longman, head of the firm that published *The Edinburgh Review*, got in touch with him to inquire whether he might contribute to that imposing periodical. "I hardly know," Thackeray replied, "what subject to point out as suited to my capacity—light matter connected with art, humorous reviews, critiques of novels—French subjects, memoirs, poetry, history from Louis XV downward or of an earlier period—that of Froissart and Monstrelet—German light literature and poetry—though of these I know but little beyond what I learned in a year's residence in the country fourteen years ago. Finally, subjects relating to society in general, where a writer may be allowed to display the humorous *ego*, or a victim is to be gently immolated. But I am better able to follow than to lead, and should hope to give satisfaction in my small way."

Confronted with this array of themes, Longman recommended Thackeray to the editor of the review, Macvey Napier, as possibly "a good hand for literary articles." Napier, a conventional sort of person, had never heard of Thackeray, and cautiously consulted one of his contributors in London, Abraham Hayward, a lawyer who dabbled in literature and was a famous gossip and party-goer. To him Napier quoted Longman as saying that "this Mr Thackeray is one of the best writers in *Punch*," and added dubiously, "one requires to be very much on one's guard in engaging with mere strangers. In a Journal like the *Edinbro'* it is always of importance to keep up in respect of names." Hayward's report was favorable enough to encourage Napier in opening direct negotiations with Thackeray.

At the same time, Thackeray was nursing plans for another book, which he regarded as so important and potentially profitable that he superstitiously refrained from telling his mother any details about it. He submitted two manuscripts simultaneously to Henry Colburn, in case they might be suitable for *The New Monthly Magazine*. One was the opening pages of a realistic novel, and the other the first part of a shorter tale—probably *Mrs Perkins's Ball*, which he had started writing at Malta. Colburn gave him a cash advance for the story.

In June Mrs Carmichael-Smyth brought the two little girls over to visit their Papa. He took them on the usual sightseeing round of the Zoo and the Tower and Westminster Abbey, and enjoyed a brief holiday with them at the home of his childhood, his great-aunt's house at Fareham. Being conveniently close to Southampton he went over to see the Brookfields, who were staying with friends there. When his mother and daughters had gone back to Paris, leaving him so lonely that he dissolved in tears whenever he thought of them, he was confronted with the disquieting news that Colburn, with characteristic impulsiveness, had sold *The New Monthly* to Harrison Ainsworth.

At a loss as to how this transaction affected his agreement with Colburn, Thackeray wrote to Ainsworth to ask whether unpublished manuscripts had been handed over along with the proprietorship. Ainsworth knew nothing about Colburn's commitments, and being busy with reorganizing the magazine he neglected to investigate the matter, assuming that Thackeray would find out about it directly from the publisher. The author, however, with his deep-rooted distaste for chaffering over his work, shrank from challenging Colburn, and inferred that Ainsworth's silence implied some shady scheme. Finally he wrote to Colburn and demanded the return of his manuscripts; but while he was still fuming, Ainsworth's prospectus of the magazine appeared, and he scanned it with a jaundiced eye. A favorite advertising device of the time, invented by Colburn and exploited by the Annuals, was to make a great showing of contributions by aristocratic amateurs, whose titles were supposed to attract readers; and Ainsworth, who rather dearly loved a lord himself, proclaimed that he had secured the aid of several writers "eminent not only for talent but for high rank." Having warred for years on exactly this form of vulgarity, Thackeray seized upon it with double fury, and dashed off a severe article for *Punch*. "Mr Ainsworth can't mean that the readers of his magazine care for an author because he happens to be a lord; a flunkey might—but not a gentleman who has any more brains than a fool. . . Don't let us talk about high rank in the republic of letters—let us keep *that* place clear."

At the very time when Thackeray was composing this blast, Ainsworth had awakened to the extent of his friend's indignation, and was demanding an explanation from Colburn. The answer was painfully blunt: the publisher was keeping the manuscript until Thackeray should refund the payment he had received. Disgusted with this typically crass conduct of Colburn's, Ainsworth had an interview with Thackeray and asked him to contribute a humorous story and also to submit the material which Colburn was holding for ransom. Thackeray was at once mollified. "Of course I'll come to dinner on Sunday," he responded; "and we are just as good friends as ever. Wasn't it much better to complain and explain? I think so—and the injured honor of Titmarsh is now satisfied."

As it was too late to recall the *Punch* article from the printers, all he could do was apologize for it candidly: "There's one thing I regret very much, too, and must be told to you now in making a clean breast of it—a certain paragraph in the next *Punch*, relating to a certain advertisement about contributors, 'not only of talent *but of rank*'. . . I always must think it a very objectionable advertisement, but shouldn't have lifted my hand to smite my friend, had explanation come earlier, so that now *you* must be called upon to play the part of forgiver, in which I'm sure you will shine."

In view of the plans that Ainsworth was making for the magazine, Thackeray knew that the manuscript previously offered to Colburn would be too long, as it would "run to 80, possibly 100 pages." With regard to the request for "a funny story," on the other hand, he considered the terms "prodigiously good," and the next two numbers of the magazine contained *The Chest of Cigars* and *Bob Robinson's First Love*, both by "Lancelot Wagstaff."

The main importance of these contributions was that they led to one of his warmest friendships. The August number contained a satire on business ethics, entitled *Jacob Omnium, the Merchant Prince*, which attracted so much notice that it was followed the next month by another sketch by the same author. Greatly interested in them, Thackeray told the publisher of the magazine that he was eager to meet the man who wrote them, and in reply he was informed that the anonymous writer had just expressed an equally keen desire to meet "Lancelot Wagstaff." When the introduction took place, Thackeray found himself gazing up at a handsome gentleman who towered over him to the height of six feet eight. Matthew James Higgins was an Anglo-Irishman of wealth, an amateur of literature and horseflesh, and a tireless supporter of humanitarian causes. Universally popular for his willingness to go to trouble in settling the problems and disputes of his friends, he was just the sort of comrade Thackeray needed.

In spite of the resolution, taken several years previously, to have no more dealings with Cruikshank, Thackeray was now persuaded to change his mind by his *Punch* colleague, Gilbert à Beckett, who was editing *George Cruikshank's Table Book* in monthly parts. From June to the end of the year it serialized *A Legend of the Rhine*, Thackeray's satirical version of a romantic story by Dumas, *Othon L'Archer*. The June number of *Fraser's* contained his usual "Titmarsh" review of the art exhibitions. FitzGerald, in a letter to Frederick Tennyson, gives a lively account of the sequel. "I met [Frank] Stone in the street the other day; he took me by the button, and told me in perfect sincerity, and with increasing warmth, how, though he loved old Thackeray, yet these yearly out-speakings of his sorely tried him; not on account of himself (Stone), but on account of some of his friends— Charles Landseer, Maclise, &c. Stone worked himself up to such a pitch under the pressure of forced calmness, that he at last said Thackeray would get himself horsewhipped one day by one of these infuriated Apelleses. At this I, who had partly agreed with Stone that ridicule, though true, needs not always be spoken, began to laugh, and told him two could play at that game. . . In the meanwhile old Thackeray laughs at all this and goes on in his own way, writing hard for half-a-dozen reviews and newspapers all the morning; dining, drinking, and talking of a night; managing to preserve a fresh colour and perpetual flow of spirits under a wear and tear of thinking and feeding, that would have knocked up any other man I know two years ago at least."

In August Thackeray gave new zest to his multifarious items in *Punch* by resuscitating the character who had first brought him fame—the irrepressible Jeames Yellowplush. England being at the moment in the grip of the railway speculation mania, Thackeray was able to satirize the money-madness of the public, and also the mercenary basis of so-called "class distinctions," by depicting the footman enriched through a lucky investment. Transformed into "C. Jeames de la Pluche, Esq.," courted by young ladies of title and offered a seat in Parliament, he paraded his illiterate vanity more complacently than ever.

As FitzGerald has reported, Thackeray's social engagements were now as strenuous as his professional ones. He was present at some of the gatherings when Dickens and Forster were conscripting almost the whole staff of *Punch* for a production of *Every Man in His Humour*—the first of Dickens's famous series of amateur theatricals. In a letter to Milnes, divulging the plans for the play, Mrs Procter added that "Mr Thackeray has offered to sing between the Acts, but they decline his services."

Mrs Procter's drawing-room was still one of his most frequent haunts. On the strength of having sustained him during his months of deepest depression, she was inclined to adopt a proprietary air toward him. Between his friends the Procters and his friends the Brookfields an intimacy had sprung up, but it was qualified by a tinge of jealousy on the part of the older woman, who could not help noticing how enthusiastically Thackeray regarded the beautiful and witty Jane.

Mrs Brookfield derived mischievous amusement from the situation. While she was spending the summer with her relations in Somerset her correspondence with her husband was full of Thackeray. She pretended to be jealous of the friendship between the two men and of their affection for Mrs Procter. A phrase in one of Brookfield's letters aroused mock annoyance: "Soh! You discussed 'matrimonial irritations' and 'domestic matters' with *yourr frriend* Thackeray!" Her husband hastily replied that the discussion had been concerned only with the family life of Douglas Jerrold. And when she remarked, "I hope you may enjoy the Procteress repast today (meant to be said in a highly satirical tone)," he gave her to understand that he and Thackeray had left early (when their host fell asleep on the sofa) and adjourned to Thackeray's rooms "where we had a weed." Tactfully he commented that "the Proctrix has not one smallest sparklet of humour. Witty, well informed—or what you like. . . but not one jot of humour. It is a sad deficiency."

Another night Thackeray dropped in at half past ten just when Brookfield's father (who was visiting him) was going off to bed. "So we kept him up $\frac{1}{4}$ hour and then dismissed him and betook ourselves to serious debauch. We smoked and 'conversed' till $1\frac{1}{2}$. We flattered you a little. He said, 'Funny little fact that—Mrs Procter being so jealous of Mrs Brookfield.' 'Oh, nonsense, it's one of the little facts you invent for the fun of it.' 'Oh, but as it's quite evident,' etc."

Every evening, if Brookfield was out to dinner, he arrived at Thackeray's rooms about eleven for two or three hours of smoking; or, if Thackeray was the diner-out, he came to Brookfield's. On his way home after one such session, Thackeray sprained his ankle. "It would make a capital advertisement for my Spirit Merchant," Brookfield said. " 'Alarming accident to the Fat Contributor. Yesterday evening, etc., late or rather early hours, etc., from the cheerful convivialities of a Revd Gent. not 100 miles from Golden Square.' "

His wife having alluded sarcastically to Father Prout, Brookfield defended him as "a very nice fellow. . . a clever scholar and pleasant companion and not indecorous." In her reply she remarked slyly, "You seem very hand in glove with Thackeray; don't become a second Father Prout." That very evening Brookfield was dining with his friend, who had been given a brace of grouse. "We ate our birds, and a plum dumpling, then set in for serious smoking, and Father Prout joined at our Schiedam, but as we retired at 12, Thackeray truly remarked, 'Well, you have neither of you been very brilliant tonight.' . . . Thackeray observed on Saturday night that you had the sweetest voice he ever heard." An ideal marriage and an ideal friendship, in which the husband described to the wife every convivial session, and proudly retailed to her the praises lavished upon her by the friend.

Struggling to complete his travel book before getting too deep in other undertakings, Thackeray in July rented a room in an Inn at Chelsea, at the end of Cheyne Row, not far from the Carlyles. They had their first intimation of his arrival when the pot-boy brought over a note asking for the loan of a Bible. He had run into serious difficulties with his section about Jerusalem, realizing that the religious complications would make his task as hard as the political complications had done for *The Irish Sketch Book*. He admitted to his mother that he was in a dilemma, "not wishing to offend the public by a needless exhibition of heterodoxy, nor daring to be a hypocrite." As he studied the Old Testament, however, the danger of heterodoxy became almost unavoidable; he got into such a rage "when reading all that murder and crime which the name of the Almighty is blasphemously made to sanction, that I don't dare to trust myself to write, and put off my work from day to day."

When he had poured out his opinions in two or three letters to his mother, she replied with such agonized protests that he canceled the whole chapter he had laboriously written. During the next month dinner parties and other social engagements prevented his resuming work, and in September he fled to Brighton to nurse his ankle and try to write undisturbed.

A few days later the devoted Brookfield came down to visit him. Arriving at ten in the morning, he found that Thackeray had not breakfasted, but was sitting at his window, drawing on wood. Later they went for a stroll and Thackeray made some sketches of the groups upon the beach. In the afternoon Brookfield wandered on the sands alone, "while Mr T. has been earning a little dinner for us by his fluent pen."

The fluent pen was racing along with its usual versatility. His latest piece of work had been the long-discussed article for *The Edinburgh Review*. As topics, Napier had proposed the memoirs of Lady Hester Stanhope or the novels of Eugène Sue, but Thackeray stood out for a suggestion of his own. He offered several arguments against writing about Sue's books—they had been too widely discussed in the minor periodicals, they were too numerous to be dealt with in a short article, and his recent ones, although cleverly evading "improprieties of expression," were among the "most immoral books in the world." But Thackeray's American acquaintance, N. P. Willis, had just brought out a book of stories, *Dashes at Life with a Free Pencil*, and might be made the subject of "a pleasant short paper."

On receiving Napier's acquiescence, Thackeray went at the task gleefully. Willis's inflated style, his absurd ideas about English aristocratic life, and the conceit that made him obviously delineate himself in the hero of every story, showed all the faults of Bulwer's society novels and none of their virtues. On receiving the manuscript, Napier realized that his premonitions of danger in encouraging an unknown *Punch* satirist had been justified. Thackeray's independence of spirit in selecting his subject had been bad enough, but the levity of the essay was intolerable. Without consulting Thackeray, he went through the review and firmly cut out all its brightest jests.

Even so, the result was unsatisfactory. When it appeared in the October number, a complaint promptly arrived from *The Edinburgh's* original editor, the redoubtable Lord Jeffrey, who still felt responsible for the standards of the magazine. "Mr Nathaniel (or Jonathan) Willis might have been as well let alone," he wrote ominously to Napier, "and his reviewer is not much better than himself." Napier made haste to assure Jeffrey that he entirely concurred in the verdict, and when he sent Thackeray his cheque he mentioned the opinion of certain friends that "Willis was too leniently used." Thackeray, however, was in no mood to accept a rebuke. His reply, couched in polite terms and expressing the confident hope that he could supply further contributions for the same liberal payment, was chiefly devoted to a burlesque lamentation for his "lovely jokes and promising *facetiae*" which had been ruthlessly murdered. The letter had an elusive tinge of sarcasm that must have disturbed Napier's complacency. After this exchange of courtesies, neither editor nor contributor felt inclined to further dealings.

As the year 1845 drew to a close, Thackeray could consider a dubious balance of success and disappointment. In his profession, the growing popularity of his *Punch* articles and the increased sums paid him by editors were offset by Colburn's duplicity with regard to a more pretentious work and by Napier's disapproval of his contribution to an influential review. It was two and a half years since he had published a book. Actually, his progress in the literary market was hard to estimate; he told his mother that he considered his reputation to be "of the best sort after the big guns. The admirers of Mr Titmarsh are a small clique, but a good and increasing one."

In private life he was gaining a few affectionate and admiring friendships, but there was a darker side to the picture. His habits of dining at clubs and taverns, where he ate and drank too much, and of prowling to a friend's house late at night for cigars and conversation to delay the return to his solitary chambers, reflected the loneliness and restlessness of his exile from his family. As late as the end of July he was entertaining the dream that as soon as the book should be finished he would try to find a pair of cottages in Hampstead or Hammersmith, so that his parents could occupy one and he and his wife and children the other, each feeling independent. But by October his wife's incoherent letters convinced him that she was no better, and he arranged to have her brought over to England to be looked after by a Mrs Bakewell. "I sate two hours with Thackeray," Brookfield reported on October 30. "He brought back his poor little wife yesterday—she is at Camberwell and he seems well pleased with the people."

In a letter to his little daughter at the end of December, Thackeray told with forced cheerfulness about his Christmas dinner with Mamma: "she was very well and happy, only she grew very grave when she talked about you; and there were tears in her eyes the meaning of which I knew quite well." Whatever he might be doing, he could never for very long forget that pretty and still youthful woman, with her vaguely troubled gaze and her pathetic, helpless sweetness.

CHAPTER 9

Can Authors be Gentlemen?

THROUGH SUCH friends as Kinglake and Milnes, Thackeray was moving into a new social orbit. Among Kinglake's closest intimates were Sir Alexander Duff-Gordon and his brilliant young wife, a cousin of Thackeray's old friend Henry Reeve. Also in the group was the beautiful, wilful Caroline Norton. It was nearly ten years since Mrs Norton's public crucifixion when her husband had sued the Prime Minister, Lord Melbourne, on the charge of seducing her. Although the defendant had been exonerated, Mrs Norton's position in society had remained equivocal, and her gay wit and unaffected manners always kept gossip alive. During the summer of 1845, when Kinglake was eager to make the Brookfields acquainted with her, the wary clergyman made inquiries, with results which he later summarized: "She does not care a bodle for what Mrs Grundy says, and like a goodish many of her charming sect I dare say she likes men better than women; but merely their talk. . . Society receives her—and does not *most certainly* receive those who are believed to be incorrect. . . And tho' I should not approve of her as an intimate friend there is nothing against a mere slight acquaintance even for the most prudent."

Mrs Norton was still the intimate friend of Lord Melbourne, and having become interested in Thackeray, she persuaded the old statesman to invite him to dinner. The other guests were the Duff-Gordons, Albany Fonblanque, and Anthony Panizzi of the British Museum Library. Panizzi was deputized by Mrs Norton to apologize to his friend Thackeray for the informality of the invitation, since the host had never met him, although, she added, she could not convince Melbourne that he was not already acquainted with Thackeray, whom he remembered vaguely as a clergyman. The dinner party was in November, and only two or three weeks later the Melbourne-Norton intimacy became for the second time a public scandal, when the lady was accused of betraying Cabinet secrets to *The Times*.

In Brighton, too, Thackeray was making new and agreeable friends. It was something of a literary settlement at the time, thanks chiefly to two veteran writers to whom Thackeray became warmly attached—Horace Smith, surviving co-author of the *Rejected Addresses*, and James Morier, whose *Hajji Baba* had accompanied Thackeray on his eastern tour. The two kindly old gentlemen provided an archaic glimpse of the dignity of letters that was soothing to Thackeray after the strivings and meannesses of his London colleagues.

Thackeray's avowed purpose in paying his visits to Brighton was to escape from the numerous dinner parties in London and to concentrate upon his work; but soon the invitations to dinner were as frequent in Brighton and as hard to resist. He had to summon up all his will-power and force himself to the hated desk. When William Archer Shee called on Horace Smith one afternoon, he found Thackeray chatting with Smith and his three bright daughters. After a while Thackeray broke off the gay conversation and rose with a sigh. "Now I must go and be funny," he announced in a disgusted tone. "You little know what dreary work it is to be obliged to be funny under all circumstances."

In January, 1846, a full year after Thackeray's return from his eastern tour, Chapman & Hall published *Notes of a Journey from Cornhill to Grand Cairo. . . Performed in the Steamers of the Peninsular and Oriental Company*, by Mr M. A. Titmarsh. In spite of some inequalities, it was an improvement upon his previous works—intimate in style, vivid in description, moving with sureness from humorous narrative of his experiences to bursts of feeling on religious and humanitarian topics. His attitude throughout was based upon common sense; he avoided sentimental raptures over the picturesque and the antique, and his occasional moments of being impressed by sublimity were hastily doused with the wet blanket of practicality or the cold water of comic details.

The book was kindly reviewed. An article in *Fraser's*, probably written by the devoted Father Prout, not only eulogized the book but surveyed Thackeray's whole literary career. Nevertheless, there were two or three less gratifying comments, and in this connection a slight mystery exists. According to Gavan Duffy, Carlyle's sense of the sanctity of authorship was outraged by Thackeray's acceptance of the free passage and his frank advertising of the company in exchange. Carlyle "compared the transaction to the practice of a blind fiddler going to and fro on a penny ferryboat in Scotland, and playing tunes to the passengers for half-pence." When Charles Buller transmitted the rebuke, Thackerary expressed his indignation, and Carlyle felt that "it was necessary to inform him frankly that it was undoubtedly his opinion that out of respect for himself and his profession, a man like him ought not to have gone fiddling for half-pence or otherwise in any steamboat under the sky."

The remarkable fact is that the identical analogy was applied to Thackeray's trip in a review in *Tait's Magazine*, an Edinburgh periodical. As there is no evidence that Carlyle contributed to *Tait's*, it must be assumed either that Carlyle was quoting the review when he made the comment, or else that the reviewer had heard Carlyle's remark and adopted it. In any case, Thackeray was goaded to publish a sarcastic retort in *Punch*; and as he knew what Carlyle had said, and Carlyle knew he knew it, some of the remarks must have been intended and accepted with a personal application. "It is that comparison of the blind fiddler who '*sends round his hat*' that ought to be devoted to the indignation of the press of these kingdoms. . . A gentleman who takes a vacant seat in a friend's carriage is not supposed to receive a degrading obligation, or called upon to pay for his ride by extra joking, facetiousness, &c.; nor surely is the person who so gives you the use of his carriage required to present you also with a guinea, or to pay your tavern bill. The critic, in fact, has shown uncommon keenness in observing the manners of his national violinists; but must know more of them than of the customs of English gentlemen. . . I think he must be a professional man of letters. It is only literary men, nowadays, who commit this suicidal sort of impertinence; who sneak through the world ashamed of their calling, and show their independence by befouling the trade by which they live."

Something of the same annoyance was aroused by the review in the *New Monthly*, which rather sneered at Titmarsh as the typical Cockney, impudent, self-satisfied, and worldly. Even though he had poked fun at himself in somewhat these terms in the book, he was insulted at being taken seriously, and his suspicion of Ainsworth was reawakened. On February 16, when he was setting off to Brighton "for two or three days' meditation," he wrote to tell his mother that a thousand copies of the book had been sold—more than the total sale of *The Irish Sketch Book*. "Haven't I gorged you with flummery from the newspapers?" he exulted. "They are all mighty polite, except one fellow, a friend of mine, who calls me a heartless and self-sufficient Cockney."

It happened that Ainsworth, who patronized Brighton as much as Thackeray did, was there when he arrived, and once again an understanding was reached. There was a touch of annoyance in Ainsworth's tone when he reported the episode to their venerable friend Horace Smith: "Titmarsh was out of humour because he was reviewed and attacked, as he thinks, in the last *New Monthly*. The paper on the contrary was very friendly. He threatened retorts, and I told him if he did he should have rejoinders. . . He went home with me to the Albion and kept me up till one o'clock, drinking brandy and soda, and abusing Byron in a ludicrously absurd and Cockney fashion." In spite of their friendship, the two men were in temperament poles apart, Ainsworth being as incurably romantic as Thackeray was satiric. In matters of taste they could seldom agree.

To make his peace with Ainsworth by public penitence, Thackeray announced in a Postscript to the second edition of his book:

Another [critic]—but this was a private friend, and I can conceive the pain it cost his amiable heart—was obliged to give judgment against the coarseness, heartlessness, flippancy, and personality of the present performance. It becomes writers to bear praise and blame alike meekly; and I think the truth is that most of us get more of the former, and less of the latter, than we merit.

About the same time, he made a move toward placating a more deeply injured adversary. When the literary friends of Laman Blanchard had rallied to the aid of his children, the most active had been Sir Edward Bulwer-Lytton. Among the schemes for raising money, Bulwer edited a collection of Blanchard's essays, and prefaced it with a memoir. This was published in February, and Thackeray wrote a review of it in *Fraser's*. Bulwer had alluded somewhat apologetically to Blanchard's poverty and had deplored the fact that he had wasted his talents in journalism and humorous sketches instead of writing a serious masterpiece. In these remarks Thackeray discerned a supercilious attitude toward professional authorship that could apply to his own work and status as closely as to Blanchard's.

With his insistent common sense, he compared the "trade of literature" with that of the shoeblack: "In some way or other, for daily bread and hire, almost all men are labouring daily. Without necessity they would not work at all, or very little, probably. In some instances you reap Reputation along with Profit from your labour, but Bread, in the main, is the incentive. Do not let us try to blink this fact, or imagine that the men of the press are working for their honour and glory, or go onward impelled by an irresistible afflatus of genius. If only men of genius were to write, Lord help us! how many books would there be?. . . To do your work honestly, to amuse and instruct your reader of today, to die when your time comes, and go hence with as clean a breast as may be; may these be all ours, by God's will. . . After all, what is this Reputation, the cant of our trade, the goal that every scribbling penny-a-liner demurely pretends that he is hunting after? Why should we get it? Why can't we do without it? We only fancy we want it. . . [Blanchard] had a duty, much more imperative upon him than the preparation of questionable great works,—to get his family their dinner."

In writing this defence of literary commercialism, Thackeray was once more assailing Bulwer's highfalutin airs. But as he had been really touched by Bulwer's consideration for Blanchard's family, he went out of his way to mention repeatedly and cordially "the kind and distinguished gentleman. . . his admirable and delicate generosity."

This discussion, and the bitter attack on the reviewer in *Tait's Magazine*, and even the spat with Ainsworth, all reveal Thackeray's concern with the problem of his own social standing. He could no longer depend on his assortment of pen-names to disguise the fact that he was an overworked hack writer. Must he therefore accept a position of inferiority? The question was linked with the oldest topic of his satire—the contrast between the patrician and the vulgarian. In his undergraduate days, the word "Snob" had been little known outside the walls of Cambridge, where it marked the ineffable distinction between the gownsman and all lesser mortals; but Thackeray's contributions to the short-lived periodical of that name showed that he was already turning his attention to a wider field and aiming his shafts at those crass and newly-prosperous bourgeois who were invading the upper world without a conception of the true feelings of a gentleman. As there was no accepted term to describe this phenomenon—Matthew Arnold not having yet proposed the adoption of "Philistine"—the short and expressive word "Snob" was beginning to gain currency.

In several stories, Thackeray exposed the social ambitions and grotesque lack of refinement on the "shabby-genteel" level. But the matter had become more than an object of impersonal observation and amusement; his own difficult position, as a hack writer who sought to remain also a private gentleman, made him painfully sensitive to the social issues involved. He saw ambitious men like Bulwer and Disraeli using literature as a means to publicity, and posing as contemptuous of the plodding professionals. Again, he saw amateur authors of small talent but noble title commanding large prices, at the expense of the publishers' hard-working drudges, simply because the public was more impressed by rank than by merit. In his own circle, he was sometimes the object of spiteful sarcasm from fellow-writers who imagined that his manner toward them was supercilious and who felt envious when they heard of his dining with people of fashion while his earnings were no better than their own.

To define the issue once for all, he planned a series of papers for *Punch* under the title *The Snobs of England*, "by one of them." The first appeared on February 28, 1846, and they continued every week for exactly a year. Only one previous series, *Mrs Caudle's Curtain Lectures*, by Douglas Jerrold, had attracted anything like the same attention, but Thackeray's essays appealed to a more cultivated class, and the circulation of *Punch* rose steadily, not only in numbers but in caste. Until then, the paper had been regarded as vulgar. In fact, most of the clever and original writing for a good many years past had emanated from the plebeians, and the people of greater refinement had shuddered in distaste. Now they had a spokesman of their own kind, and they rallied to his support.

Thackeray was no sycophant. His own background was that of a "gentleman" though definitely not of an "aristocrat." His ancestry, springing from yeoman stock and flowering in clergymen, university dons, military and naval officers, country squires, was in the tradition that produced "parliamentarians" rather than "cavaliers" two centuries before, Whigs rather than Tories later. His own political views were radical in regard to the royal family and the hereditary nobles. In the same week as his first "Snob" paper, he was writing in his Laman Blanchard article about the "real great revolution of England which is actually going on." Like Arnold a few years afterwards, he saw as many defects in the "Barbarians" of the top drawer as in the "Philistines" of the middle one. Like Arnold, he was attempting less a defense of caste barriers than a plea for genuine culture and enlightenment. But he was a satirist, and a satirist applies himself to bombarding the existing evils rather than glorifying ideal reforms.

His "Snob Papers" therefore brought him his first real renown, but also a measure of unpopularity. As he had done several times previously, he started a series with a striking central idea which could be carried on from week to week and month to month without the strain of fresh invention. By sheer pressure of momentum, he had to extend his genus "snob" into all ranks, all professions, even all countries, ranging downward from the "Snob Royal" (one of his assaults on George IV).

Several of the specimens were identified as portraits of London personalities. Stephen Price, an American theatrical manager who had led a quarrelsome faction in the Garrick Club, was depicted with all his phrases and mannerisms as "Captain Shindy;" and Wyndham Smith (a schoolmate at Charterhouse and a son of the great Sydney) was unmistakably caricatured in one of the illustrations of the paper on "Sporting Snobs." Rumor had it that Thackeray obtained permission from the secretaries of several clubs to inspect their complaint books as a source of examples.

His damnable iteration was effective in establishing the word "snob" in the English vocabulary for ever, but it also established him in the public mind as a man with a single obsession. By the time the series was complete, his lash had flicked some sensitive spot in almost every reader, and he had acquired a reputation for indiscriminate censure which he never lived down. His ironical attribution of the authorship to "one of them" could all too readily be applied seriously to him by anyone who was angered by his satire. The disapproval even invaded the inner councils of the *Punch* staff. In his essay on "Clerical Snobs," with memories of his Uncle Frank, his Cousin Elias, his friends Allen and Brookfield, Thackeray launched into praise of the Church-of-England clergy and sneered at their detractors. Douglas Jerrold, who persistently satirized the church, took this as a personal affront. Thackeray held his ground, however, and Jerrold's assaults on the bishops were discontinued.

Such arguments having revealed to Thackeray the extent of his power to give offence, he acquired an almost apologetic attitude toward the "Snob Papers." He omitted several of them when they were collected, and in his last sentence he disavowed any intention of causing pain: "if Fun is good, Truth is still better, and Love best of all." In later years he said that of all his works he liked this one the least.

When he began the series he was already hatching plans for a novel. The opening chapters had been shown to Colburn but had been rejected. The next glimpse of its development dates from Thackeray's visit to Brighton early in 1846. Among his acquaintances there was William Perry, whose father had been the wealthy and influential owner of *The Morning Chronicle;* and on a visit to Perry was his sister Kate. Frail looking, with a shy habit of holding her head on one side while she gazed admiringly up at him, she was one of those gay, witty, sympathetic women to whom Thackeray was always strongly drawn. "Mr Thackeray and I went through no gradations of growth in our friendship," she afterwards said; "it was more like Jack's bean-stalk in a pantomime, which rushed up sky-high without culture." In a letter to her sister, Mrs Fred Elliot, she reported: "The first time he dined with us I was fearfully alarmed at him. The next day we walked in Chichester Park, when he told me all about his little girls, and of his great friendship with the Brookfields."

In the same letter, she remarked that "he is now writing a novel, but cannot hit upon a name for it. I may be wrong, but it seems to me the cleverest thing I ever read." He promptly fell into a habit of coming up every evening from the Old Ship Inn, where he was staying, to read her what he had written during the day. Far from confident in the undertaking, he would say to her, "I wonder whether this will take—the publishers accept it, and the world read it." To encourage him she quoted her enthusiastic comment in her letter to her sister, and he was much cheered up, exclaiming with a laugh, "Ah! Mademoiselle, it is *not* small beer; but I do not know whether it will be palatable to the London folks." Then one evening he arrived in high glee. He had been ransacking his brain for a title for the novel, and in the middle of the night a voice seemed to whisper in his ear, "Vanity Fair." He jumped out of bed and ran three times around his room, chanting "Vanity Fair, Vanity Fair, Vanity Fair."

Shortly after this, *Mrs Perkins's Ball* was ready for publication, with a definite plan attached to it. For three years past Dickens had made a great annual success with a "Christmas Book," and Thackeray decided to attempt a raid upon the same market. *Mrs Perkins's Ball* was about the right length, and was a cheerful bit of comedy; suitably illustrated, it ought to answer very well.

As the pictures were to be a special feature, he turned his drawings over to an engraver recommended by Vizetelly. The young man felt it his duty to make improvements where Thackeray had disregarded proportion and anatomy, and thereby, in Thackeray's opinion, destroyed "a certain *je ne sais quoi*" that had been in the original sketches. "Somehow," he declared to Vizetelly, "I prefer my own Nuremberg dolls to Mr Thwaites's superfine wax models."

The business entailed anxious visits to Vizetelly's office. One day he had a brown-paper parcel under his arm, and pulled out a couple of sketches illustrating scenes in *Vanity Fair*. "Tied up with them," Vizetelly records, "was the manuscript of the earlier portions of the work, of which he had several times spoken to me. . . His present intention, he told me, was to see Bradbury and Evans, and offer the work to them. . . In little more than half an hour Mr Thackeray again made his appearance, and with a beaming face gleefully informed me that he had settled the business. 'B. & E.,' said he, 'accepted so readily, that I am deuced sorry I didn't ask them another tenner. I am certain they would have given it.' He then explained to me that he had named fifty guineas per part, including the two sheets of letterpress, a couple of etchings, and the initials at the commencement of the chapters. He reckoned the text, I remember, at no more than five-and-twenty shillings a page, the two etchings at six guineas each, while, as for the few initials at the beginning of the chapters he threw these in." In March he was confidently expecting that it would begin to appear on the first of May.

As Bradbury & Evans were the publishers of *Punch*, it was natural for Thackeray to submit his story to them, and for them to accept it on the strength of the opening chapters and drawings, since they well knew how much he was adding to the popularity of their paper. The plan of publishing it in monthly parts was the practice at that time, established by the triumph of *Pickwick* and exploited by Lever, Ainsworth, and most of the other popular novelists. The mere fact of bringing out a story in this form marked Thackeray's promotion to their category.

The effectiveness of *Punch* in influencing the public, and therefore the potential value of Thackeray in the same respect, had become recognized by propagandists. His indefatigable friend Henry Cole was just then deep in the agitation to establish a standard gauge for all English railways. He took Thackeray down to Gloucester and showed him the intolerable confusion at a junction where all the passengers and luggage had to change trains from wide to narrow gauge. Thackeray docilely wrote two *Punch* papers on the matter, in his guise of "Yellowplush."

From the beginning of the year, his rehabilitation in society continued. Acquaintances who had avoided him—or whom he had avoided—during the years of solitude and poverty now became cordial. Macready, who delighted in giving dinners and receptions for celebrities, asked him often to his house. Early in the year he dined there with Dickens, Forster, and his old friend the Rev James White, whose play, *The King of the Commons*, was read aloud, to decide whether Macready should produce it. Thackeray loyally praised it, and his enthusiasm helped to bring about its acceptance, though the advice of Dickens and others was adverse. In May, Thackeray was at one of Macready's big dinners, the guests including Panizzi, Abraham Hayward (who had reported on him to Napier the year before), Mrs Jameson (feminist and art historian), and the Rev William Harness, a minor author chiefly noted for having been at school with Byron. Another member of the Macready circle who decided to cultivate Thackeray was Frederick Pollock, an ambitious young lawyer and son of the Chief Baron of the Exchequer. He had first dined with Mr and Mrs Thackeray in the old Coram Street days, and he now entertained Thackeray repeatedly, along with such former Apostles as Tennyson, Spedding, and Frederick Denison Maurice, and other people of distinction.

In accepting such hospitalities, Thackeray felt the obligation of returning them, and his club and tavern dinners would scarcely appeal to these conventional personages. With this in mind, and encouraged by the prospect of his novel, he finally carried out his long-cherished plan of setting up a home of his own, in which his children could join him. As early as February he wrote to his mother that he was "house-hunting like a maniac," and had just come across "a perfect country domain" at two hundred pounds a year, only three miles from London, with a seven-acre farm stocked with poultry. Months went by, however, and nothing was done about the proposal. His mother strongly objected to it. She had grown devoted to the little girls and hated the thought of losing them. She was afraid, too, that their moral development would be neglected or positively injured by the unorthodox views of their father and the very mixed friendships that he enjoyed. Financial risks provoked further doubt. Thackeray had recently lost five hundred pounds in railway speculation, and was making no headway in repaying his earlier borrowings from the Carmichaels and others. On the contrary, Brookfield, though also a loser in the railway collapse, was insisting on lending him a hundred pounds.

In June Thackeray decided to force the issue by taking a house and inviting the whole family to come and live with him. He found a suitable house at No. 13, Young Street, Kensington Square, roomy, old-fashioned, and bow-windowed, and sent a tempting account of it to his mother. There would be two capital bed-rooms and a little sitting-room for herself and her husband, a handsome bed-room for her mother, Mrs Butler, two airy comfortable rooms for the children, ample space for servants, and—last and least—two little rooms "quite large enough for me." He seductively mentioned the garden, the "little courtyard," the "little greenhouse; and Kensington Gardens at the gate, and omnibuses every 2 minutes. What can mortal want more? If I ask my friends I can ask them to my own quarters. We may all be independent and together. At all events I ask it as a favour that the experiment should be tried, and am sure that we shall all be the happier and better for it." After describing his anticipations of companionship with the children, he added his indomitable refrain: "Their Mother is so well and calm that when they are of an age sufficient she will be quite able to come back to us."

To such pathetic appeals his mother could not remain obdurate. But a new conflict of duties presented itself; Major Carmichael-Smyth refused to become the pensioner of his step-son. In Paris he felt independent, with a little circle of friends of his own type and a little *ménage* that he could maintain with the remnant of his fortune. He was afraid that if he set foot in England he might be sued for a few remaining debts of *The Constitutional*; and he had developed a literary hobby that gave him the illusion of achievement—just now he was writing a history of the royal family of Lahore. To come back to London and occupy rooms in the house of his successful step-son would be to flaunt his failure before the eyes of the world. Only one solution remained. Mrs Carmichael-Smyth must give up the children to their father and find what solace she could in her loyalty to her husband. But the parting was too agonizing to face at once; she needed time to nerve herself for it.

At the beginning of July Thackeray moved into the house—a dispiriting task as he opened the trunks "full of the lumbering useless old books and woeful relics of old days." A fortnight later a first dinner-party was given, and to provide a somewhat pathetic illusion that it was a family gathering, Thackeray invited his

YOUNG STREET, KENSINGTON
FROM A DRAWING BY EYRE CROWE

step-cousin, Sir James Carmichael, and his brother-in-law, Arthur Shawe. The other guests were Kinglake, John Leech, and the Rev. William Harness, who had been at Macready's dinner two months before. Brookfield, having been detained by church duties, arrived after dinner and noted in his diary that "the evening was pleasant but lacked fire." A quarter of a century later another version of the event came out in the biography of Harness by a clerical confrère. With the lapse of time a strange metamorphosis had occurred in his memory of Thackeray's modest bachelor house-warming:

Harness thought [Thackeray's] Bohemianism and the general tone of his writings exercised an injurious influence on the rising generation. His first personal experience of the novelist was certainly not calculated to remove this impression. Thackeray invited him to dinner, and Mr. Harness accepted with delight, promising himself a rich intellectual feast . . . He found learning and talent most ably represented. The party at dinner was large, and while the ladies remained the conversation wandered softly among flowers and wine and airy compliments. At length . . . the gay *cortège* of youth and beauty made its way to the upper world . . . Now was the time for sharp repartee and for the settling of accounts between rival wits . . . He settled himself in his chair, prepared to take his part if necessary, and kept his eyes and ears open, so as not to lose a single word or gesture. "Do you smoke?" inquired the host. "Smoke?" Mr. Harness had never been guilty of such an offense against social morality. In his day, tars and bargemen were the only smokers . . . He would as soon have thought of going to carouse at a public-house as of smoking in the dining-room after dinner. "Smoke, sir? I do not." But his firm refusal had no effect whatever on the epicurean company by which he was surrounded. Cigars and tobacco were placed upon the table; punch and negus followed; and the observations which were made during the rest of the sitting consisted only of such instructive remarks as "Pass the box," and "Fill up!"

The scene was richly comic; but as filtered through twenty years of an old man's anecdotage and recorded after his death by a garrulous friend, the little six-man stag party was transformed out of all recognition.

Thackeray acquired an agreeable friend just then in the person of Robert Browning, whom he met at one of Mrs Procter's gatherings and soon again at John Kenyon's. The two got along pleasantly, and Browning even beguiled an awkward pause during one of his clandestine visits to Elizabeth Barrett by retailing one of the comical anecdotes he had just heard from his new friend Thackeray. A few days later Thackeray had Kenyon and Browning to dinner at the Garrick Club, Brookfield and Procter being the other guests. "A very pleasant evening," says Brookfield, "with several 'Sallies' which compelled three pilling-looking gents who were dining at an adjoining table to listen."

Browning was much concerned at the moment over a young poet, Coventry Patmore, who had first won his praise with a book of verse two years before. His father, Peter Patmore, a minor author in the clique of Lamb and Hazlitt, was chiefly known for having been involved in a fatal duel between a critic and an editor. Having brought up his son as a "future genius," Patmore had just lost his money in a railway speculation and had fled to France, leaving the youth helpless. At Barry Cornwall's one day Browning asked Thackeray to let him introduce the young poet. Remembering the tradition that Peter Patmore had dictated the shot that killed John Scott twenty-five years before, Thackeray violently refused, declaring, "I won't touch the hand of a son of that murderer!"

Browning and Mrs Procter then told how Coventry was working sixteen hours a day at hack-writing to earn twenty-five shillings a week. Struck by the similarity to his own misfortunes, Thackeray was at once contrite. He sent an essay of Patmore's to Nickisson, of *Fraser's*, describing the author of it as "a most deserving and clever young fellow who will be a genius some day; and his paper is so odd, humorous and amusing that I hope you will secure it, and its author as a future contributor. . . If you will use this for next month, I promise you an article (D. V.)."

The significance of this last bribe was that Thackeray had finally found himself independent enough to give up some journalistic work. In April, in spite of all Nickisson's pleas, he had stopped writing for *Fraser's*; and throughout the year he kept vowing that he would soon quit *The Morning Chronicle*. By the end of September, plans for *Vanity Fair* were so well matured that Jerrold was able to tell the news in a letter to Dickens, who was in Switzerland: "Thackeray is big with twenty parts, and, unless he is wrong in his time, expects the first instalment at Christmas."

In September Mrs Carmichael-Smyth brought the children over to their new home. The little girls were led round-eyed through the unused drawing-room, the study with its smell of tobacco—which they decided was the smell of London,—and finally their own nursery and schoolroom, gay with pictures that their father had chosen with loving care. The next morning he came into the nursery and pounced on them while they were being dressed.

Annie was nine and Minny was six. Their grandmother was beginning to find the elder a little difficult to manage—she was clever, argumentative, and thoughtless—whereas Minny was gentle and loving. After seeing them safely ensconced, Mrs Carmichael-Smyth went back to Paris, and Thackeray wrote her an unwontedly solemn letter of consolation: "It is best that they should be away from you—at least that they should be away either from you or me. There can't be two first principles in a house. We should secretly be jealous of one another. . . Now God Almighty grant I may be a father to my children. Continual thoughts of them chase I don't know how many wickednesses out of my mind; their society makes many of my old amusements seem trivial and shameful. . . Remember the children are in their natural place, with their nearest friend, working their natural influence, getting and giving the good, let us hope, which the Divine Benevolence appointed to result from the union between parents and children. May I hold fast by it I pray to God our Father."

Although he did not see a great deal of the children, their presence changed the whole tone of his life. He always started the day with them, and had them in to his study to talk for a while after breakfast; and on evenings when he dined at home alone they would come in and sit on the floor while he smoked his after-dinner cigar, after which they put a chair under his legs and left him to a nap. On Sundays and holidays there were walks in Kensington Gardens or longer outings. Although he was full of whimseys and nicknames for them, he talked to them as if they were grown women. With a serious sense of responsibility he told them about God and the Bible, and took them to church.

To fulfil his promise to Nickisson, he found time to write *A Grumble about the Christmas Books*, his last formal contribution to *Fraser's*, and a consistent conclusion to the series of criticisms on annuals and popular fiction that had begun nine years before. His discussion of Dickens's *Battle of Life* and other books of the same type was significant in view of the fact that his own first Christmas book came out just at the time.

Mrs Perkins's Ball did not exude the sentiment of the season so richly as the Dickens books did. It had no plot to speak of, but its amusing series of character studies was lavishly illustrated by the author, and the public found it a pleasant change from more sentimental tales. It was the greatest success he had yet had, he told his mother, "very nearly as great as Dickens,—that is, Perkins 500 Dickens 25000 only that difference!" The reviews were kind. An unauthorized French translation came out in *L'Illustration*, and he was more flattered than annoyed by the piracy. A greater cause for discomfiture was the fury of an Irish friend in London, who insisted that he was the original of "the Mulligan" in the story. It was reported to Thackeray that he was threatening to "kill and eat" the author the first time they might chance to meet. As a matter of fact, Thackeray knew at least four other "Mulligans" in London, and had invented the character for his story before he had even made the acquaintance of the offended gentleman; but as he had enjoyed his hospitality he was unhappy to think that he could be accused of such rudeness as to caricature his host. He was discovering the pitfalls of satirical realism by falling into them one by one.

The greatest value of the little book's favorable reception was that it paved the way for *Vanity Fair*. After telling his mother about the good sale of the first edition, he added, "My prospects are very much improved and *Vanity Fair* may make me. The thought thereof makes me very humble and frightened—not elated." This was written a week before the publication of the first number, which occurred on January 1, 1847. For the first time, his own name was allowed to appear on the title page of something he had written; but a trace of its doubtful inception and undetermined future was to be seen in the sub-title, *Pen and Pencil Sketches of English Society*, which gave no indication that a unified novel was to follow. From this description, one might infer that the eventual development of the story was almost as unforeseen as that of *The Pickwick Papers*.

His anxiety to obtain some recognition is plainly to be seen in a letter to his friend Aytoun, who was on the staff of *Blackwood's Magazine*. Writing the day after the first number of *Vanity Fair* was issued, he said, "I think I have never had any ambition hitherto, or cared what the world thought of my work, good or bad; but now the truth forces itself upon me, if the world will once take to admiring Titmarsh, all his guineas will be multiplied by 10. Guineas are good. I have got children, only 10 years more to the fore, say, &c; now is the time, my lad, to make your A when the sun at length has begun to shine. Well, I think if I can make a push at the present minute—if my friends will shout, Titmarsh for ever! hurrah for &c, &c, I may go up with a run to a pretty fair place in my trade and be allowed

COVER DESIGN FOR MRS PERKINS'S BALL

to appear before the public as among the first fiddles. But my tunes must be heard in the streets, and organs must grind them. Ha! now do you read me? Why don't Blackwood give me an article?"

For a man of thirty-five, just beginning his first ambitious novel, to talk about having "only ten years more to the fore" suggests either failing health or a strange streak of morbidity. Beyond a doubt, the presence of half-grown daughters made him feel preternaturally old, and a sense of responsibility for their future spurred him to work hard and consider finances. About this time he tried to insure his life, and was disturbed by being rejected as a bad risk. In spite of all incentives to accumulate money, however, he decided on second thoughts that literary log-rolling was an unworthy expedient, and within two weeks he wrote to Aytoun again to withdraw his request: "Puffs are good, and the testimony of good men; but I don't think these will make a success for a man, and he ought to stand as the public chooses to put him. I will try, please God, to do my best, and the money will come perhaps some day! Meanwhile a man so lucky as myself has no reason to complain. So let all puffing alone, though as you know, I am glad if I can have and deserve your private good opinion. The women like *Vanity Fair*, I find, very much, and the publishers are quite in good spirits regarding that venture."

This odd mixture of assurance and diffidence was to be seen also in the novel itself. The modest sub-title, labeling it "pen and pencil sketches;" the elaborate pretense that the author was but a "puppet-master," displaying the antics of dolls rather than the behavior of human beings; the ironical asides to the reader, dissociating the author from the serious emotions of the characters—all these were symptoms of embarrassment and efforts to prepare a way of escape if the public and critics should prove adverse. On the other hand, the same sub-title implied that the author ambitiously took the whole of "English society" to be his province; and the pose of the puppet-master and ironic commentator implied that he considered himself an omniscient analyst, aloof from mere mortal limitations. The resulting oscillations between impartiality and prejudice, between sympathy and sneering, between sentiment and cynicism, were bound to exasperate many readers; but the creative power behind the mannerisms was real enough to compel attention for the story and belief in the reality of the personages in spite of the author's own insistence upon their being marionettes.

Few novelists ever had a more thorough apprenticeship. He had learned the art of writing through ten grueling years of journalism for every type of publication and in a wide variety of forms—burlesques, travel-articles, short stories, criticism of books and pictures, factual reporting. His style, while remaining strongly individual, had become flexible, exact, and easy. To be the investigator of English society—whether in the narrow or wide sense of the word—he was qualified by the range of his experience. Birth and education made him at home in the caste which Dickens and many of the other contemporary novelists observed only as outsiders, and yet he had also seen much of the seamy side of life. Without entirely losing his insular notions, he had become more cosmopolitan than his rivals; he knew France as intimately as England, had lived many months in Germany, had thoroughly explored Ireland and the Near East. If great fiction needs to be based on wide knowledge of mankind, he was equipped to produce it.

In a profounder respect, too, his life had prepared him to be a novelist by giving him the remoteness that permits perspective. From the day when, as a six-year-old child, he had left his doting family and traveled half around the world to live among strangers and suffer loneliness and a measure of actual cruelty, he had remained an alien and an onlooker in life. By the time his mother returned to England she had a new husband to whom she was devoted, and her son spent only short holidays in the household. When he was still a child accident rendered his physical appearance grotesque. On the eve of enjoying a life of ease and dilettante interests he lost his patrimony, chiefly through the unwise trust that he and his kinsfolk reposed in the honesty of their fellowmen; and being thus cut adrift from the normal security of his caste, he was obliged to become a writer because he was unqualified for any other profession. When he married and set up a home within the limits of his narrowed income, only four years of happiness were granted to him, and the affliction which then befell his wife was more devastating to his whole future life than her death would have been. By the time he had survived these recurrent blows of destiny, he was justified in regarding life with disillusionment.

And yet he had not become a thorough-going cynic. His cynicism was nothing more than a shell, beneath which his natural generosity and sensitiveness were as active as ever. In his misfortunes he had encountered unselfish kindness as well as cold indifference, and its rarity had made him cherish it all the more. The schoolboy whose intensest delight had been the spangled fantasies of the pantomine had carried over into manhood not only an enthusiasm for the theater in its most implausible extravagances but also a tendency to look at actual life as a serio-comic melodrama. Although the title "Vanity Fair" was derived from the glum allegory of John Bunyan, there can be no doubt that Thackeray visualized it in a less austere spirit, with the bright lights and gay tunes and gaudy color of a cosmic Vauxhall Gardens. He was actuated, to be sure, by a reforming purpose, having become solemnly convinced that both the social system and the religious dogmas of his time and his nation were stupid and cruel; but his missionary zeal was brightened with laughter, and his sharpest satire gave way to unexpected gleams of tolerance.

Some of the materials for the novel had long been maturing in his mind. Nearly five years before he had thought about treating the Waterloo epoch in a less flamboyant manner than Lever's. Two years later, when reviewing *Coningsby* in *The Morning Chronicle* and *The Pictorial Times*, he had shown interest in Disraeli's fictional portraits of Lord Hertford, John Wilson Croker, and other celebrities who now appeared in *Vanity Fair* under equally flimsy disguises. Beyond these literary influences, however, there were sources for the story in his own life. The opening scene at Miss Pinkerton's Academy reflected something of his early school days in Chiswick; the Indian background of Jos Sedley and Captain Dobbin and the O'Dowds was full of reminiscences of the Thackeray and Becher and Webb clans. A good many of the names and allusions had already appeared in his earlier writings—*The Yellowplush Papers*, *The Life of Major Gahagan*, *Mrs Perkins's Ball*. This habit of carrying characters over from one story to another was evidence of the strong reality that his creations had in his imagination, and gave them an equally strong reality to any faithful reader. In conjunction with his overt use of well-known persons as models for some of his secondary characters, it gave rise to the assumption that his central ones also were portraits of people he knew.

Out of all these elements was *Vanity Fair* shaped. And whatever uncertainty and experimentation may have befogged its inception, its successive monthly numbers soon established it as an organic masterpiece of fiction, and its author as one of the leading novelists of his time.

CHAPTER 10

The Puppet-Master

IN ITS MONTHLY parts, *Vanity Fair* was by no means an instantaneous success. Among the disadvantages of serial publication were that few important literary periodicals reviewed such works until complete and that many discriminating readers also preferred to wait until the story should be available in volume form. Even though his *Punch* articles and his two books of travels were prominently mentioned on the wrapper of each part, Thackeray's name meant nothing to the general bookshop customer. His novel was therefore overshadowed by those of popular favorites who were publishing in similar monthly parts. The new Dickens novel of the year was *Dombey and Son*, and Thackeray's friends were soon drawing contrasts between the two concurrent works. In February, when the fifth number of *Dombey* told of the death of little Paul, Thackeray himself had no illusions: he confessed that he wept over the death scene—as did his friends, the elegant Milnes and the stately historian Henry Hallam; and having brought the number into the *Punch* office with him, he threw it down on the table and exclaimed, "There's no writing against this; one hasn't an atom of chance. It's stupendous!"

Even in his own household, encouragement was not profuse. Too young to understand the story, his daughters were interested in it only insofar as they enjoyed being used as models for the illustrations. As well as posing for scenes in which the Osborne or Crawley children appeared, they were called upon to stand on a chair, holding draperies and casting a shadow, while some adult friend sat for a central figure. Furniture of all descriptions was called into requisition to eke out the groupings in the improvised studio. The little girls were also fascinated when the wood-blocks were being made, for then they were entrusted with rubbing out the failures, and washing the chalk off the blocks.

His family circle was enlarged now by the addition of his grandmother, Mrs Butler, who had come over from Paris to occupy the "famous bedroom" he had allotted to her. A grim old lady, wrapped in Indian shawls, she spoke little, and remained in her room most of the time, reading devotional books. With regard to *Vanity Fair* she expressed no opinion, but when each number arrived she put on her spectacles and read it carefully. After several months she quietly parceled up the yellow-backed parts, and when the children went out with their nurse for a walk in the Gardens, she asked them to deliver the package to a friend of hers who lived on the other side. It happened that their father encountered them near the gate of the Gardens, and found out what they were carrying. Being in one of

155

his discouraged moods, in which he sometimes thought that the publication was not proving successful enough to continue, he told them a trifle sharply to take the parcel home again. As they turned to do so, he suddenly called them back: "No, stop; I've changed my mind. If my grandmother wishes it, the books had best be conveyed." It had dawned on him that in her uncompromising way the old lady had at last shown her approval.

His circle of friends, with its steady rotation of dinner parties, remained much the same, the most regular participant now being Matthew James Higgins. During that year Higgins was working on a relief committee of the Irish famine and contesting a Parliamentary seat in the cause of free trade. His first article in the *New Monthly* having gained him the permanent nickname of "Jacob Omnium," he retained it as his usual pseudonym, though his numerous letters to *The Times*' were more often signed "Paterfamilias," "A Thirsty Soul," or "A Mother of Six." He and Thackeray loomed up together so often at their friends' parties that they came to be regarded as inseparable.

The Duff-Gordons, too, were assuming a large place in Thackeray's life. In February he was at a dinner party for the fifth birthday of their precocious daughter Janet, along with Mrs Norton, Lord Lansdowne, Richard Doyle, the *Punch* artist, and Tom Taylor, a young Trinity man who had recently joined the staff of *Punch* on the strength of several successful farces. Thackeray persuaded the little heroine of the occasion to eat an oyster, assuring her that it would taste exactly like cabinet pudding; but the joke turned against him when she loved it and insisted on eating a large share of those on his plate.

As the year wore on, his novel brought him to the attention of influential personages. Mrs Norton continued to push him, and took him to call upon the Duke of Devonshire. The gratified author rewarded her by writing a poem, *The Anglers*, to accompany a silly picture in *Fisher's Drawing-room Scrap Book*, one of the Annuals with sentimental engravings and a society lady as editor, such as he had ridiculed in his articles for *Fraser's*. Lord Holland, who was always looking out for witty conversationalists to be added to the *cénacle* that he had inherited from his parents, began to invite Thackeray to dinners at Holland House. These favors were not long in reaching the ears of Lady Blessington, who rivaled Mrs Norton as a beauty and an author and sought to rival Lord Holland as proprietor of a salon. The doors of Gore House were therefore opened to the chronicler of Vanity Fair. But these more glittering occasions were not frequent enough to draw him away from the companionship of his old group.

The weekly meetings of the *Punch* staff were not neglected. At the beginning of the year he published his genial poem, *The Mahogany Tree*, which celebrated the convivial evenings about the famous round table. As the Snob papers were at last approaching their end, he cast about for a subject that might make a new series of equal popular appeal, and decided to write some parodies of contemporary novelists. On January 27 Albany Fonblanque invited him to dinner, mentioning that Bulwer might be one of the guests. Later in the day Thackeray awoke to the fact that Fonblanque knew nothing about the forthcoming burlesques and could not be aware that Bulwer was the subject of the first one. The old melodrama of George Barnwell was to be retold in Bulwer's grandiloquent style. The story was already partly written, and the wood-blocks designed. Thackeray wrote a hasty note to Fonblanque, explaining that "I can't afford to give up my plan. It is my bread, indeed, for next year. I am bound to tell you this (how the deuce did I forget it in our talk this morning?), lest you should be putting your hospitable intentions into execution, and after having had my legs *sub iisdem trabibus* with Bulwer, should seem to betray him. I can't leave him out of the caricature; all that I promise is to be friendly and meek in spirit."

Thanks to his secure income from *Punch* and his novel, he could afford to indulge scruples about other employment. One of the cheaper publishers, David Bogue, had just started a series of shilling booklets on "social zoology;" the first one, *The Natural History of the Gent*, by Albert Smith, sold phenomenally, and Bogue was eager to engage other valuable writers. When *Vanity Fair* began to be successful he asked Vizetelly to offer Thackeray a hundred guineas apiece for as many items as he would provide. Although this was twice as much as he received for each part of *Vanity Fair*, Thackeray could not bring himself to accept. In his opinion Albert Smith's brand of humor was the acme of bad taste, and he had no wish to appear conjointly with him. It was worth much to Thackeray in inward complacency to turn down several hundred guineas for reasons of literary dignity.

While Thackeray's circumstances were improving, those of the Brookfields became precarious. Brookfield had lost money through speculation in railway shares and could see no prospect of promotion from his curacy of a London church. His friends began to canvass the possibility of having him appointed an Inspector of Schools. When Thackeray set out to pull strings in the matter, he discovered that Brookfield was regarded with disfavor by some of his more earnest colleagues because of his witty conversation and worldly tastes. Their saintly college companion, John Allen, accused him of "levity and loose talk." Thackeray wrote anxious letters of protest, praising his friend to the skies and deprecating the possibility that his claims might be compromised by his intimacy with "such a reprobate as me."

Mrs Brookfield, not being at all well during these months, spent much of her time in Southampton, taking sulphur-bath treatments for gout. She was staying at the home of a clerical friend named Fanshawe, whose wife was celebrated for her intellect and wit. At the end of January Brookfield went down to join his wife, and as Thackeray was also a friend of the Fanshawes, it was natural that he should pay a visit at this time. Mrs Brookfield's doctor was an enthusiast for the newly-discovered ether; and Thackeray, after a treatment from him, was betrayed by the after-effects of the anesthetic into expressing his admiration of Mrs Brookfield so openly that her husband showed annoyance.

Startled to find that he had overstepped the limits of his friend's complacency, Thackeray devoted the train journey back to London to the composition of a long letter to the ruffled husband, explaining his "insanity" of the day before. He declared that when he contemplated "her innocence, looks, angelical sweetness and kindness" he was so charmed that sometimes he "burst out into uncouth raptures." There was no danger, he asserted, in this emotion; it was "a sort of artistical delight (a spiritual sensuality so to speak)" and he was affected in just the same way by "other beautiful objects in Nature—children, landscapes, harmonies of colour, music, etc." He assured Brookfield that "you and God Almighty may know all my thoughts about your wife; I'm not ashamed of any of them." Protesting admiration for "the generous spirit" with which Brookfield had always previously regarded his "queer raptures," Thackeray affirmed that if he had ever recognized within himself "envy, or what you call passion, or a wicked thought," he would long ago have severed all acquaintance with the Brookfields.

With his convenient classification of Jane as a species of pretty landscape, the tiff blew over. A fortnight later Brookfield, back in London, wrote to his wife with his customary amiability: "Thackwack came in at 9 last night, and we conversed till small hours. . . You alone came in for the unmeasured tempest of our abuse. He wants to know when his purse will be finished." The same day, Thackeray wrote to her about a plan for her to bring the Fanshawe's daughter to visit his children; and his letter was so exceptionally witty that she pretended to be too much overcome to answer it: "You rose grander and more awful in the majesty of your authorship each time I made the feeble attempt to write a few unpretending words."

His popularity in society was still increasing. In April, Mrs Brookfield mentioned to a cousin that "Mr Thackeray steps in more rarely now that the 'Season with unusual severity hath set in,' but he is cordial and kindly as ever." Now at last Rumsey Forster, the society reporter of *The Morning Post*, enjoyed his revenge for the "Jenkins" squibs. At the great receptions, he was customarily placed at a little table just outside the drawing-room door, to take down the names of the guests as they were announced. When Thackeray was first included among the company at the Marquess of Lansdowne's, his name was carefully omitted from the list in next day's *Morning Post*. Shortly afterwards, there was a reception at Lord John Russell's, and this time Thackeray bowed to Mr Forster, bent over his table, and said firmly, "Mr Thackeray."

"Yes, sir," replied the reporter; "I am quite aware." But again the one name was absent from the printed list.

FitzGerald, in his rural fastnesses, wrote to Frederick Tennyson: "Thackeray is progressing greatly in his line; he publishes a Novel in numbers—*Vanity Fair*— which began dull, I thought, but gets better every number, and has some very fine things indeed in it. He is become a great man, I am told; goes to Holland House, and Devonshire House; and for some reason or other, will not write a word to me. But I am sure this is not because he is asked to Holland House."

The propagator of this gossip about Thackeray's gaddings in society was Carlyle, in whom the imputation of ignorance "of the customs of English gentlemen" still rankled, and who now saw his chance to assert that Thackeray was a mere tufthunter. He sent FitzGerald the sour suggestion that Thackeray's new grandeur was making him neglect his old friends, and "Yedward" transmitted the tale to its subject. Thackeray replied: "It is not true what Gurlyle has written to you about my having become a tremenjous lion, etc., too grand to etc.; but what is true is that a fellow who is writing all day for money gets sick of pens and paper when his work is over. All that about being a Lion is nonsense. I can't eat more dinners than I used last year, and dine at home with my dear little women three times a week: but two or three great people ask me to their houses; and *Vanity Fair* does anything but pay. I am glad if you like it. I don't care a dem if some other people do or don't, and always try to keep that damper against flattery. What does it matter whether this man who is an ass likes your book or not?"

As a symbol of both prosperity and elegance, he bought a horse and took his exercise upon it regularly in Hyde Park. It was a sturdy black cob, "only fit for a bishop," as he remarked; and like a child with a new toy he boasted to all his friends about its perfections. Although "not knowing a horse from a cow," he was assured that he had got a wonderful bargain.

His letters reveal details of his family life. He told his mother about taking Annie and her governess and Mrs Brookfield and his pretty young friend Eugénie Crowe (who was posing for his illustrations to *Vanity Fair*) to see *King Lear*, and being heartily bored; about celebrating little Minny's birthday with a day at Hampton Court, with the necessary arrangements for someone to keep his grandmother company while they were out. The old lady's health was failing, but she was "in pretty good spirits, and pleased with her little household occupations, fidgetting the servants quite unrestrained, and ringing the bell with unbounded liberty." More than once he had troubles over hiring governesses, Annie being too clever to accept dull ones and her father being too distrustful of his own susceptibility to venture upon clever and pretty ones.

It is a quaint household that these glimpses disclose, with the author struggling to fulfil his responsibilities to the ancient matriarch and the two little girls, in the midst of all the writing that had to be completed by a fixed schedule—for his *Punch* contributions were as rigidly demanded as his monthly instalments of the novel. As a regular staff-member, he had his set quota of columns to be filled, including letter-press, illustrations for his own text, and drawings for jokes. The chief engraver for *Punch*, Joseph Swain, who lived in the neighborhood, used often to call on his way to the office and pick up any blocks that were drawn and ready for cutting. He would be waiting in the study when Thackeray finished breakfast, and as like as not the drawing would be made then and there, while Swain smoked a cigar and chatted with the artist while he worked. "Ah, Swain," Thackeray exclaimed one day, glancing up from the block, "if it hadn't been for *Punch*, I wonder where I should be!"

Nevertheless, for a successful novelist who was becoming a figure in society, the contributions to *Punch* were apt to be a liability. Although he had assured Fonblanque that the parodies of his contemporaries would "all be good-natured," he must have been aware that he was embarking on a risky venture. Popular authors do not enjoy being parodied, and the more skilful the parody, the greater the offense. The first of *Punch's Prize Novelists* appeared at the beginning of April. As an assault upon Bulwer it was indeed less savage than his earlier ones, in that it ridiculed only his literary style and not his private life and character; but the cleverness of the burlesque raised a chuckle very painful to the dignity of the noble baronet.

The first actual quarrel aroused by the series of parodies, however, was with John Forster. In a conversation on the subject with Tom Taylor, Forster (always prone to violent assertions) declared that Thackeray was "as false as hell." Taylor considered this so ludicrous that he reported it to Thackeray. He did not realize how sensitively Thackeray lashed back against any censure from a supposed friend. At a large party at the Procters' Thackeray publicly refused to shake Forster's hand. Prompt to avenge an insult, Forster immediately summoned Dickens as his "second," and Thackeray was obliged to ask Sir Alexander Duff-Gordon to act in the same capacity on his behalf. Dickens and Gordon conferred at the Athenaeum Club, and Dickens handed over a letter addressed to Thackeray and written by Forster in warm self-defence. It revealed Forster's knowledge that Thackeray from time to time had found his pompous manner irresistible material for burlesques in drawings and letters to amuse friends.

Upon reading the letter, Gordon declared that he was certain it would be accepted by Thackeray as closing the episode.

Dickens then took occasion to express his own opinions of the whole matter. "As far as Thackeray is concerned," he said, "and separating my remark from Forster or his affair, I should tell him, if he were here, that I think these things arise in his jesting much too lightly between what is true and what is false, and what he owes to both, and not being sufficiently steady to the former.

"I am bound to say beyond this," he went on, "that in reference to his imitations in *Punch* (out of which, as I understand from Forster, the conversation with Taylor arose), I have a strong opinion of my own; and that is that they do no honor to literature or literary men, and should be left to very inferior and miserable hands. I should like Thackeray to know this opinion of mine."

Some old grievance of Dickens's own then came to the surface. "With reference to that paragraph of retort on Thackeray, in Forster's letter, as I have reason to know its force better than Forster does even, I did not object to it, but felt that it ought to be there." He told Gordon the reason, which may have been that he had personally seen one of Thackeray's caricatures of Forster, but more likely was that he had heard of some similar gibe at his own expense.

Conscience-stricken that he had brought his friend Taylor into trouble with Forster, Thackeray wrote to Dickens expressing his regret over the whole misunderstanding. As long as Forster had reflected only upon his literary ethics and not upon his private honor, he was willing to apologize. All the friends of the disputants were agreed that the fracas ought to be promptly forgotten. When Forster carried his complaint to Macready, the actor impatiently commented in his diary, "Words, words, words." Dickens took on the role of peacemaker by inviting Forster, Thackeray, Taylor, and the Duff-Gordons to a dinner party, for a reconciliation all round. Although Thackeray had asked some of his own friends to dine with him at Greenwich on the same date, he was so ready to meet the appeasement half-way that he begged permission of his own guests to postpone his party in favor of Dickens's.

Not so easily, however, could he forget the opinions that his accepted friends, Dickens and Forster, had uttered in the heat of the dispute. With his ascent toward social and literary eminence, he encountered so much jealousy and suspicion that he began to transfer the title of his novel to the whole of the little world in which he moved. "There are no end of quarrels in this wicked Vanity Fair," he admitted to his mother, "and my feet are perpetually in hot water."

By this time the financial woes of the Brookfields had reached such a pass that they gave up their house in London, and Mrs Brookfield went to her family home in Somerset, while her husband claimed his privilege—as curate—to reside in the vaults of his church, St Luke's, Berwick Street. This gave rise to many jokes by Thackeray and his other friends about the dank and gloomy "*bouge*," but also to almost daily visits from Thackeray, intended to alleviate his loneliness, and frequent invitations from the same source to stay overnight in the more cheerful environment of Kensington. From her place of refuge, Mrs Brookfield commented on the progress of their friend's book: "The last No. of *Vanity Fair* is exceedingly good, I think, but I begin to wish he would give Amelia a few more brains. Julia [her sister] read it and rates it (even on such a mere scrap of it) much above Dickens."

At the same moment, his other Egeria decided to do something more for the novel than express private enthusiasm. Mrs Procter was exasperated with the critics for their failure to review it, and during one of her evening parties she seized upon the first of them who came in sight, Abraham Hayward, and demanded that he write an article on it for the *Edinburgh*. Hayward was placed in an excruciating dilemma. "The louse of literature," as Disraeli called him, was the last man to embark on a rash critical estimate in advance of his colleagues, and the mere thought of the *Edinburgh*'s mentioning a novel during its serial publication was horrifying. On the other hand, Mrs Procter's parties were too important in his scheme of things to be lightly foregone. He wriggled. "He was very good-natured about it," says his biographer tactfully, "but happened to be busied about other things, and fancied he could not undertake it." As a matter of fact, he had not even read the story as far as it had gone.

Mrs Procter was no woman to be deterred. She went through the published parts and marked the passages that would make the best quotations; along with these she sent Hayward a letter specifically mentioning the chief characters and incidents and suggesting the general qualities of the story. The highest praise, she declared, ought to go to "the total absence of affectation. He seems to me to excel in the pathetic parts. . . The characters are neither devils nor angels, but living, breathing people, neither above nor below one's sympathy." Thus having the whole review practically written for him, without even the necessity of reading the book, Hayward put an article together out of her notes, and sent it in trepidation to the magazine.

The writing of the novel became no easier as it advanced; rather the reverse, for Thackeray was slowly realizing how much his reputation and his future depended upon it. "Toward the end of a month," he told his mother, "I get so nervous that I don't speak to anybody scarcely, and once actually got up in the middle of the night and came down and wrote in my night chimee; but that don't happen often, and I own that I had a nap after dinner that day." Brookfield described in a letter to his wife how Thackeray was sitting beside him in *l'horrible bouge*, "brewing Vanity, in a dreadful fright lest the month of Sept. should arrive before No. next." The care that he paid to its historical details was indicated in another letter of Brookfield's, telling how, after he and Thackeray had dined well at the Garrick Club, they carried off an old medical officer who had been at Waterloo, so that Thackeray could get some hints to use in his next number.

The author was sometimes exasperated by complaints which indicated that readers were trying to equate his characters with the conventional "hero and heroine" instead of seeing in them the admixture of human failings that he intended. When his mother objected to the selfish behavior of Amelia, he answered impatiently that it was intentional; he was not trying to depict "a perfect character or anything like it." Except for Dobbin, he asserted, all the people in the book were "odious." He wanted to convey a "dark moral" by showing "a set of people living without God in the world (only that is a cant phrase), greedy, pompous men, perfectly self-satisfied for the most part, and at ease about their superior virtue." So far as the story had gone, Dobbin and the bullied lady-companion, Miss Briggs, were the only characters with real humility. Amelia would later acquire it, "when her scoundrel of a husband is well dead with a ball in his odious bowels, when she has had sufferings, a child, and a religion." Her salvation would come because she possessed "a quality above most people." This quality, Thackeray wrote in capitals, was LOVE.

Although to his devout mother Thackeray thus expounded a good religious interpretation of the story, the general public remained unenlightened. Even Mrs Brookfield was disposed to lament the dearth of agreeable characters. The October number she described as "not good—except the wicked ones." She was especially critical of Amelia because of a remark Thackeray had made to Brookfield. "Though Amelia is not exactly a copy of your wife," he had said, "I should not have conceived the character if I had not known her." In her comments on the October instalment Mrs Brookfield therefore waxed sarcastic. "Mr Thackeray has now got a 2nd Amelia, Lady Jane Sheepshanks. . . On the plan of 2 negatives making one affirmative, I suppose I may take the 2 dull ones of the book to make one Mrs B." She admitted that Amelia did resemble her in some points, but

VANITY FAIR

STORY 1^s

DESIGNS FOR THE COVER OF "VANITY FAIR"

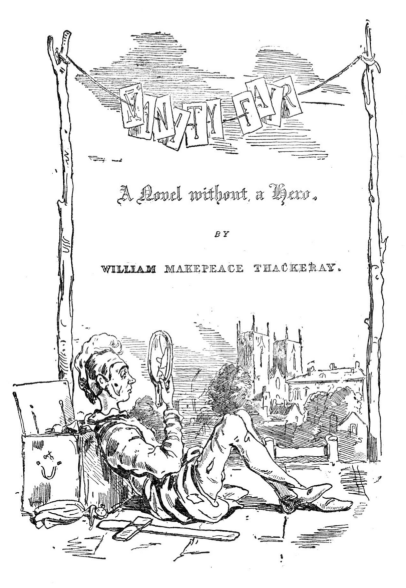

TITLE PAGE OF "VANITY FAIR"

"though she has the right amount of antiphlegm and affectionateness she is really an uncommonly dull and selfish character and very apathetic to the only person who cares for her, the quaint Capt Dobbin."

A keener feminine critic was more enthusiastic about the story at that point. "I brought away the last four numbers of *Vanity Fair*," Mrs Carlyle wrote to her husband, "and read one of them during the night. Very good indeed, beats Dickens out of the world."

In August Thackeray's grandmother was so ill that he took her and the children back to Paris, where she died two months later. After he had struggled with the details of funeral, will, and so forth, a brilliant idea struck him: the three rooms that had been originally intended for the Carmichael-Smyths and Mrs Butler being all now unoccupied, why shouldn't the Brookfields come and live with him until their future should be determined? "It will be the very greatest comfort and kindness to me," he wrote to Brookfield, "and I shall take it quite *hangry* if you don't come. . . I have got a box of preserved apricots from Fortnum and Mason's which alone ought to make any lady happy, and two shall be put under my lady's pillow every night."

He may have realized that the absence of a chaperone could be an obstacle. A little later Brookfield informed his wife that Thackeray "has engaged a Governess. . . He invites us to go there for two or three weeks. What think you? *i. e.*, after Governidge and babes are arrived."

Mrs Brookfield probably vetoed the notion firmly, and a couple of weeks afterwards she threw cold water on her husband's interest in a similar offer from the Duff-Gordons, on the grounds that their Bohemian habits might insidiously undermine the high Brookfieldian principles: "Cannot you call up visions," she warned her husband, "of cosy little Sunday dinners with Mrs Norton, Mr Thackeray, and Mr and Mrs Wigan?—and I would not vouch for your or my virtuous sense of congruities restraining our joining in such *délassements* as long as there was no intrinsic wrong in them." As Lady Duff-Gordon's tastes included cigars and a juvenile Ethiopian page-boy, the caution was probably well founded.

In October, *Punch's Prize Novelists* came to an end. In the original scheme, the series was to have included a parody of Dickens, but Thackeray's colleagues of the staff vetoed it, and the recent friction with Dickens probably inclined Thackeray to caution. This was unfortunate, as an assault upon the darling of the public might have done much to mollify his other victims. The burlesque of Bulwer could not make his relations with that author any worse than they were already; but the next story, *Codlingsby*, by "D. Shrewsbury, Esq.," with its allusions to old-clothes dealers and its mischievously confused details of university life, made an implacable enemy of Disraeli. Thereafter he cut Thackeray when they met, and he nursed his vengeance until 1880, seventeen years after Thackeray's death, when he caricatured him as "St Barbe" in his last novel, *Endymion*. The next two "prize novels" were aimed at G. P. R. James and Charles Lever. The self-important James never forgave him, but went no further than to mutter, in later years, the mild sneer, "Thackeray rhymes with quackery." Lever's more impulsive nature prompted him to write to Thackeray "to know what he meant by it," and when the reply proved unsatisfactory, he straightway introduced a heavy-handed caricature of Thackeray into the novel which he was then writing. It has been noted by critics, however, that both James and Lever reformed the conspicuous traits of their style that Thackeray had lampooned.

The other parodies, of Mrs Gore and Fenimore Cooper, were less successful. The preliminary intention had been to include Thackeray himself as one of the victims, and this presumably was the inception of the piece called *Crinoline*, which is written in the Yellowplush dialect; but instead of being an attempt to burlesque a burlesque, it is devoted to ridiculing an imaginary French author for his absurd misrepresentations of English life. The other departure from the original scheme— the omission of Dickens—evoked a letter from that novelist, ostensibly to reprove Thackeray for leaving him out, but actually to re-affirm the disapproval of the whole production that he had already uttered to Duff-Gordon. "I will tell you now candidly," he said, "that I did not admire the design and I think it a great pity that we take advantage of the means our calling gives us with such accursed readiness of at all depreciating or vulgarising each other, that this seems to me to be one of the main reasons why we are more generally divided among ourselves than artists who have not those means at their command. . . I thought your power thrown away on that series, however happily executed." It was not comfortable for Thackeray to be thus exposed to exactly the same protest that he had angrily lodged against *Tait's Magazine* and other offenders.

His work for *Punch* had been by no means restricted to the *Prize Novelists*. In addition to the usual variety of political squibs, he had supplied a number of amusing verse parodies—"Love Songs of the Fat Contributor"—and as soon as the *Prize Novelists* ended he went on with a series of *Travels in London*, by "Mr Spec." Some of these were startlingly unfunny, especially the first one, a literal account of a visit paid with Brookfield to some of the starving families in the purlieus of his parish in Soho. Such a sketch reminds one that *Punch* published Hood's *Song of the Shirt* as well as his frivolities.

A second Christmas book, *Our Street*, was published in December, and resembled its predecessor in being a series of brief character sketches, reinforced by the author's drawings, without any seasonable references; but it lacked even the vestigial plot that wandered through *Mrs Perkins's Ball*. Nevertheless, it was cordially received. "What a turmoil it is under which I live, laugh, and grow fat however," he wrote to his mother. "There's no use denying the matter or blinking it now. I am become a sort of great man in my way—all but at the top of the tree, indeed there, if the truth were known, and having a great fight up there with Dickens. I get such a deal of praise wherever I go that it is rather wearisome to hear. I don't think my head is a bit turned, please God, for I have always got my own opinion, and when men and newspapers say '*Our Street* is the finest' &c., I know a devilish deal better, and don't disguise the truth either. This London world is full of good-natured Tom Fools, and directly one begins to cry O, all the rest say Prodigious."

The publication of Hayward's article about *Vanity Fair*, in January, did much to further this recognition. But in the same month another and less conventional beam of public attention was turned upon the author from an unexpected quarter. The second edition of *Jane Eyre*, by "Currer Bell," was published with a long dedication to Thackeray:

> There is a man in our days whose words are not framed to tickle delicate ears: who, to my thinking, comes before the great ones of society—much as the son of Imlah comes before the throned Kings of Judah and Israel; and who speaks truth as deep, with a power as prophet-like and vital—a mien as dauntless and as daring. Is the satirist of Vanity Fair admired in high places? I cannot tell; but I think if some of those amongst whom he hurls the Greek fire of his sarcasm, and over whom he flashes the levinbrand of his denuncia-tion, were to take his warnings in time, they or their seed might yet escape a fatal Ramoth-Gilead. Why have I alluded to this man? I have alluded to him, Reader, because I think I see in him an intellect profounder and more unique than his contemporaries have yet recognized; because I regard him as the first social regenerator of the day—as the very master of that working corps who would restore to rectitude the warped system of things; because I think no commentator in his writings has yet found the comparison that suits him, the terms which rightly characterize his talent. They say he is like Fielding; they talk of his wit, humour, comic powers. He resembles Fielding, as an eagle does a vulture: Fielding could swoop on carrion, but Thackeray never does. His wit is bright, his humour attractive, but both bear the same relation to his serious genius that lambent steel lightning playing under the edge of a summer cloud does to the electric death-spark hid in its womb.

By this impulsive outburst of Carlylese rhetoric, Charlotte Brontë innocently touched off an explosion of scandal. When her book had first appeared, two months before, there had been immense discussion of its supposedly passionate and uninhibited emotions, and the closely-guarded mystery of the authorship increased the public excitement. Many readers assumed that its claim to be an autobiography was substantiated by its intensity of feeling. Now that the dedica-tion suddenly linked it with Thackeray, everyone who knew anything about his private life remembered that he, like the hero of the novel, had an insane wife and was in the habit of employing a governess in the motherless household. Gossips jumped to the conclusion that "Currer Bell" had actually been a governess to the Thackeray children, and more than a few of them did not scruple to add positively that she had been the novelist's mistress. As Becky Sharp had also begun life as a governess, the rumor was that a quarrel had led the former lovers to lampoon each other simultaneously in print.

Miss Brontë, in the wilds of Yorkshire, knew nothing whatever about Thackeray's personal affairs. The dedication had been her only way of proclaiming her admiration for his novel, and she had defended it somewhat defiantly in a letter to her publishers: "I do not know if the part which relates to Mr Thackeray is likely to be well received; but whether generally approved of and understood or not, I shall not regret having written it, for I am convinced of its truth."

Within a week, however, she was regretting it most heartily. Thackeray, in sending his thanks for the compliment, told his unknown admirer about the construction that was being placed upon it. When his letter was forwarded to her by the publishers—who did not themselves know her identity at this time—she could not open it until she had summoned up enough courage to be prepared for a snub if the great man should be annoyed by her temerity. Her fear was at once turned into chagrin. "His letter is most friendly in its noble simplicity," she informed her publishers, "but he apprises me of a circumstance which both surprised and dismayed me. . . Well may it be said that fact is often stranger than fiction. The coincidence struck me as equally unfortunate and extraordinary. . . I am *very very* sorry that my inadvertent blunder should have made his name and affairs a subject for common gossip. The very fact of his not complaining at all and addressing me with such kindness, notwithstanding the pain and annoyance I must have caused him, increases my chagrin. I could not half express my regret to him in my answer, for I was restrained by the consciousness that the answer was just worth nothing at all—quite valueless for healing the mischief I had done." As she made no move to emerge from her pseudonymity with a public denial of the slander, and as Thackeray was too chivalrous to say anything about it, he had to resign himself to being pointed out by quidnuncs as the original of the ferocious Mr Rochester.

He had some difficulty in persuading himself that he was really a celebrity. Such an unsolicited testimonial as that of "Jane Eyre" embarrassed him as much as it pleased him. The attentions of the great ladies of London society were equally disturbing. Probably the nearest approach to a genuine *salon* was the drawing-room of Lady Ashburton. Her husband, a shy and studious member of the millionaire Baring banking family, left her free rein for her social conquests, in which her imperious manners and brilliant wit controlled a circle of admiring friends. As her interests ran to literature, she was at home to authors more than to political potentates, and even the rugged Carlyle became her devoted vassal, to the bitter jealousy of his wife. Both in her London home and at her country house, Alresford Grange, Lady Ashburton led her guests in the display of witty, uninhibited conversation.

Thackeray had met her through Charles Buller several years before, and his *Vanity Fair* fame procured him an invitation to her house. The talk that evening was so unsparing in its raillery of some of the guests that he was positively shocked; he declined her next invitations and told a number of people flatly that he disliked her. After a while, as his annoyance simmered down, he realized how much he had misinterpreted the spirit of the hard-hitting banter. On receiving another dinner invitation from her, he followed one of his frequent habits by using a comic picture as substitute for awkward words: upon the back of her invitation card he sketched himself kneeling at her feet while she set his hair aflame with coals of fire. This wordless apology won her entire forgiveness.

In spite of the increasing evidences of his fame, he was by no means sure that authorship was to be his life work. The sales of *Vanity Fair* fell far below his expectations, and when it had only two more months to run he was lamenting that the publishers were several hundred pounds out of pocket. Retaining something of his early prejudice that authorship was not a gentleman's profession, somehow in the midst of his writing he found time to resume the legal ambitions that had been so gaily abandoned fifteen years before; and on May 26, 1848, he was duly called to the bar. Five friends combined to lend him a hundred pounds to pay his fees, for he was in lower water than ever, being repeatedly obliged to pay off further obligations of his unlucky railway company. He made no move to practice law, but stowed away the qualification for possible use in the future.

Early in the year Brookfield received his appointment as School Inspector, and in April he and his wife were able to move into a comfortable house in Portman Street. Mrs Brookfield was still in indifferent health, and had to rest a great deal, receiving her visitors while she reclined on a sofa. Thackeray became convinced that she was slowly dying, and in spite of his affection for Brookfield he attributed her illness to her husband's inconsiderate treatment of her.

As her range of pastimes was so circumscribed, and as her husband was often absent on his tours of duty, Thackeray devoted himself to the congenial task of amusing her, not only by his own visits but also by conscripting his friends to the service. Adelaide Kemble, who had enjoyed brief fame as a prima donna and then retired upon marrying Edward John Sartoris, acceded to Thackeray's request that she should go and sing to "a sick lady of his acquaintance." Mrs Brookfield was both amused and embarrassed when the impressive stranger descended upon her, "took off her bonnet and poured forth in German, Italian, and English." Uncertain of how to show her gratitude, Mrs Brookfield decided she ought to kiss the performer's hand; and then she was left, as she told her husband, "in a cold sweat (to be coarse) as to whether the kiss of the hand might not have been *un peu trop fort.*" Shortly after "the Sartoris misfortune" another of Thackeray's friends, Miss

Letitia Macready, called on Mrs Brookfield and offered to read to her; but the invalid politely and discreetly declined. She undoubtedly felt flattered by Thackeray's admiration—all the more so, now that he was hailed as a celebrity and was received in exalted social circles. His solicitude, however, when it took too practical a form, could become a nuisance.

Thackeray, for his part, in letters to his mother and to intimate friends, had no hesitation in mentioning how much he adored Jane Brookfield; but he spoke in the same way of several other women—Eugénie Crowe, Kate Perry, and Vir-

MRS BROOKFIELD ON HER SOFA

ginia Pattle, the latter being the youngest and prettiest sister in a large family that he had known since boyhood. When indulging in a playful flirtation with an attractive young woman he could momentarily make believe that he was a free agent for the enjoyment of sentimental entanglements.

His own household was complicated for a short time by a visit from his swarthy half-niece from India. He was much diverted by the girl's naïve impressions of Europe, and especially when in a letter she saluted his stately mother as "dear Grandmamma." Somewhat to his relief, she ended her visit just before the day of a big dinner party which he gave—in great trepidation—upon the insistence of Mrs Dickens and her sister Georgina Hogarth. The children and their drab governess went elsewhere for the night, several of his favorite young ladies were present to sing and sparkle, and the illusion of nonchalant social gaiety was almost perfect.

Vanity Fair was now in sight of its end. The neck-and-neck race with his chief competitor was emphasized by his attending the dinner given by Dickens on April 11 to celebrate the conclusion of *Dombey and Son*. In contrast with the rather unenthusiastic reception of that novel, the public interest in *Vanity Fair* had steadily grown, and the characters were already assuming the status of real people. In the general tendency to speculate as to their future, Thackeray was prone to join. His old school chum Liddell was now headmaster of Westminster School, and when Thackeray went riding in Rotten Row he often fell in with Mr and Mrs Liddell

and talked about what might happen in the story. "Oh, Mr Thackeray," exclaimed Mrs Liddell one day, "you must let Dobbin marry Amelia."

"Well," he replied, "he shall; and when he has got her, he will not find her worth having."

In the same spirit, when the Duke of Devonshire requested Thackeray to give him an original portrait of Becky Sharp, the author replied in great detail, recounting the present doings of all the persons of the story, as if it were the current gossip of society—several of the points differing slightly from those with which the novel actually concluded, two

months later. His description of Becky in the letter gives further validity to a theory which is suggested by the whole course of her career in the novel, that she was chiefly modeled upon the Irish novelist, Lady Morgan, who was now living not far from Thackeray in Knightsbridge and inviting him frequently to her evening conversaziones.

Another of the penalties of success was the necessity of making speeches in public. All the authors of the day responded to their duty of supporting the "Literary Fund" for distressed confrères, and of participating in its banquets. It was this institution that first prevailed upon Thackeray to break his silence. In reply to a highly laudatory toast he got upon his legs and made a few spasmodic remarks that elicited sympathetic laughter and cheers. Although he reported to his mother that "I was in such a panic that I didn't know what I said and don't know now," he was almost convinced by the assurances of his friends that he had made "an excellent funny speech."

With only one more month's installment of *Vanity Fair* to be written, he exclaimed fervently, "How glad I shall be, for I dislike everybody in the book except Dob. and poor Amelia." To increase his normal dissatisfaction with his work, his attention was distracted by the prevalence of upheaval and terror. In England the Chartist movement had burst forth once more, and the proposed delivery of the monster petition to Parliament on April 10 was expected to mark the outbreak of civil war. The evening before, Thackeray was dining out, and one of his fellow-guests, Charles Knight, records that "the cloth had scarcely been removed when he suddenly started up and said, 'Pray excuse me, I must go. I left my children in terror that something dreadful was about to happen. I am unfit for society. Good night.'"

The whole continent, too, was in turmoil, and on this account the Carmichael-Smyths were finally persuaded to remove from Paris. On June 29, with none of the delight that ought to have attended a great achievement, Thackeray announced to his mother, "*Vanity Fair* is this instant done, and I have been worked so hard that I can hardly hold a pen and say God bless my dearest old mother. I had not time even to listen to the awful cannonading in your town. Thank God you are going to leave it! . . I am very much pleased to have done, very melancholy and beat, and humble in mind, I hope. . . I get so much praise that I want keeping down."

The insertion of his personal experiences in the story continued till the end, the scenes in the Grand Duchy of Pumpernickel being derived from his own sojourn at Weimar. His affection for Dobbin and Amelia, too, among all the characters he had created, was due to their resemblance to people he was fond of in real life. His confession of Amelia's indebtedness to Mrs Brookfield has already been quoted, and the next year we find Lord Lyttelton jesting about it in a letter to Brookfield. Thackeray was only anxious to prevent this identification from being too obvious, and after the last number had gone to press he realized that he had overstepped the bounds of discretion by giving the name of Mrs Brookfield's maid to the maid of Amelia in the closing chapters. He wrote to her with an abject appeal for pardon: "Now that it is over and irremediable, I am thinking with a sort of horror of a bad joke in the last number . . I laughed when I wrote it, and thought it was good fun, but now I am in a great tremor. . . You know you are only a piece of Amelia, my mother is another half, my poor little wife—*y est pour beaucoup*."

As for Dobbin, his physical appearance in the illustrations was obviously drawn from the saintly clergyman, John Allen. As far as his performance in the story was concerned, he reproduced much of Major Carmichael-Smyth's devotion to Anne Thackeray during her married years, and his acceptance as second husband to the young widow with a schoolboy son. But in Dobbin's awkward, unspoken adoration for Amelia, his secret efforts to make her comfortable and happy, and her persistent blindness to his feelings, another and more significant element showed itself. The satisfaction with which the novelist planted the bullet in the heart of Amelia's self-satisfied husband, and eventually awarded her hand to the man who had been the husband's faithful friend, was not solely dramatic. All unconsciously, Thackeray was revealing his own growing devotion to the woman who admittedly was portrayed in Amelia—Jane Octavia Brookfield.

CHAPTER 11

In Marble Halls

NO SOONER WAS the last page of *Vanity Fair* sent off to the anxiously waiting printers—for Thackeray was getting more and more dilatory with his copy—than new schemes were clamoring for his attention. The next Christmas book had to be planned. Another novel in numbers ought to be launched as soon as possible, before the public could lose the habit of looking for an instalment of Thackeray every month. But the growing strain under which he had been working warned him that first of all he must take a holiday.

As Belgium and the Rhineland constituted one of the few areas on the Continent undisturbed by revolution, he laid plans to spend a few weeks at Spa or Aix-la-Chapelle, allowing himself freedom for any last-minute changes that impulse might dictate. Combining pleasure with business, he intended to obtain local color for a Christmas book that was to deal with the foreign travels of a comic family. As usual, he was short of cash, and asked Chapman & Hall for an advance of fifty pounds on the unwritten book. He needed the money to pay off the last remaining indebtedness of his stepfather. Now that the Carmichael-Smyths had consented to come back and live in England, they must feel no chilling shadow from the disaster of a dozen years before.

To celebrate the publication of *Vanity Fair* in volume form, which happened to occur on his thirty-seventh birthday, he was persuaded to give a tea and dinner party for some fifty friends, with Lady Pollock acting as hostess. In the glow of success he felt unwontedly amiable. Even the belligerent John Forster had made amends for the recent dispute by reviewing *Vanity Fair* generously in *The Examiner*. When they met at the home of Chapman the publisher, on the day before Thackeray's departure, Forster won his heart completely by escorting little Annie through the rain under the solicitous shelter of his umbrella.

Thackeray broke his journey at Canterbury to visit his brother-in-law, Arthur Shawe, whose regiment was quartered there; but he felt ashamed when he found himself observing the naïve anecdotes and pastimes of the hospitable Fusiliers as material for satire. This embarrassment, and an incessant downpour of rain, and twenty-four hours in the Ship Inn at Dover with nothing to do, made him feel "utterly cast down and more under the influence of blue devils than I ever remember before."

By the time he reached Brussels, however, the old spell of the Continent was strongly upon him, and he indulged in an orgy of play-going, free of the haunting

175

consciousness of the printer's devil in waiting. Somewhat wryly, perhaps, he wrote to his mother: "One comfort is that nobody here knows anything about Titmarsh the Great, and that personage is no more taken notice of than a tall ungainly man deserves to be." Even though extolling the pleasures of anonymity, he was glad to fall in with a Manchester business man who admired his books. Together they witnessed Déjazet in *Gentil Bernard,* and Thackeray described the play enthusiastically as "the wickedest I ever saw, and one of the pleasantest, adorably funny and naughty." With his mixture of sophistication and Puritanism he added that "it could only be written and admired in a society in the last stage of corruption, as ours is. I feel persuaded that there is an awful time coming for all of us."

Being in Belgium brought back vividly the story he had just written. When he visited the hotel where Becky Sharp stayed, and passed Captain Osborne's lodgings, he seemed to be remembering real experiences in which he had encountered Becky and George and Amelia. "How curious it is!" he mused. "I believe perfectly in all those people, and feel quite an interest in the Inn in which they lived."

Before leaving London he had made a compact with Mrs Brookfield for the interchange of letters. He sent long, whimsical, homesick accounts of his adventures to dispel her invalid's boredom, and called anxiously for letters from her at the post offices along his route. At Spa he spent a few lonely days in desultory sketching and in watching the *rouge-et-noir* players. He risked a small stake himself a few times, and lost about five pounds; if he was testing himself to find out whether his old penchant for gambling had been conquered, the verdict was affirmative— he found no thrill in the game and only contempt for the players, one of whom looked so like Mrs Brookfield that he could not take his eyes off her, and was strongly tempted to entreat her to desist from her sordid pastime. Then he was recognized by a lady whom he had met at Devonshire House, and who introduced him to all the fashionable guests at the watering-place; and he was at once in a busy round of visits, rides, and chatter. On the same day that he met these friends, he had at last shaken off his "blue devils" enough to make a start on his next novel.

The new book was approached with a clearer conception than *Vanity Fair* had been. That story had established a recognized "Thackeray style" which its successor would naturally maintain. *Vanity Fair,* although historical in spots, was so nearly contemporary that large segments of Thackeray's own experience had found place in it; the new story carried this trait so much further that it was virtually an autobiography. Although its hero, Arthur Pendennis, was a more egotistical and selfish young man than Thackeray had been, the satirist was only consistent in emphasizing the worse elements in his own nature as strongly as those in other people. The story began at the point where the lad was preparing to enter the University, and the opening chapters gave an almost literal account of the months Thackeray spent at Larkbeare after leaving Charterhouse.

Although he was gratified to have made a start, he did not find the atmosphere of Spa conducive to work. He did most of his writing before breakfast, and in addition to his walks and his social activities he found time to reread *Amelia* ("the most delightful portrait of a woman that surely ever was painted") and *Joseph Andrews* ("coarse and careless"). When he became thoroughly bored with the small society of the place, he moved on up the Rhine as far as Homburg.

On board the river steamer, when he was returning toward home, he struck up a friendship with Lady de Rothschild, whose husband, Sir Anthony, was one of the heads of the English branch of the firm. The vivacious, auburn-curled little woman found Thackeray a pleasant antidote to the dull trip from Mainz to Bonn. "Strange enough, we made acquaintance directly," she noted in her journal, "and he remained with us the whole day. We talked of literature, drawings, Jews, of whom he has a bad opinion, politics, etc., and we parted very good friends—at least I fancy so. He seems a good and an honest man, with a kind heart, notwithstanding a large fund of satire. I like him better than his books." She had her two little daughters with her, and Thackeray spent part of the day in carrying one or other of the children up and down the deck on his shoulder, holding her enthralled with fairy tales of the Rhineland.

By August 21 he was back in England, fussily insisting that the Brookfields ought to go at once and take the cure at a German resort that he had heard extolled. For about six weeks after his return, he did not even look at the *Pendennis* manuscript. His work for *Punch* had to be made up. A Christmas book demanded attention, and because of the uncertain political prospects abroad he set aside the projected adventures of the Kicklebury family and made a fresh start with the subject of a boarding school. Arrangements for the arrival of his parents also occupied his time, and meanwhile he was providing shelter for a friend of his artist days in Paris, Louis Marvy, who had got into trouble during the recent revolution in France. Being in bad health, Marvy remained quietly in his room at Young Street, working hard on a series of engravings of famous paintings. In the midst of all these distractions, Thackeray wrote a rather trivial sketch for *The Keepsake*, an annual edited by his friend Lady Blessington.

He had become a member of her circle at Gore House only just in time to know it before its dissolution. The extravagance of the *ménage* could not much longer be sustained. The equivocal relationship between Her Ladyship and the elegant Comte d'Orsay, too, was reaching an intolerable point of complication. During these last months of 1848, while the threats of disaster were still being defied, a sort of hysterical gaiety reigned. In that over-decorated mansion Thackeray consorted with many wits and writers, and the atmosphere of unconstrained frankness sometimes betrayed him into indiscretion.

On one occasion he told Sir Henry Bulwer his unvarnished opinion of that gentleman's brother; and the next morning, remembering the friendship between Lady Blessington and Bulwer-Lytton, he felt heartily ashamed of himself, and sent her an apology: "I have no sort of personal dislike (not that it matters much whether I have or not) to Sir E. L. B. L.; on the contrary, the only time I met him at the immortal Ainsworth's long ago I thought him very pleasant, and I know from his conduct to my dear little Blanchard that he can be a most generous and delicate-minded friend. But there are sentiments in his writing which always anger me, big words which make me furious, and a premeditated fine writing against which I can't help rebelling. My antipathy don't go any further than this. What does it matter one way or the other, and what cause had I to select Sir H. Bulwer of all men in the world for these odious confidences? It was very rude. I am always making rude speeches and apologising for them, like a nuisance to society. And now I remember how Sir B. Lytton spoke in a very different manner to a mutual friend about your very humble servant."

Obsessed with his idea that novel-writing was a precarious business from which he would like to escape, he frankly sought to use Lady Blessington's influence on his behalf. When he heard that the post of Assistant Secretary of the Post Office was about to fall vacant, he wrote to her eagerly: "What a place for a man of letters! I think if Lord Clanricarde would give it to me I would satisfy my employers, and that my profession would be pleased by hearing of the employment of one of us. I wonder might I write to him, or is there any kind person who would advocate my cause?" Under its assumed nonchalance, with the trite pun and the pretense that he was an impersonal representative of authorship rather than an anxious place-hunter, the appeal is pathetic in its diffidence. Such eagerness for the monotony of an obscure berth in the civil service seems almost hysterical in a man who had just been acclaimed as one of the master novelists of his age. The Postmaster General was quite ready to oblige his charming lady friend, but discovered that he had not the authority to appoint an inexperienced outsider over the heads of trained employees. As soon as Thackeray suspected that he would not succeed in his application, he began to assure Lady Blessington that he would regret having to relinquish his "vagabond way of life" in favor of servitude to an office routine. "Another man has got it, and deserves it too," he reported to her with positive relief.

During the weeks while his application was in suspense Thackeray saw no reason to proceed with his novel. And there were other causes for his lack of interest. Almost every afternoon his horse might be seen standing in Portman Street, while he sat by the invalid's sofa courting her smiles with his fanciful talk. At the beginning of October she went down to Somerset to stay at Clevedon Court, the home of her parents. Thackeray was desolated. In his first letter to her, he described how he rode past the house in Portman Street, just to look up at the windows. "The usual boy started forward to take the horse. I laughed a sad laugh. I didn't want nobody to take the horse."

He opened his desk and gave one glance at *Pendennis*, untouched since Spa. Then he locked it up again, for he was just setting off to visit a friend in Bury St Edmunds. He missed the train, however; and having more than four hours to wait, he went to see Bradbury & Evans, who entreated him so pathetically to get to work that he gave up the jaunt to Bury and went to Brighton instead—although, as he confessed to Mrs Brookfield, he was tempted to make it Weston-Super-Mare (close to Clevedon) "only it seemed such a hint."

On his arrival in Brighton, "ill and out of spirits" and with his "heart very sore," he called first upon the Pattles; the attractive young sisters welcomed him affectionately, and "their talk and Virginia's beauty consoled me." The fresh sea air, bright sunlight and moonlight, and gay promenading crowds completed his restoration. Then one of Horace Smith's daughters told him an anecdote that suggested to him a better opening for *Pendennis* than the one already written. With this fresh impetus he went to work more energetically. Pendennis, he decided, "is a very good-natured generous young fellow, and I begin to like him considerably."

Mrs Brookfield's family invited him to visit Clevedon, but he regretfully refused. He felt he must go back to London for the arrival of his parents and must then devote ten days or so to making them feel at home. When their coming was delayed for a week by the Major's illness he had to keep on declining invitations to dinners and evening parties, not knowing what day they might arrive. The stimulus of his visit to Brighton was quickly destroyed.

His letters to Mrs Brookfield betrayed emotional tension. Not having heard from her for some days, he composed a letter in French, giving a florid account of his anxiety, and did not post it. Three days later he sent her a long missive, partly in an assumed hand, with the explanation that the use of a different language or calligraphy produced a complete change in his character. Whimsically elaborating the theory, he declared that she, too, was a different "Mrs B." to each of her friends, whom she ridiculed privately for the amusement of her husband. "You see I am making you out to be an Ogre's wife and poor William the Ogre, to whom you serve us up cooked for dinner." In such a letter as this he jested on and on as if he were clinging to his one connection with humankind; and he ended with admitting his strong temptation to "start off this instant for the G. W. station and come and shake hands, and ask your family for some dinner."

A few days later, when the Carmichael-Smyths had arrived, the confusion in his house was so great that he had to go to his club to do any work on *Pendennis*, for which Bradbury was dunning him insistently. As usual in moments of loneliness and unrest, he sought the consolation of the back-street taverns and their rowdy entertainments. He dropped in repeatedly at the Cyder Cellars for the latest turn there—the lugubrious ballad of Sam Hall, sung by a popular comedian named Ross. The number was always given about two in the morning; and as the singer straddled a chair and glared over the back of it at his tipsy audience, even the hardiest of them was disturbed by the blasphemy and concentrated bitterness of the chimney-sweep murderer, on the eve of his hanging, epitomized in the insistent refrain,

> I hate you one and all,
> Damn your eyes.

The performance was scarcely calculated to put Thackeray in better spirits. Bad weather increased his depression, and on top of all his other work he had resumed his writing for the *Morning Chronicle*, unable to withstand the temptation of five guineas per article. Brookfield had just gone down to Somerset to join his wife. "I have passed the day writing and trying to alter *Pendennis*, which is without any manner of doubt awfully stupid," Thackeray wrote to him; "The very best passages, which pleased the author only last week, looking hideously dull by the dull fog of this day. . . . Unless you come back, and as soon as my work is done, I thought a day or two would be pleasantly spent in your society, if the house of Clevedon admits of holding any more."

His demands for a renewal of the invitation were at last heeded, and he went down to spend a few days at the beautiful old manor, most of which dated from the fourteenth century. Fascinated with the history of the estate, he explored it eagerly, making copious sketches indoors and out. After this visit, the Brookfields returned to town while Thackeray proceeded to Oxford, to make some observations for the university scenes in *Pendennis*, as they were to be a careful composite of Oxford and Cambridge. After a long session of Senior Common Room port, he retired to the bed that had been assigned to him, but lay awake wondering whether Mrs Brookfield had been made worse by her journey.

The next day he went with a party of friends to see the park and pictures at Blenheim, and was amused by the pompous evidences of Marlborough's conceit. Among those who accompanied him was Arthur Hugh Clough, who impressed Thackeray by his simplicity and earnestness, especially when he sat down in the inn yard and began to teach a ragged child to read off a page of *Punch* that had been lying on the ground. The remaining days of the visit to Oxford were spent in a conscientious round of the colleges, with special delight in the singing of the choir boys at Magdalen chapel—"children's voices charm me so that they set all my sensibilities in a quiver." Looking back to the Clevedon visit as the happiest days of his whole life, he moved in a dreamy state half way between ecstasy and misery.

His admirers were full of enthusiasm over the first number of *Pendennis*. Alfred Tennyson described it in a letter to FitzGerald as "quite delicious—so mature." In London circles Abraham Hayward, taking great credit for the perspicacity of his review of *Vanity Fair*, behaved as though Thackeray were his personal protégé. When one of his numerous lady friends asked him to obtain a drawing from Thackeray for her album, Hayward forwarded her fulsome letter to the novelist, who cautioned him not to make any more requests of the sort, and added that "these praises from all quarters frighten rather than elate me." Hayward's reply was a gem of condescension: "Don't get nervous or think about criticism, or trouble yourself about the opinions of friends; you have completely beaten Dickens out of the inner circle already. I dine at Gore House today; look in if you can." At this choice specimen of snobbery Thackeray laughed so uproariously that he was afraid his stepfather in the next room would think him insane; and he couldn't refrain from sending it on to Mrs Brookfield to see if she found it as funny as he did.

The issue of *Vanity Fair* in volume form had enhanced his renown. It bore on its title-page the apt description, "A Novel without a Hero," and was affectionately dedicated to B. W. Procter. Even this natural token of friendship became mixed up with the current mystification over *Jane Eyre*. The editor of *The Athenaeum*, Charles Wentworth Dilke, insisted that the latter novel had actually been written jointly by Mr and Mrs Procter, and he refused to believe Thackeray's protestations of ignorance in the matter. Poor Thackeray was completely dazed. "I wonder whether it can be true?" he wrote to Brookfield; "it is just possible, and then what a singular circumstance is the +fire of the two dedications."

The gossip about the authors of the two novels came to a head at this time in a review written for the *Quarterly* by Elizabeth Rigby, an arrant blue-stocking who achieved a masterpiece of feline innuendo by reviewing *Jane Eyre* jointly with *Vanity Fair* and the annual report of the Governesses' Benevolent Institution. She retailed the legend that "Currer Bell" had been the model for Becky Sharp, and ended with the suggestive remark that she was probably a woman "who has, for some sufficient reason, long forfeited the society of her own sex."

Nor was this the only pin-prick publicly inflicted upon Thackeray. Charles Lever's revenge for the burlesque of his style now presented itself in his new novel, *Roland Cashel*, wherein an obvious caricature of Thackeray was inserted as "Elias Howle," an ill-bred, supercilious English journalist touring Ireland:

Mr. Elias Howle was a publisher's man of all work, ready for everything, from statistics to satire, and equally prepared to expound prophecy, or write squibs for Punch . . . He was the creator of that new school of travel, which writing expressly for London readers refers everything to the standard of "town" . . . He was large and heavily built, but neither muscular nor athletic; his frame and all his gestures indicated weakness and uncertainty. His head was capacious, but not remarkable for what phrenologists call moral development, while the sinister expression of his eyes, half submissive, half satirical, suggested doubts of his sincerity. There was nothing honest about him but his mouth; this was large, full, thick-lipped, and sensual; the mouth of one who loved to dine well, and yet felt that his agreeability was an ample receipt in full for the best entertainment that ever graced Blackwall or the "Frères" . . . Mr. Howle made his round of salutations, and although by his awkwardness tacitly acknowledging that they were palpably more habituated to the world's ways than himself, yet inwardly consoled by remarking certain little traits of manner and accent sufficiently provincial to be treasured up, and become very droll in print or a copper etching.

Though Thackeray asserted that the lampoon only made him laugh, and provided him with a good subject for the next of a series of *Punch* drawings called "Author's Miseries," he wrote to Chapman, who was Lever's publisher as well as his, hinting that Lever ought to be rebuked for stooping to personal insult.

Even the success of *Pendennis* did not free him from other tasks. His *Punch* contributions, which he was finding harder and harder to grind out, were tending toward poetry, and in a couple of Cockney-dialect ballads he introduced an ingratiating character, "Policeman X." December brought the appearance of the Christmas book, *Doctor Birch and his Young Friends*, chiefly notable as one of the many evidences that Thackeray's memories of his school days were incurably perverted by the physical and mental cruelties—thrashings and sarcasm—that he had been subjected to. In the middle of December he felt that he must "go down to Brighton tomorrow, or somewhere where I can be alone and think about my friend Mr Pendennis, whom I have been forced to neglect. I have been working now until seven o'clock and am dead beat, having done a poor dawdling day's work, writing too much, hipped, hacked, and blue-devilled." As usual, the change to Brighton stimulated him, and he wrote doggedly on the book, with an occasional dinner at Morier's or Horace Smith's as his only relaxation. Smith's three daughters encouraged him by their interest in the story, and the youngest, Laura, was flattered to be assured that she was the model for the heroine.

A couple of weeks before, Thackeray had been horrified to hear of the death of his beloved college friend Charles Buller. Although Buller's political career had carried him somewhat beyond Thackeray's orbit, the latter had never lost his sense of almost brotherly kinship with him. In his overwrought state of feeling Thackeray applied the event to himself. "Good God!" he wrote to Mrs Brookfield, "think about the poor mother surviving, and what an anguish that must be! If I were to die I cannot bear to think of my mother living beyond me, as I daresay she will. But isn't it an awful, awful, sudden summons? There go wit, fame, friendship, ambition, high repute. Ah! *aimons nous bien.* It seems to me that is the only thing we can carry away. When we go, let us have some who love us wherever we are."

All his feelings of the moment got so mixed up with the book that he scarcely knew what he was writing. For many weeks, ever since that agonizing time when Jane Brookfield had been away at Clevedon, he had been fully aware of the depth of his feeling for her. She was now staying in Southampton again for treatment, and one of her doctors persistently lectured her with evangelical dogmas about the duty of "self-annihilation" and the suppression of all pleasant indulgences, including affection for others. In his reply Thackeray argued on behalf of love, and showed himself still preoccupied with thoughts of death. If Jane were to die first, he said, she would intercede for him in heaven; if he were the first to die, he would find his immortality in the loving memory of him that would survive in her heart. And he repeated his mystical creed: "Love proves God. By love I believe and am saved."

These thoughts had come to him while he was writing a letter to Lady Ashburton. All Buller's friends had known of the affection existing between him and this lady, the wife of one of his closest friends. It was a recognition of this further parallel between Buller and himself that prompted Thackeray to the unconventional step of sending Lady Ashburton a letter of condolence. In mentioning it to Mrs Brookfield, he showed how morbid he still felt, three weeks after his friend's death: "I feel as if I were making my will and getting ready to march too."

In Mrs Brookfield's sympathetic reply, she assured him that Lady Ashburton must have appreciated his thoughtfulness. "It is one of the most painful and absurd ways of the world," she went on, "to assume that one is in affliction for anyone who happens to have been related to us, while intimacies which must have a much deeper root from having been sought out for ourselves and made where real sympathy exists,—these are so soon to be forgotten. 'Only a friend, no relation,' you hear said many times when the words should be reversed into 'only a relation!'"

Another matter that continued to haunt Thackeray's mind was her physician's "blasphemous asceticism." He challenged it with arguments remarkably similar to those that Browning shaped a few years later in *Fra Lippo Lippi*. In an unwonted burst of rhetoric, Thackeray expatiated upon his belief that all the beauty of the physical world and all the experiences of human life were to be enjoyed as the manifestations of God's will. So long as he loved her, he declared, and knew that she and a few others were thinking of him "with a tender regard," he felt sure that Heaven might be "greater in degree, but not in kind."

Thus under such disguises as discussing one friend's untimely death and another friend's religious doctrines, they both ventured dangerously close to the forbidden ground of their feelings for one another. Thackeray, indeed, sometimes tested the frontiers of that ground with a venturesome toe. Whenever his emotions were over excited, it was his habit to pour them out in a long letter to some friend, and then—cooling off into embarrassment for his hysteria—he would burn it. At this juncture he destroyed almost as many letters to Mrs Brookfield as he posted; but even in those that were despatched there were indiscreet phrases that worried him when it was too late. He would wait in an agony of suspense, for fear she would ignore the letter or would reply only to condemn him.

After an interview with her just before she left for Southampton he had sat up all night trying to write a poem, which he mentioned in his next note, but which he changed his mind about sending. With natural curiosity she demanded it, and he obediently enclosed it in his next letter. Both the letter and the verses struck her as requiring reproof, and her reply was a masterpiece of tactful warning. She would keep the ballad, she said, "as a curiosity and perhaps leave it with all your letters as a legacy to Annie for her to work into your memoir according to her discretion 50 years hence. Do you know that if you do not write in more common-place style to me I shall be quite unable to answer you at all—I have just read your letter over again and thought how flat and dull all that I could say would be. . ."

For a writer whose work was so interpenetrated with his personal life as Thackeray's was, these emotional crises were bound to affect what he was creating. The opening scenes of *Pendennis* became a baffling mixture of satirical realism with sentimentality. He himself commented upon this new softness of his with some amazement, while telling Mrs Brookfield about his mother's unbounded devotion to him and his children. After calling her "Mater Dolorosa, with a heart bleeding with love," he added: "Is not that a pretty phrase? I wrote it yesterday in a book, whilst I was thinking about her—and have no shame somehow now in writing thus sentimentally to all the public; though there are very few people in the world to whom I would have the face to talk in this way *tête-à-tête*."

His often-reiterated vindication of the innocence of his love for Jane Brookfield was the fact that her husband was aware of it. Undoubtedly the clergyman had the fullest confidence in his wife's virtue and his friend's honor. His affection for Thackeray had grown steadily since their undergraduate days, and was now merged with an admiration for his literary achievements that made Brookfield eager to do anything that would enhance the novelist's success. Obviously Mrs Brookfield's sympathy had been for several years the only encouragement sufficient to sustain Thackeray through his loneliness and dejection. Equally obviously, she was gratified by Thackeray's allegiance. For these reasons, Brookfield felt certain that he was playing the noble rôle of the unselfish friend, and not the contemptible one of the *mari complaisant*.

Other people, however, were less charitable. A new addition to the Brook-field household was Jane's handsome and charming young cousin, Harry Hallam, who had just come down from Cambridge after a brilliant undergraduate career. Although he had a strong admiration for Thackeray, young Hallam became annoyed and a bit jealous on discovering how much his beautiful cousin was interested in the novelist, whose furrowed face and prematurely white hair made him seem much older than his thirty-seven years. Before long, Hallam's ill temper boiled over, and he gave voice to some biting comments on the frequency of Thackeray's visits. As soon as Thackeray got home after this embarrassing scene, he wrote Mrs Brookfield a note. He began by conceding that Hallam's jealousy was natural, since no man could be much in her company without feeling the same regard for her that Thackeray had acquired years before. But he was determined not to be put down by a young sprig of twenty-four, and so he returned to his argument that there could be no harm in an affection that had never been concealed from her husband. The mere fact that Hallam was a relation gave him no right to "question or supersede" Thackeray's claim to love both the husband and the wife. He suggested that if Hallam raised any question he should be told frankly that Thackeray was regarded by Jane in the light of a brother. With her permission, her husband's, and that of his own conscience, he felt justified in seeing her if possible every day, and no one else ought to have a right to deny him his greatest happiness.

Thus fortified in his platonic adoration, he continued to visit her as often as ever, and to write her long letters when they were apart, addressing her in such terms as "chère soeur, si douce et si bonne." But the recollection of Hallam's suspicion must have cast a faint but ominous shadow over the sunshine of their friendship.

At the end of January, 1849, Thackeray went off on a visit to Paris, very different from his previous sojourns there. He stayed comfortably at Meurice's Hotel in the Rue de Rivoli, and was treated with high distinction by the English Ambassador. "Lord Normanby is my dearest friend," he reported; "he is going to take me to the President—very likely to ask me to dinner. You would have thought I was an earl." The Embassy secretary got him a ticket to a debate in the Chamber of Deputies, which was still seething in the backwash of the previous year's revolution; one of the Rothschilds gave him a place in his box at the Opera; he attended a huge ball at the Prefecture of Police, at which "I felt dimly that I was 3 inches taller than anybody else in the room but I hoped that nobody took notice of me." Another evening he was at a dinner party given by the Hon Spencer Cowper, a fabulously wealthy young man, and sent Mrs Brookfield a jubilant account of "the Sybaritic repast, the magnificent apartment" and the "young voluptuaries of fashion." He added that in some of the company he "saw a chapter or two of *Pendennis*." The discovery of literary material was coming to be cited more and more often as justification for the amount of time he spent in social amusements.

To emphasize the contrast of past and present, he visited some of his old art-student haunts, and was moved to such a mood of gentle regret for those days of irresponsible poverty that he embodied it in his charming *Ballad of Bouillabaisse*. He called upon Jules Janin, the literary editor of the *Journal des Débats*, and found him so cordial and amusing that he invited him and the critic of the *Revue des Deux Mondes* to dinner. The usual observances of Thackeray family loyalty also had to be respected, though with a faint sense of martyrdom. Two of his aunts were now in Paris, for Doctor and Mrs Halliday had returned from India and joined the Ritchies there. But a more remarkable personage was his cousin, Mrs Carmichael, who made friends with him again after six years' estrangement. When she showed him all the letters from her devoted husband, who was in India, and bragged about the half-dozen admirers who were pursuing her, Thackeray contrasted the garrulous, flirtatious grass-widow with the affectionate child she had been at Larkbeare. "Oh! Becky is a trifle to her," he marveled. "By all the Gods! I never had the opportunity of inspecting such naturalness and coquetry; not that I suppose that there are not many such women; but I have only myself known one or two women intimately, and I daresay the novelty would wear off if I knew more." She insisted on taking him to consult a medium named Alexis, who—she asserted—had told the fortunes of her friends by merely touching sealed letters from them; whereupon Thackeray wrote off to Mrs Brookfield demanding a lock of her hair to be used for a consultation. "Mind you," he added, "I don't want it for myself; I pledge you my word I'll burn it, or give you back every single hair."

The chief value of the trip to France was that it provided him with subjects for several weeks' contributions to *Punch*, a task which had become so wearisome that he had been thinking of giving up the connection. To follow these Parisian sketches he started a rather mild series of "Mr Brown's Letters to a Young Man about Town," preaching a mellow tolerance that seemed like an apology for the mordancy of the "Snob" papers. About the same time, he wrote the notes to accompany a volume of engravings by his refugee friend, Marvy.

In March, when Brookfield was to spend a day in Cambridge at the beginning of an inspection tour, Thackeray took the opportunity of going there with him. As they stepped into the Bull Inn they were recognized by Jenny Lind's agent and given complimentary tickets to her concert. They devoted the day to a sentimental pilgrimage through their undergraduate scenes, and Thackeray felt very old and pleasantly melancholy. Dinner in hall at Trinity with Dr Thompson was chiefly remarkable for the familiarity of the savory accumulated smells of roast veal and mutton, that transported Thackeray back to his freshman days. When they returned to the inn, Brookfield remarked that his wife would then be at a dinner at Lady Monteagle's. "Let's drink her health," suggested Thackeray, and they pledged her solemnly in ale and soda-water, and both said "God bless her," not too loudly, to avoid waking a bagman asleep in the coffee room.

The Lind concert proved so dull that they left at the first intermission; and when Brookfield took the night train for Norwich, Thackeray was too forlorn to continue the visit and went back to London the next day. "I think," he reported to Jane, "William is a little disappointed that I have not been made enough of a lion of, whereas my timid nature trembles before such honours, and my vanity would be to go through life as a gentleman—as a Major Pendennis—you have hit it. I believe I never do think about my public character, and certainly didn't see the gyps, waiters, and undergraduates whispering in hall, as your William did, or thought he did."

He came home unwillingly, for he was finding that the constant presence of his humorless mother and stepfather made him silent and gloomy. His unlucky speculation in the Irish Railway continued to be a drag upon his resources. In April, when the departure of the Brookfields for Somerset had reduced him as usual to despondency, he received a lawyer's letter demanding immediate payment of £112 for which he was liable. As his total available cash was £120, an overdraft at his bank would be necessary to cover the month's expenses. In a letter to his brother-in-law he estimated that his income had reached nearly £2000 a year, but its sudden rise had been only a matter of the past few months, and so—in view of the railway

JULES JANIN

speculation—he was still in debt. The effect of this blow was to dispel his dreary self pity, which was largely an excuse for dodging work on the novel in hand, and he applied himself to the job with desperate energy.

The London season, however, was at its height, and neither work, depression, nor financial worries could interfere with his round of engagements. He had improved his acquaintance with Lady de Rothschild, and she saw him often not only at her own home but at those of her mother, Mrs Montefiore, and her kinsman, Baron Lionel de Rothschild. She always mentioned him in her diary as "amusing and good-natured" or "sympathetic," and in contrasting him with Charles Villiers, a wit who moved in the same orbit, she said, "I greatly prefer Thackeray because he joins to wit and humour and fun deep and good feeling, which he is never ashamed of showing and which makes one like, as well as admire him." Nevertheless, after one of his visits she was obliged to confess that "when he talked of so many of the great, the beautiful and the clever who are all anxious to attract his notice and admiration, I felt that he must be a *little* spoilt, or at least that there was not much to attract him here."

He was becoming intimate with the Earl of Carlisle, an amateur poet and scholar; he gave Vizetelly an amusing account of a dinner party at which the Earl, naïvely hoping for an evening of incomparable wit and humour, had invited nobody but the staff of *Punch*. "We all know each other's pet stories, and all the dear old jokes, and this acted as a wet blanket upon us. No one would have thought of trotting out a good new story simply for one of his *confrères* to crib for his next magazine article. If Lord Carlisle had asked half a dozen literary men and half a dozen lords, we should in this case have fit audience found, and been able to amuse the quality at the trifling inconvenience of boring ourselves."

More than all the great mansions, however, he was gratified to be admitted to the drawing-room of the two ancient Miss Berrys. Miss Mary, who had once received a proposal of marriage from Horace Walpole, was eighty-six, and her sister Agnes was a year younger. They had been familiar with all the intellectual lions from the days of Dr Johnson, and to Thackeray they were a magical link with his beloved eighteenth century. His friend Kate Perry, who was an habituée of their still brilliant little salon, praised him so highly that they gave him an invitation. He showed his delight by including a description of Miss Mary in one of his "Mr Brown" letters in *Punch:*

There sits an old lady of more than fourscore years, serene and kind, and as beautiful in her age now as in her youth, when History toasted her . . . She is as simple now as if she had never had any flattery to dazzle her; she is never tired of being pleased and being kind. Can that have been anything but a good life which, after more than eighty years of it are spent, is so calm? . . . We do not know what goodness and charity, what affections, what trials may have gone to make that charming sweetness of temper, and complete that perfect manner . . .

This device of paying compliments in print proved to be a convenient way of discharging social obligations. In the passage on maternal love, near the beginning of *Pendennis*, he uttered his tribute to Lady de Rothschild:

I saw a Jewish lady, only yesterday, with a child at her knee, and from whose face towards the child there shone a sweetness so angelical, that it seemed to form a sort of glory round both. I protest I could have knelt before her too, and adored in her the Divine beneficence in endowing us with the maternal *storgé*, which began with our race and sanctifies the history of mankind.

All the indications of social compliance in the once-intransigent Thackeray were noted by Thomas Carlyle, who voiced his disapproval to his young interviewer Gavan Duffy. "Thackeray is essentially a man of grim, silent, stern nature, but lately he has circulated among fasionable people, dining out every day, and he covers this native disposition with a varnish of smooth, smiling complacency, not at all pleasant to contemplate. The course he has got into, since he has taken to cultivate dinner-eating at fashionable houses, is not salutary discipline for work of any sort, one may surmise."

Carlyle's dour Scottish disapproval was neatly counterbalanced by an unexpected tribute that came to Thackeray from a group of Scottish admirers. Eighty residents of Edinburgh, not one of whom was personally known to him, subscribed for a silver statuette of Punch as a token of their pleasure in his work. To Dr John Brown, the physician and essayist, who had organized the subscription, he sent a reply that clearly defined the rôle he had elected for himself in literature: "Such tokens of regard and sympathy are very precious to a writer like myself, who have some difficulty still in making people understand what you have been good enough to find in Edinburgh—that under the mask satirical there walks about a sentimental gentleman, who means not unkindly to any mortal person. . . I assure you, these tokens of what I can't help acknowledging as popularity make me very humble as well as grateful, and make me feel an almost awful sense of the responsibility which falls upon a man in such a station. Is it deserved or undeserved? Who is this that sets up to preach to mankind, and to laugh at many things which men reverence? I hope I may be able to tell truth always, and see it aright, according to the eyes which God Almighty gives me. . . I can't feel otherwise than very grave, when people begin to praise me, as you do."

This expression of humility was perfectly sincere: it echoed often in Thackeray's letters to his mother and in the resolutions confided to his diary. But when he displayed the statuette to his colleagues on the *Punch* staff, they must have felt somewhat bitter that their patient labors for the paper should go unrecognized while the glittering Thackeray, the consorter with earls and dukes, was singled out as *Punch's* premier celebrity.

Being obliged to go down to Devonshire on business, he suggested that he might stop off for a couple of hours at Clifton, where Mrs Brookfield was staying with her sister. Perhaps, he hinted, he might be asked to lunch. As a result, he was able to spend nearly two days there in his lady's company. He came back to London lonelier than ever, very sorry for himself to be so overworked and over-dinnered. In spite of all his affection for his parents, he found their solemnity so depressing that he felt obliged to suggest to his mother that she might take the children over to stay in Paris for a while.

Mrs Brookfield, worrying over the neurotic tension in his letters and trying to control him with her usual mixture of elusive tenderness and mild irony, assured him that it was a good plan. He was wearing himself out, she warned him, by trying to act three or four different rôles at the same time. He was the author and the man-about-town, the satirist and the sentimentalist; at least he might gain a little rest if for a while he did not have to sustain the exacting characterization of the family man.

Teasing him about his conquest of society, she implied that he was becoming the very model of Major Pendennis, the tuft-hunting old worldling in his novel. The jest had more than a grain of truth in it. An almost childish love of admiration and an almost snobbish pride in the company of titled folk were beginning to show themselves, naturally enough after the years of obscurity when he had felt degraded from his proper rank by the hack writing that was his only support. Why should he not now enjoy moving easily in the best society by virtue of that same calling that had formerly meant his ostracism? He sometimes astonished his noble new friends by the emphasis with which he informed them that he had no source of income except his pen. With her gentle sarcasm Jane Brookfield pricked his complacency when it threatened to become pompous; but this did not deter him from continuing to retail to her the roster of his triumphs.

CHAPTER 12

The Valley of the Shadow

MORE AND MORE he found the stimulation of society essential for keeping up his spirits. The writing of *Pendennis* was unremittingly painful. At the end of April he was utterly tired out with the effort of finishing Part Seven. "I don't know whether it is good or bad," he told Mrs Brookfield; "the latter probably." Having waited at the Club for the printer's devil to bring the proofs, he went home to dress for one of his usual evenings—Lady Lovelace's drum in Cumberland Place, and a visit to the Miss Berrys—but threw himself down on his bed and slept around the clock.

When he awoke in the morning, the "great throes and disquiet" with which he had managed to complete Number Seven the day before seemed strangely far away. He set out for the day in company with his mother and the children: first to Shoolbred's to buy a gown for Mrs Carmichael-Smyth, next to Madame Victorine's to order dresses for the girls, then a heroic round of calls—on Mrs Elliot (and her sympathetic sister, Kate Perry), on Mrs Prinsep (and her beautiful sister, Virginia Pattle), on Lady de Rothschild, on Henry Hallam, on Mrs James, on Lady Pollock, on her daughter-in-law. All this feminine charm was highly therapeutic. "The children seemed to stare," he confessed to Mrs Brookfield, "to hear me laugh and talk—I never do at home." He ended the day by having Brookfield, Clarkson Stanfield the artist, and Francis Fladgate to dine with him at the Garrick. They were supposed to go on to Mrs Sartoris, but stayed where they were to chat over two bottles of champagne until too late.

The routine went on through the weeks of the Season. He was flattered by being invited to the Royal Academy banquet—"that's a great honour, none but bishops, purchasers, and other big-wigs are asked"—but he found it "a very cold and formal affair." An unexpected sequel was the heart-burning inflicted on Dickens, who had not received an invitation. According to his friend Maclise, Dickens cherished his grievance for twelve months, and—upon receiving an invitation to the banquet the next year—sent "a very stiff note" of refusal. Here again one cannot help suspecting the hand of Forster, who seldom missed an opportunity to call the attention of his friends to indignities that they might otherwise overlook.

Miss Rigby, author of the captious critique of *Vanity Fair* in the *Quarterly Review*, had just married Charles Eastlake, R.A., and she made her bridal *début* at a party given by Lady Davy, the widow of the scientist, one of Thackeray's most frequent hostesses. Whether or not he knew that she had written the review,

Thackeray made himself particularly agreeable. "He pleased me much," Mrs East-lake noted in her diary; "he bewailed himself that he had not received our cards, which were accordingly sent him the next day." During the rest of the Season they met frequently, and her comment more than once was "very diverting," or "very agreeable."

Encountering him at the Eastlakes' reception, his friend Pollock got the im-pression that he had "grown a little *blasé*, and is not quite such good company as he used to be." In somewhat the same strain of criticism, Monckton Milnes re-marked in a letter to a friend that "Thackeray is winning great social success, dining at the Academy, Sir R. Peel's, &c. I doubt whether he will be much the happier for it, though I think people generally are the better for satisfied vanity."

Even in the midst of such distractions, he did not lack a reminder of the grim depths below the glittering surface. The catastrophe in Lady Blessington's *ménage* had at last occurred, and she and D'Orsay had fled to Paris, leaving her ornate mansion to the mercy of her creditors. Thackeray went for a last glimpse of Gore House and found it "full of snobs looking at the furniture." He was disgusted to see "brutes keeping their hats on in the kind old drawing room—I longed to knock some of them off, and say 'Sir, be civil in a lady's room' . . . There was one of the servants there, not a powdered one, but a butler. My heart melted towards him and I gave him a pound. Ah! it was a strange, sad picture of Vanity Fair. My mind is all boiling up with it." Equally touched by the unexpected tip, the French *maître d'hôtel* wrote to his mistress that "M. Thackeray est venu aussi, et avait les larmes aux yeux en partant. C'est peut-être la seule personne qui j'ai vu réelement affecté en votre départ." Less than a month later the still beautiful and brilliant woman, with nothing left to live for, died in Paris of a heart attack that might be diagnosed not unjustly as a broken heart.

The apparent rivalry of Thackeray and Dickens was emphasized at this juncture by the appearance of the first number of *David Copperfield*. No reader could avoid drawing comparisons between the two semi-autobiographical novels about a young man's development into authorship. Thackeray, as usual, was enthusiastic about his friend's genius, and candidly envious of his power to touch the public's heart; but there was a tinge of irony in the praises that he uttered to Mrs Brookfield: "O! it is charming! Bravo Dickens! It has some of his very prettiest touches—those inimitable Dickens touches which make such a great man of him; and the reading of the book has done another author a great deal of good. In the first place it pleases the other author to see that Dickens, who has long left off alluding to the A's works, has been copying the O.A. and greatly simplifying his style, and foregoing the use of fine words. By this the public will be the gainer and *David Copperfield* will be improved by taking a lesson from *Vanity Fair*. Secondly it has put me upon my mettle; for ah! Madame, all the mettle was out of me and I have been dreadfully and curiously cast down this month past."

Thackeray's assumption was probably correct: the increased naturalness and simplicity of style in *David Copperfield* may well have sprung from a perception of Thackeray's adept control of easy conversational prose. At any rate, in spite of Dickens's pique over the R. A. banquet, there was no ill will between the two novelists. The dinner given by Dickens on May 12 in honor of the first number included Thackeray in a notable company along with the Carlyles, Mrs Gaskell, Samuel Rogers, Douglas Jerrold, Kenyon, Forster, and "Phiz." Thackeray's social dexterity came into play when a foggy metaphysical discussion threatened to blanket the conversation. Carlyle was seated next to the Rev. Edward Tagart, an earnest Unitarian minister who began to question Carlyle about his conceptions of heaven and hell. To everyone's relief, Thackeray blandly interrupted with, "That reminds me of our friend Macready's story about the country actor in *The Castle Spectre*," and he proceeded to tell a ridiculous anecdote with his best whimsicality.

In spite of his enviable ease in conversation, he had by no means conquered his dread of speaking in public. When asked to talk at the annual dinner of the Literary Fund, he found himself as terrified as he had been the year before. At midnight of the fatal evening he fled from the Freemasons Tavern to the Garrick Club and dashed off an incoherent note to the Brookfields, who were visiting Cambridge: "I have made an awful smash at the Literary Fund and have tumbled into 'Evins knows where;—it was a tremendous exhibition of imbecility. . . I am talking quite loud to myself at the Garrick sentences I intended to have uttered; but they wouldn't come in time."

On his way home in a cab he continued to explode with undelivered fragments of the speech, and at Young Street he found the house lighted up and his mother waiting to hear his report. He announced that he was utterly beaten and had made a fool of himself, but his mother interrupted him with a cry of protest, "No you didn't, old man." She had secretly slipped down to the tavern and listened to the whole program from the gallery, hidden by a pillar, and she assured him that his was the best speech of the evening. Furthermore, she got up very early the next morning and told the little girls all about it, so that when they came downstairs they greeted their father with raptures over his "beautiful speech." This domestic solace, reinforced by a visit to some of his most admiring lady friends, restored his equanimity, as did a visit from Lord and Lady Castlereagh and—still more gratifying—a call from his old adversary Bulwer-Lytton. By the end of the week, he was able not only to tell Mrs Brookfield that "the discomfiture will make a good chapter for Pen" but also to face a bar dinner at which he would probably be called on for another speech—"I don't mind about failing there, so I shall do pretty well."

At the beginning of June the Brookfields were back in London; Thackeray dined with them on the first with the usual circle—Kinglake, Spedding, Pollock, Higgins, Doyle, and Harry Hallam. A week later, on Annie's birthday, he invited Mrs Brookfield—"being, as I must consider you, if you please, the children's aunt" —to join an expedition to the Colosseum and the Zoo. On the eleventh he had the Brookfields, the Pollocks, and the Carlyles to dinner at Young Street. His temporary friction with Carlyle was at an end, and by this time he knew how to deal with the grumpy Sage of Chelsea. "Carlyle is a great bully," he explained, at one of the Miss Berrys' dinner parties, "but he can be silenced by persiflage."

Mrs Carmichael-Smyth, meanwhile, had gone to Fareham owing to the illness of her Aunt Becher, and the day after his dinner party Thackeray hurried down to be with them, as the doctor gave warning that the end was near. The kind protector of his childhood was so cheerful that he could scarcely believe she was in danger, and came back to London to go on with his instalment.

At the end of June he discovered that Mrs Brookfield was expecting a baby. He stayed awake the whole of that night in an agony of jealous fury, and then reconciled himself with thoughts of her future happiness. With his usual indiscretion, when he saw Harry Hallam the next day he burst out with a remark about the impending event. Brookfield, who was just setting out on his annual sea-cruise with a friend, left a letter of protest to Thackeray, including a hint that if Thackeray ate heartier breakfasts he might not drop in at Portman Square so often for lunch. Thackeray sent a contrite reply in pursuit of the yacht, and for the next week was punctilious in asking permission before he called upon the lady. She then left for her usual visit to Southampton, leaving him miserable but manfully determined not to follow her. When he wrote a letter to Adelaide Procter, two days later, thanking her for a gift, he had such a "black-edged border" around him that he was ashamed of his lugubriousness.

With the Procters he had recently renewed good relations after being upon strained terms for several months, because their daughter Adelaide, who at twenty-three was developing the soulful and moralistic tastes that were eventually to make her the author of *The Lost Chord*, had shown a tendency to find fault with his informal ways, and Mrs Brookfield had encouraged him to "give her a little quiet set-down." As a token of contrition, Adelaide had now sent him an elegant velvet purse, embroidered with his initials, and forget-me-nots on the other side, whereupon he was moved to one of his moods of feeling immensely aged. "I received this peace-offering with a gentle heart," he told Mrs Brookfield; "one must not lose old friends at our time of life, and if one has offended them one must try and try until they are brought back." And then when he wrote his letter of acknowledgment he found that instead of expressing his thanks he "only discoursed about old age, disappointment, death, and melancholy."

His despondency had several causes, but the most persistent was his worry about the financial future. He felt certain that he would not be able to sustain his success as a novelist for more than three or four years, and he was eager for some assured source of income to relieve him of the tension of depending solely on each month's stint of writing to pay for his children's bread. Medical warnings as to his health were forcing him to think somberly about providing for the future of his daughters. When he had been called to the bar in the previous year, it was with the recollection of how Henry Fielding had been able to combine novel-writing with the duties of a metropolitan magistrate. His friend Monckton

Milnes, knowing of his hopes, now made an effort to recommend him for a vacancy on the bench; but Thackeray had to notify him regretfully that he was not eligible, as the appointee would have to be a barrister of at least seven years' standing. "Time will qualify me, however," he went on, "and I hope to be able to last six years in the literary world; for though I shall write, I dare say, very badly, yet the public won't find it out for some time, and I shall live upon my past reputation. It is a pity, to be sure. If I could get a place and rest, I think I could do something better than I have done, and leave a good and lasting book behind me; but Fate is overruling." He added a query as to whether Lord Palmerston, as Foreign Secretary, might be able to place him in the Consular Service, "but," he ended, "I would rather be in London."

His family, meanwhile, blissfully unaware of the sleepless nights he was suffering on their account, finally decided on South Wales for their vacation, but he himself preferred his beloved Brighton. Even there he could not escape from morbid thoughts, for Horace Smith had died the day before he arrived, and his other literary friend, James Morier, had likewise died four months before. The sea

breeze and sunshine refreshed him, however; he ate heartily, and fell asleep over
the novel he was reading in the evening. The next day a letter from Mrs Brookfield, mentioning the incurable illness of her friend Mrs Fanshawe, plunged him
back in gloomy moralizing: "I don't see that living is such a benefit, and could
find it in my heart pretty readily to have an end of it,—after wasting a deal of
opportunities and time and desires in vanitarianism." He sought consolation in
trying to draw a likeness of Mrs Brookfield and in writing some dejected verses
about its inadequacy.

He dined alone every day and spent most of the time reading novels. One day
he devoured a Dumas novel for nine hours at a stretch. "What wouldn't I give to
have his knack of putting a story together!" he exclaimed. He confessed to Mrs
Brookfield that it has taken him many hours to write two pages of his current
story; and yet, he added, he was determined that "Mr Pendennis shan't dawdle
any more, and that I'll do something to fetch up my languishing reputation—
something uncommonly sarcastic, pathetic, humorous it must be. Can you give
me a hint or two? A guinea for a hint or two." A letter to his mother, written on
July 18—his thirty-eighth birthday—announced that his brains had almost refused
to work for several days past, but were beginning to get into action.

He had expected to spend his birthday in solitude, but Brookfield turned up
on an inspection trip, and Thackeray put in part of the day with him in the national
schoolroom, surrounded by a score of urchins writing examination papers. In the
evening the Inspector escaped early from a duty dinner to join Thackeray at his
club "where he was entertaining two dragoons with the wicked weed and wickeder
distillation."

A pleasant interlude for Thackeray was a short visit to Ryde, where Mrs
Brookfield was staying with her married brother. Having to go up to London on
the 24th, to make two plates for the next number—a task that took only two hours—
he found all his friends out of town and felt as miserable as he used to be on the
first day of school after the holidays. As soon as Number Ten was safely off his
hands, he went to Wales to join his family for a brief glimpse of rural quiet, and
then returned to his London tasks. At the end of August he was disturbed again
by the specter of death which had seemed to be dogging him for months past. This
time it was his Aunt Augusta, Mrs Halliday, who was desperately ill, and he
hastened over to Paris to be with her.

Mrs Ritchie and her daughters told him that Mrs Halliday had been wandering in her mind for weeks past; two days before her nephew's arrival she had been
imagining in her delirium that she was once more attending the deathbed of her
handsome young brother Richmond Thackeray as he wasted away with fever on
board a hospital ship in the Ganges. This reminder of his father's early death,
unexpectedly conjured up from the mists of the past and illuminated with the

ghastly vividness of hallucination, distressed Thackeray profoundly. His strong sense of family loyalty, however, obliged him to remain to "pay my last duties to one of our race who is dropping away." He therefore took a suite of rooms and settled down for an indefinite stay, which became a ghastly compound of morbid brooding and Parisian frivolity.

He began by hiring a *domestique de place,* but kept him for only two days, "for the idea that he was in the ante-room ceaselessly with nothing to do, made my life in my own room intolerable." At the art exhibition, he found "scarcely six decent pictures in the whole enormous collection." He went to the theater, but could stand only an hour of the farce, "which made me laugh while it lasted, but left a profound black melancholy behind it." A merry evening was spent with Jules Janin and two other journalistic friends at the Restaurant du Petit Moulin Rouge in the Champs Elysées; while they drank their small wine in a private room, Thackeray amused himself by stuffing the good-humored Janin with fantastic "authentic secrets" of London. There is a trace of pique in his remark to Mrs Brookfield: "Did you ever read any of the works of Janin?—No? Well he has been for 20 years famous in France, and he on his side has never heard of the works of Titmarsh, nor has anybody else here and that is a comfort." The next night he went to the play again and "I suppose because it was Sunday, was especially diverted, and laughed so as to make myself an object in the stalls; but it was at pure farcicality, not at wit."

None of these diversions dispelled his despondency for more than a moment. As the death of some other Thackeray had recently been announced in *Galignani,* all his friends in Paris had assumed it was he. "There's a glum sort of humour in all this, I think," he remarked, "and I grin like a skull." On picking up a copy of Number Seven of *Pendennis,* written only four months before, he was horrified to find "a picture which was perfectly new and a passage which I had as utterly forgotten as if I had never read or written it. This shortness of memory frightens me, and makes me have gloomy anticipations. Will poor Annie have to nurse an old imbecile of a father some day, who will ramble incoherently about old days and people whom he used to love?"

He encountered Ainsworth, with whom a slight coolness had developed in recent years; they dined next to each other at the *Trois Frères* "and rather fraternized. He showed a friendly disposition I thought, and a desire to forgive me my success; but beyond a good-humoured acquiescence in his good will, I don't care. I suppose one doesn't care for people, only for a very, very few." After expatiating to Mrs Brookfield at great length in this vein, with incoherent interjections in French about growing old and forgetful, and inflicting his egotism upon her, he ended with a sneer at himself: "Je fais de la littérature, ma parole d'honneur!—du style—du Sterne tout pur—O vanitas vanitatum."

Disturbed by the hysterical note in this letter, Jane replied with words of comfort and flattery. "When you suggested you may end in a fatuous old age without memory, &c., I merely thought how much better suited I should be for a friend to you when you are brought a little more to my level; and perhaps when you are in that state you will see what a nice provision you have made in securing an idiotic sister in your comparative early life. . . But I wish you could be made independent of having to work so constantly. I sometimes imagine legacies from unknown individuals coming in to me, and I make the handsomest settlements in an anonymous manner upon Annie and Minny. I wish they would come true some day and that I could 'hand you over your freedom.' " She quoted extensive praises for *Vanity Fair* from her brother, who had been such an "absurd Dickensite" that he had not previously read it; and she went on to a somewhat unkind anecdote of meeting Ainsworth in Venice. "I recollect saying you 'had such an affectionate nature,' which Mr Ainsworth made me repeat about 3 times, pretending not to hear, and I felt I had thrown pearls before swine and been unnecessarily frank in my praise of you, and began to think he might very possibly have a feeling of jealousy about you as an author, tho' it would be ludicrously presumptuous in him—as of all detestable writing his is the worst, I think."

These unwonted concessions to Thackeray's craving for admiration betrayed Jane's anxiety about his dismal mood. "Forgive this nonsense," she begged, later in the letter; "I wish I could make you laugh even if it were only at me." By the time it reached him, his aunt's death had occurred, and he was deep in the duties that he felt incumbent upon him. He spent many hours with the bereaved husband, bawling into his deaf ears and admiring the stoicism of old age, while at the same time he observed with a novelist's eye the ironies of the situation.

The visits of consolation were interspersed with affectionate but rather dreary sessions with his surviving aunt, Mrs Ritchie. "This isn't very amusing," he confessed, "but the sense of virtue and self-denial tickles one, as it were, and I come home rather pleased to my bed of a night." After a couple of days of the ritual, however, and with the funeral still in prospect, he felt the necessity of having a day all to himself, to restore his spirits. He spent the morning reading *Le Vicomte de Bragelonne* "with intense delight," and later turned to the new instalment of *David Copperfield*. He dined with his old crony, Roger de Beauvoir, and they went to the Théâtre des Variétés to see a popular satire, *Les Caméléons*, which horrified Thackeray, in spite of his self-elected role of misanthrope, by its callous ridicule of the most tragic events of the past sixty years in French history. "It's awful, immodest, surpasses my cynicism altogether. . . They don't care for anything, not religion, not bravery, not liberty, not great men, not modesty." At the end Beauvoir took him behind the scenes, and Thackeray was filled with schoolboy delight and awkwardness when he was brought into the dressing-room of the pert leading lady. After gazing spell-bound at the sparkling eyes and the shapely form in a revealing black satin peignoir (as he bragged in his next letter to Mrs Brookfield), he paid her several compliments, "very large and heavy, of the good old English sort," and she invited him to call upon her.

At his aunt's funeral, he chiefly noticed that the officiating clergyman would be "a good character for a book." In the midst of the service, the sonorous "Behold I show you a mystery" set Thackeray off wondering whether the disciples believed that the second coming of Christ would occur in their own lifetime. Seldom have the incongruous fancies of an author's mind been more frankly recorded than in his letters to Mrs Brookfield during these weeks.

Within a few hours of the funeral, he paid his visit to the actress. "I have but one fault in the world," she told him; "I have *trop bon coeur*." He responded with compliments even stronger than before. "I daresay that she thinks the enormous old Englishman is rapturously in love with her," he confessed; "but she will never see him again, the faithless giant. I shall pop her and her boudoir into a book some day, and that will be the end of our transactions."

With the funeral out of the way, he regained something of his normal sociability. He made the acquaintance of Macaulay, who was staying at the same hotel. At a dinner party given by Sir George Napier, with both Thackeray and Macaulay present, their host announced that one of the guests coming later was an American lady, whose greatest desire in life was to meet the author of *Vanity Fair* and the author of the *Lays of Ancient Rome*. Thackeray suggested that he and Macaulay should change identities for the occasion. "I do not approve of practical jokes," responded the historian huffily, and Thackeray was left to mourn a lost opportunity of laughter.

With customary thoughtfulness, he made an expedition to the village of Chambourcy, near Saint Germain, to visit the pathetic relics of Lady Blessington's household—her two nieces, the Misses Power, and "the poor old faded and unhappy D'Orsay," who was devoting himself with monomaniac intensity to the erection of a mausoleum to house the body of the woman he loved. If Thackeray had carried out his intention of starting for London immediately afterwards, his fortnight in France would have closed with a climax of morbidity; but fortunately a more cheering episode supervened. To his surprise, he received an invitation to dine with the President of the Republic, Louis Napoleon, and to go with a party to Fontainebleau the day following. These favors for the moment wiped out the sense of neglect that had been gnawing him.

In the middle of September he came home to London, full of determination to get on with *Pendennis*, which had been perilously delayed by his absence. A few days later, however, while dining at the house of Admiral Sir John Rodd, whose wife was one of the innumerable Thackeray cousins, he collapsed and sprained an ankle. Within a day or two a serious bilious illness had developed. For several days he struggled to write *Pendennis* in bed, and to keep his illness a secret from his family and most of his friends. He considered it to be merely a liver attack, but his doctor regarded it seriously, for cholera had been rife in Paris, and the symptoms were ominous.

Young Harry Hallam stood guard over him for two or three days, and then turned the duty over to Brookfield. By September 24, Thackeray was sure the crisis was past. He sent word to his publishers to advertise that the October number of *Pendennis* would be delayed a few days in appearing; and Brookfield, having confidence in the efficiency of Thackeray's man servant, felt no hesitation about leaving on an inspection tour.

His wife was less optimistic. With her mind full of Thackeray's recent forebodings that he would follow Charles Buller to an early grave, she also recalled his telling her once that he was unable to insure his life because of some unnamed but apparently incurable complaint. On the 27th, when she called to inquire for him (properly escorted by her sister's husband), she was told by the valet that he had been much worse, but was now slightly better after a bleeding, though extremely weak. She sent up word that she was about to write to his mother, and would be glad to convey a message; and the servant brought back an entreaty that she would grant him a minute's interview. She stood outside his room while John held open the door so that she could see him, looking shockingly pulled down and feverish. In a scarcely audible voice, he tried to assure her that he expected to be in bed only four or five days longer, but she read a very different implication in his anxious inquiries as to how soon Brookfield would be back.

A week later she wrote to her husband in something approaching terror. The Hallams had lent one of their footmen to help Thackeray's devoted John, and this man brought her bulletins of the invalid's condition. "He has had a very bad night, his room is darkened, and he is ordered to be perfectly quiet, and not to talk at all. Henry overheard the doctors say that what they are now anxious about is some former complaint of his which is more to be feared than his present attack of illness. . . Henry says the doctors are there three and four times a day and that they feared he was worse last night; but today he seemed a little better since the blister. I feel sorry that you are not able to be with him, as he can see no one to whom he can talk at all seriously, or who can really be of comfort. The day I was there he talked of the end, as possibly near at hand, and said he could look forward without dread to it, that he felt a great love and charity for all mankind, and tho' there were many things he would wish undone in his life, he yet felt a great trust and hope in God's love and mercy, and if it was His will, he would go tomorrow, and only feel about leaving his children unprotected. I did not think then that he was likely to be again in danger, and felt afraid of his exciting himself by talking in that strain, but I am now sorry I did not encourage him to say more, as it seemed a comfort to him to speak of it, and he said he felt quite happy and peaceful, that it had done him good to speak to me, and that you were the only other person he could do so to, and he spoke of you with much affection. Now I reproach myself for having rather turned off his thoughts from his own state, and tried to amuse him by talking of indifferent things, when perhaps it may have been the last opportunity he would have to talk to anyone of his feelings in dying, if that is really near at hand, which I cannot help fearing. . . I cannot feel much confidence in reports of amendment which are always contradicted by fresh relapses."

When his friends became aware of his danger, one of them insisted on calling another physician. Dr John Elliotson was among the most brilliant and most eccentric members of his profession, and Macready, Dickens, and other literary celebrities swore by him. He had been obliged to give up his professorship at the University of London hospital because of his enthusiasm for mesmerism; he held seances at his home, and shortly before the Thackeray case he had opened a Mesmeric Hospital. He was also founder of the Phrenological Society and published a magazine, *The Zoist*, in support of his theories. Nevertheless, he never inflicted his fads upon any patient who did not want them; and his mastery of the conventional arts of medicine was seldom impugned.

After Brookfield came back to town, he and Jane were able to visit the sufferer together. To Harry Hallam, who insisted on having news of him daily, she reported: "I am afraid he is not recovering as *quickly* as I had hoped when I wrote before—he is forbidden all nourishment except tea and lemonade. I suppose there is still a fear of a continuance of fever; he had better nights, however, and says he feels better. . . I only wish Mr Thackeray had anything to fall back upon when he recovers from this illness, instead of that constant writing which wears him so much and which he can never have any rest from, unless he could get some settled employment."

When his mother at last learned the gravity of his illness, she brought the vacation in Wales to an abrupt end. By the time they arrived at Gloucester, the little girls were so tired from the jolting carriage that she left them and her husband to spend the night there, while she posted on alone. On reaching Kensington, she was relieved to find him definitely out of danger, and when his daughters got home the next day they were allowed to go in and see him for a moment, appalled by how thin he was, and by his great wan eyes.

Once on the mend, he grew stronger with amazing rapidity. To Dr Elliotson he was convinced that he owed his life. Whether or not his malady was the prevalent cholera, it had undoubtedly been complicated with his latent urethral complaint. On October 21 he decided he was well enough to go to Brighton. The sea air and change of scene made him sleep soundly, and the next day he was able to write a note to Mrs Brookfield, announcing his removal. He sat out on the chain pier for a couple of hours in a bath-chair, chatting with acquaintances. "My chair anchored alongside of that of a very interesting nice little woman, a Mrs Whitmore," he reported; and after going back to his lodgings for a nap he was able to sustain "a somewhat fatiguing visit from the Miss Smiths, who are all kindness, and look very pretty in their mourning."

These details show him regaining his customary enjoyment of bright feminine company, and in her reply Mrs Brookfield teased him gaily: "I wish you would make John tell people not to talk to you while you are airing yourself, as it will do away with the good of the sea breezes if you are tired with talking, even to the fascinating Mrs Whitmore." She gave some comic details regarding the anxiety of a spinster acquaintance who was supposed to be Thackeray's infatuated adorer, and ended, "Pray be very martyrising upon yourself about your health."

He basked in these merry, flattering letters, which combined with the salt-water baths and the airings on the pier to speed his recovery. At the end of the month Harry Hallam paid him a visit. "Harry says that you won't eat your dinner well if I don't write and tell you that I am thriving," he informed the Brookfields. "I have to state that I ate a mutton chop just now in Harry's presence with great gusto, that I slept 12 hours last night and in fact advance by steps which grow every day more firm toward convalescence."

As soon as he could wield a pen, the necessity of getting on with his work beset him. *Pendennis* having already missed two numbers, he allowed it to remain in abeyance while he attacked his Christmas book. To save himself as much effort as possible he fell back on an idea which he already had in mind. Three years earlier he had published in *Fraser's* an article called *Proposals for a Continuation of "Ivanhoe."* The sequel which he there described was now developed into the burlesque romance of *Rebecca and Rowena*. Unable to face the task of making the illustrations that were an essential part of all Christmas books, he assigned it to a favorite colleague on the staff of *Punch*, young Richard Doyle.

Having to go up to London occasionally in connection with this work, he soon ventured to indulge in a few dinner parties. On November 27 he dined at Forster's in a familiar company—Tennyson, Macready, Kenyon, Kinglake, Procter, Brookfield, and Rintoul, the editor of *The Spectator*. Ten days later Fitz-Gerald remarked in a letter: "I saw poor old Thackeray in London, getting slowly better of a bilious fever that had almost killed him. People in general thought *Pendennis* got dull as it got on; and I confess I thought so too. He would do well to take the opportunity of his illness to discontinue it altogether. He told me last June he himself was tired of it; must not his readers naturally tire too?"

With returning vigor, however, Thackeray was feeling renewed interest in the book. The very day after FitzGerald wrote his complaint, Thackeray was saying to Mrs Brookfield in a note from Brighton that "the paper looks so nice and white, I should like—I should like to write a page of *Pendennis*. . . Does not this prove I am getting stronger?"

Two days afterwards he was in London again, to make the acquaintance at last of his temperamental admirer, Charlotte Brontë. During the two years since the *contretemps* over *Jane Eyre* she had obstinately refused to let him know her identity; in May, 1849, she wrote to her publishers: "Should Mr Thackeray again ask after Currer Bell, say the secret is and will be well kept because it is not worth disclosure." With unabated good-humor, he sent her a presentation copy of *Vanity Fair* with his "grateful regards," but it was not until November that he learned her name and circumstances through G. H. Lewes. A month later, when the reviews of *Shirley* had widely disseminated the certainty that "Currer Bell" was a woman, she consented to emerge from the oblivion of Haworth and spend a few days as the guest of her publisher, George Smith, and his mother. She stipulated that she should meet as few strangers as possible, but she could not withstand the temptation of seeing Thackeray, who was accordingly included in a small dinner party.

When Smith called upon Thackeray with the invitation, he was very positive in impressing him that she must not be embarrassed by any remark that would reveal knowledge of her identity. "Oh, of course," Thackeray replied. "That will be all right. One hint is enough to a man of the world, you know."

On the great day, unfortunately, Miss Brontë did not get back from a morning outing in time for luncheon; and before dinner time the combined effects of hunger and suspense had brought on a raging headache. "When Mr Thackeray was announced," she wrote, "and I saw him enter, looked up at his tall figure, heard his voice, the whole incident was truly dream-like, I was only certain it was true because I became miserably destitute of self-possession. . . Had I not been obliged to speak, I could have managed well, but it behoved me to answer when addressed, and the effect was torture—I spoke stupidly." In another letter recounting the scene she was more explicit: "At the moment Mr Thackeray presented himself, I was thoroughly faint from inanition, having eaten nothing since a very slight breakfast, and it was then seven o'clock in the evening. Excitement and exhaustion made savage work of me that evening. What he thought of me I cannot tell."

To her father she sent a less distracted report: "He is a very tall man—above six feet high, with a peculiar face—not handsome, very ugly indeed, generally somewhat stern and satirical in expression, but capable also of a kind look. He was not told who I was, he was not introduced to me, but I soon saw him looking at me through his spectacles; and when we all rose to go down to dinner he just stepped quietly up and said, 'Shake hands'; so I shook hands."

Having heard of Thackeray's tastes, Smith had gone out of his way to provide cigars for the interval after dinner when the gentlemen remained in the dining room with their wine. Thackeray was reminded of a passage in *Jane Eyre* that had been much quoted and ridiculed, the description of the "warning fragrance" of Mr Rochester's cigar as he walked amid the floral perfumes in his garden. On going up to join the ladies Thackeray could not resist asking Miss Brontë whether she noticed the "evening incense of their cigars."

In Smith's annoyed opinion, "Miss Brontë's face showed her discomposure and in a chilly fashion she turned off the allusion. She cast an accusing look at me." As a matter of fact, poor Charlotte was far too nervous to recognize the allusion at all. She had merely given a literal answer in her shy voice, and only after she looked around and noticed the expressions on the men's faces did she become aware of what Thackeray had had in mind. In confiding afterwards to Mrs Gaskell that she had "completely misunderstood" his question, she explained that she had found great difficulty in deciding "whether he was speaking in jest or earnest." Naturally serious-minded, and further handicapped by her timidity, she was sadly baffled by his glancing, ironical talk.

In her letter to her father, she made no reference to the remark about the cigars. Thackeray, she said, "spoke very few words to me, but when he went away he shook hands again in a very kind way. It is better, I should think, to have him for a friend than an enemy, for he is a most formidable-looking personage. I listened to him as he conversed with the other gentlemen. All he says is most simple, but often cynical, harsh, and contradictory."

Thackeray, for his part, went straight from Smith's doorstep to the Garrick Club, and burst into the smoking-room with the gleeful announcement, "Boys, I've been dining with Jane Eyre!" As the Brookfields had recently discovered in the matter of their expected baby, he was the last man to be trusted with a confidential secret.

On the whole the encounter had served to reinforce Miss Brontë's adulation for him. Contrasting him with the ubiquitous John Forster, whom she had met also, she explained that "I by no means dislike Mr Forster—quite the contrary, but the distance from his loud swagger to Thackeray's simple port is as the distance from Shakespeare's writing to Macready's acting." And when she reviewed her experiences, after returning to the refuge of Haworth, he figured as the climax: "He stirs in me both sorrow and anger. Why should he lead so harassing a life? Why should his mocking tongue so perversely deny the better feelings of his better moods? . . . Mr Thackeray is a man of very quiet, simple demeanour; he is, however, looked up to with some awe and even distrust." And in another letter: "Thackeray is a Titan of mind. His presence and powers impress one deeply in an intellectual sense; I do not see him or know him as a man. All the others are subordinate. . . I felt sufficiently at my ease with all but Thackeray; with him I was fearfully stupid."

She little suspected that the tremendous novelist had inwardly endured an embarrassment almost as strong as her own. But while she was scanning his every movement and painfully trying to deduce his opinion of her, he attempted no such analysis. Always uncomfortable in the presence of feminine strangers, and still weak after his illness, he carried away only a hazy impression of "the trembling little frame, the little hand, the great honest eyes." He had too much humility about his grotesque aspect and awkward manner to imagine that he could stir any emotion in the heart even of a timid country mouse before she scurried back to the bleak moorland rectory.

CHAPTER 13

Squabbles

HE HAD BARELY been able to get *Rebecca and Rowena* finished in time for Christmas; the preface was written on December 20. The twelfth part of *Pendennis*, which must have been well advanced before he succumbed to his illness, was completed in time to come out at the beginning of January—a lapse of three months. Still a little tottery, he was definitely back in harness.

Life had permanently changed its color for him. His anxiety about his health was transformed from vague premonitions to an acute sense of peril. The momentous expectations in the Brookfield household were bound to affect his relationship there. Having sorrowed over their childlessness for eight years, the worthy Inspector was looking forward to fatherhood with pride and joy, and Thackeray could not but feel himself regarded as an alien at such a time. He restrained himself from dropping in uninvited at times when Mr Brookfield was away from home. He still needed Jane's sympathy, however, for the new number of *Pendennis* had plunged him into a nasty literary dispute.

The story had reached a point where his hero was attempting to earn his living in London as a writer. Naturally, the autobiographical cast of the story induced Thackeray to use many recognizable traits of people he had been associated with during his own early struggles in journalism; and naturally, too, these portraits were not altogether kindly. Colburn and Bentley, the rival publishers, figured as Bacon and Bungay; Maginn and Jack Sheehan and the raffish gang of Fraserians plainly suggested Captain Shandon and Jack Finucane and Mr Bludyer; the dim-witted young noblemen were identified as Lord George Beauclerk and Lord William Lennox; while it was already well known, from their rôles in *Vanity Fair*, that Mr Wagg and Mr Wenham represented Theodore Hook and John Wilson Croker.

Thackeray had ample warrant for his satire on the brazen log-rolling and intrigues, which already belonged to a defunct epoch; but some of the reviewers chose to take offense at the "distortion" of the literary scene. *The Morning Chronicle* led the attack, and was promptly echoed by *The Examiner*—another instance of the ill-will displayed toward Thackeray at intervals by Forster, who was now editing that paper. The ostensible topic of the articles was whether the awarding of pensions and titles would improve the condition of authorship in England, and they disagreed on the question, but both drew their evidence from *Pendennis* and took the opportunity of assailing it. The *Chronicle* accused Thackeray of "foster-

206

ing a baneful prejudice" against literary men; *The Examiner* agreed that he "stooped to flatter" this public misconception and caricatured his fellow-authors to gain the applause of "the non-literary class."

On January 8, 1850, he wrote a long letter of protest and brought it to read to Mrs Brookfield, though confessing that he wished her husband were at home to give him a more experienced opinion. Published in *The Morning Chronicle* four days later, it was a manifesto of his views on "the Dignity of Literature," refuting the suggestion that he was ashamed of his calling or contemptuous of his confrères. He took a mild thrust at Forster's lack of judgment: "The editor of *The Examiner* may, perhaps, occasionally write, like other authors, in a hurry, and not be aware of the conclusions to which some of his sentences may lead." Elsewhere the letter hinted at greater disparagement of Forster, by implying doubts of his gentility. It was a reiteration of Thackeray's demand for self-respect among authors: "Instead of accusing the public of persecuting and disparaging us as a class, it seems to me that men of letters had best silently assume that they are as good as any other gentlemen, nor raise piteous controversies upon a question which all people of sense must take to be settled."

On another point, however, he concurred with Forster: he asserted that authors had at last achieved a position of such consequence in the social scale that they were entitled to any rewards and distinctions that would symbolize that recognition. His own hopes can be discerned in his declaration that "if it is the custom of the State to reward by money, or titles of honour, or stars and garters of any sort, individuals who do the country service, there can be no reason why men of letters should not have the chance, as well as men of the robe or the sword... Every European State but ours rewards its men of letters; the American Government gives them their full share of its small patronage; and if Americans, why not Englishmen?"

Reasonable though Thackeray's letter was, it could do little to remove the hostility that had prompted the attacks. In fact, another uncomfortable episode of the same nature soon followed. His friends were eager to make him a member of the Athenaeum Club, that most sacred resort of English intelligentsia. His nomination had been on its books for four years, and to give his candidacy the highest respectability, he was now proposed by the learned historian and revered Dean of St Paul's, Henry Hart Milman. His self-elected patron Abraham Hayward was a pillar of the club, and he received the votes of such pundits as Hallam and Macaulay, and even that of Croker, who certainly had cause to smart from the lash of his satire. But somebody on the committee was suspicious. It was well known that several of Thackeray's fellow-members of the Garrick had discovered themselves figuring in his novels, especially one Andrew Arcedeckne, a noisy, irrepressible fellow who had often irritated Thackeray by his blunt jibes, and who claimed to be proud of the fact that he was sketched to the life in *Pendennis* as Harry Foker. On the ground that Thackeray might sometime be guilty of lampooning a dignitary of the Athenaeum, he was blackballed.

Poor Dean Milman wrote to Hayward in great distress, explaining that he had been confident of Thackeray's election, or he would never have exposed him to the risk of this humiliation. The victim himself, however, took the matter in good part, and wrote gaily to Hayward, remarking that Dr Johnson would undoubtedly have blackballed Fielding, and that "as a satirical writer, I rather wonder that I have not made more enemies than I have. . . There must be thousands of men to whom the practice of ridicule must be very offensive; doesn't one see such in society, or in one's own family? persons whom nature has not gifted with a sense of humour?"

His own sense of humor was being called into play to sustain him in yet another controversy, the most ludicrous of all his series of collisions with public opinion. Somewhere in *Pendennis* he had made a passing allusion to Catherine Hayes, the callous murderess of the previous century, who had been the heroine of his *Catherine* ten years before. It chanced that Catherine Hayes was also the name of a young Irish singer who was just then at the height of her career and was being idolized by her compatriots. Some of them, having never heard of the murderess, seized on the remark in *Pendennis* as a gratuitous insult to the singer. Thackeray was amazed to receive a letter signed by one Briggs, stating that a group of young Irishmen had organized themselves to have vengeance upon him for this outrage and for his other libels upon the Irish race, and that they had sworn to come over to London one by one until successful in chastizing their victim. Mr Briggs announced that as the first emissary he had taken lodgings directly across the street from Thackeray's house, and was ready to attack him as soon as he issued forth.

The mixture of bravado, punctilio, and wrong-headedness was so precisely typical of Thackeray's own burlesque Irishmen, the Mulligan of Ballymulligan and the Molony of Kilballymolony, that he could hardly believe it real; but prudence impelled him to notify the police. A beefy detective in a mustard-colored coat arrived and stationed himself in the dining-room window. All morning he stared at the opposite doorway, while Thackeray tried to apply himself to his work. When guests arrived for lunch, the officer was sent down to eat in the kitchen; but Thackeray suddenly announced that the situation was intolerable. To the dismay of the company, he marched across the street, knocked at the door opposite, and demanded an explanation from Mr Briggs.

Taken by surprise, the youth blustered and threatened, but Thackeray's placid manner, reinforced by his mighty bulk, soon persuaded him to listen to a little lecture on the historical murderess, and within ten minutes he meekly promised to go back to Ireland that very night. In the course of the interview, Thackeray caught sight of a fine old Chippendale chair, and he paused to buy it from the landlady before he emerged to relieve the suspense of his family and friends, who were clustered anxiously in the bow-window of Number Thirteen. He soon discovered, however, that the campaign of misguided protest had spread through the Irish press and elsewhere, and he was obliged to vindicate himself in another letter to *The Morning Chronicle.*

His return to work had included resumption of the regular stint for *Punch,* and after his five months at pasture he did not welcome the yoke. Not only was it tedious to grind out a fixed quantity of humor every week, but the Wednesday night dinners of the staff were no longer wholly congenial to him. This was chiefly due to a growing incompatibility with Douglas Jerrold. As they were the two most popular contributors, there was inevitably a sense of rivalry between them. On Thackeray's side it was good-natured enough. "Let's see what Master Douglas has to say this week," he would remark, as he unfolded a new number of *Punch.* But Jerrold took it more to heart, for he had been the leading "*Punch* man" in the eyes of the public during the first few years, and had then been obliged to see Thackeray usurp the title. Besides, the bitter little satirist, who always proclaimed his proletarian sympathies, made no secret of his opinion that Thackeray betrayed the sacred cause every time he dined with a nobleman. His sneers were endured with remarkable forbearance, Thackeray's only comment on them being, "What's the use of quarreling with a man if you have to meet him every Wednesday at dinner?"

To diminish the friction he changed his place at the table, which had been between Jerrold and Gilbert à Beckett, to a seat on the opposite side. The rotund, genial editor, Mark Lemon, kept a watchful eye on the two of them, and was quick to interpose a jest whenever the remarks became barbed. Thackeray at last began to suspect that the venom of Jerrold's contempt for his exalted friendships might be distilled from envy, and he was amused one day, when visiting Lord Carlisle, to notice a presentation copy of one of Jerrold's books, with a fulsome inscription "To the Right Honourable the Earl of Carlisle, K.G., K.C.B., etc., etc." Thackeray reported this piece of evidence to Vizetelly with a chuckle, saying, "Ah! this is the sort of style in which your rigid, uncompromising Radical always toadies to the great."

On January 18, FitzGerald reported that "Thackeray is well again except not quite strong yet." A month later he was enjoying canters in the Park. A daughter was born to the Brookfields on February 26, and two days afterwards Thackeray wrote a long letter to Mrs Brookfield, seeking to amuse her with details of his doings. Then on March 4, on a sudden impulse that he would like to have a trip to Paris, he packed in half an hour and set off without even waiting to eat breakfast.

The venture did not prove a wise one. He caught such a severe cold that he was confined to his rooms at the Hôtel Bristol, unable to see his friends and feeling too stupid to work on *Pendennis*. When his cough subsided, he felt so tired that he could not face the journey to London, and so he postponed his return for some days and slaved away at the next instalment. Although he dined a few times *au cabaret*, and went to the theater for his usual orgy of laughing, he failed to find the stimulation that Paris usually gave him, and suspected that another revolution was in the air. Tormented by introspection, he began a letter to Mrs Brookfield and then discarded it as too gloomy and egotistical. One to Lady Ashburton was burned as soon as he read it over and realized that it was "too pert, and like Major Pendennis, talking only about lords and great people, in an easy offhand way." Mrs Brookfield's raillery and Jerrold's jibes were making him hypersensitive to the dread of seeming snobbish. "I think," he confessed to Mrs Brookfield, "I only write naturally to one person now, and make points and compose sentences to others. That is why you must be patient please, and let me go on twaddling and boring you."

After three miserable weeks in Paris he came back to London a day or two before the christening of the Brookfield baby, an event that he did not attend. From day to day he called at Portman Square to inquire for Mrs Brookfield, who was not yet well enough to see him. Struggling to catch up with his work, he had to refuse invitations from various friends, and was distressed to realize that they suspected him of neglecting them. Mrs Procter, still hurt over their previous falling-out, replied to his refusal of a dinner invitation, "You won't come because we haven't got a Lord." And FitzGerald asserted in a letter to Frederick Tennyson, "Thackeray is in such a great world that I am afraid of him; he gets tired of me; we are content to regard each other at a distance." Proud of himself whenever he managed to dine at home with his children two or three evenings in succession, or when he declined an invitation from a Duchess to join a house-party in Scotland, Thackeray considered his old companions very unreasonable when they displayed such jealousy.

Friends who saw more of him were worried by his grumbling over hard work. His devoted comrade, "Big" Higgins, while dining with him one evening, suddenly said, "If you are tired and want to lie fallow for a year, come to me for the money. I have much more than I want." It was a solution that he could not consider, but he was touched by the generosity of the offer.

He would have had no such scruples over an offer of an official appointment, if any friend could obtain one. This time his hopes were fixed upon Fred Elliot, Kate Perry's brother-in-law, an under-secretary in the Colonial Office, who, he remarked, "would do anything, I believe, to help me to a place." Hope deferred, however, was making him turn his thoughts toward an alternative. He was consumed with anxiety to provide for the future of his daughters by accumulating money as fast as possible. The income from his writing not being much more than sufficient to pay current expenses, he had to look for some other way to capitalize upon his fame. Dickens and other literary men were earning large fees by lecturing or giving public readings, and the United States of America was reputed to be a land of unbounded wealth and equally unbounded appetite for literary lectures. In spite of his shuddering horror of appearing before an audience, Thackeray began to consider the possibility of taking to the platform and of touring America in that capacity.

The London season being at its height, his letters to Mrs Brookfield were a recital of triumphs. At one dinner party, "the ladies, M.P.'s wives, took me aside and asked confidentially about the fashionable world in which it is supposed, I believe, that I live entirely now; and the wonder is that people don't hate me more than they do." Affecting to grumble about "an awful week of festivities" ahead of him, he added, "Isn't it curious to think—it was striking my great mind yesterday, as Annie was sorting the cards in the chimney-glass—that there are people who would give their ears, or half their income, to go to these fine places?"

He complained of being miserably tired, and yet of having such restless spells that he could not get on with his writing, but would have to wander out at random and drop in to the Miss Berrys', or the Elliots', or the Prinseps' to see the beautiful Virginia Pattle. His memory, too, remained undependable; one day he read through all the early chapters of *Pendennis*, and enjoyed them, but found them as unfamiliar as a new book. He was thereby reminded of the emotional stress that he had been enduring at the time it was written, eighteen months earlier, when his love for Jane Brookfield had first forced itself into recognition. "What a wholesome thing fierce mental occupation is!" he commented; "better than dissipation to take thoughts out of one; only one can't always fix the mind down and other thoughts will bother it."

The experiment of having his parents share his home in Kensington had continued to be unsatisfactory, and one of his objects in visiting Paris had been to arrange for their return to the little expatriate society which they had learned to love. This readjustment brought him face to face again with his responsibilities toward his growing daughters. In May they went to Southampton on a visit to the Fanshawes, and while they were away their governess, Miss Trulock, received an offer of a better position. Thackeray dreaded the prospect of interviewing applicants for her post. Perhaps the girls would be better off at a boarding school. Meanwhile, he sent them good advice—"The way to have friends is to like people yourself, you see"; and he scolded Annie because (picking up one of his favorite tricks) she had "scribbled faces" at the bottom of a letter to Mrs Brookfield— "they are not respectable or ladylike, do you understand?"

In June, Charlotte Brontë plucked up courage for another sortie upon London. She had been reading *Pendennis* every month with solicitude. "Though the story lingers," she wrote to George Smith in March, "for me the interest does not flag. Here and there we feel that the pen has been guided by a tired hand, that the mind of the writer has been somewhat chafed and depressed by his recent illness, or by some other cause; but Thackeray still proves himself greater when he is weary than other writers are when they are fresh. The public, of course, will have no compassion for his fatigue, and make no allowance for the ebb of inspiration; but some true-hearted readers here and there, while grieving that such a man should be obliged to write when he is not in the mood, will wonder that, under such circumstances, he should write so well." It was inevitable that she should have another interview with Thackeray, and that her concern for his welfare should prompt her to speak firmly to him.

"He made a morning call," she related to a friend, "and sat above two hours. Mr Smith only was in the room the whole time. He described it afterwards as a 'queer scene,' and I suppose it was. The giant sate before me; I was moved to speak to him of some of his shortcomings (literary of course); one by one the faults came into my head, and one by one I brought them out, and sought some explanation or defence. He did defend himself, like a great Turk and heathen; that is to say, the excuses were often worse than the crime itself. The matter ended in decent amity; if all be well, I am to dine at his house this evening."

It is obvious that she was as far as ever from understanding his banter. Her onslaught had startled him as much as if a little brown moor-hen had flown at him. Ten years later, after Mrs Gaskell's biography of Miss Brontë has revealed to the world all the worry he had occasioned her, he rather ruefully published his version of the encounter. "An impetuous honesty seemed to me to characterize the woman. Twice I recollect she took me to task for what she held to be errors in doctrine. Once about Fielding we had a disputation. She spoke her mind out. She jumped too rapidly to conclusions. (I have smiled at one or two passages in the *Biography*, in which my own disposition or behaviour forms the subject of talk.) She formed conclusions that might be wrong and built up whole theories of character upon them. New to the London world, she entered it with an independent indomitable spirit of her own; and judged of contemporaries, and especially spied out arrogance or affectation, with extraordinary keenness of vision. She was angry with her favorites if their conduct or conversation fell below her ideal. I fancied an austere little Joan of Arc marching in upon us, and rebuking our easy lives, our easy morals. She gave me the impression of being a very pure, and lofty, and high-minded person. A great and holy reverence of right and truth seemed to be with her always."

At the little dinner-party in her honor she did not make a very favorable impression upon Mrs Brookfield, who was apt to be somewhat feline in her observations on other women. "There was just then," she later recalled, "a fashion for wearing a plait of hair across the head, and Miss Brontë, a timid little woman with a firm mouth, did not possess a large enough quantity of hair to enable her to form a plait, so therefore wore a very obvious crown of brown silk. Mr Thackeray on the way down to dinner addressed her as Currer Bell. She tossed her head and said 'she believed there were books being published by a person named Currer Bell, but the person he was talking to was Miss Brontë—and she saw no connection between the two.' " Elsewhere Mrs Brookfield described the novelist as "the most difficult woman to talk to I have ever met." To her conversational opening, "Do you like London, Miss Brontë?" the curt reply was "Yes and no," after which she relapsed into silence.

London society was in a turmoil that summer over the High Church controversy, brought to a head by the Gorham decision of the Privy Council; and Mrs Brookfield, as the wife of a clergyman, shared in the excitement. In June the Rev William James Early Bennett, a Puseyite leader, undertook to consecrate the new church of St Barnabas, Pimlico, with a choral procession, display of images, and other abominations of Rome flaunted in the face of good protestants. Thackeray the day before heard Mrs Brookfield asking Harry Hallam to escort her, and so he also turned up in the crowd that jammed the streets around the church, and pushed his way up alongside Mrs Brookfield just as the procession emerged from the schoolhouse. "I fear," she remarked, in her report to her husband, "he scandalized some of the crowd by remarks more humorous than reverent, 'O, my dear fellow countrymen of the nineteenth century, are we gone back to this?' but he and Harry and all the men took off their hats as the door opened to admit the procession, and the Altar was revealed to view, a blaze of lights, exactly like those at the Oratory."

In *Punch* Thackeray had now started a new series entitled *The Proser*, "Essays and Discourses by Dr Solomon Pacifico," and as usual he talked about himself and his friends with very inadequate disguise. Just as he had depicted Mrs Brookfield and Miss Berry in one of *Mr Brown's Letters to his Nephew*, so now he proclaimed his admiration of Virginia Pattle, under the name of "Erminia," in an essay "On a Good-looking Young Lady." With more than usual indiscretion, however, he included an anecdote about a gentleman of distinction. Henry Taylor, a respectable permanent official of the Colonial Office, had a vast reputation in some quarters as a poet on the strength of *Philip van Artevelde* and other blank-verse dramas. His wife being a sister of Stephen Spring-Rice, who was a close friend of the Brookfields, Taylor had often amused them by his pompous solemnity and hypochondriac fussiness; but he was not impervious to feminine beauty, and after meeting Miss Pattle he addressed a florid poem to her. Thackeray seized on the episode as fair game for his irony:

This almost peerless creature, on a visit to the country, met that great poet, Timotheus, whose habitation is not far from the country house of Erminia's friend, and who, upon seeing the young lady, felt for her that admiration which every man of taste experiences upon beholding her, and which, if Mrs. Timotheus had not been an exceedingly sensible person, would have caused a jealousy between her and the great bard her husband. But, charming and beautiful herself, Mrs. Timotheus can even pardon another woman for being so; nay, with perfect good sense, though possibly with a *little* factitious enthusiasm, she professes to share to the fullest extent the admiration of the illustrious Timotheus for the young beauty.

After having made himself well acquainted with Erminia's perfections, the famous votary of Apollo and leader of the tuneful choir did what might be expected from such a poet under such circumstances, and began to sing. When poets see a beautiful creature they straightway fall to work . . . and turn out to the best of their ability, and with great pains and neatness on their own part, a copy of verses in praise of the adorable object. I myself may have a doubt about the genuineness of the article produced, or of the passion which vents itself in this way . . . Well, well, I see what you mean; I *am* jealous of him. Timotheus's verses were beautiful, that's the fact—confound him!—and I wish I could write as well, or half as well indeed, or do anything to give Erminia pleasure . . .

When Erminia got the verses and read them, she laid them down, and with one of the prettiest and most affecting emotions which I ever saw in my life, she began to cry a little. The verses of course were full of praises of her beauty. "They all tell me that," she said; "nobody cares for anything but that . . ."

Thackeray was rather proud of the skit. His friends the Elliots also knew Taylor, as Elliot was his colleague in the Colonial Office, and so at a luncheon party of theirs (as Mrs Brookfield mentioned), Thackeray "read us out his paper on Miss Pattle's tears at Henry Taylor's poem, which I believe he is now going to read to her." In spite of all the uncomfortable situations that he had got himself into, by just such mockery at the expense of fellow-authors, he remained cheerfully blind to the inevitable consequences.

At the moment, however, his connection with *Punch* became disturbed for a different reason. His clash of opinions with Jerrold had been intensified by the latter's attacks on Louis Napoleon, whom Thackeray admired. Early in July Thackeray experienced a slight attack of illness, and was more than usually bothered over what was to happen next in *Pendennis*. These annoyances wore his patience to the snapping point, and he sent in his resignation to *Punch*. He explained to Mrs Brookfield that "there appears in next *Punch* an article so wicked, I think, by poor Jerrold that upon my word I don't think I ought to pull any longer in the same boat with such a savage little Robespierre. The appearance of this

FROM A NOTE TO MRS ELLIOT

incendiary article put me in such a rage, that I could only cool myself by a ride in the Park."

    She replied with soothing words: "I am very glad you are well again, and I cannot feel sorry for the resignation from *Punch*, which is really a grand thing to have done as a testimony,—but they ought to cut out the Jerrold article and make you come back." The proprietors of *Punch* evidently shared her opinion, for his resignation was not accepted; but all through July he was absent from its pages, and on August 3 he brought *The Proser* to an abrupt end with a rather serious article defending the system by which contributors to periodicals were allowed to conceal their identity,—still harping on his fixed idea about the dignity of authorship.

    Pendennis could not be so cavalierly treated. The autobiographical element in it was so strong that he suffered the emotional stresses along with the characters, but each month's number had to be produced. Naturally he had identified Pen's mother closely with his own, and when the exigencies of the plot demanded her death he agonized so much that even his daughters shared the strain. "Oh, Papa," said little Minny, who had been imbibing some of her grandmother's fads, "do make her well again; she can have a regular doctor, and be almost dead, and then will come a homeopathic doctor, who will make her well, you know." One morning when Annie ran into his study he impatiently motioned her out again; and an hour later he came to the schoolroom, laughing in a shamefaced way, to say, "I don't know what James can have thought of me when he came in with the tax-gatherer just after you left, and found me blubbering over Helen Pendennis's death."

His household had settled into the routine of a bachelor establishment after his parents returned to France. In spite of the ministrations of Miss Trulock (who had been persuaded to retain her position) the girls were subjected to few of the restraints customary for Victorian young ladies. Their various pets had the run of the house, though the servants waged war against the increasing brigade of stray cats. The garden was a jungle of verbena and iris and London-pride; the lawn was mowed only once in years—when Lady Duff Gordon came to stay a few days—and the greenhouse was empty except for two mildewed busts—Deville's of Thackeray as a child, and another of some relation in uniform.

The *ménage* could not have functioned without the butler, who was so devoted to "the Governor" that he was able to read his unspoken wishes. A silent, sharp-eyed little man, he used to write letters to the newspapers, signing them "Jeames de la Pluche, 13 Young Street." Once when the family breakfast ware had been reduced to an irregular assortment of cracked cups and saucers, a hamper arrived containing a beautiful breakfast service, with an anonymous rhyme of presentation, made with words clipped from *The Times* and glued together. The family never tired of trying to guess who had sent the gift; and years later, when Jeames was leaving for Australia, he said reproachfully, "I sent you the breakfast things. You guessed a great many people, but you never guessed they came from me."

In the middle of July Thackeray ran over to Dieppe in the hope of being roused from his lethargy, but instead "the journey stirred up my inner man and made me ill." He described the attack as "something not at all unlike cholera," and attributed it to the biliousness of "a man who dines out every day of his life." Driving into the country, and reading the plays of Beaumarchais and a six-volume novel of Dumas *fils*, constituted his greatest exertion, and he drifted back to London in time for his birthday on the 18th.

Two days later Mrs Brookfield left for her summer visit to Southampton, and he fell to work on the next number of *Pendennis*, which was due to be published in ten days. Without her "to come and grumble to," as he wrote to her, the task was even more cruel than usual. "My groans were heart-rending, my sufferings immense," and the result, he feared, was "but stupid, rickety, and of feeble intellect." When he went back to earlier numbers to look up names and other forgotten details, he "lit upon a very stupid part, and yet how well written it is.

A REASON FOR A COUNTRY DRIVE
(DIEPPE)

What a shame the author don't write a complete good story. Will he die before doing so? or come back from America and do it?" After the wearisome day of grinding out *Pendennis*, his head was "boiling up with some nonsense that I must do after dinner for *Punch*. Isn't it strange that, in the midst of all the selfishness, that one of doing one's business is the strongest of all. What funny songs I've written when fit to hang myself!"

No sooner had the instalment gone to press than he concocted a scheme for regaining the companionship he missed so much. "I heard from Mr Thackeray," Jane Brookfield wrote to her husband on July 31, "proposing that the children and their governess should join us in taking lodgings and keeping house here, as they would be all the better for change of air, but I have said in answer that nothing is yet decided, and I fancy you would feel rather bored by the governess, however much she might stick to her schoolroom." Notwithstanding this reluctance, within a few days the arrangement was adopted; the two girls and their Miss Trulock moved into a house with Mrs Brookfield and her baby, while Thackeray took rooms at the Dolphin Inn. "You will not feel *gêné* by the governess and children," Jane promised her husband; "they use the dining room for school, and are very accommodating and good-natured."

In Memoriam had just been published, and Mrs Brookfield was reading with emotion the elegy upon the brilliant young cousin whom she only vaguely remembered, as he had died in Vienna when she was twelve years old. And while her mind was still full of it, one evening when she and Thackeray were at dinner in walked Harry Hallam, as though to restore vividness to the time-dimmed image of that elder brother, Arthur, whom he so closely resembled in brilliance and charm. Having been unexpectedly quick in carrying through his first brief on the Midland Circuit, he had found time to visit her for a few days on his way to the Continent to join his father in a tour.

Thackeray was strangely unsettled. He announced that he would wait only until Brookfield came home for the week-end, and after a day with him would set off on a long-planned visit to Scotland. But the Inspector came and went away again, and still the departure for the north was postponed. On August 18, Jane reported that "contrary to what might be expected Mr Thackeray is still at the Dolphin, having got into his new number and working hard at it; he says he had packed up to go away this morning, fancying he did not work well here, but afterwards he did a good bit of writing and came up to dine."

On the 20th he tore himself away, to get his manuscript back to London in time for the printers. In the train he encountered Miss Cissy Gore, whose mother had continued on friendly terms with Thackeray in spite of his parody of her silver-fork novels. Miss Gore claimed to be the original of the minxish Blanche Amory in *Pendennis*, a fact which Thackeray could not altogether deny, and all the way up to London they carried on a conversation of clever banter. Thence Thackeray derived a good idea for a chapter of the novel, "in which I will make Pendennis and Blanche play at being in love, such a wicked false humbugging London love, as two *blasé* London people might act, and half deceive themselves that they were in earnest. That will complete the cycle of Mr Pen's worldly experiences, and then we will make, or try and make, a good man of him. O me! we are wicked worldlings most of us, may God better us and cleanse us."

Back in his deserted house in Young Street, toiling over the illustrations for the next number, on a dismal day of pouring rain, he yearned bitterly for the delights he had left in Southampton. When he was writing to Mrs Brookfield, his eyes were so full of tears he could hardly see the paper. Perhaps never again would he have such a blissful fortnight. He would always remember the sunny days, the laughter of the children, and "the aspect of the kindest and tenderest face in the world to me." He could only pray that "her dear regard" would continue towards him till her head was as white as his.

The annual problem of a Christmas book was complicated this time by an argument with his publishers. Last year's makeshift *Rebecca and Rowena* had not been very successful, partly because it was issued too late for much of the Christmas trade, partly because a purely literary frolic was too great a departure from the expectations of the public. Nevertheless, he now notified Chapman & Hall that his price would be raised to £150 for an edition of 3000, and he intimated clearly that he would approach another publisher if his demands were not met. Chapman replied that his firm would lose money on these terms, and accordingly Thackeray opened negotiations with George Smith, who had already become his personal friend through the interviews with Charlotte Brontë at his house. One of the most enterprising London publishers, with a firm belief in the policy of generous treatment of his authors, Smith had been eager for several years to add Thackeray to his list. Thackeray candidly informed him that Chapman & Hall had not regarded *Rebecca and Rowena* as a success, and had declined to meet his demand on the next book; but the moment he stated his price Smith replied, "May I write you a cheque for it?"

Anxious to make a good showing for his new sponsor, he decided to go back to the abandoned scheme of two years before, Lady Kicklebury's tour of the Rhine. At the beginning of September he ran down to Southampton for another glimpse of his children and Mrs Brookfield, and found London intolerably "glum and dingy and smoky and dreary" on his return; but after a couple of days he set off for the Continent to refresh his memory of the Rhineland. The tour was made in company with Serjeant Gale, a congenial legal friend. Crossing to Antwerp, they went up the Rhine as far as Homburg, where Thackeray spent five days, sketching, reading novels, and watching the patrons of the Spa as they drank the waters and gambled; then he returned to Brussels and remained there quietly for several days, making a start on the next *Pendennis*.

At the beginning of October he attended the wedding of Virginia Pattle to Lord Eastnor, and met Henry Taylor for the first time since the "Timotheus" article of three months earlier. Taylor seemed friendly enough, and told Thackeray that they would soon see each other at Alresford Grange, where both had been invited by Lord and Lady Ashburton. Shortly afterwards, however, Thackeray received a letter from Lady Ashburton asking him to put off his visit, as the Taylors had let her see that they were offended with Thackeray, and she felt that it would not do to have him come while they were there.

Considering the whole business absurd, Thackeray sent her a sketch of a donkey loose in a chicken-yard, as symbolic of his flight of fancy in the *Punch* article, which he now regarded, he told her, as "unintentionally vulgar and impertinent." In great doubt as to how this would be taken, he set off to stay with the Gores in Hampshire, but all the way down in the train he brooded on the affair, and the moment he arrived at the Gores' house he wrote "a letter of contrition and apology to Henry Taylor for having made what I see now was a flippant and offensive allusion to Mrs Taylor. I am glad I have done it," he told Mrs Brookfield. "I am glad that so many people whom I have been thinking bigoted and unfair and unjust towards me, have been right, and that I have been wrong, and my mind is an immense deal easier."

This typically honest apology proving acceptable, he was asked to come to the Grange immediately. The story may here be taken up by Jane Welsh Carlyle, who was a member of the house party, and who told all the news in letters to her husband. "Thackeray is here—arrived yesterday, greatly to the discomfort of Taylor evidently, who had 'had the gang all to himself' so long. . . Taylor sulked all yesterday evening, and today is solemn as death. In fact he has been making a sort of *agapemone* here, in which he was the Mr Prince, the Spirit of Love; and no wonder he dislikes the turn that has been given to things by the arrival of the Spirit of Punch."

Thackeray exerted all his geniality to conciliate the stately poet. He told Mrs Brookfield that "I like Taylor, whose grandeur wears off in ten minutes, and in whom one perceives an extremely gentle and loving human creature, I think—not a man to be intimate with ever, but to admire and like from a distance and to have a sort of artistical good will to." And Mrs Carlyle notified her husband in her next letter that "Henry Taylor and Thackeray have fraternized finally, *not* 'like the carriage horses and the railway steam-engine,' as might have been supposed, but like men and brothers! I lie by, and observe them with a certain interest; it is as good as a play!"

Finding the atmosphere of the Grange too somnolent for writing, Thackeray spent most of his time in reading Kingsley's *Alton Locke*, which was rousing hot discussion of its Christian Socialism; and by the middle of the month he was back in London, grinding away at *Pendennis*, with the end at last in sight. As custom demanded that a novel issued in monthly parts should have a "double number" for the conclusion, he could not be so dilatory as usual; when the November one was in the press, he had to carry on with scarcely a break.

On November 4 came devastating news. Re-enacting the tragedy of seventeen years before, Harry Hallam, twenty-six years old, had died of fever in Siena. But in spite of this loss of a dear friend, and the consequent pall over the Brookfield home, to which in every other sorrow Thackeray had turned for consolation but where now he must offer the solace, he managed to compose the double number of *Pendennis* in less than four weeks, at the cost of dangerous fatigue. When the last line was written, he took a fresh sheet of paper to start a letter to his mother announcing the good news. After writing two sentences he staggered off to bed and stayed there for nearly two days. When he resumed the letter he was able to declare that he felt "as brisk as a bee and as fresh as a daisy."

He turned his attention to accumulated correspondence; a long letter that he wrote to William Allingham is a comical revelation of his habits and ideas at the time. Allingham was a young literary aspirant and customs official in Ireland. Many months before, Thackeray had met him at Leigh Hunt's, and had induced Chapman & Hall to print his first book of verses. Upon receipt of the book Thackeray had begun a letter of thanks and commentary, only to leave it unfinished. When he returned from the Continent in September, he had found a letter from Allingham awaiting him, and it had lain unopened ever since—he could not get up courage to break the seal. Now he wrote ramblingly to Allingham, on everything that was in his mind. Tennyson had just visited him, on the eve of being presented at Court as the new Poet Laureate, and Thackeray described him as "much excited about his court dress and sword (he says his legs are very good) and as much pleased and innocent about it as a girl or a page." Then allusions to Tennyson's marriage and an unhappy love affair of Allingham's led him to say, "I have passed my critical period I think and don't expect again to have my sleep disturbed by thoughts of any female." He next made an effort to discuss Allingham's poetry, but within a few sentences he was grumbling about the "turmoil" of his life in London, and after going on with his "literary woes and egotistical plaints" for half a page he tore it off and burned it. Instead, he launched into a discussion of the campaign against Cardinal Wiseman, and predicted a bitter religious war. The next morning he opened Allingham's two-months-old letter, and found that it was a request for help in becoming a contributor to *Punch*. A postscript was therefore added to the letter written the day before, saying, "If you'll send me any first-chop bits I will send them to Mr Lemon and try."

In his relief at having finished *Pendennis*, he took the public into his confidence almost as intimately as he took his family and friends. "This book began with a very precise plan, which was entirely put aside," he admitted in the preface. "Ladies and gentlemen, you were to have been treated, and the writer's and the publishers' pocket benefited, by the recital of the most active horrors... Nay, up to nine o'clock this very morning, my poor friend, Colonel Altamont, was doomed to execution, and the author only relented when his victim was actually at the window." In confessing that he had been obliged to give up his plan of delineating rascals because he discovered his "want of experience of the subject," he gave the clue to the chief charm of the book. If *Vanity Fair* was "a novel without a hero,"

Pendennis was certainly "a novel without a villain." When, in the last pages, he let Altamont escape by the drain-pipe instead of leaping to his death, he was giving in to a sort of affection he felt for that scalawag.

In the rest of the preface (with recollections of the dispute over his treatment of the literary profession) he earnestly defended the novel's realism: "Since the author of *Tom Jones* was buried, no writer of fiction among us has been permitted to depict to his utmost power a MAN. Society will not tolerate the Natural in our Art. Many ladies have remonstrated and subscribers left me, because, in the course of the story, I described a young man resisting and affected by temptation. My object was to say that he had the passions to feel, and the manliness and generosity to overcome them. A little more frankness than is customary has been attempted in this story; with no bad desire on the writer's part, it is hoped, and with no ill consequences to any reader." The whole preface was in a sincerer tone than the mocking one that had been attached to *Vanity Fair*, and showed a clearer grasp of the problems facing the honest novelist in all eras, but in the Victorian age supremely.

Since he was convinced that his life had been saved by Dr Elliotson, and since that good physician had refused to accept a fee for his services, Thackeray dedicated the novel to him in a cordial note. With this last detail out of the way, he had scarcely time to draw breath before getting to work on *The Kickleburys on the Rhine*. Smith, Elder and Company had announced it for publication on December 16, the last possible date for catching the Christmas trade; but they were not prepared for the tardiness which his previous publishers had learned to endure stoically enough. The firm's reader, W. S. Williams, remarked in a letter to Charlotte Brontë that if Thackeray "had not been helped out with the vigour, energy, and method of Mr Smith, he must have sunk under the day and night labour of the last few weeks." By these desperate efforts, the manuscript was rushed to the printers without an hour to spare.

He had hoped to take the children with him to Paris to spend Christmas with the Carmichael-Smyths, but other duties forced a postponement of the visit. His uncle's widow, Mrs Francis Thackeray, had died in November, leaving two schoolboy sons, and his poignant memory of his own boyhood loneliness prompted him to invite them to spend their holidays at Young Street. And two days before Christmas the funeral of Harry Hallam was to be held at Clevedon.

The Brookfields had closed their house and moved into the home of the Hallams in Wilton Crescent. As only the men of the immediate family were expected to attend the funeral, Jane Brookfield remained in London with her cousin, Julia Hallam. On December 20, Thackeray came in to tell them that he had decided to go down and show his sympathy by attending the ceremony. In a letter to her husband, Jane explained that "Mr Thackeray said he intended to go straight

THE HISTORY OF PENDENNIS VOL. I

BY W M THACKERAY

THE HISTORY OF PENDENNIS VOL. II

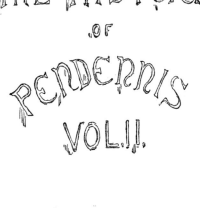

BY

W. M. THACKERAY.

to the Church and should very likely not see anybody to speak to; he said he thought it would be 'most modest' in him to keep aloof in that way as my Uncle wished for privacy, but I begged him just to call and shake hands with Arthur [Elton] and Rhoda if he could." With his habitual half-awkward tenderness, his farewell to her was "a little scolding" on the danger of giving way to dismal thoughts.

From the White Lion at Bristol he went over to Clevedon and waited at a shop in the village, watching the customers, until it was time to proceed to the church. The gloomy appurtenances of a Victorian funeral were distressing enough to him in themselves, and were now made all the more affecting by the knowledge that kind old Henry Hallam had lost nine of his eleven children. When at the final moment the old man went down into the open grave and gave the coffin a last kiss, Thackeray broke down completely.

Brookfield brought him back to Clevedon Court from the church, and when Hallam asked him affectionately whether he wasn't going to stay, he regretted having arranged to return to Bristol. It was the coldest day of the winter, and as he sat that night in the uncomfortable inn, writing to Mrs Brookfield on bad paper, he felt more than a little sorry for himself, and at the same time was able to summon up a wry smile at his own tendency to feel martyred. The whole gauche expedition was an example of that Quixotic impulsiveness of his which responded to grief or misfortune and which commanded the affection of all his friends.

A CLERGYMAN'S WIFE
AT DIEPPE

CHAPTER 14

The Tight-rope Exhibition

TO RESTORE HIS spirits after the misery of the Hallam funeral, Thackeray went from Bristol to the country seat of Sir John Cam Hobhouse in Wiltshire. Hobhouse was a monument to the glories of the previous generation as the college friend of Byron who accompanied him on "Childe Harold's Pilgrimage," and as the Radical leader who once served a prison term in the cause of free speech. Now a respected elder statesman, he was also a famous host, and the party with which Thackeray spent Christmas included "two young lords" and several brilliant wits, notably Charles Villiers, M.P., hero of the fight to repeal the Corn Laws, and Thomas Love Peacock, jovial author of *Headlong Hall* and other satires.

Memories of the Hallam tragedy were dimmed by the old English rural Christmas—snow on the woods, huntsmen in scarlet coats, church choir in smock frocks,—and Thackeray went back to London to learn the good news that the whole three thousand copies of *The Kickleburys* were sold out and a second edition was going to press. The same day, a scathing review of it appeared in *The Times*, and Thackeray was moved to one of his outbursts of wrath. In recent years he had drifted away from his association with that paper, as his friend Barnes had died in 1841 and been succeeded as editor by J. T. Delane, who made it more dogmatic than ever. Thackeray and his friends attributed the present attack to the principal reviewer, Samuel Phillips, a rabid Tory who was supposed to be largely responsible for the turgid style in most of the paper's articles.

The review heaped its condemnation chiefly upon Thackeray's old trait of despising vulgarity and pretension. "Playfully fastening his satiric fangs upon the familiar prey," said the critic, "he dallies with it in mimic ferocity like a satiated mouser. . . To those who love to hug themselves in a sense of superiority by admeasurement with the most worthless of their species, in their most worthless aspects, *The Kickleburys on the Rhine* will afford an agreeable treat. . . To our own, perhaps unphilosophical taste, the aspirations toward sentimental perfection of another popular author are infinitely preferable to these sardonic divings after the pearl of truth, whose lustre is eclipsed in the display of the diseased oyster. . . The illustrations redeem the book from an absolute ban. He cannot draw his men and women with their skins off, and, therefore, the effigies of his characters are pleasanter to contemplate than the flayed anatomies of the letter press."

These strictures might have been forgiven as legitimate opinions of a reader antipathetic to satire, but elsewhere there were nastier cuts. The charge of tuft-hunting was brought by an allusion to "a mysterious countess, spoken of in a tone of religious reverence, and apparently introduced that we may learn by what delicate discriminations our adoration of rank should be regulated." Worst of all, the book was alleged to be a pot-boiler, instigated by the author's need of ready money, and it was compared to the copies of verses which "Mr Walker, the postman, or Mr Bell, the dust-collector, leave at our doors as a provocative of the expected annual gratuity."

There was just enough of truth behind the charges to make them rankle. It was the old challenge again: "Can an author be a gentleman?" and Thackeray writhed. He needed only a few hours to pen "An Essay on Thunder and Small Beer," which he handed to his publishers for inclusion in the second edition, so that it was in the bookshops several days later. The recurrent theme of the rebuttal was that insufferable insult: "A gentleman writing a poor little book is a scavenger asking for a Christmas box!" But the whole essay was a blistering diatribe against the complacency and bombast with which *The Times* assumed to pontificate on all matters.

According to good authority, there was an ironical sequel. The real author of the review turned out to be a friend of Thackeray's, Charles Lamb Kenney, a witty and handsome young man who had sat as the model for Pendennis in the illustrations to that novel. Being Phillips's assistant on the reviewing staff, Kenney had sacrificed his own regard for Thackeray to produce the attack that his employers wanted. When he discovered the violence of Thackeray's wrath, his conscience forced him to go and confess his fault, which was at once forgiven. Having been guilty of similar verbal excesses in his Fraserian days Thackeray could scarcely bear a grudge against this offender.

His dissatisfaction with *Pendennis* continued even after its completion. In preparing it for reissue in two volumes, he cut out parts of chapters sixteen and eighteen, making two chapters out of three, and he also omitted two plates. Other people, too, were unenthusiastic. Charlotte Brontë, nursing the memory of the argument with Thackeray over his literary morals, was grateful to Smith for persuading the author not to send her a presentation copy, as he had intended; she would have been obliged to write a letter of thanks, in which "to have spoken my mind would have been to displease, and I know, if I had written at all, my mind would have insisted on speaking itself." In the same letter to Smith, she sympathized with him over the trouble Thackeray had given the firm by his undependability, and with a laborious effort at satire she proposed that he ought to do penance by building a church with two shrines dedicated to St Bacon and St Bungay, each shrine to contain "a neatly written MS., being a tale without any allusion to Belgravia in it." Apparently she was practicing sarcasm in private, to be ready to astonish Thackeray with a display of his own weapon at their next meeting.

Early in January, Thackeray was ready to go over to Paris for his delayed holiday. The day before he left, the Elliots were having a dinner party, at which the only guests were Mrs Brookfield, Serjeant Gale (who had traveled on the Rhine with Thackeray in the autumn), and Arthur Helps, a civil servant who had recently gained fame with his moralistic work entitled *Friends in Council*. Thackeray had been too busy to attend the dinner, but he knew that his friendship with the family gave him the privilege of dropping in during the evening. As a characteristic joke, he asked the servant to announce him as "Mr Sloane" (the name of a notorious criminal of the day). It chanced that the conversation had just turned to the subject of Thackeray, and Helps was expressing the unfavorable opinion that he held in common with many of the righteous. No one noticed that the door had opened and that the butler was waiting for a lull. "Is Mr Thackeray an amiable man?" Helps demanded. "His books don't give me the impression that he can possess any kind or generous sympathies toward the human race." All the rest of the company were warmly asserting his kindliness, when the butler announced "Mr Sloane," and Thackeray stepped forward.

According to Kate Perry, when she recounted the scene in after years, Helps had concluded by declaring, "I have never met him, and I hope I never shall do so"; and Thackeray stepped up to him and said in his pleasantest tone, "I, on the contrary, have always longed for the occasion when I could express personally to Mr Helps the great admiration I have always felt for him as an author and a man." Mrs Brookfield, writing the day after the event, did not mention this dénouement; but at any rate the moment was a difficult one, and Helps displayed painful embarrassment, although the other guests joined Thackeray in passing it off with laughter.

On arriving in Paris, Thackeray showed that he was determined to find the gaiety that he had missed during the past year; and for the next three weeks he was immersed in the febrile glitter of the expiring Second Republic. Leaving his daughters with the old folk, he took rooms for a day or two at the Hôtel Bristol while looking for lodgings. The first morning, he breakfasted with Edward Ellice, a popular liberal M.P., always known as "Bear Ellice." This friend promised to take him to a *soirée* that evening given by Charles Duchâtel, who had been Minister of the Interior under Louis-Philippe. Ellice also mentioned that Lady Sandwich was giving a grand ball, whereupon Thackeray wrote her a note announcing his arrival, and received an invitation by return messenger.

Apart from a call upon the Ritchies, he spent the day in showing himself at various former haunts, and inspected an art exhibition at the Palais Royal, hoping to be able to write a critique of it; but so far had he drifted away from his old interest that he found the pictures and statues merely boring. At the Duchâtel *soirée* he was equally repelled by the host's pretentious collection of paintings, and he found the company vulgar and stupid—all showing their Orléanist sympathies by ostentatious mourning for the Queen of the Belgians. Lady Sandwich's ball was better, and Thackeray jubilantly recited the roll of celebrities in his letter to Mrs Brookfield: Thiers; the Comte de Molé (the Rightist leader); "the Castlereaghs, very kind and hearty, my lady looking very pretty, and Cas (mark the easy grace of 'Cas') well, and clear-sighted; Lord Normanby and wife, exceeding gracious; Lady Waldegrave; all sorts of world." Although he laughed at himself for reveling in his social eminence, and knew that Jane would share the laughter, nevertheless he was undeniably showing signs of what unsympathetic onlookers branded as "snobbishness."

In the midst of all the frivolities, he was wondering about his next literary venture. Not for many years had he been so free of commitments. Although he had nominally remained on the staff of *Punch* after the squabble in the summer, he was becoming more desultory in his contributions. A new novel, of course, was obligatory, but he was desperately anxious to escape from the bondage of monthly parts. For the moment he kept his hand in by starting a play called *Bluebeard;* he described the first scene to Mrs Brookfield as "so witty and diabolical that I shall be curious to know if it is good." The idea of preparing a series of lectures was becoming more seductive, with a tour of America as the reward of success. And the trivial incident of Arthur Helps's disapproval bothered him unaccountably. For years he had been publicly assailed by many critics for intolerance and cynicism; only a week before he had defended himself fiercely against the same charge in *The Times;* and yet the accident of overhearing a remark at a friend's dinner table brought on a spasm of self-doubt such as he had never before admitted.

In his letter to his mother on the November day when he finished *Pendennis*, he had said, "I've got a better subject for a novel than any I've yet had." Whether in investigation of that same topic, or in preparation for his proposed lectures, he resumed his study of the Augustan Age, dormant during the six years since *Barry Lindon*. He told Mrs Brookfield that he was reading *The Tatler* of 1709 and finding it amusing. He added that "I have been advancing in Blue Beard, but must give it up, it is too dreadfully cynical and wicked. It is in blank verse and all a diabolical sneer. Depend upon it, Helps is right." Two days later, he told her that he was still at work upon it, but that it was so sardonic that he doubted "whether it is right to go on in this wicked vein; and also, I must tell you that a story is biling up in my interior, in which there shall appear some very good, lofty, and generous people; perhaps a story without any villains in it would be good, wouldn't it?"

As a matter of fact, the drama, as far as it went, was not sardonic so much as gently disillusioned. In pedestrian blank verse, suspended between poetry and conversation rather in the style of Browning's dramatic monologues, Bluebeard wistfully tells a friend about his happy school days and his dozen unsatisfactory marriages, and complains about the selfishness of the present Lady Bluebeard, who spends his money for her own amusement, while he suffers boredom and loneliness. Thackeray never carried it beyond this opening dialogue.

In the tentative plans for the American tour, it was assumed that his daughters would stay with the Carmichael-Smyths during his absence; but with something of a shock he realized that his parents were growing old. Although his stepfather was good-humored toward the children, it must have been a nuisance to have them constantly in his room. Thackeray was consumed with pity as he realized the dull trivialities that now occupied the days of a couple who had been "a famous beauty and a soldier who has been in twenty battles and led half a dozen of storming parties." They had fallen into the hands of an Indian woman who had convinced them of her occult powers, and the Major consulted her every day. Duty compelled Thackeray to make himself agreeable to their little social circle, though he hated having to "drag about in this confounded Little Pedlington." One of his mother's friends was particularly fulsome: "Papa was king, mama was queen, in this company, I a sort of foreign emperor with the princesses my daughters. By Jove, it was intolerably painful." He suspected that the girls would be far from happy if left even for a few months in this confinement.

Among his new Parisian friends, he was most taken with Theodore Gudin, the marine painter, and his English wife, daughter of Lord Hay. During the previous reign, Gudin had been the favorite artist of the king, and had undertaken vast projects; although practically ruined by the fall of Louis-Philippe, he still entertained lavishly, and Thackeray met many picturesque persons at the Gudin dinners and balls. In his letter to Mrs Brookfield he affected to complain of being lionized: "This place begins to be as bad as London in the season; there are dinners and routs for every day and night. . . . The French people talk to me about *Ponche*, when I am introduced to them, which wounds my vanity, which is wholesome very likely. . . . But with all this racket and gaiety, do you understand that a gentleman feels very lonely?"

Mrs Brookfield's answer to his long letter contained several of the little comments by which she exerted her gentle guidance of his moods: "I wish to read Bluebeard very much, and I should like you to write a novel to startle Helps and such-like objectors who think your heart does not keep pace with your head (a graceful phrase). . . I was thinking over your chafing against the petty homage and the small sets of Paris, and debating whether you ought not to chafe *as much* against the adulations on a grand scale, but I merely throw this out; I don't think you care about the sublimer flatteries in the least, but it does not irritate you in the same way."

He paid another visit to D'Orsay, whom he found in a state of paranoiac frenzy, in a studio full of mementos of Lady Blessington and Napoleon, "admiring himself in the most horrible pictures which he has painted, and the statues which he gets done for him." The usual attendance at comedies, a night of gambling in the amusing game of lansquenet (solely to observe the psychology of the players, he explained), visits to old Dr Halliday and a sick friend Tom Fraser, all filled up Thackeray's time, but failed to expel boredom. Even ventures into the half-world of the theater had lost their savor; he had an opportunity to go to an actresses' ball, but refused: "my grey head has no call to show amongst these young ones, and, as in the next novel we are to have none but good characters, what is the use of examining folks who are quite otherwise?"

A few days later, longing to be back in London, he was finding his mother's proud proprietorship more and more irksome. On the one evening which he had reserved for himself, intending to dine alone quietly and go to the play, he found that she had engaged him for Lady Elgin's *soirée*. "Was there ever such a victim?" he lamented. "I go about from house to house and grumble everywhere. . . I want to begin to write again very much; my mighty mind is tired of idleness, and ill employs the intervals of rest."

In spite of his previous resolution, he did accept an invitation to a ball "where I shall meet—I, an old fellow of forty—all the pretty actresses of Paris. Let us give a loose to pleasure." In her reply Mrs Brookfield could not restrain one of her little flashes of jealousy: "Are you going among the actresses as a kind of retort for my dull letters? That is rather unworthy in you, if it is the case. . . Now I have read over the first part of this letter I should very much like to burn it. It seems to make such a fuss about the Actresses; why shouldn't you go to their ball?"

At the beginning of February he was at home again, occupied with the duties and distinctions of his literary eminence. On February 25 the Athenaeum Club, reversing its action of the previous year, elected him to membership. His friend Macready was in the midst of withdrawing from the stage; on February 26 Thackeray was in the Procters' box at Drury Lane Theater for his farewell performance, and two days later he was one of the stewards of a testimonial banquet in his honor, for which six hundred guests assembled. Bulwer was in the chair, and the other speakers included Dickens, Forster, and Charles Kemble. Coming at the end of the list, Thackeray proposed the toast to Mrs Macready and her family. As usual, he was "all the while feeling in so terrible a panic that I scarcely knew at the time what I was uttering, and didn't know at all when I sat down." His critical friend Pollock commented that it was the only speech "out of tune," explaining that "he indulges in a humour to turn things the seamy side out, which is at least not appropriate to a festive occasion." From the summary in the newspapers, Charlotte Brontë got the same impression: "It seemed to me scarcely to disguise a secret sneer at the whole concern—the hero and his worshippers."

He was bestirring himself about the same time on behalf of a pension for Mrs Jameson, the art historian, who was one of the closest friends of the Procters. Her desperate financial straits were described by Thackeray to Lord Stanley so effectively that the case was promptly submitted to the Prime Minister, and a few weeks later Thackeray had the pleasure of telling Mrs Jameson that her pension had been granted. He served as one of her trustees for the remaining years of her life.

Few of the old friends of his Fraserian days remained among his intimates except Father Prout, whose bent little figure in the shabby clerical surtout always reappeared in Fleet Street in the intervals of his flittings about the Continent. Their old comrade Jack Sheehan, now a prosperous barrister, had recently got married and established himself at Gore Lodge, retaining the furnishings of its former occupant, D'Orsay; and here Thackeray and Mahony foregathered in surroundings very different from their wonted tavern haunts.

A more recent follower, who had attached himself to Thackeray with somewhat the same devotion as Prout, was James Hannay, an ex-midshipman who had been dismissed from the navy at eighteen by a court-martial for ridiculing his superior officers in a manuscript comic paper. Upon getting a position as a reporter on *The Morning Chronicle* he had made the acquaintance of Thackeray, who became fond of the blunt little man, with his violent Tory politics and his fiery pride in his Scots forbears. Hannay had a lively colloquial style of writing, and fought perpetual quarrels with a ferocity that won Thackeray's praise. "Hannay is a boy after my own heart," Thackeray would say. "He is a thoroughbred little fighting-cock! You can't find his match in the literary cockpit for pluck and endurance. Examine him as closely as you please, you won't find a white feather in him." Thackeray recommended him to the *Quarterly Review*, and on the strength of his first novel persuaded Smith to offer him four hundred pounds for his next. Hannay repaid these favors with loyal affection.

All through the spring Thackeray worked on his series of lectures. The subject he had chosen was "The English Humorists of the Eighteenth Century." He evolved them in close consultation with Mrs Brookfield, sometimes dictating portions to her; but even with her encouragement he found that his attention was often distracted by other themes. London was in a fever of enthusiasm over the imminent opening of the great International Exhibition, and Thackeray, as a friend of Henry Cole and several other prime organizers of it, was inspired to help it along by composing a *May-Day Ode* in honor of the event. It was a long and dutiful piece, with lush compliments to Queen Victoria, the American "goodwill" frigate *St Laurence*, the Indian cottons and Persian rugs, and all the other symbols of peace and prosperity. In order to get his details right, he was permitted a preview of the Crystal Palace with his friend Dicky Doyle, and was impressed by "the great calm leviathan steam engines and machines."

During the five days devoted to writing the ode he shut himself in his study, saw his daughters only at night, and thought about nothing but the poem. When it was finished he was left "utterly beat, nervous, bilious, and overcome." Appropriately enough for this paean of peace and goodwill, it was accepted by his late enemy, *The Times*, which printed it the day before the opening. But typical of Thackeray was the fact that he had a comic poem in the same week's number of *Punch*, describing the identical features of the Exhibition in the racy brogue and impudent rhymes of his Irish *alter ego*, "Mr Molony." Not only did journalistic economy prompt him to use a popular theme twice over, but also his schoolboyish bashfulness demanded the chance to set up a smoke-screen of ridicule around the earnestness of the *Ode*.

His chief anxiety about the lectures was the danger of breaking down from stage fright. A fortnight before the scheduled date of the first one, he went to Willis's Rooms, where he was to perform, and tested his voice by reciting the multiplication table to a waiter posted at the other end of the hall, who assured him that he could hear perfectly.

For some reason his début was postponed for a week, and it was not until May 21 that he delivered his first lecture, on Dean Swift. His mother, of course, came over from Paris for the event. All his friends responded to his appeals that they should give him confidence by the extent, distinction, and sympathy of the audience. Here was a chance to "do something to help dear old Thackeray," while at the same time enjoying an amusing performance. Seldom had such a varied group assembled in a lecture room. His admirers among the nobility—Lord Carlisle, Lord and Lady Ashburton, Lady Waldegrave, Lady Molesworth—were happy to show their patronage of literature by lending support to so presentable an exponent of it. The solemn seniors of his profession filed in—Carlyle, Hallam, Milman, Macaulay. The church was represented by Bishop Wilberforce, the law by the Lord Chief Baron Pollock; the Procters and the Elliots naturally brought all the denizens of their drawing rooms, and Thackeray's intimate friends among the writers and clubmen turned out in force—Hayward, Kinglake, Higgins, and the comrade of his school days, Venables. Nor were his *Punch* colleagues absent. His favorite among them was now the merry young Dicky Doyle, to whom he sent a comic note of instructions preparatory to the "tight-rope exhibition." Doyle was to come armed with "a very noisy umbrella" to be used at intervals, and a code of signals for applause was suggested: when the lecturer fingered his watch-chain, Doyle was to exclaim "God bless my soul, how beautiful!" when he touched his neck-cloth, Doyle was to give loud applause; when he took out his handkerchief,

Doyle was to burst into tears, or—if that were impossible—at least to blow his nose very hard.

Among those most keenly interested was Fanny Kemble, whose stage experience helped her to realize his nervousness. "Going thither before the time for his beginning," she tells in her reminiscences, "I found him like a forlorn, disconsolate giant in the middle of the room, gazing about him. 'Oh, Lord,' he exclaimed, as he shook hands with me, 'I'm sick at my stomach with fright.' I spoke some words of encouragement to him, and was going away, but he held my hand like a scared child, crying, 'Oh, don't leave me!'

" 'But,' said I, 'Thackeray, you mustn't stay here. Your audience are beginning to come in,' and I drew him from the middle of his chairs and benches, which were beginning to be occupied, into the retiring-room adjoining the lecture-room, my own readings having made me perfectly familiar with both. Here he began pacing up and down, literally wringing his hands in nervous distress. 'Now,' said I, 'what shall I do? Shall I stay with you till you begin, or shall I go, and leave you alone to collect yourself?'

" 'Oh,' he said, 'if I could only get at that confounded thing (the MS.) to have a last look at it!'

" 'Where is it?' said I.

" 'Oh, in the next room on the reading desk.'

" 'Well,' said I, 'if you don't like to go in and fetch it, I'll fetch it for you.' And remembering well the position of my reading table, which had been close to the door of the retiring-room, I darted in, hoping to snatch the manuscript without attracting the attention of the audience, with which the room was already nearly full. I had been used to deliver my reading seated at a very low table, but my friend Thackeray gave his lectures standing, and had a reading desk placed on the platform, adapted to his own very tall stature, so that when I came to get his manuscript it was almost above my head. Though rather disconcerted, I was determined not to go back without it, and so made a half-jump and a clutch at the book, when every leaf of it (they were not fastened together) came fluttering separately down about me. I hardly know what I did, but I think I must have gone nearly on all fours, in my agony to gather up the scattered leaves, and, retreating with them, held them out in dismay to poor Thackeray, crying, 'Oh, look, look, what a dreadful thing I have done!'

" 'My dear soul,' he said, 'you couldn't have done better for me. I have just a quarter of an hour to wait here, and it will take me about that to page this again, and it's the best thing in the world that could have happened.' With which infinite kindness he comforted me, for I was all but crying, at having, as I thought, increased his distress and troubles."

When he began to read, his voice was so strained by fright that his daughter did not recognize it; but he gradually gained confidence, and the audience was delighted with the ease and informality of his manner as well as the vividness of his style. He could not believe the compliments that were heaped upon him, and the next day he wrote despondently to Hayward: "The truth is the lectures won't do. They were all friends, and a packed house; though to be sure, it goes to a man's heart to find amongst his friends such men looking on kindly."

The only significant disapproval of the lectures was indicated by John Forster. Thackeray was becoming steadily more convinced that Forster was so unjustly biassed against him by his jealous championship of Dickens and Bulwer that he kept spreading insidious anti-Thackeray propaganda. Forster regarded himself as an expert in the eighteenth-century English authors; and three years before, when his *Life of Goldsmith* was published, Thackeray was indiscreet enough to tell him of his own hope of sometime writing biographies of Goldsmith and Fielding. When the lectures began Forster was prepared to be hypercritical, and he reviewed the first one in *The Examiner* with damnatory faint praise, disagreement over details, and a patronizing explanation that Thackeray had to "sacrifice much to effect."

Thackeray was deeply incensed. He would have had no objection to unfavorable criticism, if it were fairly based; but he knew how blindly Forster overpraised his favorites, and he could not forget the remark that "Thackeray is as false as hell." Feeling that the falseness was entirely on the other side, he chafed against the hypocritical pretense of friendship between them. In reviewing the second lecture the cocksure critic played into Thackeray's hands by attributing a quotation to Congreve instead of Steele; and with silent satisfaction Thackeray gave the correct fact in his next lecture.

Meanwhile, having invited Thackeray to dinner, Forster told him with customary bluntness that his lectures were intended only to entertain his lady friends, and were devoid of humor or cleverness. In a burst of temper Thackeray replied as rudely that he might say the same of Forster's *Goldsmith*. This open battle ended in immediate reconciliation; Thackeray went home mollified, assuring himself that Forster was merely jealous of his popularity in high society. Within six weeks, however, he was once again so infuriated that he wrote to Forster and threatened to set up a paper in rivalry to *The Examiner*. He took a vow that he would never regard Forster as a friend again.

Otherwise, Thackeray received only a few hints that lecturing was not a seemly performance for an author. The tactless Mrs Norton reported to him that Julia Hallam had said after the first lecture, "I saw by Papa's face, he was trying not to say 'Pooh! Pooh!' all the time." As a special effort to appease the great historian Thackeray inserted in the second lecture the remark, "how can I ask my superior to say that I am a wonder when he knows better than I?" and called it to Mrs

Brookfield's attention when rehearsing the lecture before her and Mrs Elliot the day before it was given.

It was "much more successful and more popular than the one before," Mrs Brookfield told her husband; "Mr Thackeray was much less nervous, indeed quite cool and collected, and gave out his voice, so as to be well heard, and had his paper on the desk instead of in his hand, which gave a freer look to the thing. The room was very much fuller, indeed it appeared quite full, tho' there might have been room for more, and there were all the Duchesses and Marchionesses that were there before with sundry additions to the number, and some of the big wigs among the men, Lord Clanricarde, Sir J. Hobhouse, etc. . . Uncle Hallam was there and was much pleased this time; of course Maria had told him of Mrs Norton's treachery in repeating the 'Pooh! Pooh!' at which he was in a great rage and declared he would punish her by believing all the stories told against her."

Charlotte Brontë had decided to pay another visit to London, to see the Exhibition, and she hastened her arrival to be in time for his second performance. "I did not at all expect," she wrote to a friend, "the great lecturer would know me or notice me under these circumstances, with admiring duchesses and countesses seated in rows before him; but he met me as I entered—shook hands—took me to his mother, whom I had not before seen, and introduced me. She is a fine, handsome, young-looking old lady." All the people within earshot of the introduction craned their necks to stare at "Jane Eyre," and Thackeray embarrassed her still further by pointing her out to various friends, so that glasses were turned upon her from every direction, and Lord Carlisle and Mr Milnes came up and introduced themselves. "I am afraid Mr Thackeray has been playing me a trick," remarked Miss Brontë primly to Mrs Smith, who was chaperoning her.

The lecture pleased her, however. "Thackeray just got up and spoke with as much simplicity and ease as if he had been speaking to a few friends by his own fireside. The lecture was truly good: he had taken pains with the composition. It was finished without being in the least studied; a quiet humour and graphic force enlivened it throughout." As soon as he ended, Thackeray stepped down from the platform and came over to ask for her opinion, but she was too much abashed to reply. In a scene of her next novel, *Villette*, she expressed in the guise of fiction the comments that she could not utter directly: "He should not have cared just then to ask what I thought, or what anybody thought; but he *did* care, and he was too natural to conceal, too impulsive to repress his wish. Well! if I blamed his overeagerness, I liked his *naïveté*. I would have praised him; I had plenty of praise in my heart; but alas! no words on my lips."

Mrs Smith, realizing that most of the audience was lining the aisle for a better view of the author of *Jane Eyre*, grasped her trembling hand and hurried down the "avenue of eager and admiring faces," in dread that Charlotte might faint before they reached the exit. The next day Mrs Carmichael-Smyth brought the two girls to call on her, and Thackeray also called separately. Her host, George Smith, later reported the interview. "When I entered the drawing-room I found a scene in full progress. Only these two were in the room. Thackeray was standing on the hearthrug, looking anything but happy. Charlotte Brontë stood close to him, with head thrown back and face white with anger. The first words I heard were, 'No, Sir! If *you* had come to our part of the country in Yorkshire, what would you have thought of me if I had introduced you to my father, before a mixed company of strangers, as "Mr Warrington"?'

"Thackeray replied, 'No, you mean "Arthur Pendennis." ' "

" 'No, I *don't* mean Arthur Pendennis!' retorted Miss Brontë; 'I mean Mr Warrington, and Mr Warrington would not have behaved as you behaved to me yesterday.'

"The spectacle of this little woman, hardly reaching to Thackeray's elbow, but, somehow, looking stronger and fiercer than himself, casting her incisive words at his head, resembled the dropping of shells into a fortress. By this time I had recovered my presence of mind, and hastened to interpose. Thackeray made the necessary and half-humorous apologies, and the parting was a friendly one."

In her own report of the episode, Miss Brontë was more concise. "I had a long talk with him, and I think he knows me now a little better than he did, but of this I cannot be sure; he is a great and strange man."

The triumph of this second lecture was a good omen for the four that were to follow. "Mr Thackeray is in high spirits about the success of his lectures," Miss Brontë informed her father on June 7. "It is likely to add largely both to his fame and purse. He has, however, deferred this week's lecture till next Thursday, at the earnest petition of the duchesses and marchionesses, who, on the day it should have been delivered, were necessitated to go down with the Queen and Court to Ascot Races. I told him I thought he did wrong to put it off on their account— and I think so still."

Jane Welsh Carlyle wrote confidentially to her sister that "the lectures be-tween you and me are no great things—as *lectures*—but it is the fashion to find them 'so amusing'!" Other observers, however, were kinder. After the third lec-ture, Macaulay noted in his journal that "he is full of humour and imagination, and I only wish that these lectures may answer both in the way of fame and money. He told me, as I was going out, that the scheme had done wonders for him; and I told him, and from my heart, that I wished he had made ten times as much." At two guineas for a reserved seat for the series, and seven shillings and sixpence for single unreserved admissions, he could see a pleasant accession of funds every time he faced a crowded hall.

Among the audience at the lecture on Steele was John Chapman, the chief publisher of books by advanced free-thinkers, and a man of doubtful personal reputation. His diary records that he was "much disappointed. The lecture was more like a long sermon than anything, and did not gain by being read." When Chapman was introduced to the lecturer by Thornton Hunt, Thackeray remarked jocosely that he wanted to buy some of Chapman's "atheistic publications" at the "trade price." It was arranged that he should call on Chapman two days later, and upon this occasion Chapman was agreeably surprised by his frankness. "I find that his religious views are perfectly *free*, but he does not mean to lessen his popularity by fully showing them; he said he had debated the question with himself whether he was called upon to martyrize himself for the sake of his views and concluded in the negative. His chief object seems to be the making of money. He will go to America for that purpose. He impresses me as much abler than the lecture I heard, but I fear his success is spoiling him."

The interview had not been arranged merely for rationalistic discussion. Chapman was in the process of purchasing the *Westminster Review*, and he wanted Thackeray to write for it an article on the modern novelists. Thackeray prudently declined, for reasons which Chapman chronicled: "That his writings were so much more valuable, pecuniarily, if published in other ways; that he, from his position, could not criticise his contemporaries, and that the only person he could thoroughly well review and cut up would be himself! He complained of the rivalry and partizanship which is being fostered—I think chiefly Fo(r)ster'd—in respect to him and Dickens by foolish friends." Thackeray took the opportunity to suggest that the commission to write the article be offered to Charlotte Brontë; but this idea was vetoed by Marian Evans (not yet known as "George Eliot"), who was Chapman's protégée and literary adviser at the time, and who pointed out that Miss Brontë would suffer under the same handicaps as Thackeray.

Under the impulsion of the Exhibition, the London season was of unparalleled brilliance, with even the Court discarding some of its dignity to lead the revels. Charlotte Brontë watched the frivolity with a somber eye. "A new toy," she wrote to her father, "has somewhat diverted the attention of the grandees lately, viz., a fancy ball given last night by the Queen. The great lords and ladies have been quite wrapt up in preparations for this momentous event. Their pet and darling, Mr Thackeray, of course sympathises with them. He was here [at the Smiths'] yesterday to dinner, and left very early in the evening in order that he might visit respectively the Duchess of Norfolk, the Marchioness of Londonderry, Ladies Chesterfield and Clanricarde, and see them all in their fancy costumes of the reign of Charles II before they set out for the Palace!" He took his daughters with him on this pilgrimage; and the glimpses of the vast old London mansions, with the throngs of gracious, laughing courtiers in Restoration costume, stayed in their memories throughout their lives like a vision of fairyland.

Now half way through the lectures, Thackeray was at last assured that he had not failed. "His lectures, it appears, are a triumphant success," wrote Miss Brontë. "He says they will enable him to make a provision for his daughters; and Mr Smith believes he will not get less than four thousand pounds by them. He is going to give two courses, and then go to Edinburgh and perhaps America, but *not* under the auspices of Barnum. Among others, the Lord Chancellor attended his last lecture, and Mr Thackeray says he expects a place from him; but in this I think he was joking. Of course Mr T. is a good deal spoiled by all this, and indeed it cannot be otherwise. He has offered two or three times to introduce me to some

MRS BROOKFIELD AND HER TWO MAIDS

of his great friends, and says he knows many great ladies who would receive me with open arms if I would go to their houses; but, seriously, I cannot see that this sort of society produces so good an effect on him as to tempt me in the least to try the same experiment, so I remain obscure."

In the hope of doing her honor in a style that would not afflict her with too much shyness, he hit upon the rash scheme of giving a party consisting only of his women friends. "There will not be a Jack amongst us," he said in his invitation to Mrs Elliot and Miss Perry. In view of the coolness previously developed, he did not have Mrs Brookfield, but asked Mrs Procter and Adelaide, Mrs Carlyle, Mrs Crowe, and one or two others. Unable to realize that his wife might be invited anywhere without him, Carlyle presented himself along with her, and monopolized much of the conversation by "railing at the appearance of Cockneys upon Scotch mountain sides. There were also too many Americans for his taste, but the Americans were as gods compared to the Cockneys."

The guest of honor proved to be no more at her ease among these witty ladies than in mixed company; and the scene engraved itself upon the memory of Anne Thackeray, who at fourteen was developing a keen eye for social comedy. "It was a gloomy and a silent evening," she tells in her memoirs. "Every one waited for the brilliant conversation which never began at all. Miss Brontë retired to the sofa in the study, and murmured a low word now and then to our kind governess, Miss Trulock. The room looked very dark; the lamp began to smoke a little; the conversation grew dimmer and more dim; the ladies sat round still expectant; my father was too much perturbed by the gloom and the silence to be able to cope with it at all. . . My sister and I roamed about excitedly, and in one of my incursions crossing the hall, towards the close of the entertainment, I was surprised to see my father opening the front door with his hat on. He put his fingers to his lips, walked out into the darkness, and shut the door quietly behind him. When I went back to the drawing-room again, the ladies asked me where he was. I vaguely answered that I thought he was coming back." But he had fled to his club, and after a while the guests straggled home.

His mother returned to France on June 24, after trying to convert all his friends to her latest craze for mesmerism. She made an effort to take little Minny back to live with her, but Thackeray refused to countenance her being separated from him and her sister.

The fifth lecture, on June 26, dealt with Hogarth, Smollett, and Fielding. Miss Brontë listened to it with pain. Her natural puritanism having been intensified by the fatal dissipations of her brother Branwell, she was horrified by the levity with which Thackeray talked of Fielding's delinquencies. "Had Thackeray owned a son," she declared, "grown, or growing up, and a son, brilliant but reckless— would he have spoken in that light way of courses that lead to disgrace and the grave?. . . Had I a brother yet living, I should tremble to let him read Thackeray's lecture on Fielding. I should hide it away from him. If, in spite of precaution, it should fall into his hands, I should earnestly pray him not to be misled by the voice of the charmer, let him charm never so wisely."

Although Miss Brontë was carried away by personal prejudice, her protest impinges upon the central problem of the lectures. Thackeray's choice of a subject had been congenial, and yet perilous. The eighteenth century was his favorite epoch, and its authors, with their realism and satire, were his literary forbears. But in offering an extended critical survey, he incurred the duty of basing it upon clear standards of judgment, both ethical and literary. His early journalistic experience in criticizing pictures and current books had not provided him with such standards. To deal fairly with the great Augustans in the heyday of Victorian prudery would have needed courage of a high degree, whereas Thackeray was mainly concerned with titillating his audience. Although Charlotte Brontë was shocked by his tolerant attitude toward Fielding, modern readers are more apt to be annoyed by his contempt for Swift and his emphasis upon the coarseness of Sterne. The black misanthropy and smoldering rage of the Dean disturbed him, and the sly lewdness of *Tristram Shandy* poisoned the urbane sentimental wit that would otherwise have charmed him. With one of the contemporary allusions that besprinkled the lectures, he ended the discussion of Sterne by contrasting him with Dickens, in a handsome compliment: "I am grateful for the innocent laughter and the sweet and unsullied page which the author of *David Copperfield* gives to my children."

Addressing a non-scholarly audience, Thackeray was wise to avoid pedantic minuteness. But in crowding twelve authors into the six lectures he had to be unduly superficial, and he evaded the real challenge of the theme in a sparkle of irony and sophistication. He was not enough of a Victorian to reprobate the Augustans as Charlotte Brontë would have liked; and yet he was too much of a Victorian to vindicate their frankness. "I wish," remarked Carlyle to Venables, "I could persuade Thackeray that the test of greatness in a man is not whether he would like to meet the man at a tea party."

CHAPTER 15

The Best of Friends Must Part

AFTER THE HARD labor of the lectures Thackeray wanted to be off as soon as possible for a holiday on the Rhine. The day before his departure he was astonished to receive a message from the Lord Chancellor requesting an interview at half-past four that afternoon. Confident that at last he was to be offered an official position, he broke other engagements to keep the appointment. As Lord and Lady Truro insisted on his sharing their early dinner at that impossible hour, he had to suffer agonies of suspense and make polite conversation until Lady Truro at last went off to a concert and the Chancellor worked around to his objective. He wanted Mr Thackeray's support in some trivial literary scheme.

When Thackeray dropped in at Mrs Brookfield's the next morning to say good-bye, he made good comedy out of his disappointment. He also offered to sell his horse and newly-renovated carriage at a bargain for thirty-five pounds. Brookfield's health had collapsed, with symptoms of lung trouble, and Thackeray insisted that he ought not to tire himself with walking. But as Thackeray was beginning to break up his establishment for the proposed American tour, the offer may not have been wholly disinterested.

With some hesitancy, he had decided that his daughters were now old enough to explore the Rhine in his company. He soon began to find that the unaccustomed duty of looking after them was less irksome than he had feared. He felt obliged to be dignified and circumspect, avoiding all his usual conversations with strangers and devoting himself to pointing out the proper sights. But he was rewarded by their enthusiasm for all they saw, and as he became better acquainted with them he discovered unsuspected merits, especially in Annie, who delighted him by her considerateness and her humor. For appropriate reading, to while away the tedium, he had brought three of his own works, *A Legend of the Rhine*, *Rebecca and Rowena*, and *The Kickleburys*, and he confessed that he found all three "capital," adding that "*R. and R.* not only made me laugh but the other thing."

After a day of sightseeing at Antwerp, they proceeded by way of Cologne and Mayence in a river steamer to Wiesbaden. On board they encountered Charles Kingsley and his parents, who were making the tour in the hope of warding off a nervous breakdown that was threatening the young clergyman-novelist. His recent books, *Yeast* and *Alton Locke*, had provoked charges of "heresy" and "socialism," and by a sermon at a special service for working-men he had just roused such a furore that he was temporarily banned from all pulpits in the diocese of London.

241

Thackeray felt toward him very much as toward Charlotte Brontë; a condescending pity for their unworldliness was admixed with envy of their earnestness and driving idealism, the lack of which left him rudderless. "A fine go-ahead fellow," he described Kingsley, "who charges a subject heartily, impetuously, and with the greatest courage and simplicity, but with narrow eyes (his are extraordinarily brave, blue, and honest), and with little knowledge of the world, I think. But he is superior to us worldlings in many ways, and I wish I had some of his honest pluck."

Full of paternal responsibility, he had a solemn talk with the children one night about their mother, impressing on them how "humble minded" she was, and how Mrs Brookfield possessed this same virtue. On reaching Baden-Baden, he encountered several acquaintances, and determined to stay for two or three days. Feeling that after five days devoted to the girls he had earned a little freedom, he went out alone for a walk; and when he met Mme de Bonneval he accepted her suggestion of an evening of social gaiety. On his return to the inn he found Annie holding Minny on her knee and maternally telling her a story, a scene which touched him so deeply that he stayed with them till their bed-time, dropped in at the de Bonnevals' for only half an hour, and did not go near the *rouge-et-noir* at all.

Realizing that "the impure atmosphere of the pretty, witty gambling place" was "not good for my young ones," he firmly departed the next morning, and in the luxurious privacy of a first-class railway compartment they proceeded to Basel, so enchanted by the "calm sweet landscapes" that he entertained passing fancies as to whether "a residence in this country would ennoble one's thoughts permanently, and get them away from mean quarrels, intrigues, pleasures? make one write good books—turn poet perhaps or orator—and get out of that business of London?" His fortieth birthday was passed at Berne, and by the time they reached Lucerne his devotion to his charges was confirmed. He gave thanks to Heaven for "such an artless affectionate companion" as Annie. "Oh! may she never fall in love absurdly and marry an ass!" he soliloquized. "If she will but make her father her confidant, I think the donkey won't long keep his ground in her heart."

They went on as far as Milan and Venice before returning home, and as soon as they were back in London Thackeray set to work vigorously on his next novel. Plans were afoot for repeating his lectures, and a stack of requests came in from all parts of the country to deliver them for the literary clubs and mechanics' institutes that had sprung up. He was amused to receive also a number of invitations from his friends in society asking him to give private readings—unpaid, of course,—at their receptions.

The American project, too, was never far from his thoughts. James T. Fields, a Boston publisher who specialized in promoting the works and personal appearances of English writers, was paying a visit to London, and heard so many favorable opinions of Thackeray's lectures that he sounded out some members of the

Garrick Club as to the likelihood of being able to persuade the novelist to visit the United States. The clubmen with one accord declared that old Thackeray would never bestir himself to such an effort; but one of them must have mentioned the inquiry to him, for the very next morning he presented himself at Fields' lodging while the publisher was at breakfast, and revealed his eagerness for an engagement. William Allingham, who had been renewing his acquaintance with Thackeray, received the impression that the American tour was in immediate prospect, and on August 25 Carlyle grunted in a letter to Emerson that Thackeray "is coming over to lecture to you: a mad world, my masters."

But the lectures must not be allowed to take precedence over authorship. George Smith had commissioned the new novel as soon as he heard of it, paying six hundred pounds immediately on account, as half of the payment for the first edition of 2500 copies. Encouraged by this generosity and the consequent release from the agony of monthly parts, Thackeray was sanguine enough to promise to have the book finished by the beginning of the new year, after which he would be free for the American visit.

For the setting of the story, his lectures had immersed him in the Augustan Age so deeply that he sometimes felt as if he were living in it. His letters tended to drop playfully into the mannerisms of Addison and Steele, and even such a fortuitous event as the Queen's costume ball had helped to bring the age to life in his imagination. He selected an unusual technique: the story was cast in the form of memoirs, and yet written with old-world formality in the third person. This gave all the advantages of reality and vividness, while diminishing the impression of egotism that is the bane of the autobiographic device. And as Henry Esmond, his hero and narrator, was supposed to be a man of action rather than a scholar, any errors or confusion in the telling could be accepted as plausible instead of being attributed to the carelessness of the real author.

Within a few weeks of his return from the Rhine, the long-avoided crisis in his relations with the Brookfields suddenly exploded. In the days of their unclouded friendship, Thackeray had held it as one of Brookfield's special merits that he had conquered certain handicaps of birth and early environment. His father had been a solicitor in a midland city, of strict evangelical tenets, and the young man had spent a year or two of apprenticeship to that profession before persuading his parents to send him to Cambridge. All the more credit to him, Thackeray had argued when promoting his qualifications to be a School Inspector, that he had revealed such social graces as soon as he entered the urbane world of the university, while yet remaining unashamed of his provincial parents. But in recent years, as Thackeray grew exasperated with what he regarded as the neglect and indignities visited upon the angelic Jane, he could not help wondering whether Brookfield was, after all, altogether a gentleman.

How much his suspicions were entirely due to jealous devotion to the lady and silent observation of Brookfield's behavior, or how much may have been conveyed to him by confidential hints from Jane herself during the years of their intimacy, is impossible to decide; but upon his return from abroad Thackeray became convinced that Brookfield had progressed from mere selfish inconsideration to positive harshness.

If Thackeray's opinion had any grounds beyond his own unhappy, frustrated idealization of Jane Brookfield, the causes must be recognized in her husband's career. Ambitious and popular, he had expected his marriage into a family of higher social rank to help him to success in his profession. Jane had probably accepted him upon the same subconscious assumption. But somehow he had never risen above an underpaid curacy, and had been obliged to accept the dull routine of his inspectorship. Jane's ill health, and perhaps her social affinities, prevented her from fulfilling the ordinary duties of a parson's wife.

He proved, therefore, to be a querulous invalid, and in Thackeray's eyes his wife was a long-suffering nurse. Goaded to fury by some display of impatience toward her on Brookfield's part, Thackeray lashed out with accusations of selfishness and cruelty. Brookfield retorted hotly, insisting that the friendship between Jane and Thackeray must be totally ended, or else that there must be a separation from her husband. He went so far as to say that he ought to have married a cook. To Jane there was only one conceivable course of action: whether or not her enjoyment of Thackeray's company and gratification in his devotion could be accurately described as "love," there was no shadow of doubt as to her dutiful loyalty to her husband and her home. Bowing to his authority, she declared all communication with Thackeray at an end.

Their social position and responsibility to their families demanded that no hint of the incident must reach the outside world. As the friendship had never aroused a breath of scandal, so the breach must be masked with the conventions. Each victim, however, sought a confidante: Mrs Brookfield turned to her closest friend, Mrs Fanshawe, and Thackeray to the ever-sympathetic Kate Perry. As each of these ladies remained intimate with both the sufferers, an indirect contact was maintained.

In helpless misery, Thackeray fled blindly from London and took refuge in the depths of Derbyshire. He tried to get a grip upon himself by working on his novel, but soon realized that the resulting story would be "diabolical." His moods were uncontrollable. At one moment, he condemned his own attack upon Brookfield as unjustifiable, praised him for acting nobly, and pitied him as much as he pitied himself and Jane. While in this state of remorse, he even went so far as to claim that he had intentionally behaved so as to alienate her—that his insulting remarks to her husband had been planned to rouse her wrath and make any reconciliation impossible. When Mrs Fanshawe forwarded to him a letter that Mrs Brookfield had written to her with the obvious intention of its being transmitted to him, he requested Mrs Fanshawe to warn Mrs Brookfield against this "round-about correspondence."

Three days later his state of mind had changed from abnegation to bitterness; he wrote a sneering letter to Jane about the "hypocrisy" that her husband's attitude was imposing upon her and everyone else in the situation, and then sent it to Miss Perry instead—perhaps hoping that she, like Mrs Fanshawe, would promote the "roundabout correspondence" he had recently condemned. And yet with the novelist still asserting himself through the pangs of the lover, he closed his note to Miss Perry with the assertion that he would soon be better, "and if it's out of mere spite I'll do something Big yet."

At other times he adopted a more fatalistic view, and distributed the blame equally among all three of them. He ought to have broken away, but was too complacent in the certainty of his own and Jane's continence; she or her husband ought to have dismissed him, but Brookfield's conceit had fed on the admiration his wife received; they all had been playing with edged tools until without any single wrongdoing they had found themselves enmeshed beyond escape. Regrets were vain. He had been played with by a woman, who discarded him the moment her lord and master gave the word. Nor could he at the moment face the thought of ever again seeing the two Brookfields together.

Throughout, however, his love and sympathy were always primarily for Jane, his greatest misery was the thought of the torments she must be suffering, and he recurrently appealed to Miss Perry to try to comfort her. "Duty" was a keyword in the letters, and it was not Jane's duty only—his own duty to his career and his children had to be remembered. Gradually he forced himself back to work.

By the time he returned to London, their intimates had set themselves to patch up the ruins of the friendship. The domineering Lady Ashburton probably took a hand in the affair; at any rate, after a morning of "parleys" Thackeray and Brookfield shook hands, and Thackeray told Miss Perry of his thankfulness that Jane's "dear little heart is made tranquil on the score of our enmity at least." But it was a constrained truce, and Thackeray could not help noticing with scorn certain "queer ceremonies" and petty "punctilios" in his former friend, such as indicating his state of grief by letting his hair grow long. At the end of October, the Brookfields left for Madeira and stayed there for eight months in the hope of restoring his health.

In some respects, this separation was more disastrous for Thackeray than the loss of his wife had been. Jane Brookfield was an ideal companion for him, stimulating his wit, understanding his moods, guiding him with a tactful mixture of raillery and sympathy, as the meek, anxious little Irish girl could never have hoped to do. During the five years of his intimacy with Mrs Brookfield, he had written his two greatest novels, risen to a place of eminence and respect in society and literature, and enjoyed a large measure of genuine happiness. Subconsciously, he must have realized how vulnerable their intimacy was, and this vague menace made it all the more precious. Now middle-aged, and seeing clearly that one of the things he loved best in Jane was the steadfast constancy that must set up a barrier between them for ever, he could hope for no future comrade that would replace her. Nor must it be forgotten that William Brookfield had been the idol of his college days and the best loved of all his friends during the twenty years that followed. The deepest foundations of his happiness were destroyed, and the whole structure tottered.

Written in the midst of this anguish, the opening parts of his novel were repetitive and confused. In spite of the century and a half which supposedly isolated it from his own time, he put as much of his personal experience into it as into *Pendennis*, save only that the experience was of inner conflict rather than of external detail. The story was bound to be identified in his mind with Jane Brookfield, for the scene of it, Castlewood House, was unmistakably derived from her family home, Clevedon Court; and his visit to Clevedon Court had been at the time when he first recognized how deeply he cared for her. The central theme of the novel— the partly-suppressed love of Henry Esmond for a woman who seemed to be separated from him by an unbridgeable chasm of duty and convention—reflected the exact situation of Thackeray and Mrs Brookfield; and through the words of Esmond he was able to pour out the devotion and the longing that were consuming him. Lady Castlewood was a more exact portrait of Mrs Brookfield than Amelia Sedley had been, in her beauty and dignity, her unwavering fidelity as wife and mother, her religious earnestness, even her little outbursts of jealousy. Lady Castlewood was represented as being set apart from her worshiper not only by her family loyalty—first to her husband and later to her children—but also by the fact of being eight or nine years his senior. This unusual feature concealed in some degree the autobiographic basis of the theme.

As the writing of *Henry Esmond* proceeded more slowly than he had hoped, the American tour retreated into the future. On October 12 Allingham reported to Emerson that it had been postponed until next year. Meanwhile, arrangements were being made for lecturing closer to home. With regard to Scotland, Thackeray consulted John Blackwood, who recommended Dr John Brown as the best possible sponsor. On the strength of their previous correspondence over the Punch statuette, Thackeray wrote to ask for Brown's advice and aid, with somewhat pathetic insistence upon the great success of the lectures in London and his anxiety not to fail in Edinburgh, lest the prospects of future engagements be imperiled. In apology for his concern over financial details, he explained that "as I don't intend to touch the proceeds of the lectures myself (beyond actual travelling charges) and resolutely invest all the winnings for my two girls, I'm bolder than I should be otherwise in the business." Foreseeing offers of hospitality, he added that he would have to devote part of each day to his novel, and so "I must have my own way, my own lodgings, factotum, liberty, cigar after breakfast, etc., without all of which I can't work."

The first repetition of the lectures was to be at Oxford and Cambridge, requiring the sanction of the University authorities. When he went up to Oxford to apply for it, the Vice-Chancellor showed blank ignorance of his identity, and asserted he had never heard of *Vanity Fair*. Thackeray had to cite his friendship with the Bishop of Oxford in order to establish his respectability. For the Cambridge venture he took the precaution of writing to his cousin, the Vice-Provost of King's, asking him to negotiate with the Vice-Chancellor.

All the haggling and self-advertising produced a sense of humiliation which he tried to suppress by blatantly proclaiming himself a mountebank. "I propose to mount my tub and send round my hat," he said in his first letter to Brown, and again, "I can't say when the Titmarsh Van will begin its career." To Dr Thackeray at Cambridge he emphasized his hope that the American tour would produce "a little fortune for my little people. If I ever get *another* fortune, I will keep it." And in a letter to his mother he uttered the same vow: "Cowardly self-love cries out Save—save, or you may starve. . . So please God we will, and do that work resolutely for the next year." While assuring her that he was in much improved health, he confessed to "the absurd fancy that, now the money-making is actually at hand, some disaster may drop down and topple me over."

After some postponement, the Oxford and Cambridge lectures were given during November, and went off without mishap. At Oxford his host was his school friend Stoddard, now a tutor at St John's, and the first night's audience was so good that he reported gleefully to his mother, "The young ones will probably be worth £30 apiece tonight." In addition to the money, he was gratified to receive the approval of the university audiences, for the judgment of the "dons and their donnas" was likely to be the most searching he would meet.

Still feeling that the lectures were *infra dig.*, he spoke slightingly of them to his friends. "Thackeray says he is getting tired of being witty, and of the great world," FitzGerald remarked to Frederick Tennyson. Dining with the Miss Berrys, on the eve of his departure for Scotland, he gave the old ladies a contemptuous picture of the lectures, "what humbug he thought them all" (Kate Perry noted in her diary), "and how impossible it was for him to believe in himself, or in anyone listening to him." At this dinner he was finally accepted by Miss Berry in the inmost circle. Kate Perry and her sister, tireless in praising him and in bringing him to the soirées in Curzon Street, suspected that the two old ladies had never fully appreciated him. On this occasion Miss Berry startled the company by announcing that she could not read Jane Austen's novels, which were nothing but "long drawn out details of very ordinary people;" and then she added, "Thackeray and Balzac write with great minuteness, but with a brilliant pen." Thackeray stood up and made her a solemn bow, and then a second one, pointing downward to indicate that it was on behalf of the recently deceased Balzac. After he left, the Miss Berrys gave their pontifical verdict: "We have perceived for the first time what a very remarkable man he is."

The Edinburgh lectures had been efficiently prepared for by Dr Brown, who also tried to arrange for a series in Glasgow, though he was handicapped by Thackeray's carelessness in failing to answer letters promptly. When Thackeray arrived in Edinburgh, invitations to dinner greeted him, and he was assured that the lectures were well subscribed for—though he suspected that "there will be more praise than money at this town." For the first lecture he had a hundred subscribers and two hundred others in the audience. "Isn't that handsome?" he exclaimed. "It is such a good audience that I begin to reflect about going to America so soon. Why, if so much money is to be made in the empire, not go through with the business and get what is to be had?" Dr Brown reported to a friend that "he has been so surprised and pleased at his success last night that he longs to harry Glasgow of £100." Franklin Lushington, a brother-in-law of Tennyson, being in Edinburgh the next week as a candidate for a professorship, fondly imagined that he was cheering Brookfield in his exile by informing him that Thackeray had delivered his lectures "with great success to enthusiastic audiences."

Dr Brown was delighted with the visitor, whom he described to a friend as "a strong-headed, sound-hearted, judicious fellow. . . He is much better and greater than his works. . . He is 6 feet 3 in height, with a broad kindly face and an immense skull. . . He makes no figure in company, except as very good humoured, and by saying now and then a quietly strong thing. . . He is as much bigger than Dickens as a three-decker of 120 guns is bigger than a small steamer with one long-range swivel gun."

On the way home Thackeray bought a copy of *Punch* to read in the train, and was confronted with a cartoon of Louis Napoleon, who had just seized dictatorial power, as a "Beggar on Horseback," galloping to hell with a sword dripping with blood. Thackeray's annoyance against the policy of the paper had been repeatedly rekindled since the squabble over Jerrold, and he had protested against the abuse of Prince Albert, of the Crystal Palace, and of Lord Palmerston, as well as the unrelenting campaign against Louis Napoleon. On all these topics, he felt, *Punch* was slavishly echoing the fulminations of *The Times*, and he sincerely believed that such attacks were not only unjust but actually "dangerous for the welfare and peace of the country." No longer dependent upon the income he received from *Punch*, he had written scarcely anything for it during the past six months; and as soon as he got back to London he marched into the office of the proprietor, F. M. Evans, and presented his resignation. As he emerged he encountered his old school-friend, John Leech, now the chief cartoonist on the staff, and told him of his action, to strengthen its finality.

His disgust with the English press and his apprehension over the international crisis aroused him to a sense of political responsibility. For years he had been convinced that the whole fabric of European culture was tottering to a fall, that the organizations of church, school, social classes, and government would tumble in the imminent crash. Previously he had been content to let his radical, anti-monarchical views find vent in private letters and arguments, or indirectly through his satirical representations of snobbery, bourgeois prejudice, and aristocratic corruption. He flattered himself that his little pinpricks were beginning to contribute to the great collapse.

Lord Palmerston having now been forced out of office for his approval of the French *coup d'état*, Thackeray hoped that old "Pam" would capitalize upon his popularity by leading a bold attack upon the hide-bound dogmas of the Whigs. Until this time, Thackeray's ambitions for an appointment in the public service had been frankly in terms of financial security, but now he confessed to a crusading impulse. To his particular friend Lady Stanley, whose husband had been Under-Secretary for Foreign Affairs with Palmerston, he wrote eagerly offering his services in any campaign of advanced Liberalism. He would be willing to work on a new newspaper, or even to go back to writing for *Punch* if his assistance seemed more valuable there. All he demanded was that some positive move be made to seize the opportunity for establishing a progressive political drive.

Over the New Year's holidays of 1852 Lady Ashburton asked him to bring his daughters to The Grange for their first glimpse of a great country-house. Only the hostess knew of his emotional disturbance, and she tried to shield him from any friction. In a letter to Mrs Brookfield, after conveying messages from Annie and Minny to the Brookfield baby, she added, "as for the Elder Gentleman, he is socially tabooed by his assiduous writing of a new novel, and appears only when Nature requires periodical restoration." Carlyle, who was a member of the house party, scowled at him with more than his normal crankiness. "I had never seen him so well before," the Sage rumbled in a letter to his brother. "There is a great deal of talent in him, a great deal of sensibility,—irritability, sensuality, vanity without limit,—and nothing, or little, but sentimentalism and play-actorism to guide it all with: not a good or well-found ship in such waters on such a voyage."

After visiting at another great house for a few days, Thackeray went back to London to complete arrangements for repeating his lectures, having been offered £150 to perform at the Portman Square Rooms—"pretty well for six hours," he gloated. The novel, however, hung heavy on his conscience. He had now reached the date when the manuscript was to have been handed to the publishers, and instead he was not able to give them much more than enough for the first of the three volumes. To Smith's surprise, when the date arrived with the contract unfulfilled, Thackeray immediately returned to him the cheque for six hundred pounds, which he had never deposited at his bank. With difficulty the publisher persuaded him to retain it, insisting that he had no misgivings whatever as to the fulfilment of the pledge.

All his friends knew about his problems. Lushington wrote to Brookfield that "he professes to be in a fix about his novel, which has been advertised some time, and for which the public are naturally becoming impatient, while he wishes to re-write it altogether." One reason for his dissatisfaction was the tone of unhappiness that pervaded it. "I wish the new novel wasn't so grand and melancholy," he wrote to his mother; "the hero is as stately as Sir Charles Grandison—something like Warrington—a handsome likeness of an ugly son of yours. There's a deal of pains in it that goes for nothing." And in a letter to Lady Stanley he grumbled, "I am writing a book of cut-throat melancholy suitable to my state, and have no news of myself or anybody to give you which should not be written on black-edged paper, and sealed with a hatchment."

In the struggle to master his misery he sometimes affected indifference toward all deep feeling. In a conversation with Lady de Rothschild he could not conceal from that intuitive lady that he was speaking of personal experience. In her diary she recorded his assertion "that love is short-lived and that without any apparent reason the being who has inspired us with passionate affection, at whose dear presence our heart has throbbed and our cheek turned pale, becomes perfectly indifferent to us. I had never experienced it, but I felt such might be the case, and with Thackeray it evidently has been the case."

Smith had sent the manuscript of the first volume of *Esmond* to Charlotte Brontë, and she replied with a long letter of characteristic criticism. "I feel full as much ire and sorrow as gratitude and admiration. . . In the first half of the book, what chiefly struck me was the wonderful manner in which the writer throws himself into the spirit and letters of the times whereof he treats. . . But what bitter satire, what relentless dissection of diseased subjects! Well, and this, too, is right, or would be right, if the savage surgeon did not seem so fiercely pleased with his work. Thackeray likes to dissect an ulcer or an aneurism; he has pleasure in putting his cruel knife or probe into quivering, living flesh. Thackeray would not like all the world to be good; no great satirist would like society to be perfect.

"As usual, he is unjust to women, quite unjust. There is hardly any punishment he does not deserve for making Lady Castlewood peep through a keyhole, listen at a door, and be jealous of a boy and a milkmaid. . . But I wish he could be told not to care much for dwelling on the political or religious intrigues of the times. Thackeray, in his heart, does not value political or religious intrigues of any age or date. He likes to show us human nature at home, as he himself daily sees it; his wonderful observant faculty likes to be in action. . . Some people have been in the habit of terming him the second writer of the day; it just depends on himself whether or not these critics shall be justified in their award. He need not be the second. God made him second to no man. If I were he, I would show myself as I am, not as critics report me; at any rate, I would do my best. Mr Thackeray is easy and indolent, and seldom cares to do his best." Smith forwarded these astringent comments to Thackeray in the hope of goading him to fuller achievement.

His lectures in Glasgow had been hanging fire for two months. In February, although in the midst of a "working fit" on the novel, he had to leave Brighton, where he had been staying for change of air, and travel to the north, taking the manuscript with him. During the twelve-hour train journey he made notes from a volume of Swift, and in Glasgow he tried to write. The "infernal noise" of the city kept him from sleeping, the smoke-laden air seemed to choke him, even the number of Irish faces in the streets made him uncomfortable. He felt something like terror at the prospect of remaining for a fortnight, and was certain that the lectures would be a failure. To crown his annoyance, when he presented a letter of introduction to a wealthy merchant, he was told brusquely to call the next day at one o'clock. "He thinks I'm a sort of actor," Thackeray wrote crossly to Dr Brown, "and he's quite right too. I shall go, I think, and be very respectful and humble. MOI! Well, I think it's good fun, and am laughing, I think, quite sincerely at the joke. We all think too strong beer of ourselves, or our friends for us." His old obsession had returned in a new guise. No sooner had he proved to his satisfaction that a novelist could indeed be a gentleman than he was faced with the ominous question, "What about a lecturer?"

The next morning the rich merchant came puffing up the stairs of his lodging, exuding apologies. Thackeray was mollified, accepted an invitation to dinner, and wrote hastily to the Browns to declare that he was "a very kind and worthy old gentleman." Later he fled to the Trossachs and stayed for two days at Balloch, "scribbling away, but in quiet and fresh air;" and on returning to Glasgow he was able to feel grateful for the efforts of the worthy burghers to make themselves agreeable to this strange visitant—an author.

Another trouble that now afflicted him was the inadequacy of facilities for research. "I wish I had six months more to put into the novel," he grumbled to his mother; "now it's nearly done, it's scarce more than a sketch, and it might have been made a durable history, complete in its parts and its whole. But at the end of six months it would want other six. It takes as much trouble as Macaulay's History almost, and he has the vast advantage of remembering everything he has read, whilst everything but impressions—I mean facts, dates, and so forth—slip out of my head, in which there's some great faculty lacking, depend upon it."

Nevertheless, the diversions that interfered with historical thoroughness were helping him to forget the Brookfield quarrel, and the second volume of *Esmond* proceeded more buoyantly in consequence. On February 26 he wrote to his mother: "My book has got into a more cheerful vein, that's a comfort, and I am relieved from the lugubrious doubts I had about it." He even considered for a day or two the possibility of its being issued in monthly parts, but gave up the idea, as he explained to his mother, because it was "much too grave and sad for that, and the incident not sufficient. It was written at a period of grief and pain so severe that I don't like to think of it, and am ashamed now to be well so soon and rid of my melancholy."

In spite of his regret at its insufficiency of historical detail, the chief defect of the story is that it contains too much. After steeping himself in contemporary journalism and diaries, Thackeray tended to manipulate his plot too obviously in order to introduce all the celebrated personages and great events. "I have been living in the last century for weeks past," he said in a letter, "in the day, that is; going at night as usual into the present age, until I get to fancy myself almost as familiar with one as with the other, and Oxford and Bolingbroke interest me as much as Russell and Palmerston—more, very likely." He even became personally stirred by long-buried disputes. One episode was dragged in with no conceivable purpose except a humiliation of Jonathan Swift. And there was rancor in his portrait of Marlborough. With characteristic family pride, he had allotted a conspicuous part in the story to General John Richmond Webb; and as Webb had nursed a grievance against the great Duke, Thackeray revived the feud. He had by this time adopted the Webb crest and arms, as "much prettier and more ancient" than his own; and he accepted the family tradition that the hero of Wynendael was a direct ancestor. After *Esmond* was published, he learned that his grandmother belonged to a collateral branch.

Another personal grudge was inserted by means of a dialogue between Dick Steele and Henry St John, obviously reproducing Thackeray's dispute with John Forster. The mistake over the authorship of Steele's *Tatler* essay was here attributed to a blundering Grub-street critic named Tom Boxer; and in the subsequent conversation Boxer was accused of being so blind a partisan of Congreve that he would not review Steele's latest play. When the book came out, Forster and his friends immediately recognized the allusion. A new outbreak of the quarrel ensued, and was patched up, as usual, with insincere reconciliation. Thackeray, in his habitual belated attack of conscience, canceled the passage in his revised edition of the novel.

Interpolation of his own prejudices, indefensible enough upon either artistic or prudential grounds, had the advantage of intensifying the author's imaginative participation in his story. Although some of the chapters read like a text-book on the campaign in Flanders, Thackeray elsewhere succeeded in bringing the period vividly to life. As he strolled through the Kensington streets surrounding his home, he used to picture the spacious Jacobean houses as the actual settings of parts of his story; once he pointed out No. 7, Kensington Square, to his daughter with the remark, "That is where Lady Castlewood lived." He briefly entertained thoughts of moving into one of the mansions—perhaps this same Number 7—but when he found it would cost five hundred pounds he yielded to his newly cultivated sense of economy. It was not only familiar spots, however, that he introduced with assurance. To his surprise, he began to find that his imagination was acquiring a fulness almost amounting to "second sight." Sometimes when he was describing a scene, he could hardly believe he had not been there; in one of the battles in *Esmond*, every detail of the foreground was visible to him as he wrote, such as the clump of reeds by the stream and the curve of its bank.

The increasing complexities of research induced him to engage a secretary. He offered the position to Eyre Crowe, eldest son of his old friends. As Crowe had been trained in art, he could serve as drawing master for the girls; and later he would be useful as traveling companion and business manager during the American tour. "Six months' tumbling about the world will do you no harm," said Thackeray breezily; and when Crowe doubted his own competence to handle business arrangements, Thackeray pointed out that he would have half a year of apprenticeship in England before the journey began.

Early in March Crowe took possession of the battered green-leather despatch box, which had knocked about Europe with Thackeray for years, and acquainted himself with the manuscript of the first half of *Esmond*, neatly written on small strips of note-paper and held together with an elastic band. At first, Crowe was sent to the British Museum with lists of questions to be answered; but as the historical events became more complicated, Thackeray found it necessary to be on the spot himself. He applied to his friend Anthony Panizzi, the Keeper of Printed Books, who assigned a special desk in the gallery where eighteenth-century periodicals were shelved, so that Thackeray could verify his material in the midst of dictating the story to his amanuensis. At the Athenaeum Club, also, permission was granted for the use of a side room off the library; and the novelist's voice, sometimes raised in the excitement of narration, shattered the somnolence of the club. Crowe became so absorbed in the story that he soon found himself hating Marlborough as fiercely as Esmond did.

By May, the end was in sight, and at this moment the American expedition took positive form, when the American Minister transmitted to Thackeray a letter from the secretary of the Mercantile Library in New York, with a definite offer for lectures in that city, and a promise of help in making engagements in other parts of the Union. Once again, the currents of his own life showed themselves in the novel in hand, as he ended it with the unexpected removal of his hero and heroine to Virginia, and laid an obvious foundation for a sequel by implying that their twin grandsons took opposite sides in the War of the Revolution.

Edward FitzGerald, reporting on one of his brief and unwilling visits to London, told Frederick Tennyson: "Thackeray I saw for ten minutes; he was just in the agony of finishing a novel, which has arisen out of the reading necessary for his lectures. He will get £1000 for his novel; he was wanting to finish it and rush off to the Continent to shake off the fumes of it." The last pages were written on May 29, and a dinner party in the evening celebrated the event. Within two or three days, he was on his way to the Rhine.

His parents joined the party to travel as far as Zurich and stay there for the summer, and by the time they reached that city Thackeray had decided to leave the girls with them and to go on alone. The ostensible reason was that the children had grown "too big to sit three on a side;" but actually the chief trouble was divided authority arising from the old lady's jealous love. "My mother wanted the children so much," he told Dr Brown, "that I gave them up, nor was it possible that we could travel together, and the girls have two powers over them. So I had a dismal holiday alone, in place of a pleasant one with them."

His "dreary lonely journey" took him through the Tyrol, the Salzkammergut, and Franconia, with stops at Munich and other cities, to Vienna. His pocket-book containing ninety pounds was stolen, and the heat was too great for sightseeing or even writing. In Vienna, where Lord Westmoreland, the English Ambassador, was most cordial, he spent the days in reading and went out to a series of "fine dinners" followed by the play or the opera. Thence he traveled to Dresden to "see if I can paint a bit." While he was making a copy of the boy angels at the feet of the Sistine Madonna, he was recognized by two vacationing Cambridge undergraduates, Arthur Coleridge and his cousin John Patteson. When Patteson expressed admiration of the drawing, Thackeray answered sharply, "Sir, I am quite impervious to flattery; it's my intention to burn that sketch when I get back to my lodgings." Then, noticing that the young man was hurt by the snub, he added, "I'll call on you tomorrow morning." At ten a.m. he came to their inn, full of amiability, and ordered Lager beer. As the home of the Coleridges was Ottery St Mary, he soon had the youths deep in jolly talk about the old Larkbeare neighbors.

He had started the tour with some ideas of writing a book about it, but the places he visited failed to arouse enough interest. Another scheme was to explore Hanover and observe the local background for a series of lectures on the four

Georges; but on realizing that his hopes for a police-magistrateship or other public office depended upon his keeping in favor with the authorities, he put aside a topic that would inevitably lead him to "say something impudent" about the royal family. Nevertheless, he confessed wryly that "because it *is* a needless job, and because I might just as well leave it alone," he felt much more drawn to it than to innocuous themes.

His greatest satisfaction was in verifying his descriptions of places mentioned in *Henry Esmond*. He found Blenheim exactly as he had pictured it, except that the village was larger; he discovered the brook that Esmond crossed, and almost the spot where he fell wounded; and he walked down to the Danube, "and mused mighty thoughts over it."

Having ended his wanderings in Berlin, he got back to London early in August, and set to work on reading the proofs of the novel. Smith had decided to produce the book in appropriate form by imitating the make-up used in the time of Queen Anne; and as the type-face was available only in limited quantities, the proofs came slowly, only a hundred pages a week. "Esmond looks very stately and handsome in print," the author found, "and bore as he is, I think will do me credit."

With his daughters gone from Young Street, he felt desperately lonely in London. Mrs Brookfield had returned from Madeira about the time he had started on his continental tour, but the illness of her father kept her at Clevedon Court, and so he was spared the pain of encountering her. With these loosings of ties, he was drifting back into the aimless current of club life. The Garrick always remained his first love: "We, the happy initiated," he once said, at one of its annual Shakespeare birthday dinners, "never speak of it as the Garrick; to us it is the G, the little G, the dearest place in the world." Some of the members, however, were inconvenienced by its refusal to serve late suppers, and they formed an auxiliary group to supply that need. At first it was known as the C.C.C. ("Cyder Cellars Club") in reference to the tavern where it originated; but Thackeray was soon asked to propose a more dignified name, and he selected "the Fielding."

Among the members of the Fielding were many of his closest cronies, but also others who were sometimes rumored to be on bad terms with him, such as Andrew Arcedekne, whom he had depicted as the blatant Foker, and Albert Smith, his predecessor at the *Punch* table. Smith, like Arcedekne, grated on Thackeray by the studied crudity of his sense of humor. Whenever they met, however, Thackeray contrived to get on with him well enough, and Smith was even heard to declare roundly (after a session at the Cyder Cellars till three a.m.) that the novelist was "a very jolly fellow, with no 'High Art' about him." But there is perhaps a trace of sarcasm in the compliment that Smith paid him at the end of a versified roster of the Fielding's founders:

And then there came a mighty man who, 'tis but fair to state,
Among the small is Affable, though Great among the great—
The good Pendennis.

Even those who accused Thackeray of snobbery had to admit that in the convivial atmosphere of the Fielding he made no effort to dictate the selection of members according to his private preferences.

In the intervals of proof-reading he paid visits to Birmingham and Manchester to negotiate about giving lectures. The visit to Manchester was for a special occasion. As the first city to take advantage of the Public Libraries Act, Manchester was organizing a great opening ceremony, with leading authors and other celebrities taking part. James Fields being in England again, Thackeray thought he saw a good opportunity of impressing this influential American with his ability as a speaker, and so he asked Fields to go with him. All the way down in the train, probably to bolster his ebbing courage, he kept up a burlesque braggadocio. Each part of his speech was specially planned for its effect on some particular element in the audience. The other speakers, including Dickens, Bulwer Lytton, and John Bright, would be outshone by his eloquence.

When he stepped forward to face three thousand people, he gave a reassuring wink to Fields in the front row, and began to speak clearly and gracefully. After three minutes he stopped dead in the middle of an elaborate sentence, gazed up at the ceiling with a look of comical despair, crammed his hands into his trouser pockets, and returned to his seat.

After the meeting he said blandly to Fields, "My boy, you have my profoundest sympathy; this day you have accidentally missed hearing one of the finest speeches ever composed for delivery by a great British orator." To John Bright, however, he was franker. "Who will ever come and hear me lecture," he lamented, "if I break down like this before such a number of people?"

"Never you mind," Bright answered. "Very few people don't break down at one time or another. You come along with me this evening; I'm going to another meeting—not fine fal-lal folks, but a set of good, honest working-men, and you must try again." Thackeray took himself firmly in hand, reasoning that "there's nothing more wicked in breaking down in a speech than in slipping on a piece of orange peel." The result was "a capital speech," in Bright's opinion. The audience was delighted.

Until the novel was through the press, the date for his departure for America could not be fixed. His friends could still hardly believe he was serious in the scheme. "Dear old Thackeray is really going to America!" exclaimed FitzGerald on August 10. A whole month later, Thackeray was thrown into a panic when the publishers told him they had lost the third volume. He was reconciling himself to a delay of at least six weeks, when the manuscript turned up.

In his letters to his daughters, full of good advice about working hard on their French and music, coupled with anxious hints that they ought not to become too deeply imbued with the Evangelical religious views of their grandmother, he emphasized that he was going to America not because he liked it, but because a six months' tour of the States might earn nearly a third of the sum of money he must secure for them and their mother.

At the end of September he and Crowe went down to Liverpool, and during the next three weeks the lectures were given in Manchester on Tuesdays and Thursdays, and in Liverpool on Wednesdays and Fridays, with consequent train journeys back and forth. The attendance was rather disappointing. At Liverpool, he reported, "not above 200 people come to the lectures, and the Philharmonic Hall, the most beautiful room I've seen, is made for 2500, so that the little audience shudders in the middle, and the lecturer stands in a vast empty orchestra, where there is space for 150 musicians." The local newspapers printed bitter comments on this betrayal of Liverpudlian culture. "At Manchester," the lecturer explained to Dr Brown, "the audience isn't greater, but looks greater for the room is small. And though pecuniarily the affair is a failure it is not so really. I aid my reputation and the people who come seem to like what they hear hugely." By the end of the series, the audiences had increased.

While in Liverpool he took the decisive step of booking passage on a ship to sail for Boston on October 30. Another experience also brought the adventure uncomfortably close. In the reading room of the Liverpool Athenaeum he picked up a New York newspaper and came upon a violent denunciation of his projected visit. It asserted that he would be another in the parade of lecturers who came over to line their pockets with good American dollars and then went home to lampoon the manners and customs of their hosts. At first Thackeray felt depressed by this assault; but as he remembered the unfavorable reports on America published by Mrs Trollope, Marryat, Dickens, and many other English writers, he recognized the grounds for the assumption, and made up his mind that he would take the warning to heart.

The latter half of October was given over to preparations for departure and farewell visits. While spending a day with Lord and Lady Stanley at Alderley, he discussed, half in jest and half in earnest, a suggestion that his friends in England should all preserve the letters he would send them from America, and give them back to him on his return to form the materials for a book. Later he visited the Ashburtons; Carlyle, who was there again, wrote to his mother in a slightly gentler mood, "Thackeray is coming, for whom I care nothing, tho' he is a clever and friendly man; he comes today with a nobleman and a Portrait-Painter: comes but is soon to go."

In the intervals of packing, Thackeray sat for his portrait to Samuel Lawrence, who made a specialty of authors. The picture had been commissioned by Smith, who had a duplicate made for Charlotte Brontë, and sent another to the two girls in Paris. Mrs Carmichael-Smyth presented her son with a lifebelt and made him promise to take it with him. These preparations were so suggestive of mortality that he fell into an almost sacramental mood. He was not yet entirely cured of his unhappiness over the Brookfield quarrel. "The wound's healed," he told Dr Brown, "but the weakness is not over quite; a little change of air and scene will end that, and who knows when I come back I may tell you I'm in love with somebody else, and have begun Act I of another tragedy or farce, which is it?"

Two days before leaving home he wrote in a gloomier vein to his oldest friend, FitzGerald: "If anything happens to me, you by these presents must get ready the *Book of Ballads* which you like, and which I had not time to prepare before embarking on the voyage. And I should like my daughters to remember that you are the best and oldest friend their Father ever had, and that you would act as such; as my literary executor and so forth. My Books would yield a something as copyrights: and should anything occur, I have commissioned friends in good place to get a Pension for my poor little wife. . . Does not this sound gloomily? Well: who knows what Fate is in store: and I feel not at all downcast, but very grave and solemn just at the brink of a great voyage. . . The great comfort I have in thinking about my dear old boy is that recollection of our youth when we loved each other as I do now while I write Farewell." So might Columbus or Magellan have written as they faced the unknown.

CHAPTER 16

Land of the Free

ON THE MORNING of October 30, when Thackeray and Crowe were standing on the dock at Liverpool, waiting to board their ship, a messenger caught up with them, to deliver a batch of letters and a parcel containing copies of *Esmond*. Well pleased with the appearance of the three neat volumes, the author was cheered by the good omen as he put out in the tender and from it climbed the swinging ladder to the deck of the Royal Mail Steamship *Canada*.

Among his fellow-passengers he caught sight of a burly figure and swarthy face which he recognized as Arthur Hugh Clough, the friend of his Oxford visits. Having given up his Oxford fellowship from motives of religious doubt, and spent three uncomfortable years as principal of a students' hall of London University, Clough was now on his way to Massachusetts in the hope of finding more congenial environment. Another literary celebrity on board was James Russell Lowell, on his way home with his family after a year in Italy.

Clough did not receive his old acquaintance with much enthusiasm. "Lowell is very friendly," he wrote in his diary; "Thackeray and I also get on." In Thackeray's opinion, too, Lowell was "very pleasant," and for Mrs Lowell he whiled away time by drawing whimsical sketches on a pack of cards. Her ardor in the causes of abolition and temperance proved wearisome, however, and before the voyage was over he was regarding her with mock dread as "an awful superior woman."

During the crossing, which lasted two weeks, Thackeray suffered his share of sea-sickness. When, about six hundred miles out, they came into bright weather, his appetite returned and he started to scribble a penciled letter to his daughters, but the pitching made his sentences "lurch about and grasp hold of anything to support themselves," until he had to stop. As he lay awake in his tiny cabin, "tumbling and rolling and bumping and creaking in the roaring black midnight," feeling as if *Esmond* and everything connected with his normal life were a hundred years away, he thought much about his girls at home, and about the unknown experiences ahead. One vague project he had already discarded: he would not stir up ill will among the Americans by publishing his impressions of them. "It seems imprudent to write a book," he decided, "and mere sketches now are somehow below my rank in the world—I mean, a grave old gentleman, father of young ladies, mustn't be comic and grinning too much."

Boredom gradually overcame the voyagers. "Who less likely to come to their wits' end than W.M.T. and A.H.C?" wrote Lowell in his account of the journey; "yet I have seen them driven to five meals a day for mental occupation." Clough later wrote a poem, *Mari Magno*, which told of the uneventful voyage and included portraits of his companions. Thackeray appeared under the disguise of "the lawyer:"

> By nature he to gentlest thoughts inclined,
> To most severe had disciplined his mind;
> He held it duty to be half unkind.
> Bitter, they said, who but the exterior knew;
> In friendship never was a friend so true:
> The unwelcome fact he did not shrink to tell,
> The good, if fact, he recognised as well . . .
> Often, I think, he suffered from some pain
> Of mind, that on the body worked again;
> One felt it in his sort of half-disdain,
> Impatient not, but acrid in his speech . . .

The *Canada* had to fight against head winds all the way. When the vessel was near Cape Race, Thackeray began some letters, but as the cabin table quivered and creaked under his hand and the dishes rattled all around him, the effort was disastrous. He retired to his berth in such misery that Clough, now entirely amiable, sat for half an hour in the cramped cabin to divert his mind with conversation. Thackeray and Crowe did not feel like going ashore during the pause at Halifax, but as they neared Boston they were on deck to enjoy the view of the city silhouetted against a frosty sunset.

No particular welcome was accorded to Thackeray when he went ashore. Much diverted by the crowds at the pier and the squabbles in the customs-shed, he and Crowe picked up their portable luggage and found seats in a ramshackle omnibus, which, at the exorbitant price of four dollars each, rattled and bumped them to the Tremont House.

The excitement and novelty of the adventure had raised Thackeray to a pitch of boyish high spirits. At the Tremont House Fields was waiting for him with the cheering news that dinner was about to be served and that several congenial souls were assembling for the occasion. Clough reached the hotel in time to be included. As Thackeray had expressed incredulity to Fields in London regarding the magnitude of American oysters, Fields arranged to have the largest ones procurable served at this first meal. "I'm sorry," Fields explained, while Thackeray gazed in horror at the half-dozen immense bivalves in front of him, "that these are so extremely small; but we'll do better next time."

"How shall I do it?" Thackeray demanded in an anguished whisper, with his fork suspended in mid-air.

Fields explained the American method of oyster-eating. The visitor picked up a large specimen, inspected it, and put it back. "It looks," he murmured, "just like the High Priest's servant's ear that Peter cut off." After bowing his head as if saying grace, he took the smallest oyster, opened his mouth very wide, made a desperate gulp, and all was over. The whole party had been watching the struggle in spell-bound silence.

"How do you feel?" Fields inquired.

"Profoundly grateful," he gasped, "and as if I had swallowed a little baby."

Later the party adjourned to the smoking-room to introduce the newcomer to the delights of sherry-cobbler, and the proceedings lasted hilariously far into the night. These enjoyments may have had something to do with the fact that both Thackeray and Crowe felt their beds lurching all night as if they were still at sea; in fact, Thackeray averred the next morning that he had been pitched out on the floor by the imaginary heavings.

They stayed in Boston for four days, to get their "land legs." Clough was persuaded to wait over a day to "lionize with Thackeray and his friend Crowe through the streets," before proceeding to Concord. The buildings were draped with mourning for the funeral of Daniel Webster, which had been held a fortnight before. On his third evening in Boston, Thackeray was entertained at dinner in the home of William Hickling Prescott, and was much taken with the cheerfulness and courage of the almost blind historian.

As well as meeting the local literary celebrities, Thackeray encountered several people who, like himself, were touring America for profit. At the Revere House he called on one of the characters of London, Alfred Bunn, manager of Drury Lane and librettist of many operas, who was equally noted for his inordinate vanity and for having chewed Macready's finger in a backstage brawl. Although Thackeray had shared in *Punch's* relentless war on "the poet Bunn" and had caricatured him again and again, from *Flore et Zephyr* to *Pendennis*, the interview was cordial.

Another guest at the Revere was Mme Sontag, whom Thackeray had adored from a distance, twenty years before. She told him in her lively French that she hoped to earn enough in her present tour to "close her *gosier*" and retire into private life. As Sontag was to sing at the Melodeon, where Thackeray expected to deliver his lectures, he went to her concert to study the acoustics of the hall. Fields accompanied him, and while they were waiting Thackeray extemporized biographies for members of the audience who passed down the aisle. As Fields knew most of the people, he was convulsed by the interpretations. "I remember," he narrates, "a pallid, sharp-faced girl fluttering past, and how Thackeray exulted in the history of this 'frail little bit of porcelain,' as he called her. There was something in her manner that made him hate her, and he insisted she had murdered somebody on her way to the hall. . . There is one man still living and moving about the streets I walk in occasionally, whom I never encounter without almost a shudder, remembering as I do the unerring shaft which Thackeray sent that night into the unknown man's character."

On November 16, the travelers proceeded to New York. When a rosy-cheeked newsboy, passing down the aisle of the train, shouted "Thackeray's works" among his wares, the novelist was touched as by a friendly welcome to a strange country. Since these American reprints contained many of his writings that had not been collected in England, he bought a copy of *A Shabby Genteel Story* and read it for the first time in twelve years, with poignant recollections of the tragedy that cut it short. Crowe at the same time bought *Uncle Tom's Cabin*, but Thackeray refused to read it, asserting that such painful themes were scarcely legitimate for fiction. Besides, he had been warned by friends to avoid committing himself on the vexed question of slavery.

At a wayside station Crowe got off to eat lunch, and the train went on without him. As he had the baggage checks, he came on by a slow train in an agony of anxiety, only to find that Thackeray had calmly identified the bags and was already ensconced at the Clarendon Hotel, receiving a visit of welcome from George Bancroft, the historian and diplomat.

Thackeray's approach had been trumpeted in the New York papers every day since the *Canada* touched at Halifax. Henry James, Sr., in the *Tribune*, announced him as "the most thoughtful critic of manners and society, the subtlest humorist, and the most effective, because the most genial, satirist the age has known." On his arrival, therefore, he was greeted by a stream of reporters and other visitors, in contrast with his quiet début in Boston.

Suggestions were made that it was customary for visiting lecturers to pay a round of calls on the newspaper editors, "hat in hand," to ask for puffs. Mr Bunn had done so, he was told; but Thackeray's abhorrence of servility rose in revolt. "I'll see them damned first," he blurted.

The Mercantile Library Association had engaged a Unitarian Church for the lectures, and Thackeray was greatly amused at the prospect of performing in a pulpit. When he was shown over it by Millard Felt, the secretary of the Association, he made various facetious suggestions: "Will the organ strike up when I enter? . . . I suppose I shall have to come in by the sacristy. . . ."

Among the earliest callers at the hotel was Legrand Smith, the business agent for P. T. Barnum, with a message that the great showman wished to see Mr Thackeray at his museum. After traveling up town in the Broadway omnibus (which was repeatedly detoured into side streets because Broadway was torn up for repaving), and threading the grimy monstrosities of the museum to the proprietor's little office, plastered with photographs of General Tom Thumb, Thackeray was told that Barnum was preparing to launch a weekly paper, *The Illustrated News*, and wanted the English author to write his impressions of America for the first number. Still inflated by his triumphant management of Jenny Lind, Barnum also hinted about other profitable engagements, but Thackeray politely explained that he wished to maintain his independence and avoid any over-publicized schemes.

Such is Eyre Crowe's account of the interview. Barnum himself, as might be expected, gave a somewhat different version in his autobiography: "Thackeray called on me at the Museum with a letter of introduction from our mutual friend Albert Smith. He spent an hour with me, mainly for the purpose of asking my advice in regard to the management of the course of lectures which he proposed to deliver. I gave him the best advice I could as to management, for which he was very grateful, and he called on me whenever he was in New York." At any rate, there is no doubt that the two gentlemen made favorable impressions on one another.

George Bancroft had invited the novelist to spend an evening at his house, and it turned out to be a spiritualistic séance conducted by Daniel Dunglas Home, then at the height of his fame. Thackeray was impressed by the messages rapped out by the table, of which the most coherent was, "I merely wished to say Makepeace you argue of importance." During the next few days he tried several times to repeat the experiment, but without success; and he sent full instructions home to Mrs Brookfield.

His first lecture was given on November 19. Tickets for the whole series had been sold out in advance, and an audience of nearly two thousand greeted him enthusiastically. As was his custom, he had asked the newspapers not to print detailed summaries of the lectures, and therefore the reporters devoted their space to his personal appearance, his habit of plunging his hands into his trouser pockets, and other mannerisms. The best of the descriptions was written by William Cullen Bryant for the *Evening Post*:

Few expected to see so large a man: he is gigantic, six feet four at least; few expected to see so old a person; his hair appears to have kept silvery record over fifty years; and then there was a notion in the minds of many that there must be something dashing and "fast" in his appearance, whereas his costume was perfectly plain, the expression of his face grave and earnest, his address perfectly unaffected and such as we might expect to meet with in a well-bred man somewhat advanced in years. His elocution also surprised those who had derived their impressions from the English journals. His voice is a superb tenor, and possesses that pathetic tremble which is so effective in what is called emotive eloquence, while his delivery was as well suited to the communication he had to make as could well have been imagined.

His enunciation is perfect. Every word he uttered might have been heard in the remotest quarters of the room, yet he scarcely lifted his voice above a colloquial tone. The most striking feature in his whole manner was the utter absence of affectation of any kind. He did not permit himself to appear conscious that he was an object of peculiar interest in the audience, neither was he guilty of the greater error of not appearing to care whether they were interested or not . . .

Thackeray frankly enjoyed the praise of the newspapers; but he got fun also out of the *Herald*, which chose to wage a campaign against him as a "snob"; six different people were reading the latest attack when he came in to breakfast one morning, and as he sat down a man across the table slipped it guiltily under the cloth.

He found himself enjoying America much more than he had expected. The unaffected friendliness and interest made him feel at home, and he confessed in a letter to Kate Perry that "the jolly manner answers here very well, which I have from Nature or Art possibly." He admired the ladies, who struck him as being "as lean as greyhounds" and "all dressed like the most stunning French actresses." He loved the "rush and restlessness," the fast-moving traffic on Broadway, the railway trains puffing into the very heart of the city, the houses being pulled down to make way for new ones, the barricades and scaffoldings in every street. All the residences he visited seemed to be in the process of remodeling, with carpenters hammering and the stairs or a wall torn out. The furnishings were like those of "the most splendid gambling houses. . . The houses are all so new that the walls are not even papered, and on the walls in the midst of the hangings of brocade and the enormous gold frames and mirrors you see little twopenny pictures and coloured prints." He summed up New York as being "the most curious varnish of Civilization."

Among the gentlemen presented to him was a genial Mr Baxter, who got up courage to invite him to his home on Second Avenue, and was astonished by the promptitude of the acceptance. The Baxter family included two pretty daughters; the elder, eighteen-year-old Sally, was the first specimen of lively American girl to cross Thackeray's field of vision, and he fell victim to her first sparkling glance. "She is exactly my idea of Beatrix Esmond!" he exclaimed.

To the delight of the Baxters, the admired celebrity proved pathetically grateful for their hospitality, and was soon devoted to Mrs Baxter and her girls. Lonely for the sympathetic ministrations that he had come to depend upon, from Mrs Brookfield and other charming ladies, as the only solace of his broken home, he was even more than usually responsive to the happy atmosphere of a united family. He begged leave to drop in for dinner with them as often as possible, before his lectures, and soon the place at Mrs Baxter's right hand was regularly reserved for him on lecture nights, with a pitcher of claret set within reach. He would listen with interest to Miss Sally's chatter about her dances and her beaux, toward whom he expressed melodramatic jealousy. His parting prophecy to Brown seemed in a fair way to being fulfilled, and there was a hint of seriousness in his jesting comment in a letter to Mrs Brookfield: "I expect when I am sixty I shall be marrying a girl of eleven or twelve, innocent, barley-sugar-loving, in a pinafore."

A very different household that received him was that of Henry James, the one-legged philosopher, who led the novelist into his study and settled down to intellectual debate. Thackeray's attention must have wandered, for he soon noticed that the door was ajar and hovering outside was the ten-year-old son and namesake of the host, garbed in the tight little brass-buttoned coat that was in style for urchins. Thackeray suddenly interrupted the Swedenborgian monologue by shouting, "Come here, little boy, and show me your extraordinary jacket!"

Shyly the small boy edged up to the visitor's chair. Thackeray, with a kind but heavy hand on his shoulder, gazed in wonder through his spectacles and asked, "Is that the common uniform of your age here?"

"Y—yes, sir."

"If you were to go to England in that costume, you would be addressed as 'Buttons'."

Without understanding the allusion, little Henry received in a flash the disturbing conviction that Americans were "queer"—a discovery that provided him with a life-long series of novels.

No matter how busy he might be, Thackeray did not overlook opportunities to promote the artistic career of his diffident protégé, Crowe. Mr James was one of the celebrities he persuaded to sit for a portrait, and it was another unforgettable experience for Henry, Jr., to watch a "real painter" at work.

In spite of feeling genuine affection for Thackeray, Mr James was pained by his levity toward metaphysical problems and his consorting with the New York "wits" whom James despised. Months afterwards, in a conversation with Emerson, James quoted some of Thackeray's flippant remarks and expressed the opinion that the novelist "could not see beyond his eyes and has no ideas, and merely is a sounding board against which his experiences thump and resound: he is the merest boy."

Other literary men showed him every courtesy. He was visited by Horace Greeley, who enlightened him on the puzzling complexities of American political parties. Of an older generation, but still spry, was Washington Irving, ruddy of nose and husky of voice, who would drop in for a chat and complain of his friend Dickens's imprudence in embittering Anglo-American relations. William H. Appleton, the publisher, who had made Thackeray's acquaintance in Paris as early as 1835, introduced him at the Century Club, where he soon felt at home; when enjoying a supper and a smoke and a glass with such members as George W. Curtis, the handsome young traveler and essayist, and Frederick S. Cozzens, wine-merchant and humorist, he might almost have been in his beloved Garrick or Fielding in London.

During his stay in New York he made profitable arrangements with publishers. His experience was more satisfactory than that of Dickens and other English authors had been. Harper and Brothers had paid him five hundred dollars for *Henry Esmond,* and so there was no sting in his jest when the publisher brought in his little girl to meet him, and Thackeray remarked as he shook hands, "So this is the Pirate's Daughter, is it?" The firm of Putnam made him a liberal offer for the American rights of the lectures, but he gave the preference to Harpers, who promised him a thousand dollars for the privilege of printing them from the sheets of the English edition as soon as it should be published. He had no intention, however, of letting them get into print while they were still being offered to audiences. "The goosey is much too good a goosey to be killed," he wrote to Kate Perry.

Meanwhile, Appletons were already issuing a cheap reprint of all his writings, in twelve volumes; and on the strength of his old acquaintance Appleton asked him to write a preface. As the edition included many examples of his journalistic work that had never been republished in England, he commented on them rather disparagingly, and explained that since he could not prevent their reproduction in America, he was glad that at least the Appleton series had forestalled other schemes for their exploitation. He also took the opportunity to make overdue amends for his affronts to Bulwer-Lytton:

> The careless papers written at an early period, and never seen since the printer's boy carried them away, are brought back and laid at the father's door; and he cannot, if he would, disown his own children . . . I own to a feeling of anything but pleasure in reviewing some of these misshapen juvenile creatures . . . I ask pardon of the author of *The Caxtons* for a lampoon, which I know he himself has forgiven, and which I wish I could recall. I had never seen that eminent writer but once in public when this satire was penned, and wonder at the recklessness of the young man who could fancy such personality was harmless jocularity, and never calculated that it might give pain.

In the same preface, he touched tactfully on the sore subject of American literary piracy, giving credit to the American publishers for the fact that "our names and writings are known by multitudes using our common mother tongue, who never had heard of us or our books, but for the speculators who have sent them all over this continent." He added that "it is, of course, not unnatural for the English writer to hope that some day he may share a portion of the profits which his works bring at present to the persons who vend them in this country; . . . and the present writer, having long since ascertained that a portion of a loaf is more satisfactory than no bread at all, gratefully accepts and acknowledges several slices which the book-purveyors in this city have offered to him of their own free-will." He concluded with further allusions to "the goodwill from publishers and public." Thus quietly he sought to counteract the rather strident crusade that Dickens had fought on behalf of his financial rights.

In spite of his intention not to publish any comments on American life, he allowed himself one small skit at the expense of the reporters and their appetite for personal details. This he sent to *Fraser's Magazine*—his only contribution after *Vanity Fair* rescued him from the drudgery of magazine work. It appeared in the January number under a pseudonym, but was readily recognized as his. In the guise of a burlesque on American journalism, it was a somewhat naïve notification to the English public of his great success across the Atlantic. And to mollify the possible annoyance of his hosts he concluded it by quoting the glowing tribute to American hospitality that formed the peroration of his closing lecture.

The demand for tickets to the lectures so far exceeded the supply that a second series had been organized, and the first lecture was repeated on December 1, when two of the original six still remained to be given. An engagement in Brooklyn was also filled, followed by a hilarious supper party. By the time Thackeray moved on to Boston, his earnings amounted to nearly five thousand dollars, which he left with the New York agents of Baring's Bank to be invested in favor of his daughters.

His departure from New York was clouded by real grief over parting from the Baxters, and anxiety as to whether he had given offense by impulsively kissing the girls good-bye. As soon as he reached Boston he started to write them a long letter, only to put it in the fire as too fond and sentimental; a second suffered the same fate; and only the next day was he able to phrase his gratitude in his customary vein of whimsical banter. The letter contained also a strong hint that he could make a special journey back to spend Christmas with them; but as the scheme proved impractical on second thoughts, he had to content himself with sending Sally a pretty gift.

As well as the series in Boston, lectures were delivered in several other cities, that in Providence being distinguished by its lack of a jolly after-party, as the state of Rhode Island had a prohibition law. The Lyceum committee provided only cold boiled veal and coffee. Mr Thackeray was observed to be looking bored, and he retired to bed early.

The Boston lectures promised to be as popular as the New York ones, and when Fields informed him that the tickets for the series were all sold he burst into "uproarious shouting and dancing." The presence of Fields always seemed to incite him to his most juvenile clowning; Fields tells the amazing tale that on the way to the lecture hall for the first performance he insisted on thrusting his long legs out of the window of the carriage, "in deference," he said, "to my magnanimous ticket-holders." Some twelve hundred people attended the lecture, and at the end of it an ungainly man pushed up to him, grasped his hand, and announced, "I'm the proprietor of the Mammoth Rat. I'll be happy to present you with a free ticket to my show, in exchange for a pass to your lectures." With grave politeness, Thackeray exchanged cards with him, and promised to visit the rodent.

The literary circle of Boston received him as a brother. Prescott again made haste to give a dinner for him. Fields met Thackeray one day ploughing through the snow in Beacon Street with a copy of *Esmond* under his arm. Having hailed Fields from a distance with shouts and brandishing of the parcel, he exclaimed, "Here is the *very* best I can do, and I am carrying it to Prescott as a reward of merit for having given me my first dinner in America. I stand by this book, and am willing to leave it when I go as my card."

Another favorite host was George Ticknor, the historian of Spanish literature, whose Burgundy and claret were as good as Prescott's, and to whose cosy library Thackeray was happy to adjourn for a pipe and a chat after his lecture. He soon felt free to banter his host. In the course of a discussion, Ticknor asserted that one mark of a gentleman was a handsome face, for good blood showed itself in good features. "A pretty speech," Thackeray broke in, "for one broken-nosed man to make to another!" Lowell, in recording the anecdote a few days later, added that "all Boston has been secretly tickled with it." Naturally it was soon misquoted, and a pointless version was widely retailed.

Oliver Wendell Holmes called on him, and impressed him as "a dear little fellow, a true poet. I told him how much I liked his verses, and what do you think he did? His eyes began to water. Well, it's a comfort to have given pleasure to that kind soul."

On New Year's Eve he invited himself to Ticknor's to watch the new year in, and as midnight struck he rose and offered a toast with tears in his eyes, "God bless my girls and all who are good to them."

Lowell asked him over to Cambridge for January 5, promising that there would be "only *clubbable* men, and such as can't make speeches." One of them was Longfellow, who had already attended one of the lectures, and who described the party in his diary: "Lowell gave a supper to Thackeray. The other guests were Felton, Clough, Dana, Dr Parsons (Dante's translator), Fields, Edmund Quincy, Estes Howe, and myself. We sat down at ten and did not leave the table till one. Very gay, with stories and jokes." Several of the other participants also described the memorable evening. Clough was not greatly entertained by the hilarity. "Puns chiefly," he noted, "but Dana is really amusing." He was pleased to observe that "Thackeray doesn't sneer; he is really very sentimental; but he sees the silliness sentiment runs into, and so always tempers it by a little banter or ridicule. He is much farther into actual life than I am." And Richard Henry Dana's impression was that "Thackeray is not a great talker. He was interested in all that was said, and put in a pleasant word occasionally. Felton, Lowell, and I did nearly all the talking."

"It is like the society of a rich Cathedral town in England," Thackeray decided, "grave and decorous, and very pleasant and well read." In another letter he compared Boston to Edinburgh—"a vast amount of Toryism and donnishness everywhere." To the Baxters he remarked that "it is quieter, but I think we drink more than in New York."

The Bostonians, for their part, did not allow their liking for the man to dull their judgment of his lectures. "I do not think he made much impression as a critic," Prescott commented; "but the Thackeray vein is rich in what is better than cold criticism." Another sort of opinion was reported by Clough in a letter to Lady Ashburton, who passed the word gleefully to Mrs Brookfield: "Some of his lectures have been thought dangerous in their tendencies for the Moralities of the young Yankee men!"

His final Boston lecture was given on January 7. The next day he went back to New York, hoping to see as much as possible of the Baxters. With Mrs Baxter, whom he had taken to calling "Lady Castlewood," he was already on the terms of half-ironic, half-tender confidence that he reserved for two or three of his women friends in London. One day he picked up a copy of *Pendennis* in her parlor, glanced at a few pages with his whimsical smile, and finally burst out, "Yes, it is very like—it is certainly very like."

"Like whom, Mr Thackeray?"

"Oh, like me, to be sure; Pendennis is very like me."

"Surely not," protested Mrs Baxter; "Pendennis was so weak!"

"Ah, well, Mrs Baxter," he replied, with a shrug of his broad shoulders, "your humble servant is not very strong."

After a week's holiday, he had to set off for Philadelphia. Irving happened to be taking the same train, *en route* to Washington. "In the gentlemen's cabin on the ferry boat," he wrote to a friend, "whom should I see but Thackeray? We greeted each other cordially. . . We took seats beside each other in the cars, and the morning passed off delightfully. He seems still to enjoy his visit to the United States exceedingly, and enters into our social life with great relish. . . Said the Bostonians had published a smashing criticism on him; which, however, does not seem to have ruffled his temper, as I understand he cut it out of the newspaper, and enclosed it in a letter to a female friend in New York."

His reception in Philadelphia was made pleasant by a letter of introduction from Lord Mahon (author of a notable history of eighteenth-century England) to William Bradford Reed, who was holding the two diverse posts of District Attorney for Philadelphia and Professor of American History at the University of Pennsylvania. As grandson of Washington's adjutant-general, Reed enjoyed family prestige; but his austere manner was unpopular. He was a man of genuine literary taste, however, and was immediately captivated by Thackeray's easy friendliness.

The novelist had been anxious about how Swift and Fielding and Sterne might be regarded in the city of the Quakers, but his lectures in the Musical Fund Hall were crowded, and he was specially touched by the sincerity of the tributes he received. "There's something simple in the way these kind folks regard a man; they read our books as if we were Fielding and so forth." He was delighted to be told by "the prettiest girl in Philadelphia" that she had read *Vanity Fair* twelve times. In fact, the beauty of the Quaker girls particularly charmed him—"hundreds of airy-looking little beings, with camellia complexions."

When Clement C. Biddle presented him with a gold pen in a handsome case, he described it to Mrs Brookfield with boyish pride, and he assured Biddle earnestly that, "Please God, the gold pen shall tell no lies while it lives with me." Another hospitable friend was Morton McMichael, editor of the *North American*, who escorted him to such impressive institutions as the Mint and the Free School, and also to a less dignified one, "Prosser's," which, being smoky and stuffy and located in a cellar, reminded him forcibly of his favorite Evans's in Covent Garden, except that the waiters were black.

With his friends at home in mind, he called upon Pierce Butler, the estranged husband of Fanny Kemble, knowing that she would be anxious for a report upon her children; but in spite of his broad hints they were not produced for inspection.

One moonlight night, as he and Reed were walking across Penn Square on their way home from a dinner party, Reed asked him, "What has most struck you in America? Tell me candidly, for I shall not be at all angry if it be unfavorable."

Standing still to deliver his dictum, Thackeray replied, "You know what a virtue-proud people we English are. We think we have got it all to ourselves. Now, what most impresses me here is that I find homes as pure as ours, firesides like ours, domestic virtues as gentle; the English language, though the accent be a little different, with its home-like melody; and the Common Prayer book in your families. I am more struck by pleasant resemblances than by anything else."

Nevertheless, he was growing weary of the whole affair. After a week of Philadelphia's hospitality, out to dinner and supper every night, he wrote petulantly to Mrs Brookfield: "Oh! I am tired of shaking hands with people and acting the lion business night after night. Everybody is introduced and shakes hands. I know thousands of colonels, professors, editors, and what not, and walk the streets guiltily knowing that I don't know them and trembling lest the man opposite to me is one of my friends of the day before." He was counting the weeks until his return to England, and yet already making plans for another tour as soon as he could prepare the necessary lectures. If the second course should prove as profitable as the first, his mind would be at rest regarding his wife and daughters, and he could "sing Nunc Dimittis without faltering. There is money-making to try at, to be sure, and ambition—I mean in public life," he added to Mrs Brookfield; "perhaps that might interest a man, but not novels, nor lectures, nor fun any more. I don't seem to care about these any more, or for praise, or for abuse, or for reputation of that kind. That literary play is played out and the puppets going to be locked up for good and all."

In giving his lectures he had got over his nervousness and was beginning to enjoy himself. "The curious thing is that I think I improve in the reading; at certain passages, a sort of emotion springs up. I begin to understand how actors feel affected over and over again at the same passages of the play." And his success had helped him to conquer any lingering doubts about the respectability of lecturing. In a letter to Lady Stanley, he attributed the ill-will of some Boston newspapers to the fact that "Boston is the center of lecturing; lecturers go out thence to all quarters of the Union, lecturers who only get one dollar to my ten, and who are at least quite as good as I am, hence animosities and natural heart-burnings; and I don't care, so long as the reason is with them, and the dollars with me. . . Everybody lectures in this country, and it isn't, nor any trade or calling else, for that matter, thought *infra dig.*"

At the end of his Philadelphia series, he went back to New York for a few days, having promised to give a benefit lecture for a "Ladies' Society for the Employment and Relief of the Poor." His subject was to be "Charity and Humor," but until the last moment he had not found time to prepare it. He then devoted a day to the task, lying on the bed in his hotel room, smoking steadily, and dictating to Crowe with unusual fluency. "I don't know where it's all coming from," he exclaimed delightedly. By the time the dinner-gong sounded, the manuscript was complete. Forming a pendant to the series he had been giving, it contrasted the eighteenth-century humorists with those of his own day, and he took the opportunity to pay a hearty tribute to Dickens. It brought in some twelve hundred dollars for the funds of the society.

His next engagement was in Washington, which was at the height of festivities leading up to the inauguration of President Pierce. He also gave the lectures on alternate nights in Baltimore, where he drew a larger audience than in the capital, but where he spent little time, as the Washington gaieties occupied him to the full. Irving, who was still sojourning there, reported that "he is well received here, both in public and private, and is going the round of dinner parties, &c." The English minister, Philip Crampton, gave several dinner parties at the legation, and brought his whole staff to the first lecture—"very much bored," Thackeray suspected. Edward Everett, Secretary of State, also gave a dinner; so did Senator Hamilton Fish. General Winfield Scott, the defeated Whig presidential candidate, was his host at the war department. In a party that included both the incumbent and the prospective presidents, Millard Fillmore and Franklin Pierce, he took part in an official inspection of the new and revolutionary steamship just completed by the ingenious John Ericsson. The visitors were supposed to gaze reverently upon the expensive "caloric engine" and other novelties; but as it was a bitterly cold day Thackeray preferred to seek a snug corner between decks—at imminent danger of braining himself on the beams—for a chat with Washington Irving. The same evening he was a guest at dinner in the White House.

As lonely for the Baxters as ever, he invited them to come to stay for a few days in Washington at his expense, promising to give up to them his poky little rooms above Anderson's Music Store, and to take them to the British legation, and the President's *levée*, and Baltimore and Mount Vernon; but an accident to their younger girl prevented their acceptance.

When he was still in Washington a disturbing suggestion reached him. The British consul in Philadelphia suddenly died, and Reed wrote to Thackeray on behalf of his friends in that city to request that he apply for the appointment. In pondering the idea, Thackeray found how much he had grown to like the country. "There's a rush and activity of life quite astounding," he wrote in a long earnest letter to Albany Fonblanque, "a splendid recklessness about money which has in it something admirable too. You get an equality which may shock ever so little at first, but has something hearty and generous in it. There's beautiful affection in this country, immense tenderness, romantic personal enthusiasm, and a general kindliness and serviceableness and good nature, which is very pleasant and curious to witness for us folks at home who are mostly ashamed of our best emotions." Even the costumes of the New York ladies, which had made him laugh by their "splendaciousness," now seemed pleasingly handsome. If he had been ten years younger, he might have seriously considered making a fresh start in the new world. But the ties of habit were too strong to break. "Home among my parents there," he replied to Reed, "and some few friends I have made in the last twenty-five years, and a tolerably fair prospect of a livelihood on the familiar London flagstones, and the library of the Athenaeum, and the ride in the Park, and the pleasant society afterwards; and a trip to Paris now and again, and to Switzerland and Italy in the summer—these are little temptations which make me not discontented with my lot, about which I grumble only for pastime, and because it is an Englishman's privilege."

His concluding lecture in Washington, on February 26, was distinguished by the attendance of the two presidents. Two days later he started on the southern leg of his tour, still uncertain as to its extent. He had planned to go as far as New Orleans, and come back *via* St Louis and Ohio; but when he was offered only $2500 for appearing in New Orleans, instead of the five thousand he hoped for, and when he heard disquieting tales of Mississippi steamboats hitting snags or blowing up their boilers, he allowed these facts to strengthen his growing dislike of lecturing, and he began to mutter about "striking work any day."

As his boat passed down the Potomac he gazed with interest at Mount Vernon and tried to pick out the site of the "New Castlewood" which Henry Esmond had built and which was already inhabited in the author's imagination by his hero's daughter, Madame Esmond Warrington, and her twin sons, as mentioned in his preface to the novel.

Owing to a missed connection between boat and train, Thackeray and Crowe were late in reaching Richmond, and the waiting audience had to be dismissed until the next day. In spite of this inauspicious start, the three lectures were so popular that the "Athenaeum" was not half large enough to accommodate those who wanted tickets.

Some anxious moments were caused by Crowe's imprudence in dropping in at a slave auction and making a sketch of the proceedings until he was chased out as a suspected abolitionist spy. For a little while, Thackeray was afraid that his whole southern tour might be jeopardized by the escapade, but it was soon forgotten. It was probably a mere coincidence that his lecture in Petersburg, Virginia, was thinly attended. Thackeray insisted on remitting half of the stipulated fee. "Nobody must lose money by me in America," he declared.

After a week in Richmond they went on by the steamer "Governor Dudley" to Charleston. There were the usual dinners and receptions, at which Thackeray shared the honors with Professor Agassiz, who was giving a course of scientific addresses. Having repeatedly declared that he had no intention of being "lionized," he sometimes grew impatient with the social engagements. One of those in Charleston was a supper at the home of Mrs Henry King, a lady with a vast local reputation for her wit and daring. When Thackeray was unresponsive to her conversational challenges, she announced that she was disappointed in him. "I don't care a fig, ma'am," he replied bluntly, "whether you are pleased with me or not." The anecdote spread widely and in various forms, none of them to the credit of Thackeray's courtesy.

Having heard so much condemnation of slavery in the North, he was surprised to find that it did not horrify him at all. The masters seemed to him consistently kind and generous, the slaves well-fed, happy, and leisurely. In each household he noticed the old slaves who were cared for when they could no longer work, and the laughing pickaninnies who seemed to make a game of waiting on table. In Charleston he attended a negro ball, where he was mightily amused by the gorgeous costumes, the energetic orchestra, the full-throated merriment. He drank spruce-beer with the guests, and saw no reason to pity them for their servitude.

His three lectures in Charleston drew the largest audiences ever seen in the Hibernian Hall, earned him $665, and created such enthusiasm that he arranged to come back in ten days and give the other three. In the interval he proceeded to Savannah, Georgia, where his experience was less satisfactory. The proceeds of the three lectures were smaller than anywhere else; one of them had to be given in a "dirty little theatre," as his hall was otherwise engaged; the damp heat was enervating; and the hotel was so infested with fleas that his bedroom floor in the morning was strewn with burnt matches, expended in efforts to catch his tormentors. On the second day the British consul, Andrew Low, a wealthy cotton broker, came to the rescue, and gave Thackeray and Crowe comfortable quarters in his house for the rest of the week.

By the time he had fulfilled his return engagement in Charleston, Thackeray's disgust with "this ambulatory quack business" had become intense. "The idleness of the life is dreary and demoralizing, "he wrote to Dr Brown, "and the bore and humiliation of delivering these stale old lectures is growing intolerable." He returned to New York with vague intentions of going on to Canada, but for a fortnight enjoyed a vacation, with two lectures in Albany as the only exertion. He saw much of the Baxters, and on April 15 wrote a pretty set of verses for Lucy Baxter's seventeenth birthday. Plans for the Canadian tour had matured to the point of newspaper announcements of the Montreal dates, when on the morning of April 20 he looked up from his newspaper and remarked to Crowe, "I see there's a Cunarder sailing this morning. I'll go down to Wall Street and see whether I can secure berths in her. Meanwhile, you might try and get all the traps packed up and ready." At eleven o'clock their cab was clattering down Broadway; they tumbled into a boat in the East River amid shouts of "Hurry up, she's starting;" and by noon they were steaming out toward Sandy Hook.

The American tour, undertaken with such misgivings, had proved an entire success. His twenty-five hundred pounds, already invested at the comfortable American rate of eight per cent, relieved his mind of the anxiety about his wife and children which had haunted him ever since the doctors had warned him of his precarious health. But he carried home with him less tangible assets also. He had found how easily he could get along with the people of a strenuous new world, and had proved that in spite of all the accusations of snobbery leveled against him in England, he could be more at home in an equalitarian society than the great proletarian, Dickens. He had seen something of the power and vastness of a nation of twenty-six million people who spoke English with a quaint accent, and where the lowest wage for a laborer was a dollar a day. "The young blood beating in its pulses warms one, like the company of young men in England," he exclaimed. His tentative scheme of writing about the States had been obliterated by a profound conviction of inadequacy. "No man should write about the country under five years of experience, and as many of previous reading." "A deal of Cockney arrogance" had been rubbed off, he confessed. In short, he had acquired yet another angle for that prism of aloofness and estrangement through which he viewed his fellow-countrymen, and which displayed them so clearly and yet in such unaccustomed lights.

Lady of the House.

CHAPTER 17

To be a Peacemaker

THE EUROPA HAD a calm and speedy crossing of ten days, and Thackeray was able to enjoy the company of congenial passengers of both sexes. Several times he composed letters to Sally Baxter, only to tear them up when he realized that their scornful jibes were unsuitable for sending to a young lady. In spite of all resolutions to be decorous, his pen would run away with him into sarcasms that might have passed in conversation under cover of his kindly smile, but which looked startlingly bitter in black and white.

After spending the night of May 1 at the Adelphi in Liverpool, he reached London the next day, and devoted himself immediately to calling on friends. As Lady Stanley was giving a ball that night, he marched into it unannounced and enjoyed the sensation he made. Invitations to dinner arrived from "some of the immensest big wigs," but he refused them all on the ground that he was hurrying off to Paris to see his family as soon as some pressing business was attended to. An infected tooth kept him for several days longer in London, but was accompanied by an unsightly facial eruption that precluded appearances in public.

Meanwhile, the news spread that he did nothing but praise the United States. At Lady Stanley's ball he had pulled out his watch, which he had not set since leaving New York, and said, "There! That's the *real* time." He disparaged the dancing and the ladies' dresses in contrast with the racing polkas and brilliant toilettes of New York. As usual, no one was sure how much of all this was seriously meant and how much was raillery. Lady Stanley protested that his praises of the American women were "outrageous." There was no doubt, however, of the seriousness of his outburst whenever he heard a complacent English sneer at anything American: with unwonted earnestness he would dilate upon the kindness and worth and good breeding that he had found. Henry Greville, who met him at Lord Granville's, remarked somewhat skeptically upon his enthusiasm: "He says that he never heard an uncivil expression towards this country or himself, and that he met with constant kindness and hospitality. He says the feeling of the upper classes toward us is most friendly, but he admits that the lower orders abhor the name of England."

He was disturbed to discover that everybody was reading *Uncle Tom's Cabin*, for he felt that the book would do harm by inflating the English with a sense of their superior virtue in having freed their slaves. In his determination to promote better understanding between the two countries, the signification of his second name assumed the importance of an omen. "I pray Heaven," he wrote to Mrs Baxter, "it may be my chance as it will be my endeavour to be a Peacemaker between us and you and to speak good will towards you." When Clough got home two months later, he was greeted with the news and relayed it to his friend Norton at Harvard: "Thackeray, they tell us, is full of the kindheartedness and generousness of the Americans, and is faithful to his purpose of writing no book."

The reputation he had left behind him was on the whole likely to fulfil his hope. Writing to Carlyle in August, Emerson reported what he had heard during a visit to New York: "Thackeray has made a good mark in this country by a certain manly blurting out of his opinion in various companies, where so much honesty was rare and useful." Carlyle's reply contained what is perhaps the best of his various analyses of his friend's character: "Thackeray has very rarely come athwart me since his return: he is a big fellow, soul and body; of many gifts and qualities (particularly in the Hogarth line, with a dash of Sterne superadded), of enormous *appetite* withal, and very uncertain and chaotic in all points except his *outer breeding*, which is fixed enough, and *perfect* according to the modern English style. I rather dread explosions in his history. A *big*, fierce, weeping, hungry man; not a strong one."

Now that the lectures had earned all he could expect, he permitted their appearance as a book, which had been prepared for the press and provided with footnotes by his friend Hannay. And publishers were bidding against each other for his next novel. As their offers grew more tempting, he realized that his second lecture tour across the Atlantic, which he had planned for the coming autumn, might have to be postponed. After all, authorship was still his profession, and he had to admit that he could earn as much during the next twelvemonth by staying at home and writing a novel as by preparing a series of lectures and traveling thousands of miles to deliver them. Unable to reach a decision, he went off to Paris for leisure to think it over.

After the vastitude of America he found more than his usual difficulty in adjusting himself to the limitations of his parents' life. His stepfather had suffered a cerebral attack during his absence, and had to live carefully. The small-talk of the "twaddling society" that was ruled by Mrs Carmichael-Smyth, endlessly discussing "the misdeeds of maids-of-all-work," exasperated Thackeray, and not the less because he was aware of how easily he might drop into similar triviality. Her possessive affection, and the dutiful homage of her friends, embarrassed him; he felt guiltily conscious that he was giving himself airs as he talked to them. The life-size portrait of him seemed to swagger in the little drawing-room so that he couldn't evade his pompous stare.

His stepfather looked almost gratified when he had an attack of illness, for it gave the good old major an opportunity to administer pills. His daughters proudly displayed their progress in piano-playing, and he was touched that they had devoted themselves to his favorite music, the stately airs of Haydn and Mozart, but their strumming bored him none the less. Annie had also been applying herself to authorship, and showed him the manuscripts of several novels and a tragedy; but he brought this activity to a halt by ordering her not to waste her time with scribbling, but to read other people's books.

He was further bothered by the problem of the girls' education. Faithful Miss Trulock had given up her position when he went to America, and although their new Parisian governess was excellent she was "much too young and pretty to come to a single man's house," as well as being too proud for the indignities of a governess's place in London.

He saw none of his French friends. When he got out for a few hours one day he went all alone to a picture gallery, dinner at the Trois Frères, and a theater, reveling in the solitude. Paris was full of American visitors, and whenever he heard a transatlantic twang he felt tempted to hail the speaker as a friend.

At the beginning of June he returned to London for three weeks of "idleness and lounging and gourmandizing." The Season was at its height, and his constant round of luncheons, dinners, and even breakfasts soon brought him to a state of mental confusion in which the throngs of fellow-guests flitted like figures in a dream. Never before had he been quite so conscious of the artificiality and pretension, the toadying and money-worship, in this "belle société" that was his normal environment. He wondered whether he might be wrong in bringing up his girls in such an atmosphere; but he argued with himself that human nature was the same in all ranks, and the highest society had the advantage of giving the best dinners.

He could not do much entertaining on his own account, as his house was partly shut up, and his plate at his banker's; when he asked two American friends to dinner, a tea-cup had to be used for a soup-ladle, and he suspected that the story would find its way into the New York papers with embellishments.

At one luncheon he met Harriet Beecher Stowe, who was visiting England to enlist sympathy for abolition, and he was surprised to find her gentle, sweet-looking, and sincere. He decided that he must "buckle to" and really try to read *Uncle Tom's Cabin*. Nevertheless, he made a point of remarking to Mrs Stowe's chief supporter, Lord Shaftesbury, "After all, there are other people besides blacks in America; there are twenty-three millions of whites who interest me still more than the niggers." So many friends were urging him to give a lecture on the United States that he began to feel tempted to do so, but his lack of a secretary was a sufficient excuse for not preparing it.

Of the Brookfields he saw but little. Their second child had been born shortly before his return from America, and Brookfield's pride in his new son made him a much tenderer husband. "I'm not in the least annoyed," remarked Thackeray, in describing their domestic happiness to Mrs Baxter, to whom he had confided the whole affair.

About this time he found an opportunity of helping an old friend. One day in the Strand he met Charles Mackay, who was editing the *Illustrated London News,* and Mackay asked if he could recommend a Paris correspondent for that paper. "Had I been asked ten years ago," Thackeray replied, "I should have offered myself for the place; and I don't know that I shouldn't like it even now. What do you say to Mahony? . . . But stay! I know somebody still better, who writes, if not so

THE CARMICHAEL-SMYTHS AND THEIR
GRANDDAUGHTERS

brilliantly as Mahony, quite brilliantly enough for any newspaper in the world, and to whom the salary would be a perfect godsend. I mean Miss Margaret Power, niece of Lady Blessington. If you appoint her you will do a good action, get a good correspondent for the *Illustrated,* and greatly oblige your old friend—me." Miss Power duly received the appointment, and retained it for the few remaining years of her life.

In the intervals of entertainment, Thackeray continued the search for a governess, and had more success in engaging a highly-recommended valet for himself. He also paid some attention to business affairs. His banker, Mr Baring, worried him by shaking his head glumly over American railroad shares and their glittering

eight per cent. The first edition of the lectures was almost exhausted. The impor-
tunities of the publishers finally drove him to accepting an agreement with Bradbury
& Evans to write a new novel in twenty-four numbers. For this he was to receive
£3600, and he counted on an extra five hundred for the American and Continental
rights. "It's coining money, isn't it?" he exclaimed gleefully to Mrs Baxter. If the
second American tour could be achieved, he calculated that in two years he would
reach his objective of providing fully for his daughters' future.

His power of self-restraint being inadequate to withstand invitations to dinner,
he fled from London as soon as the contract was signed; to have stayed another
week, he felt certain, would have been fatal. Having crossed the Channel in a gale,
he reached Calais feeling so unwell that he decided not to go on that night, and put
up at Dessein's Hotel, always a favorite of his for its old-world dignity. This time
he was given the very same bedroom that Sterne had occupied when he was setting
out on his Sentimental Journey. As the sardonic face looked down at him from a
picture over the chimney-piece, Thackeray's mind went back to the unfavorable
comments on Sterne in his lectures, and he seemed to hear Mr Yorick say, "You're
right, I *was* a humbug; and you, my lad, are you not as great?" Recollecting some
recent sneers at his own expense in London newspapers, he was stirred with a fellow-
feeling for his spectral room-mate.

He lingered for a while in Paris, trying to make up his mind where to go for the
change of scene that he needed to stimulate his wits. His favorite journey up the
Rhine to Switzerland beckoned him, but he pondered the possibility of Devonshire
instead, and even remarked only half jestingly to his daughters that he might take
them across the ocean and settle down to write his novel at Saratoga Springs. A
winter in Rome having long been a cherished prospect, he tentatively planned to go
there in December; and then when he realized how frail his stepfather was becoming and how much the old couple delighted in having him and the girls, he felt that
he ought to resign himself to wintering in Paris instead.

The new novel was torturing him so that he wandered aimlessly about, avoiding company and wrestling with vague ideas. As so often before, recent experiences
of his own suggested themselves. Telling Mrs Baxter that his hero might fall in love
and be jilted, he added: "He won't break his heart. I don't think he'll have much of
a heart. . . I wonder whether all literary men are humbugs and have no hearts. I
know one who has none." Thus sneering at himself, he finally got away to the
Rhine at the beginning of July, accompanied by his two girls and attended by his
new valet, Charles Pearman.

He set out with the conviction that the novel would not be a good one—"not a
step forward, but a retreat, rather." The naïve chatter of the girls, however, with
the bland summer weather and ever charming scenery, put him in a more hopeful
mood, and as soon as he reached Baden he went resolutely to work on the intro-

THE CALAIS PACKET

ductory chapter. While still engaged on *Esmond,* more than a year before, he had thought about a novel depicting a boy born in India, and having a half-brother and sister, and had gone back to his own childhood days at Fareham as suitable for the opening scenes. He now embodied this reminiscent material in his picture of the Newcome family.

He spent ten agreeable days in Baden, reading *Don Quixote* with delight, chatting with friends, and completing a draft of the first number of *The Newcomes.* In spite of this good progress, he felt unenthusiastic about it, seeing it as only "a repetition of past performances" and aware that he had almost reached the end of his resources. He acknowledged the immense advantage over him that Dickens enjoyed in "the great fecundity of his imagination," and added frankly that the once-despised Bulwer-Lytton was proving in this respect to be better than both of them, his latest novel being his freshest and richest.

He realized that the girls were growing bored in Baden, and on his forty-second birthday he took advantage of a rainy day to pack up and move on to Basle. When they sat down to supper in the hotel there, Thackeray heard unrestrained American chatter from a large touring party occupying the main table. "There, my dears," he remarked to his daughters, "I've been telling you what pleasant folks the Americans are. It makes me feel comfortable to see some of them again."

At that moment no less than five of the party—two of them ladies—put their knives half-way down their throats. The Thackeray girls burst out giggling, and in horrified haste their father had to think of an excuse. "My dears," he protested, "your great-great-grandmother, one of the finest ladies of the old school I ever saw, always applied cold steel to her wittles. It's no *crime* to eat with a knife."

His next move was to Neuchâtel. Still uncertain about the novel, he kept on preparing for possible failure by insisting in his letters to his friends that he was "too old for story-telling," that if he lived a few more years (this "if" was now attached to all his forecasts of the future) he would devote himself to politics or history, but that meanwhile he still needed money for his family, and of the four thousand pounds which *The Newcomes* would earn, he hoped to lay aside three.

His discomfort with the story arose from a sense that the autobiographical element was all too conspicuous. On July 25, at Vevey, a solution occurred to him. The new book by Lytton that had impressed him so favorably was *My Novel,* which the author had linked to his preceding work, *The Caxtons,* by having it narrated by Pisistratus Caxton. Such carrying over of characters from novel to novel was already a favorite device of Thackeray's (in fact, Lytton may well have borrowed it from him), but Thackeray was candid in admitting that Lytton's particular example gave him the idea of writing *The Newcomes* in the guise of Arthur Pendennis, thereby enabling himself "to talk more at ease than in my own person."

With this fresh start, he was able to finish Number Two by the end of July.

An infallible symptom of better spirits was the appearance of his sketch-book, and during this happy week at Vevey he spent every morning in drawing the summer-softened Alpine scenery, while the afternoons were devoted to dictating the story to Annie. Then restlessness gripped him again, and they wandered on to Geneva, Lausanne, Bulle, Fribourg, Berne. He never knew when a sudden impulse might send him back to England at a day's notice. His enthusiasm for the story was waning. His letters resumed the old lament: *The Newcomes* was "stupid," it was "rubbish," he ought to leave novel-writing to younger, more inventive men. For days at a time he would scarcely be able to bring himself to open his mouth, even though aware that his moodiness made him seem haughty to people he encountered.

One day, while at Berne, he went for a walk with his girls, preoccupied with his difficulties in Number Three. As they strolled down a sloping stubble-field, he noticed a little wood at the foot, and asked them to wait for him while he explored it. In a few minutes he came back with lightened step and beaming face, explaining that in a miraculous flash the whole future development of his plot had been revealed to him. Thus encouraged, he finished Number Three at Thun a few days later, began the next number at Zurich, and worked on it in the train as they traveled by way of Basle and Heidelberg to Frankfort. As a result of all this effort, he suffered an attack of illness which kept him in bed for some days, well looked after by his competent new man-servant.

When he got back to London at the beginning of September, with the four completed numbers, he was eager to see them in print. Warned by his relapse of health, he had given up the idea of illustrating the novel himself, and he suggested to Bradbury & Evans that they employ his friend Doyle. During the three weeks of waiting while Doyle produced his first drawings, Thackeray busied himself with the interminable search for a governess. A "Ger-woman" came on trial, with excellent credentials, but he soon found that she was one of the many people "who shut me up or drive me to my own room," and so she was sent off. He was still uncertain as to whether he would spend the winter in Rome. Meanwhile, he suddenly decided to buy a house—No. 36, Onslow Square, Brompton. Although it was not so roomy as his house in Young Street, it appealed to him by its outlook on the elms in the square and its arrangement which would enable the girls to have a floor for themselves, with their own bathroom—a feature that pleasantly reminded him of America.

Another touch of illness prompted him to draw up a will, in which he appointed his two oldest friends, FitzGerald and Brookfield, to serve as guardians for his daughters in the event of his death. The combination of illness, governess-hunting, house-buying, and receiving visits from many friends made it impossible for him to do any work. He paid a visit to Mr and Mrs Higgins in Oxfordshire and spent a few days in Brighton, which braced him up as promptly as ever, so that he even wrote a ballad, *The Organ Boy's Appeal*, and sent it to *Punch*, his first contribution in two years.

When the proofs of Number One of *The Newcomes* finally arrived, accompanied by Doyle's engravings, he decided that they were not so good as the sketches he had originally made himself. Disgruntled, he hastened his arrangements for returning to the Continent, until he was halted by a proposal from a publisher that he should undertake an edition of Horace Walpole's letters. Historical research had given him so much enjoyment while preparing his lectures that he was looking forward to it as the chosen occupation of his later years; but he realized that at this moment it would compete disastrously with the task in hand, and so he repelled the temptation and on October 4 returned to Paris.

His hopes of going later to Italy were dimmed by the unsettled state of European politics, but in a short time the annoyances of Paris convinced him that at all costs he must make the move. No sooner would he try to settle down to work in his apartment in the Maison Valin, Avenue Champs Elysées, than it was time to visit his parents or take the girls for a walk. As his numerous friends in Paris belonged to three or four distinct sets, the problem of seeing and entertaining them was complicated. He gave several restaurant dinners that revived something of the old bohemian jollity, and thought about paying for them by writing a series of gastronomic articles for *Punch*. But during the whole of October he produced only one number of *The Newcomes*. Often he would sit at his desk for hours at a time, with a blank sheet in front of him, unable to write a sentence. Secretly he longed to go to Rome for a month all by himself, but he was well aware of how this would hurt his daughters' feelings.

To increase his demoralization, news reached him during November that an absurd storm had arisen in the United States over a tactless sentence in the second chapter of *The Newcomes*. In a passage summarizing the state of England under George III, Thackeray had included the remark that "Mr Washington was heading the American rebels with a courage, it must be confessed, worthy of a better cause." This was seized upon as an insult to both the nation and its hero, with such fury that the New York correspondent of *The Times* considered it worthy of a despatch. Thackeray was horrified. After all his extravagant praises of the United States, in his self-elected function of apologist for America among the English, he was deeply wounded by the abuse and by the distrust that it implied. His English friends, smarting from his sneers at their misunderstanding of Americans, were not slow to ridicule him. "It serves you right," they jibed; "you see what good you have got by praising the States."

In his rage and contrition, he told himself that his second lecture tour would now be impossible. The thoughtless blunder had cost him ten thousand dollars. Although he felt that "there's no use explaining and apologizing to an angry, half-educated man," he sent a letter to *The Times*, pointing out the obvious fact that his words had been intended to echo the feelings of the English public in 1776, and not to express his own opinion; and he earnestly protested that "I think the cause for which Washington fought entirely just and right, and the Champion the very noblest, purest, bravest, best of God's men."

He apparently besought his friends to support him. Thornton Hunt, for example, sent a long letter on the subject to an American literary man:

I happen to have met Thackeray in a company where he could, with the most unqualified confidence, and where he must have conversed without study, and without thought of what would be repeated . . . I wish what he then said could have been overheard by the whole Union, because I never heard but one Englishman so heartily acknowledge the noble qualities, the worth, and the estimable traits of Americans generally . . . I heard him talk of giving his impressions of the Union publicly, and I joined with others in urging him to do so. What was his objection? That he would not make money by his sense of the kindness which he had received; and that if he did it without payment it might be misconstrued into an invidious contrast of his own better feeling as compared with that of others who had not so well understood the American people. I wish that his over-delicacy had not restrained him . . .

War meanwhile had broken out between Russia and Turkey. In the middle of November, when Thackeray was briefly back in London, he received a proposal from Charles Mackay that he should go to the seat of war as a special correspondent of the *Illustrated London News*. He did not consider the offer, of course, but once more he grasped the opportunity of helping a friend. Young Joseph Crowe, brother of his erstwhile secretary, was struggling to launch a literary career, and was at the moment so penniless that he had not been able to go from London to Paris, three weeks before, to attend his mother's funeral. Lauding Crowe's talents in both writing and drawing, Thackeray impressed upon Mackay that he was just the man for the post, and then hastened to seek out Crowe and tell him of his impending good luck. "I cannot help asking," Crowe remarks complacently in his reminiscences, "whether it was not providential that just at the point when my affairs were at so low an ebb, I should have such a stroke of good fortune." Perhaps for his reference to Providence he might have substituted a more specific name.

When at last Thackeray summoned up energy to gather the necessary impedimenta and detach the girls from their grandmother's tearful embraces, they left Paris on November 27 and proceeded by way of the Rhône, in dreary snowy weather to Marseilles, where they took ship. The last stage of the journey, the coach drive from Civita Vecchia to Rome, gave Thackeray some anxiety, for there was much talk about banditti, and he had ninety *louis* or so in his pocket. There was no excitement, however, except that a postillion was accidentally killed; but the very next day a party was robbed, and Annie and Minny expressed disappointment that they had missed the adventure.

They first put up at the Hotel Franz in the Via Condotti, where Thackeray had stayed nine years before; but Browning soon helped them to obtain a vast and over-furnished suite of rooms in the Palazzo Poniatowski, in the Via della Croce. Thackeray felt obliged to devote the first week to sightseeing with the girls. Although enjoying their raptures, he was not greatly taken with Rome: his innate Protestantism was irritated by the "enormous pile of fiction and ceremony" which entirely obscured Christ at St. Peter's; and he asserted grumpily that everyone he met in Italy was either a thief or a beggar.

A week after arriving, he was laid low by a sharp attack of his malady. A gruff and slovenly Irish doctor, who lodged in the same palace and had few patients, devoted himself to the case, and after four days of leeches, blisters, and calomel, Thackeray was well enough to face the fact that he had not written a word of *The Newcomes* since leaving Paris, and was rapidly losing the advantage of the four numbers he had accumulated before publication began.

The story was remaining just as close to its author's early life as *Pendennis* had done—indeed closer, for the whole Anglo-Indian clan of Newcomes was derived from his own kindred. He merely picked up the strands of his youth that had been omitted from the earlier novel. His hero, Clive Newcome, studied art instead of becoming a journalist. If Helen Pendennis had been a portrait of the author's mother, Colonel Newcome was an equally faithful reproduction of his generous, unworldly stepfather; the kindly aunt in Brighton, who looked after little Clive on his arrival from India, was "Aunt Becher" of Fareham; and pretty Rosey Mackenzie bore a close resemblance to Isabel Shawe. But in the midst of this family gallery, one figure appeared from a very different world. As the character of the heroine developed, readers across the Atlantic did not hesitate in recognizing the original of the frank, witty, capricious girl, with her gay scorn for her suitors and for the whirl of parties in which she dwelt; Thackeray's New York friends told each other knowingly, "Of course, Ethel Newcome is Sally Baxter."

Setting a routine for himself of early rising and early to bed, he worked on the novel in the mornings from seven till noon, dictating to Annie until he came to a crucial scene, when he would send her away: he could always think more clearly pen in hand. They worked in a huge colonnaded room hung with pictures and swinging lamps, while pigeons cooed from the deep window-sills and the hum of the streets rose muffled from far below.

Afternoons and evenings were free for social visiting. They went to John Gibson's studio to see his famous "tinted Venus," and the Thackeray girls were equally impressed by the close-cropped head of his American pupil, Harriet Hosmer. Fanny Kemble was in Rome, as impulsive as ever; she puzzled the girls with her diatribes against slavery, and embarrassed them by bursting into song while driving with them through the streets in her carriage. Her sister, Adelaide Sartoris, was also established in Rome, with her children. Thackeray had always liked her much better than the hard, brilliant Fanny, and though she had grown massively fat he could still see her as the "Tot Kemble" of twenty years before. At her house he met "the best society in Rome" and heard exquisite music.

The Brownings were cordial, too; Mrs Browning vied with Mrs Sartoris in providing feminine attentions to Annie and Minny. Still, the sensitive spirit of the poetess was ruffled by the novelist's worldly pose. "Mr Thackeray complains of dulness," she wrote to her sister; "he is disabled from work by the dulness. He 'can't write in the morning without his good dinner and two parties over-night.' From such a soil spring the *Vanity Fairs!* He is an amusing man-mountain enough and very courteous to us—but I never should get on with him much, I think—he is not sympathetic to me."

The Brownings' greatest friends, however, saw a different side of him. The American sculptor and poet, William Wetmore Story, had spent the summer with the Brownings in Lucca; just after he brought his family back to Rome in the autumn his little son died suddenly of gastric fever, and his only other child, nine-year-old Edith, fell desperately ill with the same disease. Thackeray, always mindful of the loss of his own infant, won the undying gratitude of the Storys by his kindness. "We often urged him," Mrs Story later explained, "to forget us and not to be drawn down into the depths of our sorrow, but rather to disport himself in the cordial sunshine of appreciation, among his own people. But he would not hear of this, and came again and again, listening to our tale of grief as if it had happened to himself, with a kindness and sympathy never to be forgotten. Once he surprised me when I had in my hand a little worn shoe which had for me an intense association; he shed tears over it with me and understood what it meant to me as few could have done. Under what people called his cynical exterior and manner, his was the kindest and truest heart that ever beat."

From the Brookfields he had acquired an interest in the Anglo-Catholic movement, and he was glad of a chance to investigate the mentality of the converts with whom Rome was liberally supplied. To one of them, Pollen by name, he had an introduction from his devout Catholic friend, Doyle. As Pollen was an Oxford man, with congenial views on literature and the fine arts, they became good friends, but Thackeray made little headway in comprehending "the secret of the religion for which he has given up rank, chances, and all good things of this life." He was gratified to learn from Pollen, however, that Father Newman had read the first two numbers of *The Newcomes* and praised the style. He also made the acquaintance of the latest distinguished convert, Dr Manning, as well as various English abbots and friars, and admitted himself to be "touched by their goodness, piety, and self-negation."

Outside of the English colony he made no acquaintances, and even the most renowned works of art no longer roused any thrill of rapture. He confessed that he could have written his book just as well in Brompton as in Rome; but he derived some glow of satisfaction from the knowledge that he was doing his paternal duty and supplying the girls with lifetime memories of the Eternal City. The only positive pleasure that he found was in the "flaming splendour" of the sunsets behind St Peter's, and the brilliance of the stars when the nights turned frosty.

Just after New Year's day the girls gave a party for their young friends. Refreshments were easily obtained from Spillmans, the famous pastrycooks that were located in the ground-floor of their *casa*, but the hostesses found themselves at a loss for entertainment without the magic lantern or the "tuppence-coloured" cardboard-theater characters with which they were accustomed to celebrate Twelfth Night at home. They appealed to their father to sketch some figures, to be shaken up in a lottery and drawn for prizes. With memories of his beloved pantomimes, he produced a grotesque series of characters; and when the little Sartorises and Denmans, and four-year-old Pen Browning, had eaten their cream-tarts and gone home, he came on the bright-colored sketches scattered on a table, and began idly to arrange them in the sequence of a plot. Growing interested in the fantasy, he dug a few older drawings out of his portfolio and adapted them to the new theme. As each episode of *The Rose and the Ring* was composed, he took it over to entertain little Edith Story in her tedious convalescence. He would sit beside her bed and read the tale, and then would discuss the characters in it as if they were real people, and tell their further adventures; or for a change he would ask her to tell him a story, and drawing his chair up to a table he would illustrate it with sketches as she went on.

By the end of January, enjoying an unusual spell of good health, he had finished Number Eight of *The Newcomes*. His social engagements were limited to gentle tea-parties or dinners with the Brownings, the Storys, and other friends. Mrs Browning described him as bringing "small-talk by handfuls of glittering dust swept out of saloons," but she admitted that by his kindness to her little boy he had "won her heart rather," and without qualification she added that "as to the Thackeray girls I am inclined quite to love them!"

Early in February he was laid low with Roman fever, and decided to move on as soon as possible to Naples. While he was recovering, he was saddened to hear of the death of his aunt, Mrs Ritchie, who had given him such motherly kindness when he arrived from India, thirty-six years before. In his deep distress, he told the girls to hasten their packing, and they left Rome several days sooner than had been planned.

They reached Naples by moonlight, after two days on the road. For a week they enjoyed the beauties of the region, making excellent headway on the novel in the intervals of the usual visits to Herculaneum and Pompeii. Then Annie came

down with scarlatina; thirteen-year-old Minny revealed an astonishing gift of healing in nursing her, but caught the disease herself within a week. Their father
promptly suffered an attack of his own old complaint. He was able to hire an excellent Irish nurse, and for some days all three of them were confined to their beds
with nothing to do but gaze at the Mediterranean, "so provokingly bright and
blue."

After this interruption he found it impossible to get on with Number Eleven.
Musicians distracted him by bawling songs under his window; his recent fright over
the girls' health made him specially solicitous of them; and he felt that he ought to
be back in London reading for his next lectures if they were to be ready to take to
America in the autumn. There was no time for any more sight-seeing; in fact, if it
had not been for the amusement he derived from going on with the "nonsensical
Christmas book," he would have been in a miserable state. Not until March 17 was
he able to resume *The Newcomes*, and at the end of the month they embarked for
Marseilles.

The long-anticipated winter in Italy had proved a failure. He felt sure that it
had contributed nothing to the five numbers that he wrote there; and his sense of
impending death had been strongly intensified. "I do feel twenty years older than
when I was in America," he wrote to Mrs Baxter, "and three months of ill health
and gloom in this charming climate have made me about seventy . . . I sleep like a
monk with a death's head in my room! 'Come,' says the cheerful monitor, 'rouse
yourself, finish Newcomes . . . for your time is short, and the sexton wants you.
You have had enough champagne and feasting, travelling, novel-writing, yawning,
grumbling, falling in love and the like . . . Get £200 a year apiece for your girls and
their poor mother, and then come to me!' "

The persistence of the *idée fixe* is shown by its reappearance in a letter to a
Punch comrade, written in Paris after a conversation with his old crony, Father
Prout. In his usual fund of gossip, Prout had included the news that Douglas Jerrold was making a great success as editor of *Lloyd's Newspaper*. "Please the gods
D.J. will lay by a little money," Thackeray wrote. "What's the business of us fathers
of families but that? When we are in the *domus exilis Plutonia*, we shall have a consolation in that glum limbo by thinking we have left some bread behind us for our
young ones here under the sun."

After staying ten days or so in Paris he left his daughters there and crossed to
London for the tiresome details of moving into his new home. He was in time for
the annual Shakespeare dinner at the Garrick, and was glad he attended, because
Dickens, who was in the chair, made flattering allusions to him. "Though I don't
care for the compliments," he told his mother, "I do for the goodwill and peace
among men."

The house in Onslow Square pleased him as much as in the first hasty inspection, but he realized that his old possessions would look decrepit in the freshly-decorated rooms, and he was determined to make a handsome showing. Accordingly, he spent a month in haunting furniture sales, chaffering with upholsterers, carpeters, fenderers, and mirror-makers, and paying interminable bills. He made no calls in society, but dined every night with bachelor cronies. After his virtuous months of family duties, he was enjoying the reversion to the habits of the years before his daughters were old enough to make claims upon him.

When he moved into the house on May 18, only two of the rooms were fully ready, but he sent word to the girls that he would meet them in Boulogne and bring them home. They were charmed with the taste in which he had provided the rooms with green carpets and curtains to harmonize with the trees outside the windows. Until the very day of their arrival, he was fumbling as ineffectually as ever with the problem of finding a governess or companion for them; and when the search led him to an efficient "College for Ladies" under German management, he wished he had solved the whole matter by sending the girls to board there two years before. His decision was left in abeyance, however, for the summer.

Even after he was in the new house, there was still so much hammering and bell-ringing and general confusion that for three weeks he could not concentrate on *The Newcomes*. Besides, Doyle was so dilatory with the plates that Thackeray began to think he might have to take over that task himself at any moment. Nor did he make a start on the lectures. The subject that he had projected was "Men of the World," including Chesterfield, Wharton, Walpole, and Brummell, and offering ample scope for satire and Augustan wit, but in the absence of any definite offer from America he hesitated to attack the necessary research.

Having rented a château in Boulogne for the summer, he had to salve his conscience with regard to the extravagance by undertaking a "piece of buffoonery" for *Punch* that would pay the rent. This series of articles, which ran through six issues, under the title *Important from the Seat of War*, was the sort of burlesque that he could always dash off with little effort.

During June he was busy with his seasonal round of dinner parties and receptions, and was particularly pleased to be invited to dinner by Lord Palmerston, who, as Home Secretary, was "the man who has Police Magistrateships in his gift." In spite of years of disappointment, Thackeray was as hopeful as ever of stepping out of authorship and into public affairs.

Only five weeks after occupying the house in Onslow Square, the family went over to their Château de Brecrecque, with a retinue of three household servants and an amanuensis. As the Carmichael-Smyths were joining them for the summer, even the spacious château was too small to hold them all, and Mr Sleap the amanuensis had to find lodgings in the town. Mr and Mrs Charles Dickens were also summering in Boulogne, with their nine children, and there was much intercourse between the Château de Brecrecque and the Villa du Camp de Droite. A particular friendship sprang up between Minny Thackeray and Katie Dickens, a few months her senior. The amusements of the Dickens ménage were somewhat too strenuous and juvenile for Thackeray, and after a whole evening of playing forfeits and the game of "buzz" he observed drily that even "buzz" might tire him after a certain number of repetitions.

LORD CLARENDON, VICEROY OF IRELAND,
AND HON. GERALD PONSONBY, HIS GENTLEMAN OF THE BEDCHAMBER

The Thackerays' residence proved to be more impressive than comfortable. Dickens described it in a letter to Forster as "a melancholy but very good château on the Paris road, where their landlord (a Baron) has supplied them, T. tells me, with one milk jug as the entire crockery of the establishment." Besides, the air of Boulogne was not so salubrious as he had hoped, and soon they all had colds. The news that Mme Sontag had died of cholera, at the height of her triumphal tour, moved him to start a poem, as he recalled his youthful admiration for her and their pleasant interview twenty months before; but he desisted on realizing that it was about himself rather than her.

After two weeks of concentrated work, he treated himself to a week in Paris, where he called on nobody, spent his days in buying clocks and other knick-knacks for the new house, and went to the theater every night. By the time he made a flying visit to London, in the middle of August, he could announce that he had written five numbers of *The Newcomes* and suffered four sharp attacks of illness during his two months' absence. He found a letter which had been waiting for him for weeks, and in which the New York Mercantile Library Association offered him one thousand dollars for a series of four lectures. In reply he explained that as his illnesses had not only prevented all preparation of lectures but also held him at least six months behind his schedule with *The Newcomes*, he could not possibly come; and in a private note to Mr Felt he added that the inadequacy of the offer was a further reason for declining. Moreover, the American railway share market was going through such a crisis that he felt terrified about the survival of his profits from the previous tour.

Still, he was deeply disappointed by this further postponement of his visit. Professor Henry Reed, a brother of his friend in Philadelphia, had been spending the summer in Europe, and when Thackeray called upon him at his hotel he felt transported back to "grave, calm, kind old Philadelphia" the moment he heard his voice. Reed was to sail for home a few weeks later in the steamer *Arctic*. "How much I should like to be going with you!" exclaimed Thackeray, as they parted. The words came back to his mind with a shudder when the news arrived that the *Arctic* had been lost off Newfoundland with all on board.

A gleam of an old hope was kindled by his hearing that the secretaryship of the British legation at Washington was vacant. He instantly applied for it, but the Foreign Secretary, Lord Clarendon, explained that the new appointment had already been made, and besides, it was necessarily filled by promotion within the diplomatic service. Realizing that this fact was a permanent barrier to ambitions in that direction, Thackeray went gloomily back to the interminable "old mill-wheel" that ground out *The Newcomes*.

CHAPTER 18

In the Sea of Life Enisled

WHEN THE TENANCY of the château expired in the autumn, the girls went to Paris to stay with their grandparents until after Christmas, and Thackeray resumed a bachelor existence in London. His attacks of spasms recurred so regularly every few weeks that he was beginning to accept them as part of the routine of existence. To all the ordinances of destiny that had combined to make him an exile and an on-looker in the world was now added this last and most inexorable decree—perpetual warnings of an early death.

Ever since his homeless childhood had first taught him to curb his affectionate impulses and protect himself against bullies, his life had been too bitter a sequence of ironies and frustrations to be indemnified even by his long-deferred fame when it arrived in full measure. Nothing would have pleased him better than to give up his eminence as a novelist in exchange for the obscure and monotonous work of a police magistrate or a minor diplomatic official. But even this humble request to be an active participant in the affairs of life was stonily denied, and he had to re-main the spectator.

No wonder that by the time he was forty gray hair and wrinkles made him ap-pear as old to others as he felt himself inwardly to be. No wonder that he had to burn many of his intimate letters instead of posting them, lest their cynicism should sear the happiness of the recipients. No wonder that readers of his books com-plained uncomfortably about the dark abysses that he would sometimes momen-tarily reveal beneath his urbane banter. If he was to make a living by his novels, he knew he had to humor the complacent illusions and fetishes of his public; but he was too honest an artist to conceal the fact that in his own personal universe the axioms of happy men were mocking shams.

It was only the fitting sequel that just when his daughters were growing old enough to provide some of the domestic life and love that had been snatched from him, the symptoms of progressive disease admonished him that he might not long enjoy vicariously the pleasures of their girlhood. His doctors advised him, to be sure, that by regular habits and abstinence from liquor he might postpone the final chapter; but will-power had never been one of his merits, and life had not endeared itself to him sufficiently to be worth purchasing at the expense of the only anodynes that made it endurable. Instead of reforming his habits, he allowed them to drift into greater irregularity. With his very existence thus in pawn, he had reached the ultimate detachment from human hopes.

When his application for a diplomatic post was rejected, he felt a revival of a long-dormant interest which early disasters had not totally destroyed—the management of a newspaper. Such work could employ his pen more congenially than the painful gestation of novels, and might also open a door to political opportunity. His friend and publisher, George Smith, was always eager for new enterprises, and Thackeray felt under an obligation to him after having allowed his old loyalty to Bradbury & Evans to influence him in the sale of *The Newcomes* to that firm, even though Smith had offered higher terms. With Smith, therefore, he discussed a project of establishing a periodical to be called *Fair Play*, a small daily sheet of literary criticism and political comment, a modernized equivalent of the *Spectator*, *Rambler*, and other "personal" newspapers of his beloved eighteenth century.

Meanwhile, he found some gratification in writing an article for the lordliest of the reviews, the *Quarterly*, on John Leech's *Pictures of Life and Character*. It was a chance to praise the friend who had been his protégé ever since their boyhood at Charterhouse, and he wrote about Leech's humor with the same enthusiasm that he had expressed for Cruikshank's in his article for the *London and Westminster Review* fourteen years earlier.

He also enjoyed completing his whimsical Christmas fairy-tale, *The Rose and the Ring*, and thereafter devoted himself happily to cutting the wood-blocks for it. He bought a new horse and felt the benefit of resuming his canters in the Park, until one day a stirrup-leather broke and he was ignominiously thrown in the midst of Rotten Row, and thereafter laid up for several days.

In planning the concluding events of *The Newcomes*, he decided to have the Colonel end his days as a gentleman-pensioner at Charterhouse. Thus he emphasized a change of heart towards his old school. In *Pendennis* and other earlier stories it had been depicted with obvious traces of the dislike that Dr Russell had implanted in him. But in *The Newcomes* his feelings had changed to mellow, amused affection. To refresh his memory, he visited the school and asked one of the boys to introduce him to a pensioner. Leading him across into Pensioners' Court, the boy made him known to a kindly old "Codd" named Captain Light, who took Thackeray to his room for a long chat. The novelist visited him several times, and the veteran was proud to boast, "I'm going to sit for Colonel Newcome." At the end of the term, Thackeray made a speech to the boys of the school, dwelling kindly and comically upon his early experiences there.

As the necessary seven years since he was called to the bar would be completed in the spring of 1855, his expectations of a magistracy seemed to be on the eve of fulfilment. Early in January his political friends assured him that the administration was well disposed toward him, and that if he made a formal application it would be promptly acted upon. Should he receive the appointment, of course his projected newspaper would not materialize. Accordingly he suspended his negotiations with Smith, and went over to France to visit his family. While he was there the Aberdeen government fell, and all his claims fell with it.

In Paris he encountered the Storys, full of joy over the recent birth of a son. Almost every day his afternoon walk would take him to their house, where he would chat with his young admirer, Edith, and let her show him the wardrobe of her infant brother. When Annie Thackeray went to her first ball, at the Hôtel de Ville, Mrs Story was her chaperon, and was delighted by Thackeray's interest in his daughter's dress, and by his sitting up till her return, so that he could enjoy her report while her enthusiasm was at its height.

On bringing the girls home to London at the beginning of February he solved the problem of their chaperonage with characteristic unconventionality and kindness. The recently-widowed Crowe was preparing to remarry, and so Thackeray took his daughter Amy into his household, ostensibly as companion for his girls— though she was not much older than they—but actually almost as a sister to them. Nor was this the sum of his services to his old friends. Joe Crowe having just arrived home from the Crimea with a red beard and intermittent fever, Thackeray went to much trouble in recommending him for lecturing and writing engagements.

His own journalistic prestige, however, was going through one of its recurrent crises. Upon his return from Paris he had been greeted with the bad news that the whole staff of *Punch* was in arms against him because of certain passages in the essay on Leech. With only the vaguest recollection of the words he had used, he had to re-read the article to discover the cause of offence.

In the course of a mainly favorable survey of *Punch's* history, he had touched upon its occasional intolerances, alluding to the fact that Doyle had withdrawn from the staff because of its anti-Catholic bias, and that "the biographer of Jeames, the author of the 'Snob Papers,' resigned his functions on account of Mr Punch's assaults upon the present Emperor of the French nation, whose anger Jeames thought it was unpatriotic to arouse."

This was perhaps an indiscreet bit of autobiography under the protection of an anonymous article; but worse was to come. In his glorification of Leech, he declared, "Fancy a number of *Punch* without Leech's pictures! What would you give for it? The learned gentlemen who write the work must feel that, without him, it were as well left alone." When he read these sentences, Thackeray awoke to their offensiveness. As in his "Timotheus" skit on Henry Taylor, and his "Mr Washington" allusion in *The Newcomes*, and half-a-dozen other *faux pas* in the course of his career, he had thoughtlessly wounded the self-respect of people to whom he bore no ill will.

When Mark Lemon, as editor of *Punch*, disputed the accuracy of his statement about his resignation, he defended himself with a detailed narrative of what had happened three years before. But the other remark he knew to be indefensible, and for it he could only abjectly apologize. The loudest objections had come from Douglas Jerrold, including the harsh words "snob and flunkey," and by this, Thackeray said, "I feel rather comforted." But to each of his well-loved old colleagues of the *Punch* table he could only repeat that he had used phrases he did not mean, that he had let his pen run on without keeping his mind on his words. Although he was too loyal to Leech to retract the opinion that his drawings were "a hundred times more popular" than any of the literary contributions (his own included), he knew he ought not to have said so in terms that affronted the writers.

His friendship with them survived the squabble, and he remained a welcome guest whenever he chose to attend the weekly dinners; but he did not resume contributing. In fact, he felt distinctly aggrieved toward the business management of the paper. His series of articles in the previous summer had been paid for at less than his former rate. A further annoyance arose from reports that a volume of *Poetry of Punch* was being planned. Thackeray was intending to issue his ballads in collected form, and realized that there would be little sale for the book if three-quarters of them had just appeared in another. Notifying F.M. Evans that he retained the copyright of all his *Punch* contributions, he did not refuse to permit reprinting, but asked that the anthology be delayed until after his book of ballads came out.

In this affair, as in his rejection of the lecture offer from New York, his peevishness over finances suggested that his determination to provide for his daughters was growing into an obsession. Aware that his complaints were hardly dignified, he explained to Evans that he would not have quarreled over a few guineas except "as a point of honour;" and he reminded the publisher of the favorable terms on which *The Newcomes* had been given to the firm, solely because the author respected old allegiance.

There were other repercussions from the dispute over the Leech article. The next time Thackeray met John Murray, publisher of the *Quarterly*, he suspected a touch of coolness in his manner; and this may have been the reason why no further contribution by Thackeray appeared in the review. Furthermore, Thackeray told George Smith that the affair made him unwilling to go on with plans for *Fair Play*. If he could not write a literary criticism, on an apparently innocuous subject, without hurting people's feelings so as to cause himself misery and even illness, he would be unwise in committing himself to a periodical that would probably ruin his temper and his health.

Still restlessly looking for a new literary medium, he wrote a comedy, *The Shorn Lamb*, and offered it to Alfred Wigan, of the Olympic Theater, but it was not accepted. In March the members of the Fielding Club were busy with plans to raise money for a young journalist, Angus B. Reach, dying of a brain disease, and

Thackeray helped by giving his lecture on "Charity and Humor" for the first time in England. Its concluding passage of praise for Dickens, on being quoted in *The Times* next morning, evoked a letter of warm gratitude from its subject: "I do not know how to tell you what a glow it spread over my heart. Out of its fulness I do entreat you to believe that I shall never forget your words of commendation. If you could wholly know at once how you have moved me, and how you have animated me, you would be the happier I am very certain."

Both novelists were aware that their intemperate partisans pitted them against each other, and that the public was inclined to take sides. "We shall never be allowed to be friends, that is clear," Thackeray once remarked, on hearing some gossip about the supposed jealousy between them. Temperamentally they were too unlike to become intimate, and each of them kept a watchful eye on the career of the other; but they had a strong appreciation of each other's talents, and both took every opportunity to express it. When *Blackwood's Magazine* printed an article on the three leading novelists of the era, Thackeray commented to Dr Brown: "I don't believe Bulwer is the first of the triumvirate the reviewer talks of: I think Dickens is (not that I have read him of late; but thinking back of him, I think he's the greatest *genius* of the three). But what after all does it matter who is first or third in such a twopenny race?"

At the great Twelfth-night party in the "little theater" at Tavistock House, when Dickens and Mark Lemon and all their children performed in Planché's extravaganza *Fortunio*, Thackeray was present and laughed so heartily at some of the solemn juvenile actors that he positively rolled off his chair, and infected the whole audience with mirth. Five months later, he and his daughters again attended the little theater to see the more ambitious adult performance of *The Lighthouse*, by Wilkie Collins.

Being now almost eighteen, Annie Thackeray was taking her place as her father's official hostess, presided at his dinner parties, and in a state of mingled pride and terror—with occasional flashes of satirical observation—made the rounds of tea-parties and receptions. Thackeray's women friends exerted themselves to ensure her success. Mrs Procter, Lady Rodd, Mrs Elliot and Miss Perry invited her and escorted her. Mrs Brookfield, too, was full of thoughtful little attentions. Thackeray went to one or two dinner parties at the Brookfields', but remained faithful to his resolution of avoiding seeing Jane alone. In the eyes of their friends, however, the breach between the families was healed.

The removal to a new neighborhood had brought new acquaintances. Next door in Onslow Square lived Baron Marochetti, a famous sculptor, with a charming wife and family. Not far away were Theodore Martin and his wife Helena Faucit, the great Shakespearian actress, "one of the sweetest women in Christendom," in Thackeray's opinion. Martin, who began his career as "Bon Gautier," author of comic ballads very like Thackeray's, and ended it as the biographer of the Prince Consort, has left a pleasant portrait of Thackeray as a neighbor:

> He used to pay us long visits at breakfast, and then he talked with frankness and unreserve more like those of a large-hearted boy than of a man who had seen life in so many phases, many of them of a kind to induce the *pensieri stretti*, for which strangers thought he was peculiar. His nature was obviously one that yearned for sympathy. It was full of tenderness, and showed it, where he was sure that it would be understood. In fact, of all men I have known he was the most tender-hearted; in this respect, indeed, almost womanly. He always showed a marked respect for my wife's opinion in all matters of literature and art.

Though his home was fuller of social stir than ever before, the welcome for old friends was not diminished. Annie's diary repeatedly records her father's Cambridge comrades coming to dinner—Spedding and Frederick Tennyson and above all FitzGerald, grumbling that he wouldn't come again, because "everybody had had enough of Fitz"—and then coming again within three weeks.

During the summer of 1855 Thackeray began to show a more active concern with politics. He attended some of the mass meetings held at Drury Lane Theater by the Administrative Reform Association, at which Dickens and others, embittered by maladministration in the Crimean War, voiced violent disapproval of the dominance exerted in Parliament by the aristocracy and their sycophants. Thackeray associated himself also with a similar agitation that was started inside the House of Commons by W. S. Lindsay and A. H. Layard, seeking to establish public appointments upon a basis of merit rather than personal influence and traditional routine. The overwhelming defeat of their resolution in the House intensified Thackeray's skepticism about the existing system.

He uttered his opinions freely to Charles Gavan Duffy, who had printed his contributions in *The Nation* a dozen years before but who now met him personally for the first time. Upon being introduced to Thackeray by Carlyle, Duffy felt some disappointment in his facial expression. "The damaged nose and bad teeth mar its otherwise benign effect, and were imperfectly relieved by a smile which was warm but hardly genial. He is near-sighted, and said 'he must put on his glasses to have a good look at me.'"

Duffy questioned him about the reform agitations. "They ruined an excellent cause among them," Thackeray replied. "Lindsay made some remarkable statements certainly, but unhappily they did not bear investigation. Sir Charles Wood made pie of them. Layard is a good, simple soul, altogether unfit for the task he took in hand; he set himself to overthrow the aristocratic scheme of patronage, and quite recently he complained to me that the aristocracy had ceased to ask him to dinner! The constitutional system is getting frightfully damaged in England, and we can't count on a long life for it in its present relations."

With the end of *The Newcomes* in sight, he took the girls over to Paris in June. In order to have more convenience for working, they did not stay with the Carmichael-Smyths, but borrowed the apartments of his cousins, the Ritchies, in the Rue Godot de Mauroy. In approaching the pathetic scenes at the close of the novel, Thackeray began to feel how deeply the characters had taken hold of his emotions. At the end of chapter 79, as he dictated the scene in which Clive's little son is put to bed and says his prayers while his grandfather looks on, Thackeray almost broke down, and glanced at Annie to see whether she had noticed the tremble in his voice. He continued dictating to her, however, until midway in the last chapter; then he sent her away, and wrote the death of Colonel Newcome alone. Thereupon he went out and dined by himself and attended a vaudeville, at which he fell asleep. The girls were seeing Ristori in *Maria Stuart* that night, but he did not feel in the mood for tragedy.

His sense of personal concern in the lives of his creations was a natural outcome of his detachment from the affairs of actual life. In his relations with living persons, he repeatedly annoyed or wounded them by his inability to see their point of view, to comprehend them as having susceptibilities; he was astonished and remorseful when they displayed human feelings. The beings that owed their existence to his imagination, however, were less remote; he could enter into their souls and share their destinies. Hence his habits of apostrophizing his characters, of lauding or condemning them, of transferring them from book to book. After ending *The Newcomes* he was so loath to "part with a number of kind people with whom I had been living and talking these twenty months past" that he discarded the disguise of Arthur Pendennis, which he had assumed so gladly to conceal the autobiographical element, and appended an epilogue frankly discussing how real the characters had become, and hinting a sequel.

Indeed, one of the final events was a subconscious clue very similar to one in *Vanity Fair*. If the killing of Osborne and the eventual marriage of Amelia to his best friend was a revelation of Thackeray's suppressed desires in the Brookfield triangle, so the opportune death of the pathetic little Rosey and her widower's marriage to Ethel Newcome had more than a hint of the author's impossible dreams of being free of his wife and young enough to be a suitor for Sally Baxter.

On his way to the post-office with the manuscript of the last instalment, he met an old friend. "Come into this archway," said Thackeray, "and I'll read you a bit of *The Newcomes*." As he listened to the scene of the Colonel's death, the friend became more and more deeply moved, and at the end he burst into tears. "If everybody else does like that," he exclaimed, "the book's fortune is made!"

This prediction, however, was not wholly fulfilled. Some reviewers condemned Thackerary for "cynicism" that made out people to be worse than they really are. *The Times*, in particular, attacked the book as prejudical to morality and religion.

Grieved by this onslaught, Thackeray appealed to a new friend, Whitwell Elwin, the editor of the *Quarterly Review*. "With regard to religion," he wrote to Elwin, "I think, please God, my books are written by a God-loving man; and the morality— the vanity of success, etc., of all but love and goodness—is not that the teaching *Domini nostri?*" Elwin earned his lasting gratitude by defending the novel in the *Quarterly*.

Unexpected antagonism to the book was displayed by Dickens. He was conducting a campaign against the administration of the Charterhouse charity, in his paper *Household Words*, and he saw that Thackeray's idyllic picture of the old pensioner was a strong argument for his adversaries. In addition to remonstrating personally with Thackeray, he arranged to have a rebuttal published in his paper. In his instructions to his sub-editor he explained that he wished, "of course with all respect for and praise of Thackeray, to knock that destructive bit of sentiment in connexion with the poor brothers slap over as with a rifle shot." For once, the charge of sentimentality, under which Dickens had suffered so often, could be brought against his rival.

Thackeray had not been too busy with finishing the novel to enjoy some of the Parisian social amenities. He visited his friend Henry James, who had just arrived from New York to educate his sons in European civilization. A more congenial type of New Yorker, however, was discovered in the person of Sam Ward, a famous wit and *bon vivant*. Ward escorted Thackeray's daughters and their grandmother to the opera on nights when the novelist preferred less solemn entertainment. With the artist, Daniel Maclise, once his comrade on the staff of *Fraser's*, Thackeray went to the Château des Fleurs, the most notorious vaudeville of the day, and was inspired with "mortal melancholy" by the sight of "Lais and Phryne dancing the cancan." Dining out as much as in London, he complained of "too much Burgundy, too much Bordeaux." He had a merry breakfast with Jules Janin in his humble *cinquième;* and at Lady Ashburton's he encountered Prosper Mérimée and felt a strange antipathy toward him, in spite of admiring his books.

Now that the novel was off his hands, he had no obstacle to the second American tour, but the prospect no longer appealed to him. He did not want to leave the girls; he lacked energy for the research necessary in preparing new lectures; and he dreaded a recurrence of his malady when far from home. During July he visited Baden and Homburg, still wondering what subject to choose for the series. The "Men of the World" were discarded, and he was considering a plan to "repeople Holland House, to revivify the old *Edinburgh Review* clique, to light up again the poor dear old dead lights in Curzon Street and set the kind old souls [the Miss Berrys] talking round the hissing silver cauldron."

He realized, however, that these names would mean little to the American public, and so he reverted to a topic that had tempted him three years before and had been rejected as dangerous—the House of Hanover. It was symptomatic of his waning hopes of preferment, the growing urgency of his money-getting, that he chose the subject that would be sure to titillate American audiences, though equally sure to offend English prejudices. He had also acceded to the New York suggestion of limiting the series to four lectures, and the "Four Georges" were obviously destined to fit the scheme.

Back in London in August, he assiduously cultivated American relations. A rendezvous of transatlantic visitors was the mansion of Russell Sturgis, a young American partner in the Baring banking firm; here one day he encountered Story, Lowell, and Christopher Cranch, another American poet, and straightway invited them to dine at the Garrick.

Both Lowell and Cranch wrote accounts of the characteristic evening. It began inauspiciously with Thackeray's discovery that he had ordered dinner for only two instead of four. He divided his attention between scolding the waiter and chaffing his friends. When an attenuated dish of cutlets appeared, he exclaimed solicitously, "Eat one of 'em, Story. It will make you feel a little hungry at first, but you'll *soon* get over it."

After dinner he took them to the snug private parlor over the Cyder Cellar. When cigars were lighted and glasses of gin and water filled, Thackeray asked his friends if they had seen the last number of *The Newcomes*. On their admitting that they had not, he said, "I'd like to read you a part of it," and sent out the waiter with a shilling to buy a copy.

In the midst of reading one of the tirades of Mrs Mackenzie, "the Campaigner," he broke off to remark, "That's my she-devil of a mother-in-law, you know, whom I have the good luck to possess still." As he was working up to the pathetic death scene, a tall man in shirt sleeves blundered into the room. "Well, Thack, I've read your last number," he shouted. "Don't like it. It's a failure. Not as good as the rest."

"Be off with you, Morgan John," growled Thackeray; "can't you see I'm busy?" The big man good-humoredly withdrew. "That's Morgan John O'Connell," explained the host, "nephew of the Liberator, and one of the merriest dogs of our low Bohemian set."

Thereafter the reading proceeded undisturbed to its pathetic climax. The hearers were moved by the death of the Colonel, but Lowell complained that the marriage of Clive and Ethel was an artistic blunder. The author readily agreed with him. "But then, you see, what could a fellow do?" he went on. "So many people wanted 'em married. To be sure, I had to kill off poor little Rosey rather suddenly, but shall not a man do what he will with his own? Besides, we can hope they won't have any children." At this point a noisy party came in, and put a stop to the discussion.

By the time Thackeray had made his choice as to the subject of the lectures, scarcely two months remained before he would have to start for America. Struggling with masses of material, he recognized the urgent need of an amanuensis who could serve him as Crowe had done. Just three months earlier, he had given financial aid to a journalist named George Hodder, a satellite of Jerrold and other *Punch* writers. Thackeray kept a sort of "revolving fund" to meet the frequent crises among his Grub Street acquaintances; the memory of his own days of indigence made him particularly considerate toward them. On hearing that Hodder had lost his job, he had sent him a few pounds, with a tactful note explaining that another friend had just repaid a loan and that whenever Hodder should have tided over his difficulty, someone else would be grateful for the money. As Hodder was still unemployed at the beginning of September, he asked him to come around to Onslow Square for an interview.

Hodder was ushered first into the study, but Thackeray immediately led him upstairs to his bedroom, where elaborate writing equipment was laid out. Hodder's duties, he learned, were to comprise coming every morning to write the lectures from dictation, and spending the rest of the time in transcribing extracts, either at Thackeray's house or in the British Museum. The task proved an easy one, for Thackeray dictated clearly and deliberately, maintaining an unmoved expression even when Hodder laughed at some witticism that he uttered. The only indication of effort was to be seen in his restless movements—now sitting down, now prowling about the room, again standing still, or throwing himself on the bed. In fact, he seemed to be most at ease when in some distorted posture. Whenever his ideas ceased to flow smoothly, he would light a cigar, puff it for a few minutes as he paced the floor, and then deposit the butt on the mantel-piece, and resume work with restored equanimity.

The subject, he had to confess, did not become any more congenial as he progressed. "I sometimes ponder the question," he remarked to Gavan Duffy, "whether every soul of these people I have to speak of was not damned in the end."

In his concentration on work, he neglected even his favorite friends. Mrs Brookfield reported to her husband, who was on a long holiday tour in Scotland, that on her way to the French Exhibition she had met Thackeray in Pall Mall: "He went in to the Exhibition with us, and told us he had been very ill, and had been a good deal out of Town. His daughters were in the Isle of Wight. He put us into our carriage at the door of the Exhibition and bade us good-bye. I did not think that he looked well. Mrs Elliot says she has hardly seen anything of him since she returned from abroad." This account shows clearly that in her husband's absence Thackeray saw Mrs Brookfield only in one accidental encounter, and restricted it scrupulously to a very public spot.

One day, when he waxed expansive with Hodder and talked about his improved finances, and his esteem for the *Punch* staff, and his hope of establishing a magazine of his own after returning from America, the meek secretary plucked up enough courage to volunteer to make the trip with him. After considering the idea overnight, Thackeray decided he would have to take his valet with him, to look after him in the inevitable seizures of illness. "I can ask a servant to hold a basin to me," he explained to Hodder; "but I doubt if I could so treat a secretary—at least, he *might* object."

When the news of his definite plans reached New York, the Baxters sent a cordial invitation to Annie and Minny to come with him and be their guests while he made his tour, but after long discussion it was reluctantly decided that the girls must remain behind and look after their grandparents.

In spite of his hard application and Hodder's assistance, only three of the four lectures were completed before his departure. The books from which he would obtain his material on George IV had to be packed and carried with him. Perhaps because of this difficulty, he changed his mind on the question of bringing a secretary. Less than two weeks before his sailing date, he looked out of his window and saw the handsome young son of Baron Marochetti standing on his own doorstep. "Maurice," he shouted, "will you come to America with me?" The offer was instantly accepted, but at the last moment a death in the Marochetti family caused the arrangement to be cancelled.

Elwin's review of *The Newcomes* had now appeared, but for so far his acquaintance with Thackeray had been by correspondence. When they met on October 8, at a dinner party given by Forster, Elwin was deeply impressed. "His unbounded frankness," he wrote to a friend, "surpasses what I have ever seen in any other man."

Thackeray declared flatly that his book had been overpraised in the review.

"There is probably more in your novels," suggested Elwin, "than you are yourself aware of. I suspect you write by a sort of instinct, without marking the full import of your narrative as you go along."

"Yes," Thackeray replied, "I have no idea where it all comes from. I have never seen the persons I describe, nor heard the conversations I put down. I am often astonished myself to read it after I have got it on paper."

He had to leave unfinished the preparation of the first volumes of a collected edition of "Miscellanies," containing the ballads, *The Book of Snobs*, and other sketches. The responsibility of seeing them through the press was left in the hands of Hodder.

Thackeray's literary friends were busy with arrangements for a farewell dinner. Peter Cunningham was appointed secretary, and every care was taken to ensure having only congenial men in the company. Even though he knew that none but intimate friends would be present, Thackeray was worried by the prospect of having to make a speech before all these wits. "It's very kind of my friends to give me a dinner," he said to Hodder on the morning of the appointed day, "but I wish it was over. That sort of thing always sets me trembling. Here, take a pen in your hand and sit down; I'll see if I can hammer out something. It's hammering now; I'm afraid it will be stammering by and by." With remarkable fluency he dictated a draft of his speech, but as his purpose was merely to organize his ideas, he did not take the notes with him to the London Tavern, or even look at them after dictating them.

Several of the company wrote down their impressions, differing only slightly in details. Dickens, as chairman, proposed Thackeray's health in a speech which Macready described as "very good, but not his very best," although another observer said that "Dickens—the best after-dinner speaker now alive—was never happier. He spoke as if he was fully conscious that it was a great occasion, and that the absence of even one reporter was a matter of congratulation, affording ample room to unbend." As summarized by Forster, his remarks were concerned with "telling Thackeray not alone how much his friendship was prized by those present, and how proud they were of his genius, but offering him in the name of the tens of thousands absent who had never touched his hand or seen his face, life-long thanks for the treasures of mirth, wit, and wisdom within the yellow-covered numbers of *Pendennis* and *Vanity Fair*."

With regard to Thackeray's speech in reply, there is much more difference of opinion. Frederick Pollock, never given to enthusiasm, said that "neither of the two principal speeches was very felicitous." Edmund Yates remarks that "Thackeray was plainly moved, so much so that his reply was very short; he tried to pass off his emotion with some joke about the coming voyage and the steward, but it was too much for him." On the other hand, the unidentified guest who gives the fullest report asserts: "Thackeray, who is far from what is called a good speaker, outdid himself. There was his usual hesitation; but this hesitation becomes his manner of speaking and his matter, and is never unpleasant to his hearers. This speech was full of pathos and humor and oddity, with bits of prepared parts imperfectly recollected, but most happily made good by the felicities of the passing moment. It was a speech to remember for its earnestness of purpose and its undoubted originality." Nobody knows whether it had any resemblance to the preliminary draft that was preserved by Hodder and eventually published.

Thackeray, as usual, was far from satisfied with the speech. In particular, he thought he had made a mess of a carefully planned tribute to Macready. As a matter of fact, Macready described the dinner in his diary as "a great success," but Thackeray was so well aware of his touchiness that he worried all the way across the Atlantic for fear he had offended the tragedian, and wrote him a long letter from America, to explain what he had really meant.

When the arranged program was at an end, Dickens got up to leave, and the guest of honor started to follow his example. On an impulse Douglas Jerrold slipped into the chair, motioning Thackeray to remain; the *Punch* contingent and other convivial souls did likewise. It was a gracious gesture on Jerrold's part to cancel any recollection of previous disagreements. All constraint was now at an end, wit and sarcasm flashed on every side, toasts were proposed to each remaining guest in turn, and the merriment lasted most of the night.

Two days later the moment of departure arrived. Mrs Sartoris had undertaken to escort the girls to Paris, after their father left. Hodder, coming in for last-minute instructions, found Annie and Minny weeping in the dining-room and Thackeray in his study in an equally tearful condition. Taking a grip on himself, he attended to last-minute money matters, and talked to Hodder about proof-reading and footnotes for the *Miscellanies*. Then the cab arrived at the door. "This is the moment I have dreaded," said Thackeray, as he went in to say good-bye to his daughters.

On emerging from the dining-room, he ran down to the cab without looking back at the window where the girls were watching him. "Keep close behind me," he muttered to Hodder, "and let me try to jump in unseen." As the cab door closed, Hodder had a last glimpse of him throwing himself back in the seat and burying his face in his hands.

CHAPTER 19

Home of the Brave

LEAVING LIVERPOOL by the steamer *Africa* on October 13, he was full of anticipation of renewing friendships on the other side. At his request, the Baxters came to Boston to meet him, and he hoped they would go with him to see Niagara Falls; but they were obliged to hurry home to continue arrangements for Sally's approaching marriage.

When Thackeray reached New York, he was enthusiastically welcomed. "The papers announced him with two colours," his valet boasted. Requests for his autograph poured in, as did invitations, but the latter were firmly declined until he had finished writing the final lecture. He would send his key down to be hung on its hook at the hotel desk, to convince visitors that he was out; and he kept the door shut between his room and his valet's, to be able to test his sentences aloud as he wrote them, without embarrassment. Not until November 13 could he report in a letter home, "Now I may look out for some sound sleep without being woke up by that confounded nightmare of George IV, and eat my dinner in peace, and hear what people say to me."

The series had been begun in New York on November 1, with some trepidation. "The lecture was too smutty for the fair sex," observed the valet candidly, in his diary; and Thackeray admitted the same fact in a letter to Frank Fladgate, one of his greatest friends at the Garrick Club: "The people did not know what to make of George I and his strumpets. Morality was staggered." As the series went on, however, they became triumphantly successful, and (as before) so many people were turned away that a repetition was arranged.

Among the reporters who covered the lectures was Thackeray's very first American sponsor, N. P. Willis, who had engaged him for *The Corsair* sixteen years before. Willis described his success in glowing terms. Of the first performance he said: "Although the lecture was an hour and a half long—and curtailed at that, unfortunately for the delighted listeners—it was heard with the closest attention from beginning to end." Nevertheless, Willis did not become at all intimate with his old *protégé.* He cannot have known that Thackeray was the author of the disrespectful review of *Dashes at Life*, and of two other anonymous burlesques at his expense, one in *Fraser's* and the other among the *Proser* papers in *Punch*. But he may have suspected that he was the original of John Paul Jefferson Jones in chapter fifteen of *Vanity Fair*. In their first conversation, the journalist asked why Thackeray was not making notes of his impressions. A caustic reply was on the tip of his tongue, when he happened to remember that Willis had made his reputation by just that sort of international gossip, and he managed to withhold his comment.

One of the friends he had made on his previous visit was far from pleased with the lectures. Fitz-Greene Halleck had been in his youth an American version of the Regency dandy, and had become in his old age a sentimental royalist; on both counts he was so incensed by the lecture on George IV that after the first few minutes he muttered to the friend who was with him, "I'm going. I can't listen any longer to his abuse of a better man than himself." And the old poet marched out.

As before, the *Herald* distinguished itself by its attacks. Thackeray assured Fladgate that he was "too old a hand" to read "that sort of thing," but it rankled none the less. At a reception given by George P. Putnam, the host came up while Thackeray was talking to a lady, and broke in to introduce Dr Griswold. Thackeray bowed stiffly and resumed his conversation; but when Griswold moved away, he turned to Putnam and inquired, "That's Rufus, is it?"

"Yes, that's he."

"He's been abusing me in the *Herald*," continued Thackeray. "I've a mind to charge him with it."

"By all means," responded Putnam, "if you're sure he did it."

"Positive," growled Thackeray; and he stalked across the room and towered over the critic, scowling down upon his bald head. "Doctor," he announced, "you've been writing ugly things about me in the *Herald*. You called me a snob. Do I *look* like a snob?"

His most pleasant contacts with the journalistic world were made through William Young, an Englishman who was editing *The Albion*, a weekly of British news. A new friend among the writers, who appealed to him strongly, was Bayard Taylor—young, handsome, as tall as himself, and bubbling over with experiences of his travels in many lands. "I have met Thackeray and like him very much," Taylor wrote to his mother. "He likes me too, for he has said so to all my friends." In a letter to England, Thackeray declared that Taylor "is one of the most interesting men I have ever seen in my life."

Thackeray's health continued to give him trouble, though the invigorating atmosphere of New York produced a restlessness that delusively resembled energy. He slept, most nights, three hours less than in England, making it up by a prolonged sleep every fourth night or so. He found peculiar difficulty in putting down the correct words when writing, and even in keeping his thoughts coherent in conversation. The day after his arrival in New York, when someone asked him how long he had been there, he hesitated and then was astounded to hear his own voice reply, "A week." He attributed his absence of mind to "some electric influence in the air and sun. People can't sit still, people can't ruminate over their dinners, dawdle in their studies and be lazy and tranquil—they must keep moving, rush from one activity

to another." With the first shower of rain he experienced relief from the tension—
"I felt a leaden cap taken off my brain pan and began to speak calmly and reasonably, and not wish to quit my place."

His program was more crowded than on the previous visit, and without rest he
was unable to shake off his malady. At the end of November he reported that "I
have been lecturing every night except two in the week, and in the intervals fever
and ague. Isn't it good fun? Four attacks this month; and yet mussifully I have
never missed a lecture—only a dinner or a breakfast or two which would be more
pleasant than shuddering in bed but which I don't care for losing." The dinner he
missed was given at the Astor House in his honor by the Press Club. He was able
to come into the dining-room for a few minutes, shook hands with a few of the men
nearest him, and then was helped out. The staff of the hotel would not let him try
to go back to the Clarendon, but put him to bed, heaped him with blankets, and
tended him solicitously till the fit wore off.

To make up for this disappointment, Bayard Taylor a little while later arranged a Sunday morning breakfast at Delmonico's for a group of admirers. This
time Thackeray was in good form; he sang his favorite "Doctor Martin Luther,"
and the party lasted five hours. Another entertainment at Delmonico's was a dinner given by his friend Sam Ward. On getting back to the Clarendon from this
affair at a late hour, Thackeray had a misadventure that seemed to be plagiarized
from a story by his great rival. When he was taking off his clothes in the dressing-
room, a sweet feminine voice from the inner room exclaimed "Georgie?" Realizing that he was on the second floor instead of the third, he gathered up his garments
and dashed upstairs.

The Century Club remained his favorite haunt. Among the men he met there
was Dr Elisha Kent Kane, just back from his second Arctic voyage with the Grin-
nell expedition. Thackeray was touched when Kane told him of having noticed one
of the seamen crouching for hours over a book in the hold of the ship, and the book
proving to be *Pendennis*.

Thackeray also enjoyed foregathering with an old crony of the Garrick Club,
James Wallack, who, after acting alternately in London and New York for many
years, had now opened his own theater on Broadway, with his son Lester as leading
man.

The strain of Thackeray's work was relieved for him as much as possible by
assiduous friends. Some of the young men of the Mercantile Library Association
undertook his secretarial work—writing business letters, planning his itineraries,
calling for him in cabs and accompanying him if he had to go to the suburbs. As
well as giving his course twice over in New York City, he lectured in Brooklyn to
one of his largest audiences, some twenty-five hundred people, and was relieved to
get through it with ease. In fact, as he wrote home, he "ended rather the better for

having talked. Had a good supper, a good sleep, woke early, actually dreaming that I was lecturing in London to three boys and three reporters."

When he went to lecture in Troy, he stayed with English friends who had a pretty country place between Troy and Albany. He admired the old-world atmosphere of the two cities, and found the Hudson reminiscent of the Rhine; but he suffered painfully during the five-hour journey "in the stifling cars where your feet freeze whilst your head throbs with heat." A few days later he made a similar excursion to Yonkers, as the guest of his Century Club friend Frederick Cozzens, who had by this time gained fame as the author of *The Sparrowgrass Papers,* and whose rural home, "Chestnut Cottage," figured in many of his writings. They took the opportunity of driving the nine miles to Irvington to visit its most famous inhabitant, Washington Irving. Thackeray was delighted to find his friend in excellent health, and half way through an ambitious book, his life of Washington. The visitor described Sunnyside as "a funny little in-and-out cottage." Everything about it was toy-like. After Thackeray had been regaled with cakes and wine, and had inspected his host's curios, Irving accompanied them back to Yonkers for a dinner party at Chestnut Cottage, and the subsequent lecture on "Charity and Humor." The whole outing formed one of Thackeray's pleasantest recollections of the tour.

Early in December he moved on to Boston, where his lectures were to begin on the seventh. On the afternoon of that day he drove over to Cambridge to call on Longfellow, escorted by the poet's brother-in-law, Tom Appleton, one of the merriest wits of Boston. As they sat chatting in the twilight, a servant came in with the news that the visitors' horses had run away with their carriage. Longfellow hastily ordered another, and they got back to Boston barely in time for the lecture. The hall was so crowded that Longfellow had to sit in the back row, and could hear only about half of what the speaker said.

The next evening Thackeray went out to Cambridge again for supper at Longfellow's,—"a very pleasant little partykin," the novelist called it, the only other guests being Fields and Ole Bull, the fantastic Norwegian violinist. Thackeray was charmed with his incredible playing, and still more by his eccentricities of manner. He also liked his host's historic old house and pretty children. The poet, he decided, was "a kindly, pleasant gentleman."

The Storys, who were spending the winter in their homeland, had Thackeray to dinner on the ninth to celebrate the first birthday of their son, whom he tipped with the inevitable sovereign—his donation to all boys, from infancy to the end of school days.

Less enjoyable was a meeting of a Boston scientific club, to which Fields had been delegated to invite the distinguished visitor. It was held at the home of an important pundit, and Thackeray was installed in a seat of honor in the front row. An insufferably dull lecture on the Arctic regions began. After a while Thackeray rose and stalked into an alcove. Fields, in an agony of embarrassment, could not take his eyes off him, but his misery was changed to suppressed mirth as Thackeray proceeded with an elaborate pantomime. Grappling with an imaginary adversary, he threw him to the floor and stabbed him several times with a paper-knife he had seized from a desk. He may have intended to depict his feelings toward the lecturer, but Fields' conscience told him that he himself was the victim, for having lured Thackeray to the meeting. Next Thackeray shot his enemy several times through the head with an invisible revolver. As the lecture droned on, he looked around for new weapons, found a small vial on the mantel-shelf, and vividly enacted the murder of King Hamlet by Claudius. Fields hoped that the attention of the audience was absorbed by the lecturer; but some years later a stolid member asked him seriously, "Whatever was the matter with Mr Thackeray that night the club met at Mr ———'s house?"

Sally Baxter's wedding was on December 12, and her parents had invited Thackeray to come back to New York to attend it; but after lying awake all night in an agony of indecision, he had refused. It would have meant canceling two lectures, and making nine-hour journeys on two successive days, a strain that his health could certainly not have stood, as even the four-hour trip to Providence, where he was lecturing on alternate nights, sent his temperature up and obliged him to lie down for a rest. He therefore decided that his "duty was to stay away;" and he felt vindicated when a particularly violent attack of spasms seized him on the day of the wedding, and became so painful the next day that he had to stay in bed and postpone his lecture in Providence. During the rest of the week it was only by the greatest effort that he was able to resume the course. "O my!" he wrote wryly to Baxter, "what twinges I had yesterday as I was lecturing! No one would have thought from the sweet serenity of my countenance what hagonies were going on within!"

With regard to the reception of the lectures in Boston, the evidence is contradictory. Thackeray himself announced his gratification that they were far more enjoyed in this hyper-critical city than in New York. Story, however, sent a less rosy report to Lowell:

> Thackeray has been lecturing here to crowded houses, but people did not want to be pleased, and he was severely criticised. He was not heavy and instructive enough for Boston, and only a few dared thoroughly to like the light and genial sketches of manners and society he gave us in his inimitable way . . . Oddly enough, *our* people objected to him that he pitched into the Georges and called names. P. M. objected to them on the score that he could find all the facts and anecdotes in books he had in his library . . . Thack has been far from well here, and I'm afraid that he's in a bad way.

On the other hand, George Ticknor, who had listened with a professional historian's discernment, uttered unqualified praise:

I have heard Thackeray's four lectures on the four Georges, truculent enough in their general satire—though not much beyond the last half-volume of *Harry Esmond* about Queen Anne—but full of generous passages about individuals. The sketches of the German princes of the seventeenth century, and down to the middle of the eighteenth, with which he opened, amused me more than anything else. They were capital. The passage most applauded was a beautiful tribute of loyalty to Queen Victoria and the tone and manners of her Court. It was given, on his part, with much feeling, and brought down the house— always crowded—very fervently . . . His audience was the best the city could give, and above twelve hundred strong, besides which, he repeated the lecture about George III to an audience of two thousand, two or three evenings ago.

His choice of this lecture as his encore was dictated by his discovery that it was much the most popular of the four, not because of that king's connection with the American Revolution, but "on account of the pathetic business." In a letter to Macready, Thackeray explained that "what the people like is sentiment, and I could not give them any of this article except about old George III, whom they received very tenderly."

From Boston he went on Christmas eve to Greenfield, where he stayed with the Hon. George Thomas Davis, an ex-congressman and noted conversationalist, and where in spite of heavy snow large crowds flocked to hear him. The next day he traveled on to his friends the Dunlops at Albany, and thence on the 27th to Buffalo, where three thousand people came to his two lectures. He enjoyed sleigh rides in these cities, the one at Buffalo taking him along "the darkling lake" to a point where he could see "a bowshot across the Niagara River the black firs and glittering white houses in Canada."

On the last day of the year he returned to New York, full of admiration for the railway system that carried him five hundred miles in twenty hours in spite of the driving snow, and enabled him to earn his dollars in so many localities at such rapid succession. He was enthusiastic about the West, too, on the strength of his brief glimpse of it, and advised Fladgate to send his sons out there as soon as they grew up.

In Philadelphia he was welcomed as warmly as before, but he was not well enough to enjoy it to the full. He rested as much as possible, and was able to get through an unusual amount of reading: Prescott's *Philip II*, which the author had given him in Boston; Dickens's new Christmas book, *The Holly Tree Inn*, which he considered to be in his "best manner"; *The Life and Letters of Cicero*. He cast longing eyes at the latest volumes of Macaulay's *History of England;* but as he had already been obliged to discard the trunk-full of books that he had brought with him for use in writing the last lecture, he was unwilling to burden himself with more.

His circle of familiars in Philadelphia was enlarged by the inclusion of George Henry Boker, poet and dramatist, a friend of Bayard Taylor, whom he resembled in gigantic stature and handsome face. It was from Thackeray's first lecture that Boker derived the idea for *Königsmark*, one of his best plays. And he made a point of boasting to his friends that he had persuaded Thackeray to sit for a photograph especially for him.

William B. Reed, however, remained his most intimate friend. Almost every day—sometimes more than once a day—he would drop in at Reed's house, where he could be sure of quietness and understanding. He told quaint fairy-tales to Reed's children, and took them out walking. One evening, when he was to attend a dinner given in his honor at an important club, he went round to Reed's house first, and found it in some confusion, as Mrs Reed was feeling ill. "You must excuse me for a while," explained Reed, "while I go and carve the boiled mutton for the children."

"I love boiled mutton," said Thackeray, "and children too, and I'll dine with them." He accompanied Reed to the nursery, where a merry feast was enjoyed by all; and at the subsequent banquet the clubmen wondered why their guest of honor showed so little appetite for the lavish courses that were set before him.

Thackeray developed a strong liking for Reed's sister-in-law, widow of the young professor who had been lost in the shipwreck. Her sadness and quiet common-sense appealed to him, and he was astonished when she made her young son hand back a five-dollar gold piece that the novelist had given him. In vain Thackeray protested that it was his invariable habit to tip schoolboys; he had encountered another difference between English and American customs. He made up for the lad's disappointment, however, by sending him autographed copies of *Vanity Fair* and *Pendennis* before leaving the country.

Although the weather continued to be severe, his audiences were large; the last one in particular he described as "proh-digious." As usual, one of the local newspapers—in this case, the *Bulletin*—elected to attack him, with the old charges that he was uncharitable and sneered at virtue. He took the assault calmly, "remembering," as he remarked to Reed, "how I used to lay about me in my own youthful days, and how generally I took a good tall mark to hit at." The crowd at the last lecture was so dense that Reed suggested he come back in the spring and give the old series on the humorists.

His next stop was Baltimore, where the weather remained bitterly cold and his malarial attacks left him too miserable to go out much. He usually stayed in bed at the Gilmore House till noon, reading a cheap reprint of the new Macaulay and planning the history book he intended to write when he should have made his fortune. He became friendly with John Pendleton Kennedy, novelist and ex-secretary of the navy. "Thackeray tells me," said Kennedy in his diary, "that he is going to write a novel with incidents of our revolution introduced into it. To give him some information he is seeking with this in view, I lend him some books."

Kennedy entertained him at his club, but Thackeray's mood was perverse. "O Gods, such a dreary club!" he groaned in a letter; "such a desperate dinner! such a stupid man that *would* talk!" And when his sense of obligation made him drag himself to a supper party after his lecture, even the beauty of his hostess could not stimulate him to more than two remarks: one, that the terrapin was good; the other, that she had some interesting old china. He felt painfully conscious that he must be appearing stupid and ungracious; but as a matter of fact the literary lights of Baltimore for the next half century cherished legends of his geniality and his witticisms.

The first two lectures in Baltimore were sparsely attended, because an opera company was performing on the same nights. Thackeray's local manager scolded furiously at the intruders, but Thackeray remarked with good humor that "they are a hundred in their company, wanting bread many of them; and shall I be angry, because they take a little of the butter off my enormous loaf?"

He was already struggling against violent impulses to stop the tour and rush back to England. Until almost the end of his stay in Baltimore he had not decided on his next step. A circuit of the West tempted him, but as the exceptional snowstorms continued he heard terrifying reports of trains buried in drifts and the passengers burning the seats to keep themselves from freezing; and in his infirm state he seriously doubted whether he would emerge from such an ordeal alive. He therefore chose an itinerary through the South, though it would probably be less remunerative.

His brief visit to Washington was overshadowed by international complications. His friend Crampton had just been charged with trying to recruit American volunteers to fight in the Crimean war, and the newspapers were clamoring for his recall. Loud war talk was in the air; on the last night of Thackeray's visit, at a dinner given by Senator Fish and attended by several senators and cabinet officers, one oracular gentleman announced that there would be war within ninety days. Admiring the equanimity with which Crampton endured vilification and misstatements in silence, Thackeray also remained calm, though he was worried about the probable effect of war upon his investment in American railway shares.

When he reached Richmond, on January 18, there was still much snow on the ground, but the air was mild enough to permit open windows. At his first lecture, a hundred people were turned away, and just as he was embarking on the questionable narrative of the royal favorites he was horrified to notice a score of little school girls occupying the front rows.

He took the opportunity while in Richmond to explore some of the scenes connected with the early life of George Washington, in preparation for *The Two Virginians*, as he called the novel that he was planning to write. He also made an expedition through the snow to Charlottesville to see the University of Virginia.

He faced his visit to Charleston with mixed emotions, for this was now the home of Sally Baxter and her husband, Frank Hampton, and he was not yet entirely reconciled to her marriage. The peculiar mixture of sentimentality and jealousy in his attitude toward the marriage of any woman that he liked was a natural result of his own marital disaster. He repeatedly spoke, only half in jest, of how grimly he would hate any prospective wooer of his daughters. The painful meeting with the Hamptons was successfully passed over, however, and he soon found himself on good terms with the bridegroom.

Lucy Baxter was visiting her sister at the time, and accompanied Thackeray to several parties. At one dinner, she was startled by her first glimpse of the sternness with which he could snub what he considered presumption. Mrs Sue Petigru King, the same lady who had crossed swords with him on his previous visit, was evidently waiting for revenge. Among her claims to local fame was the authorship of several novels, and when the conversation touched on the tribulations of authors, she leaned across the table and declared, "You and I, Mr Thackeray, being in the same boat, can understand, can't we?" Thackeray glared at her, made no reply, and then addressed a remark to somebody else; and constraint fell upon the company until he went off to his lecture.

He found as much pleasure as before in the negro life, particularly the children. He never tired of sketching them, tipping them, and asking them questions. The numerous colored servants of his various hosts were as cheerful and under-worked as before. And yet the shadow of the slavery controversy hung in the background of his thoughts. One friend had sold his estate since the previous visit, and Thackeray could not summon up courage to ask him what had become of the merry darkies he remembered so well.

From Charleston he went to the quaint old city of Augusta, and liked its "happy dirty tranquillity." He chuckled to find that while he was lecturing in one portion of the Masonic Hall, another was given over to a performance by "The Wild Men—Admission 25 cents—Ladies and Children can visit the Wild Men, as there is neither word, action, nor deficiency of dress to offend the most delicate eye or ear." Thackeray's dignity was no longer so sensitive as to be wounded by the juxtaposition.

In Savannah, he again enjoyed the hospitality of Andrew Low, calling it "the most comfortable quarters I have ever had in the United States." The southern composure charmed him after the strenuous atmosphere of the North—"no row, no tearing northern bustle, no ceaseless hotel racket, no crowds drinking at a bar —a snug little audience of two or three hundred people, far too lazy to laugh or applaud." He reveled in having some time to himself without disturbance, and was so bored with the tour that he obtained a passport for Havana, planning to go there for a week or two and rest. Demands for his lectures in other southern cities, however, obliged him to give up the idea; as long as the five hundred dollars a week continued to roll in, his responsibility to his daughters would not permit him to refuse.

He was annoyed to learn at this time that his lectures were being decried in the English press as disloyal. The newly-established *Saturday Review*, in particular, complained that he was ridiculing the royal family in order to curry favor with the Americans. In his letters home he pointed out that he not only brought his audience to the verge of tears over George III, and omitted all reference to George IV's treatment of Caroline, but also digressed in the lecture on George II to pay his tribute to Queen Victoria, which never failed to bring down the house: "I salute the Sovereign, wise, moderate, exemplary of life; the good mother; the good wife; the accomplished lady; the enlightened friend of art; the tender sympathiser in her people's glories and sorrows."

He declared roundly that if the criticisms continued after he came home, he would fight them to a finish. "I have always told you," he wrote to Mrs Elliot, "I can hit harder than any man alive, and I never do—but o! I think a little exercise would do me good."

His adventures in the smaller southern cities proved dispiriting. The long journeys through monotonous pine flats were dreary; his fellow-travelers in the trains and river steamers and hotels wore dirty linen, and ate with their knives, and seldom washed their hands; the hotels had greasy glasses and a sour stench of whiskey. At Macon—"a great, big, rambling, shambling village, which they call a city here,"—the largest element in his audience was 125 girls from a Methodist Seminary, and after a three-day visit he received only $170. Eight hours across the Georgia plain to Columbus, seven more hours to Montgomery, and then down the Alabama River to Mobile, where he was relieved to find a comfortable hotel that could provide a warm bath. Mobile proved also to have an agreeable social circle, but his lectures were unlucky: one night there was such a rainstorm that he could scarcely make himself heard, and only 120 people attended, which left him a net profit of three dollars; and on the final evening, with a large audience, he found the last pages of his lecture disarranged, and, being unable to improvise his conclusion, in spite of having given it so often, he was obliged to dismiss his hearers abruptly. To offset these discomforts, his health was better in Alabama than anywhere else during his tour.

New Orleans made up for any shortcomings in other parts of the South. Feeling immediately at home in its French atmosphere, he reveled in the wine and the food, and found convivial friends. In an essay written six years later, he eulogized its charms:

As for New Orleans, in springtime,—just when the orchards were flushing over with peach-blossoms, and the sweet herbs came to flavour the juleps—it seemed to me the city in the world where you can eat and drink the most and suffer the least. At Bordeaux itself, claret is not better to drink than at New Orleans. It is all good, from the half-dollar Médoc of the public hotel table, to the private gentleman's choicest wine. Claret is, somehow, good in that gifted place at dinner, at supper, and at breakfast in the morning . . . At that comfortable tavern on Pontchartrain we had a *bouillabaisse* than which a better was never eaten at Marseilles; and not the least headache in the morning, I give you my word; on the contrary, you only wake with a sweet refreshing thirst for claret and water.

Spending a fortnight in this agreeable city, he gave his four regular lectures, plus the "Charity and Humor," and had plenty of time to take leisurely walks along the levees. He bought himself a broad-brimmed soft hat, and, being mistaken for a Kentucky farmer, was asked if he knew of anyone who wanted to buy a field hand. His supply of small change was constantly diminished by endless five-cent tips to the grinning black children.

When one of the local newspapers attacked him, he was in far too good a humor to be annoyed, and excused it because it was an Irish one. His only concern was the prospect of traveling up the Mississippi by river steamer. He was not encouraged by hearing that the boat in which he had gone from Montgomery to Mobile had blown up on its next trip; he remembered uneasily that his cabin had been alongside the boiler room. One of his New Orleans friends, too, during a walk along the quays, regaled him with the gruesome details of an explosion, pointing out the spot where a mule had been cut in two by one fragment of the machinery, and the coffee-house window through which another piece had entered to kill a waiter.

On the day of his departure, his landlord of the St Charles Hotel presented him with two bottles of the finest Cognac; and on board his steamer three separate friends arrived to see him off, each bringing him a dozen bottles of his favorite Médoc. Thus fortified, he endured the nerve-wracking creaking, and groaning, and quivering of the boat for five days. Whenever he looked out at the vast yellow stream, he saw the vicious snags sticking up; and after nightfall the smoke-stack belched showers of sparks that fell all over the deck and the passengers. Indeed, the boat caught fire twice, once resulting in the destruction of the galley; but by that time the traveler was resigned to any fate. One day of the journey was rendered miserable by a recurrence of his chills and fevers, but the rest of the time passed pleasantly enough with the novels of Marryat—"a vulgar dog but he makes me laugh and very few can now."

There were not many passengers on board the *Thomas Small*, but at Memphis their number was increased by a party whom Thackeray had seen depicted on posters wherever he had stopped—the Kentucky Giant, the Bearded Lady, and her three-year-old son, who already had flourishing black whiskers. These celebrities were not so awesome as they had looked on the bill-boards; in fact, apart from their following the universal custom of eating with their knives, Thackeray found them very mannerly, for the giant had a small appetite, and the lady spent her time in needlework, and kept her beard modestly swathed in a red handkerchief. Thackeray, for his part, as a fellow-exhibitionist, was punctilious in treating them as if they were ordinary people; but he felt sorry for the lady's small daughter, who, being blond and smooth-faced, was slighted by the others, and looked melancholy.

Parting regretfully from his traveling companions at Cairo, which was still as dreary as when Dickens saw it fourteen years before, he proceeded overland to St Louis, where he lectured on March 26 and 27. In his audience was a lanky lawyer and rural politician from Illinois, Abraham Lincoln, who described the occasion to a friend in later years. One day, too, an impecunious farmer, who had driven in from his log cabin at Gravois to sell a cord of wood, was chatting to a fellow-veteran of the Mexican war, when the latter broke off to point out a tall man who was strolling past and say "That's Mr Thackeray, the English writer." The name of the farmer was Ulysses S. Grant.

A conversation of two Irish waiters at the Planter's Hotel provided Thackeray with his favorite anecdote of the trip. The man who was serving his table nudged a comrade and whispered loudly, "D'ye see that man?"

"Av coorse I do. What the hell is the matter wid him?"

"Why, that's the great Thacker."

"Ye don't say so! What's he done?"

"I'm damned if I know. But he's the great Thacker!"

By this time intolerably weary of his task, he fulfilled a two-lecture engagement in Cincinnati and then hastened back to New York—forty hours in the train. Arriving on April 5, he found quarters prepared for him in a bachelor establishment headed by one of his friends of the Century Club, William Duer Robinson, whose two house mates moved out to accommodate Thackeray and his valet. Nicknamed by Thackeray "the Bower of Virtue," the house was Number 604 Houston Street, near Broadway.

Bayard Taylor breakfasted with him the morning after he arrived, and reported that "he looks jolly and rosy, although he had a few chills on the Mississippi . . . It is refreshing to see his good face and big body among us once more. He says he will stay until June 1st, but I expect he will disappear suddenly some Wednesday morning."

Meanwhile, he enjoyed his release from duty. He would stroll over to the office of *Putnam's Monthly*, invade his friend Curtis's room, lay his watch on the desk, and announce, "Howadji, I will give you just fifteen minutes," or "My dear boy, can you waste a quarter of an hour on a hidle Hinglishman?" The young actor, Lester Wallack, living next door but one to the Bower of Virtue, also became a favorite. "It was understood," he says in his memoirs, "every night when I came home from acting, that if I saw a light in a certain window I was to go in. When I did find them in we never parted until half past two or three in the morning. Then was the time to see Thackeray at his best, because he was like a boy: he did not attempt to be the genius of the party: he would let Robinson or me do the entertaining, while he would be the audience. It did not matter how ridiculous or impossible might be the things I said, he would laugh till the tears ran down his face: such an unsophisticated gentle creature as he was."

Fulfilling his promise to Reed, he went back to Philadelphia to give the lectures on the Humorists. At the suggestion of his friend Boker, he stayed at the La Pierre House, in Broad Street, an older but more comfortable hotel than the Girard. Among the residents of the hotel was another local literary man, Charles Godfrey Leland, newly married to "the prettiest girl in Philadelphia," as Thackeray declared. Admiring Leland's translations of Heine and other German poets, Thackeray got on well with the young linguist and humorist.

The lectures drew only small audiences. It was too late in the season, and everybody had read the lectures in book form. Thackeray's chief concern was for the young bookseller who was trying to establish himself as an impresario, and had invested more than he could afford in hiring Thackeray. "I don't mind the empty benches," he would say, when he resorted to Reed's house for a quiet supper after each lecture; "but I can't bear to see that sad, pale-faced young man as I come out, who is losing money on my account."

Back in New York in the later part of April, he gave a dinner at Delmonico's for all his special friends. It was a memorable occasion. The host announced that there would be no speeches, but that every man must sing a song or tell a story. When James Wallack protested his inability to do either, Thackeray replied, "I tell you what you can do better than any living man—you can give us the great scene from *The Rent Day*;" and without rising from his seat the old actor stirred them almost to tears by his recitation. His son and Curtis sang several duets, and Thackeray contributed his old stand-by, "Little Billee."

There was an atmosphere of farewell about the gathering, but nothing definite had yet been said as to his departure. A few days later, on April 25, as he was walking down Broadway the weather seemed so propitious for a voyage that he stepped into the shipping office and arranged to sail the next day. Farewells made him feel so "sad and guilty" that he preferred this sudden disappearance. His final dinner at Houston Street depressed him with its "forced jokes, dreary songs, deadly lively jollification." "Thackeray went off in the *Baltic* on Saturday," wrote Bayard Taylor, "running away from his friends, for fear of having to say good-by. I saw him off; he seemed sorry to leave."

He had despatched a handsome silver tankard to Robinson, a silver teapot to Sally Baxter Hampton; and one of his last acts was to send back twenty-five per cent of his Philadelphia fee to the distressed manager.

CHAPTER 20

The Rostrum and the Hustings

THE VOYAGE WAS miserably stormy and uncomfortable. After the first day out Thackeray fell victim to a violent attack of his spasms, after which a recurrent infection of the mouth broke out, so that he landed at Liverpool with an eight-days' beard. He resolved that as soon as he got home he would lay himself up for three months in London or Paris in a determined effort to "patch up" his "crazy old hull."

When he reached London, on May 8, he learned that the great annual event of the Garrick Club—the Shakespeare dinner—was taking place that night, two weeks later than usual. He could not resist the temptation of greeting so many friends; he attended it, made a "Yankee speech," and woke up the next morning with an agonizing headache. He began to realize how seriously his internal seizures were now complicated by the fever and ague that were the permanent legacy of his winter in Rome. His doctor admitted that he had trembled at the risk which he had run in making the tour, and ordered him to refuse all social engagements and attempt no writing. By submitting to the discipline, he began to have relief from the malarial attacks about the end of May.

This wretched health combined with the political tension between the two nations to render his opinion of the United States far less enthusiastic than it had been after his previous visit. Charles Greville, meeting him on June 1, recorded his views on the crisis: "He thinks there is every probability of the quarrel leading to war, for there is a very hostile spirit constantly increasing throughout the States, and an evident desire to quarrel with us. He says he has never met a single man who is not entirely persuaded that they are in the right, and we are in the wrong, and they are equally persuaded if war ensues they will give us a good thrashing; they don't care for consequences; their riches are immense, and two hundred thousand men would appear in arms at a moment's notice."

Within three weeks the strain was allayed by the recall of Crampton from Washington; but Thackeray grumbled that England had been obliged to "eat humble pie," and he predicted that "that kind of humility never will appease your Anti-English over the water or be understood by them." His friendship for Crampton was an additional cause for his disgust. Ticknor, who was in London, wrote to a friend at home that "Thackeray, who has a strong personal regard for him, was outrageous on the matter, and cursed the Ministry by all his gods for making him, as he said, their scapegoat." He confessed, however, that his views were probably prejudiced by the abuse with which he had been bespattered by certain newspapers during his tour. He was determined not to incur the "degrading ordeal" again by returning as a lecturer. "Those scoundrels," he told the Baxters, "managed to offend and insult the most friendly stranger that ever entered your country or quitted it."

He had been looking forward to initiating Annie into the delights of a London season, and so he made two or three attempts, as soon as he was well enough, to escort her to parties, but the experiment was pitiful. He had to leave the balls at one o'clock, "just when the fun is at its best;" and when Annie realized that he paid for each outing with an attack of ague the next day, she assured him that she would prefer to stay at home, because she wouldn't enjoy the balls half as much if she went to more of them.

He was distressed by the fact that many of his American friends were visiting England that summer, and that he could not repay the hospitality they had accorded him. The Ticknors had taken a house for July. "Thackeray has been to see us a good deal," Ticknor reported in a letter to Prescott, "but he is very poorly, and has troubles that may wear him out." Tom Appleton, on the other hand, who met him at dinner at Ticknor's, sent a different opinion to Longfellow: "Thackeray seemed to remember the Yankee sunshine, and expand, and looked well, though but lately recovered from an illness." After dinner, Thackeray proposed adjournment to Evans's "Singing-room," which vied with the Cyder Cellar as his favorite nocturnal resort. They were led to seats of honor at the head of the table, and the famous proprietor, Paddy Green, discoursed to Appleton about Beethoven and Mozart, and displayed some of his rare first editions. Interspersed with the comic songs, a chorus of sixteen boys (who in daylight hours were the choir of a neighboring church) enraptured Thackeray, as usual, with their limpid sopranos.

This convivial evening, however, was exceptional. With a feeling of guilt toward both his daughters and his friends, Thackeray spent most of his time "skulking about at clubs" and talking to nobody. He was worried, too, about the reception awaiting his lectures when he should be well enough to give them in England, for he remembered the unfavorable opinions that the reports of them had evoked.

He summoned up enough strength to read the first three to a small audience of his intimates. He was particularly anxious about the effect on George Venables, his friend since schooldays, not only because Venables was noted for his incisive frankness, but also because he was a regular contributor to the *Saturday Review*. It was a relief to Thackeray, therefore, when his verdict on the first one was enthusiastic. Another listener whom the lecturer eyed with trepidation was his own sixteen-year-old Minny, since there had been some complaints that parts of the lecture were unsuited to innocent young ears; but she, too, was satisfied.

He received an equally favorable response when he read the third lecture to a select party at the Procters'. "It was very pleasant," commented Procter, in a letter to Fields, "with that agreeable mixture of tragedy and comedy that tells so well when judiciously managed. He will not print them for some time to come, intending to read them at some of the principal places in England, and perhaps Scotland."

By the middle of July he was accepting invitations: on the 18th he was at a dinner given by Milnes and attended by the Brownings, the Procters, Venables, and Spedding, with Leigh Hunt (who never ate dinner) coming in at nine o'clock.

A few days later, Bayard Taylor arrived from America, bringing a young brother and two sisters to see the sights of Europe. Thackeray was determined to fulfil his promise of making this favorite American friend acquainted with literary London. "I found him as jovial and tenderhearted as ever," Taylor reported. The Thackeray girls took the Taylor girls for a long drive, after which the two families dined together; and on August 1 Thackeray gave a dinner party, his first in the Onslow Square house. Story and two other Americans were present, in addition to Taylor, with five principal members of the *Punch* staff, and Messrs Bradbury and Evans, its publishers. As the dining-room was far from big enough, its furniture was carried up to the drawing-room, which was denuded of its usual equipment. The girls of the household, enjoying the fun of a picnic supper in the ravaged dining-room, went out into the square every now and then for the view of the affair upstairs, for it was a hot night, and the windows all stood open; but by the sounds that issued forth they inferred that the party was not proving so amusing as some of the smaller ones they had listened to. English humorists and American poets were perhaps a little shy of each other on a first encounter. "Not a single joke," lamented Taylor, "did I hear during the whole blessed evening."

At last Thackeray was receiving testimonies that his position in English literature was secure. One day a stranger called and sent in word that he was a Russian admirer of his books who wished the privilege of meeting him. In the drawing-room Thackeray found a handsome, bearded man, as tall as himself. "My name is Ivan Turgenev," said the visitor. The two authors took an immediate liking to each other, and before long Turgenev was regaling Thackeray with a Russian folksong that made him shake his sides with laughter.

Having concluded an agreement with Bradbury & Evans to write another novel in numbers, Thackeray as usual could not get to work upon it until he wandered on the Continent for a while. He took his daughters to Calais and thence to Spa and on to Düsseldorf for a couple of days, enjoying himself at all these places in spite of the restrictions which his duties as *père de famille* set upon the range of his acquaintance. Next he tried Aix-la-Chapelle, although he knew the place always disagreed with him. While he was being ill there, news of the death of his stepfather's sister-in-law summoned him to Paris, where the girls went to stay with their cousins and he took a room at the Hôtel Bristol.

He no longer felt at home in Paris. All his old favorite dining places seemed to have been demolished to make room for palaces, and he had to find solace in the Louvre pictures and the shabby loneliness of the Palais Royal. He went twice to the theater, and left each time at the end of the second act, finding the plays "too wicked"—one was *Le Juif Errant* and the other *La Dame aux Camellias.* The chief reason for his depression, of course, was that he was "haunted by No. 1 of Mr Thackeray's new serial, which won't leave me alone, which follows me about in all my walks, wakes me up at night, prevents me from hearing what is said at the play, and yet seems farther off than ever." He felt convinced that anything more he wrote would be mere repetition. that the public would accuse him of being written out. Only the six thousand pounds bribed him to go on, and for that he was willing to incur the unfavorable opinion of posterity.

His ideas on the subject were reinforced by news of the death of his friend Gilbert â Beckett, one of the founders of *Punch*, who—in spite of seven years' service as a London magistrate—left no money, not even a life insurance policy, to his wife and children. As à Beckett was almost exactly of his own age, he drew the inevitable comparison: three years earlier he had been in no better position to leave his wife and daughters provided for. He wrote to à Beckett's *Punch* colleagues proposing that they "do something to show his poor widow and family our sense of his worth," and offering a hundred pounds to start a fund for enabling the elder son to complete his course at Oxford.

A visit to Mrs Norton suggested to him what good characters for fiction she and her son Brinsley would be—"if one could but say all one thought—but in England we are so awfully squeamish. Ah, if one's hands were not tied there might be some fun in that forthcoming serial!" As long as he was in such a pessimistic mood, even when he managed to draft the opening of a story it aroused no interest in him.

During this month of frustration he was visited by Allingham, who paused in Paris during a continental tour. He found that Thackeray usually stayed in bed at his hotel until mid-day or later, in combined illness and literary travail, but was likely to recover himself in the evenings.

Allingham mentioned the Brownings, who were also in Paris. "Browning was here this morning," said Thackeray. "What spirits he has—almost too much for me in my weak state. He nearly blew me out of bed!"

"A wonderful fellow, indeed," Allingham replied.

"Yes, and he doesn't drink wine."

"He's always screwed up to concert pitch," added Allingham.

"Far above it. But I can't manage his poetry. What do you say?"

Allingham praised it enthusiastically.

"Well, you see," protested Thackeray, "I want poetry to be musical, to run sweetly."

"So do I—" Allingham began.

"Then that *does for* your friend Browning."

Allingham launched out into further rhapsody, but Thackeray merely smiled and said, "He has a good belief in himself, at all events. I suppose he doesn't care whether people praise him or not."

"I think he does, very much."

"Oh, does he? Then I'll say something about him in a number."

Thackeray invited his friend to dinner at a favorite restaurant in the Palais Royal. "One's first glass of wine in the day is a great event," he announced, looking solemnly at Allingham through his spectacles, as he sipped it. They had intended to go to the Palais Royal Theater, but after dinner Thackeray suggested that instead they should visit Father Prout, who lodged nearby. The Padre, lounging in unbuttoned comfort with a book and a bottle of Burgundy, greeted them in a low voice. "Evening, boys. There's a young chap asleep there in the corner." It was a youth from Cork who had spent all his money and was receiving shelter until his family could rescue him.

Refusing the Burgundy as "too strong," Thackeray asked for brandy and water. Literary conversation ensued, and Allingham remarked that a story of Dickens might be improved if a man of good taste would run through it and strike out unnecessary passages.

"Young man," said Thackeray, in a rich brogue, "ye're treadin' on the tail o' me coat." Seeing that his hearers were puzzled, he added, "What you've just said applies very much to your humble servant's things."

Although he undoubtedly enjoyed the protestations with which his remark was contradicted, it was consistent with his policy of refusing to countenance any criticism of his rival in his presence.

At the beginning of October he returned to London to make arrangements for his lecture tour in Scotland. Whitwell Elwin, meeting him in Piccadilly one day, walked home with him and questioned him about what he had been doing.

"I began a story," Thackeray answered, "was dissatisfied with it, and burnt it. I can't jump further than I did in *The Newcomes*, but I want to jump as far."

"What was the matter with the piece you burnt?"

"It ran in the old track. I have exhausted all the types of character I am familiar with, and it's very difficult to strike out anything new. I have thought of two or three schemes. One was to lay the scene in the time of Doctor Johnson."

"Don't do that," advised Elwin. "*Esmond* is a good piece of imitation but you are obliged to take the accessories at second hand. A novelist can only describe his own age. You intimated in *The Newcomes* that you meant to give us the history of J. J."

"That was what I had begun," Thackeray replied, "but it was commenced in too melancholy a strain. I want to have a cheerful hero, though this is very difficult, for a cheerful character must have some deeper element to give enough dignity and interest. It is hardly possible to have a hero without a dash of melancholy. I think the cheerful man must be the second character—a good-humored, pleasant rogue. But people are always complaining that my clever people are rascals and the good people idiots."

"Why don't you describe a domestic family, enjoying the genuine blessings of calm domestic felicity, put in contrast with the vexations and hollowness of fashionable life?" Elwin, it may be recalled, was a clergyman.

"How can I describe that sort of domestic calm?" Thackeray asked in a pathetic tone. "I have never seen it. I have lived all my life in Bohemia. Besides, there would be very little to describe. It must of necessity want movement. I intended to show J. J. married, and exhibit him with the trials of a wife and children. I meant to make him in love with another man's wife, and recover him through his attachment for the little ones."

Elwin begged him not to go on with that story; but his relinquishing of it was more likely to be due to his realization that it was even more perilously autobiographical than his previous plots.

According to first intentions, his daughters were to go with him on the Scottish tour. He accepted invitations to various pleasant country houses, and Mrs Sturgis gave a provisional coming-out party for Minny so that she would be qualified for all social events. Then came a telegram from Major Carmichael-Smyth, announcing the illness of his wife, and the family rushed back to Paris, to find the Major in violent alarm, which had communicated itself to the patient. When a succession of her favorite homeopathic doctors had treated her unavailingly, she became sufficiently frightened to accept a regular practitioner, and soon improved; but her son was at least convinced that the old couple ought not to continue to live alone.

In his own state of illness and depression he could not help feeling some impatience with his stepfather, in spite of his sincere respect for him. At seventy-six, the old gentleman had become tedious and fussy, refusing to go out or receive visitors, endlessly reading the newspaper and bewailing the state of the world. As he demanded the perpetual attendance of his wife, Thackeray attributed her illness to the strain on her nerves, and became alarmed for her reason, for she could not sleep unless she had social amusements such as her husband denied her. Her son felt that he must either give up his own home and come to live with them in Paris—a step that would preclude lecturing and might be the death blow to his waning creative powers—or else bring them to Onslow Square, although the Major's pride still rebelled against accepting such protection. Meanwhile, the girls had to forgo the tour they had been looking forward to, and remained to cheer the old folk with their company.

During this disturbance Thackeray had not been able to do anything about the new book, which continued to prey on his mind; nor had he even felt free to accept future lecturing engagements, though he was besieged with offers. When he went back to London he came down with a bad attack of his malady, and was groaning in bed the very day before he had to start for Edinburgh.

The lectures there were cordially received, but as usual he contrived to wound the sensibilities of a portion of his audience. These *faux pas* occurred so often that one wonders whether they resulted from thoughtlessness or a mischievous love of teasing. This time, the cause of annoyance was Mary Queen of Scots. In his discussion of Sophia Dorothea, he went out of his way to disparage the Stuart queen:

Like Mary of Scotland, she finds adherents ready to conspire for her even in history, and people who have to deal with her are charmed, and fascinated, and bedevilled. How devotedly Miss Strickland has stood by Mary's innocence! Are there not scores of ladies in this audience who persist in it too? Innocent! . . . So was Helen of Greece innocent . . . Yes, Madame Laffarge never poisoned her husband, and Mary of Scotland never blew up hers . . . and Eve never took the apple—it was a cowardly fabrication of the serpent's.

When these heresies were uttered in Edinburgh, a good many people in the audience hissed him roundly, and even his friend Aytoun was moved to the blunt remark that he ought to "let the Georges alone and stick to his Jeameses."

The unlucky beginning was soon forgotten. After hearing the third lecture, John Brown gave a rapturous report: "We liked it better than the first time. What power and gentleness and restraint! I wonder at and love him more and more. To-night he took the whole house by the heart, and held them; they were still, and serious, and broke out wildly at the end. We have seen a great deal of him; he comes and sits for hours, and lays that great nature out before us, with its depths and bitternesses, its tenderness and desperate truth. It is so sad to see him so shut out from all cheer and hope."

In spite of this inward gloom, shown only to most intimate friends, he was able to enjoy the hospitalities showered upon him by the literary circle. He stayed with John Blackwood in Randolph Crescent, "the most hospitable and magnificent inn I ever put up in," with an inexhaustible supply of "the most prodigious good claret." Aytoun was almost next door, and another friend in Edinburgh was Colonel Edward Hamley, a Crimean hero and contributor to *Blackwood's*, who had him to dinner at the Artillery Mess. He received kind attentions, too, from the proprietor of *The Scotsman*, John Ritchie, and his editors, J. R. Findlay and Alexander Russel. As this newspaper was violently Whig in its politics, and the Blackwood family as violently Tory, there was little friendship between the two camps. Thackeray, as an outsider who liked both factions, decided to heal the breach. One evening he marched into Blackwood's den, bringing Russel with him, and a convivial night ensued.

On November 19 he moved on to Glasgow and gave his first lecture to an audience of two thousand; then went back to Edinburgh to begin a second series and attend a dinner given in his honor by Ritchie. A particular effort was made to have Thomas De Quincey present, but the invitation was politely declined on the excuse of "a most distressing affliction of the chest."

For the next week Thackeray alternated between the two cities, lecturing every night and dosing himself unmercifully with calomel in the hope of staving off his attacks. Then he pushed on to Inverness, though he almost gave up the expedition when his train ran into a violent snow-storm just after leaving Aberdeen. Part of the journey had to be made by stage-coach, and he dreaded the discomfort. It turned out to be enjoyable, however, reviving boyhood delights and making the past live again. In the sincere, archaic surroundings of Inverness, he felt almost ashamed to stand before his audience of "honest squires and country gentlemen" to utter his "dreary scepticism about George I" and sneer at "loyalty, courts, and king-worship."

He also gave a lecture at Paisley and one at Dumfries, and by the time he reached Hull, on December 2, he ventured to boast that his health was amazingly improved and his waistcoat was getting tight again. The whole month he had been in Scotland he had felt uncomfortably that he did not understand the temperament of his audiences—they were as alien as the Americans, and he did not think he could ever depict any of them in fiction; but as soon as he crossed the border he felt at home and began to observe types that he might use. Even though he found Hull hideous, and his hosts all fat philistine merchants, he enjoyed his week there mightily.

The Scottish tour had proved that the lectures would be as profitable as in America; but still more gratifying was his discovery that they were far more thoroughly enjoyed. His hearers responded to many little allusions that had been lost on the Americans. At last he could smile at a jibe of the New York *Herald* that had rankled in his soul ever since—"that any young man could sit down in their office and write such lectures in an evening." Although he insisted that "praise does not produce the least elation," he was thriving on being appreciated. There was a trace of pride in his reiterated complaints that his correspondence averaged ninety letters a week—that he would have to write four thousand in a year. He estimated that by the end of the next year he would be worth £20,000, which he had fixed as the sum he wished to leave his daughters. Then he would be able to devote himself to politics, or any other gentlemanly hobby that attracted him. To symbolize his restored equanimity he invested a thousand pounds in shares in the new transatlantic cable, regarding it as "a thread that shall tie our two countries together."

After proceeding from Hull to Bradford he suffered a sharp seizure, and had to cancel two lectures; but he was able to fill his engagements in Liverpool and

Manchester later in the week. Although he admitted to his daughters that they "would have been a clog sometimes" during his wanderings, he missed them so much that he now sent them peremptory orders to meet him in London. If the old couple would not come with them, a lady companion for his mother would have to be obtained. He was therefore able to spend a happy Christmas season with his

A LECTURE AUDIENCE

girls in Onslow Square, and to go with them to Dickens's usual Twelfth Night play at Tavistock House—this time *The Frozen Deep.*

His northern tour had netted him nearly a thousand pounds, but the burden of business correspondence was proving almost intolerable. In a letter to a cousin, defending himself from the charge of "being haughty and supercilious to old acquaintances," he complained, "This opinion once put forth against a man, all his friends believe it, accommodate themselves to the new theory, see coolness where none is meant. They won't allow for the *time* an immensely enlarged acquaintance occupies, and fancy I am dangling after lords and fine people because I am not so much in their drawing-rooms as in former days. They don't know in what a whirl a man plunges who is engaged in my business. Since I began this work, besides travelling, reading, seeing people, dining—when I am forced out and long to be quiet—I write at the rate of five thousand letters a year. I have a heap before me now. Six of them are about lectures. One from an old gentleman whom I met on the railroad and who sends me his fugitive poems. I must read them, answer them, and compliment the old gentleman. Another from a poor widow, in bad spelling, asking for help. . ."

At the beginning of 1857 he was relieved from the worst of this burden. The firm of Cramer, Beale, & Co., music dealers and entertainment agents, aware of the large audiences he was drawing, requested his former amanuensis, Hodder, to open negotiations on their behalf. As the suggestion was favorably received, Hodder brought Mr Beale to Thackeray's house one morning for an interview. With his usual repugnance to business discussions, the novelist treated the visitor brusquely, and accepted the proffered fifty guineas a lecture without a word of comment; but when Hodder, who was to travel as his manager, came round the next day to talk about details, Thackeray greeted him with jubilant exclamations: "What terms! fifty guineas a night! Why, I shouldn't have received one half that sum for an article in *Fraser's* a few years ago."

FitzGerald, being in town, described his old friend as "looking gray, grand, and good-humoured. He goes lecturing all over England; has fifty pounds for each lecture; and says he is ashamed of the Fortune he is making. But he deserves it." Mrs Browning heard one of the lectures under the new management, "and thought it better than good—fine and touching," as she told Miss Mitford. "To what is it that people are objecting? At any rate, they crowd and pay."

The first result of the expert management was the use of modern publicity methods. For the opening of his series at the Surrey Zoological hall, London was plastered with huge garish posters. Half amused and half chagrined, he discovered that many of his fashionable friends were horrified at such vulgarity, quite as much as at his lack of respect for the royal family, and conveyed to him plainly that he need no longer expect invitations to their houses. "Having pretty nearly enough of the halls of splendour," he wrote to his mother, "I shall be quite resigned to a quiet life without them."

Occasionally a shaft penetrated his armor. One day Charles Mackay found him alone in the library of the Reform Club, with a scowl on his face and a newspaper crumpled up in his hand. When Mackay asked what was the matter, he handed over the paper, which was the local publication of a town where he had recently lectured.

The rector of the parish had received the valuable living in succession to his father, on whom it had been conferred by George IV. Enraged by Thackeray's opinion of that monarch, the clergyman wrote an article for the paper, beginning: "An elderly, infidel buffoon of the name of Thackeray has been lecturing in town on the subject of the Four Georges." On reading this far, Mackay burst out laughing.

"It's no laughing matter," declared Thackeray. "I've a mind to bring a libel action for a thousand pounds."

Advising him that no court would regard the abuse as libellous, Mackay tried to talk him out of his fury. "Yes, that's all very well," Thackeray grumbled, "for you have not been attacked. We all bear with perfect equanimity everybody's annoyances but our own."

About this time he was astonished to receive overtures from the chief whip of the Whig party, asking if he would be interested in contesting a seat. A political crisis was brewing, and plans were being quietly laid. In spite of his frequent hints, in recent years, about turning to a parliamentary career, he was hesitant over the proposal. He would hate to give up profitable lecturing for the hazards of an election. Ironically, his long-deferred dreams of wealth and public preferment were now being fulfilled so plenteously that they threatened to impede each other. And yet he was strongly tempted by the offer of a seat. "I shan't be happy in politics," he wrote to his mother, "and they'll interfere with my digestion; but with the game there, it seems faint-hearted not to play it."

Meanwhile, his surrender to professionalism had subjected him to a crowded schedule. For a while the series was being given in Brighton and London simultaneously—Brighton in the afternoons and London in the evenings. "Thackeray we see very little of," Kate Perry told Brookfield on January 26, "as he is always on the move, one day at Bath and another at Brighton. He has made a much better bargain for himself now, having found a Barnum, and in 3 or 4 months he says he will be able to rest on his oars, having then made enough to endow his daughters."

His first lecture in Bath was disappointing. After four hours in the train from London he had only time for a hasty dinner before going to the hall, which was "crammed with 400 genteel folks and 350 of the wulgar." The genteel portion sat with blank faces, revealing no understanding of what he said, whereas the groundlings responded to every allusion and laughed at every joke. He attributed the dulness of the polite section to the preponderance of clergymen, and heard so many complaints about their autocratic control of the community that he wanted to declare war on the whole tribe of them. The Bath committee must have been better satisfied, however, than he suspected, for a representative called at his hotel the next morning to ask for the rest of the series. On the same day he received offers from Ireland (promptly declined), Devonshire, Bristol, and Yorkshire (for an extensive tour in the summer).

On his visit to Devon he took the girls with him, and enjoyed showing them the surroundings of his boyhood. When they spent a night at an old inn at Exeter they recognized it at once as the "George" in Chatteris, and felt that they were living in a chapter of *Pendennis.* He took them on a pilgrimage through the town, including visits to old family friends, more than one of whom could be identified as the originals of characters in the novel.

On February 9 he started on an extended northern circuit. Hodder had discretion enough to travel always in a different railway carriage and put up at a different hotel, showing himself only on business occasions or when Thackeray felt sufficiently genial to ask him to dinner. At the very beginning of the tour, a bout of illness in Halifax necessitated cancellation of lectures, but a good doctor was obtained, whose rigorous treatment soon made the victim feel better. After spending a week-end at Fryston, where he found old Mr Pemberton Milnes as quaint and hospitable as sixteen years before, he made his headquarters for a week at a comfortable hotel in Sheffield. Lectures in Leeds and other northern towns occupied him until the end of the month, when he went on to Scotland, with engagements (not handled by his London "Barnum") for the whole month of March.

The next day, the Palmerston ministry was defeated on a want-of-confidence motion over their policy in China, and a general election was called. Thus abruptly faced with the dilemma, Thackeray could not see his way to accepting a nomination. He would have to give up his Scottish lectures, and break his contract with Beale for April and May. Besides, a large part of his recent earnings might be eaten up by the campaign. As it was, the election meetings proved damaging rivals to his lectures. Although he complained that the month in Scotland was "a failure as regards money," he was pleased to be told that the audiences in Edinburgh amounted to three per cent of the whole population. "Ah!" he exclaimed, "if I could only get three per cent of London!"

Edinburgh was again lavish with dinner parties and good talk. Ritchie made another effort to entice De Quincey to dinner. This time the Opium-eater vaguely accepted, but on the appointed evening a friend found him placidly reading proofs. To the friend's urging, he replied, "No; much as it troubles me to see people, if it had been Dickens, now, I might have gone—I *should* have gone. But not Thackeray. There is a *benignity* in everything that Dickens has done."

A public dinner in Thackeray's honor, which was to have been held in Edinburgh on March 28, had to be postponed three days because of his health. When the chairman, Lord Neaves, emphasized the quality of sympathy in his work, saying that it was just as important as his satire, he was particularly touched, after all the trite accusations of cynicism he had endured. He got up to reply to the toast, in his usual agony of discomfort, and Brown was struck by his "pathetic, dumb face, like a great child going to cry."

He had made up his mind, however, to vindicate himself from the charge of disloyalty that was being hurled against the lectures. He described the overwhelming applause that had invariably, on both sides of the Atlantic, greeted his tribute to Queen Victoria, and he went on earnestly:

Suppose in Philadelphia or in New York I had spoken of George IV in terms of praise or affected reverence, do you suppose they would have hailed his name with cheers or have heard it with anything like respect? They would have laughed in my face if I had so spoken of him. They know what I know and what you know, and what numbers of squeamish loyalists who affect to cry out against my lectures know, that that man's life was not a good life—that that king was not such a king as we ought to love or regard or honor. And I believe, for my part, that in speaking the truth as we hold it of a bad sovereign, we are paying no disrespect at all to a good one. Far from it. On the contrary, we degrade our own honor and our Sovereign's by unduly and unjustly praising him; and the mere slaverer and flatterer is one who comes forward, as it were, with flash notes, and pays with false coin his tribute to Caesar. I don't disguise from you that I feel somehow or other on my trial here for loyalty, for honest English feeling.

As usual, "he thought he had made an immense fool of himself in his speech till he saw it next morning."

At this time he had an opportunity of doing a good turn to the most suspicious of his friends. Douglas Jerrold had been invited by Charles Mackay to join the Reform Club, and was hesitating to let his name be put up, for his Radical opinions had often annoyed the orthodox Whigs. When Mackay suggested enlisting the aid of Thackeray, Jerrold replied in alarm, "Thackeray and I are very good friends, but our friend T. is a man so full of crotchets that, as a favor, I would hardly ask him to pass me the salt. Therefore, don't write to him."

Mackay disregarded this request, and received so cordial a reply that Jerrold admitted contritely, "I was both pleased and rebuked by T's letter. I suppose that *I* at least must henceforth say nothing of 'crotchets.' " When he was put up for membership, Thackeray figured as his proposer and Mackay as his seconder.

Having returned to London on April 3, Thackeray started on the series of appearances that his managers had been arranging in the home area. His popularity, however, was wearing thin. Charles Lever, who was in London on one of his infrequent visits from Florence, told the news about his old friend in letters to his wife. When he first arrived, during Thackeray's absence in Scotland, the gossip in London literary circles was that "Thackeray is lecturing away at a guinea a minute, or 60 guineas each lecture! he says he'll not write any more so long as this hunting lasts." A few weeks later, however, Lever's report was very different. "Thackeray's lectures have come to a dead stop. After an overwhelming success in Scotland he came to Brighton last Saturday [April 11] and only *three* tickets being sold, the lecture was put off. In London Beale, who acted as his Barnum, has lost fifty pounds per night by him. T. affects to laugh and says that there was a giantess who drew all the people away, but that he'll be tumbling away, fresh as ever, in a week or so. He told me himself that one year like the last would secure him an independence for life—he has already laid by above £10,000."

Later in the month he lectured in Cambridge, apparently in good form, for Pollock, who was there at the time, told Macready that "the four Georges have been good friends to him, and many parts of the country remain to be perambulated with them." On May 7 he dashed up to London, in the interval between lectures at Leamington and Oxford, to vote for Jerrold at the Reform Club, and was delighted when the candidate was accepted. "We've got the little man in," he exclaimed to Hodder, as soon as he saw him; and on noticing his manager's mystification he told him the reason for the hurried trip to London, and explained that there had been some fear "that the minnows of the institution would rather forgo the questionable pleasure of having a Triton amongst them."

At Oxford the lecture on George III was so exceptionally appreciated that Thackeray exclaimed to Hodder as he stepped off the platform, "There's an audience for you! Gad, I would lecture to those young fellows for nothing!" At a breakfast party in Lincoln College one of the company was a young mathematical don, Charles Lutwidge Dodgson, whose diary contains his impression of "Thackeray (the author)": "I was much pleased with what I saw of him; his manner is simple and unaffected; he shows no anxiety to shine in conversation, though full of fun and anecdote when drawn out. He seemed delighted with the reception he had met with last night; the undergraduate seems to have behaved with most unusual moderation."

His last engagement for Beale was at Norwich, where he gave the four lectures on successive nights. The proprietor of a newspaper there had invited him to stay at his home, but had received no reply. When Thackeray put up at an hotel in the town he received an aggrieved note from the magnate, who shortly afterwards called on him to remonstrate. "No doubt," said Thackeray, "your letter is among the packet of unopened ones I left in town." Then in one of his bursts of impatience with people he suspected of trying to patronize him, he picked up the gentleman's note and said, "I'm going to light my cigar with your very valuable autograph."

His friend Elwin—"Parson Primrose," as he had now taken to calling him—came up with his wife and children from his country rectory, to hear the lecture and be his guide in exploring the quaint old city. Mrs Elwin kept full notes on the conversations.

"I think I'll take the girls to India next year," Thackeray announced. "I should like to see my native city, and I have friends in almost all the judgeships. Twelve lectures would pay for it."

Expressing amazement at the idea, Elwin added, "I take it you like a roving life."

"Yes, I like it. I should never be at home if I could help."

"But can you write away from home?"

"I write better anywhere than at home, and I write less at home than anywhere. I didn't write ten pages of *The Newcomes* in that house at Brompton. I wrote two lectures in it. This [an hotel] is the best place to write in."

After complaining about the strain of the lecture tours, he went on, "There is something very sweet about it too. I meet everywhere such kindness and hospitality—taken into families, and making friends among them—so that there is quite a little heart-pang at parting."

Although he enjoyed his sight-seeing with Elwin, and wanted to be taken to Yarmouth "to see where Peggotty lived," Thackeray was on the verge of breaking down. Ominous symptoms of his illness appeared, and for the final lecture he had difficulty in getting to the hall in time. Hodder sent him onto the platform with encouraging words, and the burst of applause gave him energy to begin, but soon his voice was faltering, and he struggled painfully to his conclusion. The next morning he summoned his manager to his hotel room. "Don't look at me, Hodder," he gasped from his bed; "I know I'm a hideous object." All offers of service were declined, with the request that Hodder hand over the remainder of his fee and go home to London, leaving him to fight out his seizure as best he might.

Funerals, too, cast a shadow over those months. On May 12 he attended that of Lady Ashburton, which brought together the brilliant political and literary group that she had so often assembled at Alresford Grange—Carlyle, Henry Taylor, Venables, Brookfield, Lord Dufferin and nine other peers. A very different circle gathered on June 15 for the funeral of Douglas Jerrold; Thackeray and Dickens walked side by side as pall-bearers, along with Milnes, Forster, Mark Lemon, Shirley Brooks, and other journalists. For this irascible, downright little man who had been his friendly adversary for so many years Thackeray mourned sincerely, and he volunteered his aid toward raising a fund to assist the widow and children.

At the beginning of June Bayard Taylor reappeared in London. Thackeray could not ask him to stay in Onslow Square, as he had just "pulled part of his house down," but begged him to take quarters nearby and come in and out as he pleased. He also gave Taylor an introduction to Tennyson which was deeply appreciated.

Another acquaintance from over the ocean also called upon him. Phineas T. Barnum, after a spectacular bankruptcy trial, had decided to recoup his fortunes by a European tour with two of his greatest attractions, General Tom Thumb and Cordelia Howard, the most popular "Little Eva." According to Barnum's autobiography, "When I called upon [Thackeray] at his own house, he grasped me heartily by the hand and said, 'Mr Barnum, I admire you more than ever. I have read the accounts in the papers of the examination you underwent in the New York courts; and the positive pluck you exhibit under your pecuniary embarrassments is worthy of all praise. You would never have received credit for the philosophy you manifest, if these financial misfortunes had not overtaken you.'

"I thanked him for his compliment, and he continued: 'But tell me, Barnum, are you really in need of present assistance? for if you are, you must be helped.'

" 'Not in the least,' I replied, laughing; 'I need more money in order to get out of bankruptcy and I intend to earn it; but so far as daily bread is concerned, I am quite at ease, for my wife is worth £30,000 or £40,000.'

" 'Is it possible?' he exclaimed, with evident delight. 'Well, now, you have lost all my sympathy. Why, that is more than I ever expect to be worth. I shall be sorry for you no more.'

"During my stay in London I met Thackeray several times and on one occasion I dined with him. He was a most genial, noble-hearted gentleman."

The general election had been held at the end of April, and Thackeray must have smiled a little wryly at the fact that it was a triumph for the government party, which was returned with an enhanced majority. If he had chosen to accept a nomination he would almost certainly have been elected on the wave of Palmerston's popularity. Then in June the Whig member for Oxford was unseated on a technicality ("for a twopennyworth of bribery which he never committed," as Thackeray remarked), and the seat was offered to the novelist. This time he had no excuse for refusing, and so he established himself at the Mitre, appeared at a meeting of supporters, and issued his "Address to the Electors."

His promises were moderately expressed, and conformed to the conventional objectives of his party:

> . . . With no feeling but that of goodwill towards the leading aristocratic families who are administering the chief offices of the State, I believe it could be benefitted by the skill and talents of persons less aristocratic, and that the country thinks so likewise . . . I think that to secure the due freedom of representation, and to defend the poor voter from the chance of intimidation, the ballot is the best safeguard we know of, and would vote most hopefully for that measure. I would have the suffrage amended in nature, as well as in numbers, and hope to see many educated classes represented who now have no voice in elections . . . I promise to use my utmost endeavour to increase and advance the social happiness, the knowledge, and the power of the people.

In his first speech from the hustings, the same emphasis was laid upon the proletarian appeal, as he contrasted the university quarter with "your new city, which is not picturesque or beautiful at all, but which contains a number of streets, peopled by thousands of hardworking, honest, rough-handed men." He paid unqualified compliments to the unseated Mr Neate, modestly declaring, "I cannot hope, I never thought to equal him; I only came forward at a moment when I felt it necessary that someone professing his principles, and possessing your confidence, shall be ready to step into the gap which he had made." Replying to the charge of incompetence as a public speaker, he asserted: "I cannot spin out glib sentences by the yard, as some people can; but if I have got anything in my mind, if I feel strongly on any question, I believe I have got brains enough to express it."

His Tory adversary, Viscount Monck, was a gracious gentleman, and the campaign was begun in terms of high courtesy. Happening to meet in the street one day, the two opponents shook hands heartily and discussed the trend of events. As they parted, Thackeray uttered the trite phrase, "May the best man win."

"Oh, I hope *not*," replied Lord Monck, with a polite bow.

Thackeray had retained a sneaking fondness for elections ever since his youthful exploit of canvassing for Charles Buller in Cornwall. His glimpse of the South Durham campaign in 1841 was also a bright spot in his memory. But he soon found that the position of candidate was less amusing than that of supporter. In the opening days of the contest he summarized the situation for his daughters in doggerel:

> My dearest little women, as far as I can see,
> The independent woters is all along with me,
> But nevertheless I own it, with not a little funk,
> The more respectable classes they go with Wiscount Monck;
> But a fight without a tussle it is not worth a pin,
> And so St. George for England, and may the best man win.

As the Oxford City constituency was divorced from the University, he had no dealings with his academic friends and admirers, and the worthy citizens were oblivious to his literary reputation. In some anxiety, he appealed for aid to his most popular colleague. Dickens later told how Thackeray "despatched his agent to me from Oxford with a droll note, urging me to come down and make a speech, and tell them who he was, for he doubted whether more than two of the electors had ever heard of him, and he thought there might be as many as six or eight who had heard of me."

Against Lord Monck, Thackeray stood a good chance of being elected; but at the last moment the situation entirely changed. The Tories were desperately anxious to rebuild their representation after their disaster, and among their defeated leaders one of the ablest was Edward Cardwell. Lord Monck therefore suddenly withdrew, and Cardwell was put up instead. "I never would have stood against Cardwell," said Thackeray, "if I had known he was coming down." Indeed, in the privacy of his family Thackeray admitted that he was himself a Cardwellite.

The twelve days of canvassing were hard on Thackeray's temper. He felt humiliated by marching into some little shop, introducing himself to the woman behind the counter, and being told stolidly, "Are yeow Mr Neate's friend? My measter's aout; 'e said I were to say 'e would vote for yeow." When he and his agent ran one voter to earth in a beer house, the man talked vaguely about "considering," with obvious hints for a bribe. "Come on," exclaimed Thackeray, turning away in disgust, "We'll leave the fellow alone." They next solicited a more respectable citizen who answered openly, "No, sir, I am a supporter of Mr Cardwell."

"Shake hands, sir," said Thackeray. "It's a pleasure to meet such a man as you, that can speak out plainly. Though you're an opponent, I'm glad to make your acquaintance. But as for such damned shilly-shallying fellows as the one we've just left, I'd kick them."

Perhaps the most exasperating trial of all, to the old scourger of snobs, was the patronizing air of his more prosperous adherents. One loud-voiced auctioneer always addressed him familiarly as "Thackeray." If the poll had been postponed for a single day, he remarked afterwards, he would not have been able to refrain any longer from kicking him.

Thackeray's agent was naturally convinced that the Tories had used as much corruption and intimidation as the Whigs in the previous campaign and that they were resorting freely to bribery in the present one, on the theory that the constituency would not risk disenfranchisement by lodging another protest. In any case, the contest was not decided by the large abstract principles of secret ballot and extended franchise that Thackeray had announced, but on a trivial issue. During those years the question of Sunday observance was being bitterly disputed, and the Evangelical party was just then in a fury against a proposal that museums be allowed to remain open on Sundays. The bigotry of the Sabbatarians was so typical of what Thackeray despised in his countrymen, and he had been so annoyed by other recent experiences of clerical despotism, that he ignored all advice to temporize, and openly proclaimed himself in favor of liberalizing the law on Sabbath observance. Thereby he alienated many solid Whig voters.

Even so, the contest was close. The final count stood at 1085 for Cardwell, 1018 for Thackeray. When he appeared on the platform at the close of the poll the defeated candidate addressed his supporters with equanimity. "You have fought the battle gallantly," he told them, "against great influences, against an immense strength which has been brought against you and in favor of that honored and respected man, Mr Cardwell." At this name, some of the crowd hissed, but he silenced them sharply: "When Lord Monck came down here and addressed the electors, he was good enough to say a kind word in favor of me. Now, that being the case, don't let me be outdone in courtesy and generosity." Later in his speech, another allusion to the adversary brought forth a shout of "Bribery." "Don't cry out bribery," he admonished. "If you know it, prove it; but as I am innocent of bribery myself, I do not choose to fancy that other men are not equally loyal and honest." And his closing words seemed unmistakably tinged with relief: "I will retire and take my place with my pen and ink at my desk, and leave to Mr Cardwell a business which I am sure he understands better than I do."

CHAPTER 21

An Immoderate Use of the Fleshpots

WHEN THACKERAY returned from Oxford to his disappointed family he was in good spirits, and full of anecdotes about the campaign. It was a lesson to his vanity, he said, to discover how little he was known to the man in the street. The following night he gave his lecture on "Charity and Humor" for the Jerrold memorial fund, and brought down the house by beginning solemnly, "I happened yesterday to be in an ancient city, called Oxford, of which some of you may have heard . . ."

For the next two weeks he paid the penalty of his exertions by a severe bout of illness, although "so busy that the nurse has had to sit in the antechamber all the while." On August 4 he removed to Brighton to spend a month in recuperation, while his daughters enjoyed riding lessons and sea bathing. A short visit to Homburg and Paris was his only continental excursion. The Carmichael-Smyths had been persuaded to come to England in August for a long stay, and Thackeray rejoiced to see a steady improvement in his mother's health.

In the autumn he settled down in Onslow Square on a more pretentious scale of living than before. Ever since the American tour Charles Pearman had suffered from delusions of grandeur, wearing a black coat instead of a livery; and the fact that the house next door kept both a butler and a footman was his excuse for insisting that the Thackerays must do likewise. His master gave in and hired a "Jeames," although quizzically amused at the spectacle of two imposing menials serving him and his girls their simple mutton chops. Although the expenses of the election, totaling £887, had obliged him to sell out his stock in the transatlantic telegraph, he felt safe in incurring this and other outlays.

His spirits, however, did not keep pace with his prosperity. Confessing himself to be growing steadily more "silent and selfish," he spent much of his time at his clubs. His towering figure became a more and more familiar sight of the West End, sauntering, usually alone, along Pall Mall, or mounting the steps of the Garrick, or seeking a quiet corner in the Athenaeum to write for an hour or two, or gazing dreamily—often with a weary expression—out of the window at the Reform Club. Stories of his moodiness were current in literary circles. George Augustus Sala, for instance, who had known him for some years, called on him one day to ask for advice about writing a biography of Hogarth. "He gave me, as usual, the heartiest of receptions," says Sala. "He was delighted with the idea, and sagaciously added that the first thing to do in the matter was to secure a first-rate publisher for the work.

So he sat down and wrote a letter introducing me in terms far more eulogistic than I deserved to Mr George Smith. . . . It was a fine day, and Thackeray and I walked from Brompton to Piccadilly, gossiping the whole time on a hundred and one topics . . . Halting just opposite Morell's, the well-known Italian warehouse, Thackeray observed that he was about to order some wine. He made me a bow which in its sweeping stateliness would have done honour to Sir Charles Grandison, concurrently giving me his hand, which was cold enough to have belonged to a professor of swimming who had just emerged from his tank; and then he stalked over the way, leaving in my mind a perplexed impression that he had suddenly forgotten who I was, or that, knowing me, he had arrived at the conclusion that I was a confounded bore . . . When I came to know him intimately I fully understood the reasons for these sudden reactions of apparent hauteur. He could not help that which probably was due either to an acute spasm of bodily pain or the sudden passing of a black cloud across his mind."

The first time Hodder saw him after the painful scene in the Norwich hotel, Thackeray alluded to his health, and Hodder asked whether he had ever sought the best medical advice.

"Certainly I have," was the reply; "but what's the use of advice if you don't follow it? They tell me not to drink, and I *do* drink. They tell me not to smoke, and I *do* smoke. They tell me not to eat, and I *do* eat. In short, I do everything that I am desired *not* to do, and therefore what am I to expect?"

In this gloomy frame of mind he set to work on the new novel that had already been under contract for more than a year. For his subject he finally adopted the idea of a sequel to *Henry Esmond*, which he had foreshadowed in the preface to that book, and which had been so vivid in his imagination during his visits to the United States. The theme of the story, and the main characters, were no more fully developed when he began to write it than they had been five years before. In view of his difficulties with Doyle over *The Newcomes*, he decided to draw his own illustrations, in spite of the additional effort entailed. On October 10, only three weeks before the first number was to appear, he wrote to John Brown, enclosing a sketch of the design for the cover: "This is the best part of *The Virginians* which is done as yet. I have been working hard and don't like what I have done."

On account of its American setting, he was particularly pleased that Harper and Brothers had arranged to receive the proof-sheets of each number in order to run it serially in their magazine. He felt that the £480 which they paid for the privilege was a generous sum. Then at the end of October came a report of another panic in the New York stock market, and he jumped to the conclusion that all his investments there were lost, and the Harper fee as well. He announced dramatically to his daughters that they would have to give up the "carriage and one," and dismiss one or both of the men-servants; but the next day better news arrived, and he could laugh at his fright. Hard times were prevalent in England, too, as a result of the "accommodation-bill crisis," and during November no less than fifteen men came to him with urgent appeals for loans, so that every penny of his available cash was absorbed.

Even this condition could not put a stop to his impulsive generosity. Bayard Taylor came back from the Continent just then with a German bride, and a dinner party was given for them in Onslow Square. When the gentlemen joined the ladies in the drawing-room, the host suddenly said, "By the bye, I must give you a wedding present. What shall it be?"

Going to a what-not in the corner, he glanced over its crowded shelves and took down a handsome silver ink-stand.

"Oh! not that one, Papa!" exclaimed Minny, in an agony. But Thackeray ignored her protest, and a few days later the ink-stand, suitably engraved, was delivered at the Taylors' hotel. About this time, too, Thackeray gave Taylor one of his most cherished mementos—the sword of Schiller.

The first number of the new novel was far from satisfactory. "I don't think *The Virginians* is good yet," he told the Baxters, "though it has taken me an immense deal of trouble, but I know it will be good at the end." Feeling guiltily that Bradbury & Evans would lose money by paying him three hundred pounds a number, he feared that he would have "the melancholy duty of disgorging." In January he explained to another American friend that he was drawing only £250 per month; "but I like everybody who deals with me to make money by me so I cede those £50, you see, until better times."

A further embarrassment was the immediate pirating of the book in the United States. It was serialized in the weekly edition of the New York *Tribune*, and the London representative of Harpers protested to Thackeray against this infringement of the authorized publication in their magazine. Reasonably enough, Thackeray pointed out that if Harpers could not protect their own rights at home, he was helpless in the matter: "Could English writers have remonstrated with any effect we should have done so years ago: but I am sure that an outcry at present would neither be useful nor dignified, and can only express my regret that I don't see how, in the present instance, I can be of service to a House which shows itself inclined to act in a kind and friendly manner to English literary men."

The year 1857 closed agreeably enough. His parents had gone home to Paris in November in improved health and spirits. He and the girls spent Christmas with such festivities that his work on Number Four was sadly impeded. He longed for three days at home alone for uninterrupted work, but he could not bear to deny his daughters any pleasure. So he went with them to stay with Mr and Mrs Sturgis at Walton-on-Thames amid "lavish splendours and magnificence. . . fountains of champagne and hock, drives in coaches and four." One day of the visit was spent in composing a speech that he was to deliver on behalf of the Commercial Travelers' School; after dictating it to Annie he was chagrined to find that she remembered it verbatim while he could not retain a single phrase. When he went up to London on Boxing Day to deliver it, his only hope was that it would be so flat a failure that he would be spared similar demands in future.

Not until January 2 was he able to settle down to Number Four. He behaved "as one distraught" when struggling with a number, and yet if he desisted from it he was unable to fix his attention upon anything else. Four days later Elwin met him at dinner at Forster's, and the two friends were so openly delighted with each other's company that Forster took offence at their neglect of him and his wife, and announced indignantly that he would never invite them together again. Still in his mood of dispensing souvenirs, Thackeray gave Elwin the gold pencil case that he had used for years. As they walked home after the dinner, Thackeray held forth about his plans for the novel. "I'll bring in Goldsmith, representing him as he really was, a little, shabby, mean, shuffling Irishman. And Dr Johnson, and all of them. It will be easy—I feel that I know them so well. Why, if I were to hear Garrick's laugh, I'd identify it from the look in his portrait."

His conscience told him he ought to get several numbers ahead, in case of a severe illness; but his growing laziness made it impossible for him to work except under the pressure of the "deadline." He did not finish Number Four until January 22. Although his spare time was spent in poring over newspapers and magazines of 1756, he encountered unsolvable problems as to the details of events in America. He could not find out the color of the Washington livery. When he realized that his plot required the disappearance of one of his twin heroes for a year and a half, after Braddock's defeat, he wrote in despair to New York, begging that Cozzens or Curtis would suggest a good way of managing it. Cozzens replied in detail, but not helpfully, for he proved by statistics that no prisoners had been taken by the Indians. As problems of this sort would inevitably multiply when he reached the chapters dealing with the Revolution, Thackeray toyed with the idea of returning to the United States in the autumn to write the last half of the story on the scene of action.

Apart from the tortures of composition, he was feeling fairly complacent. Because of the election and other extravagances, he admitted that he was no richer than twelve months before: he estimated his annual expenses at £2600, which ought to have kept two families on the same scale; but he realized that he "somehow" gave away £500, and celebrated the ending of each month's number by buying "pooty things," such as silver spoons. He bragged about paying a hundred pounds for eighteen dozen of 1848 claret, to be laid down in his cellar for four more years. In February he bought "a famous little cob that carries me to perfection." The ill-will aroused among his fashionable friends by his treatment of the Georges was fading, and he was gratified that "the Earls and Marquises" were "beginning to come back."

He was able to indulge himself also by giving an occasional lecture as a favor, instead of for hire. For a year past he had been receiving treatment from Dr Henry Thompson, a leading genito-urinary specialist, who had refused to accept a fee; and when Thompson went with him to hear him give one of the old lectures on the Humorists in a London suburb, Thackeray handed over to him the cheque for twenty-five pounds. A month later Macready, who had settled down as a country squire in Dorset and was full of local philanthropies, offered him fifty pounds to come and lecture on the Georges in two little towns of his vicinity; Thackeray replied that he would give the lectures but not accept the fee.

During the first three weeks of February he had three bad attacks, admitting that he was falling victim to "claret drunk not wisely, but too well, an immoderate use of the fleshpots." He was able to go for a ride on his new horse only about once a fortnight. His imposing butler-valet, Charles, was replaced with a Frenchman. And Numbers Five and Six were toilsomely composed.

The Oxford election ought to have cured his political hankering, for a few months afterwards he discovered that—in defiance of his strict orders—his agents had indulged in corrupt practices that would probably have unseated him, if he had been elected. And yet at the beginning of March the prospect of a dissolution caused him to tell Dr Brown that he was "afraid I shall try Parliament again." To another friend he elaborated the idea: "Having tasted of the excitement, I have a strong inclination to repeat it. Novel spinning is not enough occupation for a man of six-and-forty, and though I am so dilatory with my own work, I think I should be all the better for having a good deal more." On April 4 he remarked to Sir Mountstewart Grant Duff that his chief reason for wishing to be in the House of Commons was that he could stand up once a year and warn his countrymen of what would happen "when the French invade us." Toward the end of the month he told the Baxters that he had seen his name suggested as a candidate for four different constituencies, "but don't want one now for a while" because of the expense.

There was also some talk of his being tendered the Lord Rectorship of Aberdeen University, but he expressed relief when the nomination to "that quaint office" went to a graver character, his friend Lord Mahon. In spite of these enticing gestures from the world of affairs, his conscience told him that he ought to be giving undivided attention to the novel. On April 10 he had done only three pages of the current number. He excused himself on the ground that during the previous fortnight he had suffered two attacks, "each attack throwing me back a week or two;" but he added candidly that he had being going out with the girls to a round of parties and dinners. In May it was the 21st before he finished the number, barely in time for the American copy to catch the boat at Liverpool. John Blackwood, who was staying in London and seeing much of the Thackerays, commented anxiously in a letter to G. H. Lewes: "He says he cannot get ahead with *The Virginians*, and was desperately pushed with the last No., having written the last 16 pages in one day, the last he had to spare. The last two Nos. are, I think, better than their predecessors, but he must improve much or the book will not keep up his reputation."

Thackeray described the novel aptly as "clever but stupid," and admitted that the reason was his growing distaste for plot-making. He had begun to hate the conventional materials—surprises, love affairs, and so forth. Already one-third of a long novel was completed and nothing had happened in it.

In this respect lies the book's charm as well as its weakness. It is actually more pleasantly readable than *Henry Esmond*. It lacks the artificiality which chilled that novel by the attempt to recreate an Addisonian style and to reveal Esmond's despondent temperament through his own words. Instead, *The Virginians* wanders in ample leisure among events and celebrities with whom Thackeray had become intimate while reading for his lectures.

The original plan for it was Thackeray's best. To write a novel about the American Revolution showing the partisans of both sides as human beings with the usual proportion of wisdom and folly, generosity and selfishness, idealism and prejudice, was a bold scheme. The central characters—two contrasted brothers remaining devoted to each other in spite of rivalries—were thoroughly true to human nature; and the further theme of the domineering mother, almost ruining the lives of her sons with the highest motives, was more consistent with twentieth-century psychological realism than with the Victorian idolatry of The Family.

Thackeray must have foreseen that the story would rouse resentment in the United States. In view of modern revelations, it is amusing to find even his admiring friend Cozzens protesting, more in sorrow than in anger: "I must except to your making George Washington use language unbecoming an officer and a gentleman, as you do. If you look at the courteous language of old 'Virginny,' you will see nothing there but pure and polite English." The American press and public, in no sympathetic mood toward England, were unmeasured in their condemnation. Thackeray, however, was not the man to be intimidated. His persistence in lecturing in England on the Georges is evidence enough.

His uncertain handling of *The Virginians* was due to more immediate causes. The difficulty in finding details of American history made him dread to undertake the chapters about the war. Besides, having placed the opening events twenty years earlier, he was going to have a technical problem in handling the time-lapse. Meanwhile, he had inexhaustible material for his picture of London and Tunbridge Wells in the days of Dr Johnson and Lord Chesterfield and Jack Morris and General Wolfe. Therefore, having arbitrarily expelled George Warrington from the story,

THE VIRGINIANS

VOL. I

THE VIRGINIANS

VOL. 2

he lingered lovingly over brother Harry's escapades in England. The baseness of the noble Esmonds was elaborated in contrast with the honest kindness of the Lambert family. Thackeray admitted on occasions that the two Lambert girls were remarkably like his own daughters (even to the plumpness of the elder), and his Annie expressed the opinion in later years that General Lambert was a recognizable portrait of Thackeray in his domestic rôle. With all these elements of the character-sketch and the history of manners and the personal essay, he could get on well enough from number to number without a plot.

An irruption of American authors had by now become an adjunct of the English summer. This year the most prominent was John Lothrop Motley, whose letters home to Boston provide a lively word-portrait of Thackeray in his forty-seventh year. They met first at a dinner at Robert Mackintosh's. Motley was delighted to hear Thackeray, further down the table, suddenly say to somebody, "Have you read *The Autocrat of the Breakfast Table*, by Holmes, in the new *Atlantic Monthly?* No man in England can write now with that charming mixture of wit, pathos, and imagination. Holmes's papers are better by far than anything in our magazines." Motley was so delighted by this unsolicited tribute to his friend that he hurried back to his hotel, tore open a letter to Holmes that he had already sealed, and added a postscript.

In a letter to his wife he gave a fuller description. "Thackeray has the appearance of a colossal infant—smooth, white, shiny, ringlety hair, a roundish face, with a little dab of a nose upon which it is a perpetual wonder how he keeps his spectacles, a sweet but rather piping voice, with something of the childish treble about it, and a very tall, slightly stooping figure. . . . His manner is like that of everybody else in England—nothing original, all planed down into perfect uniformity with that of his fellow creatures. There was not much more distinction in his talk than in his white choker or black coat and waistcoat. I shall endeavor to Boswellize him a little, but it is very hard work. Something was said of Carlyle. Thackeray said, 'Carlyle hates everybody that has arrived; if they are on the road, he may perhaps treat them civilly.' . . . Of the Cosmopolitan Club, Thackeray said: 'Everybody is or is supposed to be a celebrity; nobody ever says anything worth hearing; and everybody goes there with his white choker at midnight, to appear as if he had just been dining with the aristocracy. I have no doubt,' he added, 'that half of us put on the white cravat after a solitary dinner at home or at our club, and go down among the Cosmopolitans.' . . . Thackeray invited me to dine next Sunday, and he went off very soon, as he confessed, to work at *The Virginians*."

At the dinner at Thackeray's, Motley found the two daughters of the house "both intelligent and agreeable." Thackeray remarked to him that "he hated *The Book of Snobs* and could not read a word of it. *The Virginians*, he said, was devilish stupid, but at the same time most admirable; but that he intended to write a novel of the time of Henry V, which would be his *capo d'opera*, in which the ancestors of all his present characters, Warringtons, Pendennises, and the rest, should be introduced. It would be a most magnificant performance, he said, and nobody would read it. After the ladies had left the house we went downstairs and smoked cigars till into the small hours."

The next night Motley came again, to a "drum" that Thackeray had unwillingly consented to let Annie give. He was sure that "this horrible tea-fight" would cause all sorts of ill-feeling, because of the peculiar range of their acquaintance: "we know great people and small, polite and otherwise; the otherwise are not a bit comfortable in company of the others but yet angry if they are not asked." The kindly Blackwoods invited him to dinner with them that evening, "to be out of the way of the preparations." At the party Motley found various agreeable people, but complained that "there was a tremendous screeching lady, who stunned the company with Italian music, with a voice which wanted elbow-room as much as it did melody."

On the following evening Thackeray was giving a private reading of "George III" in the drawing-room of Lady Stanley, and he took Motley with him. "I was much impressed with the quiet, graceful ease with which he read—just a few notes above the conversational level, but never rising into the declamatory. This light-in-hand manner suits well the delicate, hovering rather than superficial, style of the composition. He skims lightly over the surface of the long epoch, . . . running along from grave to gay, from lively to severe, moving and mocking the sensibilities in a breath, in a way which I should say was the perfection of lecturing to high-bred audiences . . . I was somewhat surprised at the coolness with which he showed up the foibles and absurdities of kings, and court, and court folks in a former but not remote reign, before a small company which consisted of the cream of London cream. They seemed to enjoy it, and to laugh heartily at all the points without wilting."

Motley and Thackeray next met in the dean's pew at St Paul's Cathedral, on an annual occasion which was one of Thackeray's sentimental indulgences—the charity children's service, at which hymns were sung by some four thousand pupils from the endowed schools, whose treble harmonies and rosy faces never failed to bring tears behind Thackeray's spectacles. Leaning over to Motley (who was also feeling that the effect "suggested the choir of the angels in Paradise"), Thackeray whispered, "It's the finest thing in the world—finer than the Declaration of Independence."

The historian dined several times more at Thackeray's, and became convinced that his host was "very kind-hearted and benevolent." Their final meeting seemed to have an unaccountable touch of pathos. Working in the reading room of the British Museum one morning, Motley happened to look up from his notes, and "I found seated next to me Thackeray, with a file of old newspapers before him, writing the ninth number of *The Virginians*. He took off his spectacles to see who I was, then immediately invited me to dinner the next day (as he seems always to do everybody he meets), which invitation I could not accept, and he then showed me the page he had been writing, a small, delicate, legible manuscript. After this we continued our studies. I can conceive nothing more harassing in the literary way than his way of living from hand to mouth. I mean in regard to the way in which he furnishes food for the printer's devil. Here he is just finishing the number which must appear in a few days. Of course, whether ill or well, stupid or fertile, he must produce the same amount of fun, pathos, or sentiment. His gun must be regularly loaded and discharged at command. I should think it would wear his life out."

Although Motley only intuitively guessed that something was wrong, Thackeray was deeply sunk in vexation. Five weeks earlier, in a letter to Mrs Baxter, after enumerating his blessings—"good daughters, good wine in the cellar, easy work, plenty of money in my pocket, a fair reputation,"—he declared that he was not happy "above four days in the month. A man without a woman is a lonely wretch." This curiously statistical estimate of his happiness was invalidated within three weeks, when he got into a miserable broil.

For nearly twenty years he had been fighting a losing battle against the vulgar gossip and personalities of the press. He had two reasons for his persistence: as a celebrity, he wished to retain a gentleman's privilege of privacy; as a former journalist, he hoped to endow that profession with dignity and ethics. He had hectored the publisher of *Fraser's Magazine* for the impertinent verbal caricature that had been smuggled into Keane's *Illustrations of Discount*. In his *Essay on Thunder and Small Beer* he had belabored the potent *Times* for an affront implied in some phrases of a review. In spite of his determination to make allowances for the free and easy manners of Americans, he had been gradually infuriated by newspaper familiarities during his visits to the United States.

The latest outrage was far more galling. Edmund Yates was a twenty-seven-year-old journalist who had grown up in the atmosphere of the newspaper office and the green room, being the son of a popular actor and actress. By cool misrepresentation he had got himself elected to the Garrick Club at the age of seventeen, and later he had been one of the foundation members of the Fielding Club. Through connivance with the secretary of the dinner on the eve of Thackeray's second American tour he was included among the sixty "special friends."

At the end of May Yates joined the staff of a new and insignificant weekly named *Town Talk*. When he went to the printers' to see the issue of June 12 through the press, he was informed that, as a contributor had defaulted through illness, a column of material must be immediately forthcoming. Having written for the previous number a personal article about Dickens that had been well received, Yates sat down and scribbled what came into his head about Thackeray.

Although the article contained words of praise for some of Thackeray's writings, its general tenor was neither sympathetic nor in good taste. It began with a description of his appearance and manners:

... His face is bloodless, and not particularly expressive, but remarkable for the fracture of the bridge of the nose, the result of an accident in youth. He wears a small grey whisker, but otherwise is clean shaven. No one meeting him could fail to recognize in him a gentleman; his bearing is cold and uninviting, his style of conversation either openly cynical or affectedly goodnatured and benevolent; his *bonhomie* is forced, his wit biting, his pride easily touched; but his appearance is invariably that of the cool, suave, well-bred gentleman, who, whatever may be rankling within, suffers no surface display of his emotion.

Proceeding to Thackeray's career, Yates remarked:

... In the *Punch* pages appeared many of his wisest, most thoughtful, and wittiest essays ... Here, too, were published his buffooneries, his Ballads of *Policeman X*, his *Jeames's Diary*, and some other scraps, the mere form of which consisted in outrages on orthography, and of which he is now deservedly ashamed.

Regarding the novels, Yates interspersed compliments to *Vanity Fair* and *The Newcomes* with statements that *Vanity Fair* "had been offered to, and rejected by, several of the first publishers in London;" that *Esmond* "fell almost stillborn from the press;" and that *The Virginians* "lacks interest of plot, and is proportionately unsuccessful."

It was the lectures, however, that inspired Yates to his most insolent remarks:

His "Lectures on the English Humourists" ... were attended by all the court and fashion of London. The prices were extravagant, the lecturer's adulation of birth and position was extravagant, the success was extravagant. No one succeeds better than Mr. Thackeray in cutting his coat according to his cloth. Here he flattered the aristocracy; but when he crossed the Atlantic, George Washington became the idol of his worship, the "Four Georges" the objects of his bitterest attacks. These last-named lectures have been dead failures in England, though as literary compositions they are most excellent. Our own opinion is that his success is on the wane. His writings never were understood or appreciated even by the middle class; the aristocracy have been alienated by his American onslaught on their body; and the educated and refined are not sufficiently numerous to constitute an audience. Moreover, there is a want of heart in all he writes, which is not to be balanced by the most brilliant sarcasm and the most perfect knowledge of the workings of the human heart.

Until the end of his life, Yates would never admit that the article could be considered "offensive or objectionable." In fact, he was so well pleased with himself that he discussed his contributions to *Town Talk* that same evening with a friend at the Garrick.

Thackeray, however, was justifiably angry. A preceding issue of the paper had printed an incorrect account of his private dealings with his publishers. Now this article revived all the imputations of snobbery and heartlessness that he had combated for so long. There was just enough modicum of truth in the comments to make them rankle the more. When he learned (presumably from the Garrick member to whom Yates had boasted) that the writer of the libel was a man who had been for ten years a fellow-member of the club, he decided to take action.

He wrote the journalist a strong letter of protest. Admitting Yates's right to praise or condemn the books "as a literary critic," Thackeray could not extend the same liberty to the description of his conversation, the imputation of insincerity, and the charges of "advancing statements which I have never delivered at all." Other calumnies, by unknown persons, Thackeray had ignored; but the present assailant was a supposed friend, with whom he had "shaken hands more than once," and whom he had recently and warmly praised to one of the editors for whom Yates worked. After pointing out these circumstances, he described the articles as "not offensive and unfriendly merely, but slanderous and untrue;" he then gave the culprit a brief but pointed lecture on the ethics of club membership and the enormity of making newspaper copy out of the unrestrained talk that might be overheard at the Garrick; and he closed with a positive demand "that you will refrain from printing comments upon my private conversations; that you will forgo discussions, however blundering, upon my private affairs; and that you will henceforth please to consider any question of my personal truth and sincerity as quite out of the province of your criticism."

Yates saw that the emphasis upon the sanctity of private behavior gave him an opportunity for retort. He composed a defiant letter, pointing out not only Thackeray's lampoons of Bulwer but also his recognizable use of Garrick Club habitués as models for characters in *The Book of Snobs* and *Pendennis*. Before sending the letter, however, he sought advice from his friend Charles Dickens.

If Dickens had been in his normal senses, he would undoubtedly have mediated the affair. But by an unlucky chance he was in a state of blind misery and rage that bordered on madness, and was busily committing the great indiscretion of his career. His separation from his wife had just occurred; and on June 12—the very day of Yates's article in *Town Talk*—he printed in *Household Words* a public defence of his conduct, with details of his domestic troubles that even his best friends deplored. Defying their advice, he insisted that the statement be given the widest circulation, and when it was refused republication in *Punch* he was bitterly offended. The editor, Mark Lemon, was his good friend, and the proprietors, Bradbury & Evans, were his partners in publishing *Household Words*; he promptly declared his intention of severing relations with the firm and of terminating intimacy with all former friends who did not justify his actions.

Now, Yates had just earned his gratitude by supporting him. Furthermore, Thackeray was an intimate of Lemon and the whole *Punch* staff, and Bradbury & Evans were publishing *The Virginians*. Besides, Dickens was uncomfortably aware that Thackeray was just the sort of person who would be sure to stigmatize his behavior as "caddish," and he was especially infuriated over the issue of "freedom of the press" involved in Lemon's rejection of his statement. He was in no mood to be judicious over a question of "good taste." Like a goaded bull, he was ready to gore anybody as a vengeance for his misery; and when Yates was accused of publishing intimate details in disregard of gentlemanly reticence, he saw a situation in which he could indirectly vindicate his own course.

Upon reading the draft of Yates's letter, therefore, Dickens condemned it as "too flippant and too violent." In a subsequent effort to mollify Thackeray, he asserted that "I told [Yates] that his article was not to be defended; but I confirmed him in his opinion that it was not reasonably possible for him to set right what was amiss, on the receipt of a letter couched in the very strong terms you had employed." Yates, in his later account of the affair, was carefully ambiguous as to whether Dickens actually approved the letter that was substituted for his intended reply; Yates's words are that "after a little discussion, the following acknowledgment was sent:"

You will excuse my pointing out to you that it is absurd to suppose me bound to accept your angry "understanding" of my "phrases." I do not accept it in the least. I altogether reject it.

I cannot characterise your letter in any other terms than those in which you characterised the article which has given you so much offence. If your letter to me were not both "slanderous and untrue," I should readily have discussed its subject with you, and avowed my earnest and frank desire to set right anything I may have left wrong. Your letter being what it is, I have nothing to add to my present reply.

Whoever had a hand in the retort, it was abominably rude. Thackeray forthwith turned the evidence over to the committee of the Garrick, with the request that they decide "whether the practice of publishing such articles will not be fatal to the comfort of the Club, and is not intolerable in a society of gentlemen."

Now thoroughly alarmed, Yates appealed to the committee to give him time to consult his friends and prepare his own version of the dispute. He declares that he held "frequent councils" with Dickens, Forster, Albert Smith, and Dickens's sub-editor, Wills. His statement to the committee, however, consisted only of the assertion that, as the Club was not mentioned in the article, the committee had no jurisdiction in the quarrel. Rejecting this protest, the committee gave him the alternative of apologizing to Thackeray or retiring from the Club, with the proviso that otherwise the matter would be referred to a general meeting of the members.

Hoping to be able to drum up a sufficient faction in his defence, Yates demanded the summoning of the general meeting. By the advice of Dickens, who was now restored to some prudence, he did not attend it in person, but submitted a letter, based wholly on the contention that he was really the injured party, owing to the insolence of Thackeray's letter to him. Though refusing to apologize to Thackeray, he offered to humiliate himself to the extent of apologizing *to the Club* "for any unpleasant feeling that I may have awakened" in it. Thackeray also, of course, stayed away from the meeting.

Dickens, meanwhile, presented his version of the case in a letter to one of Thackeray's warmest friends in the Club, W. H. Russell, who was in India. He spoke of Thackeray's "amazing want of discretion" in appealing to the committee. "The article is in bad taste, no doubt," he admitted, "and would have been infinitely better left alone. But I conceive that the committee have nothing earthly, celestial, or infernal to do with it . . ."

At the general meeting, Dickens took the lead in his friend's behalf. With protestations that he and Thackeray had been on good terms for many years, and that he was sorry to be obliged to oppose him, he presented his argument that the dispute was no concern of the Club. Others who spoke on Yates's behalf included Wilkie Collins and Samuel Lover; but the vote went two-to-one in support of the committee's decision. In a haughty letter, Dickens immediately resigned from the committee.

In various letters that Dickens wrote during the turmoil, his state of mind can be easily read. He was not actuated, as some people thought, by literary rivalry toward Thackeray; but having rashly put himself in the position of Yates's champion, he found that his prestige in the Club was going to be at stake, and he was humiliated to discover that he could sway so few of the members.

For the same reason, Thackeray was determined not to give way an inch. When a journalist friend, John Cordy Jeaffreson, had the temerity to tell him that many people thought he was going too far in his punishment of Yates, he answered grimly, "You mustn't think, young 'un, that I am quarreling with Mr Yates. I am hitting the man behind him."

Thackeray had conducted himself with due gentlemanly restraint, but he gave vent to his annoyance in one indiscretion. In the current number of *The Virginians*, after one of his ironical digressions—on the theme that "there are few better ways of securing the faithfulness and admiration of the beautiful partners of our existence than a little judicious ill-treatment"—he went on:

I should not be surprised if young Grubstreet, who corresponds with three penny papers and describes the persons and conversation of gentlemen whom he meets at his "clubs," will say "I told you so! He advocates the thrashing of women! He has no nobility of soul! He has no heart!" Nor have I, my eminent young Grubstreet! any more than you have ears.

A few chapters later, he returned to the touchy subject:

> There are certain lines which must be drawn: and I am only half pleased, for my part, when Bob Bowstreet, whose connection with letters is through Policeman X and Y, and Tom Garbage, who is an esteemed contributor to the *Kennel Miscellany*, propose to join fellowship as brother literary men, slap me on the back, and call me old boy, or by my Christian name.

These flashes of pique were ammunition for his foes. Yates and his party built up the legend that Thackeray was using his great fame and his secure social position to exterminate honest and struggling young writers for daring not to worship him. George Augustus Sala, for example—who, like Yates, was a satellite of Dickens's editorial throne—took up the gage in another of the penny weeklies, *The Welcome Guest*:

> The great Mr. Polyphemus, the novelist, is bidden to the Duke of Sennacherib's, and as he rolls to Sennacherib House in his brougham, meditates satiric onslaughts on "Tom Garbage" and "Young Grubstreet"—those Tom Thumb foes of his—in the next number of the *Pennsylvanians* . . . And where are the working men of literature, the conscripts of the pen, doomed to carry Brown Bess for sixpence a day all their lives? Where are Garbage and Grubstreet? . . . Grubstreet, is he in some murky den, with a vulture's quill dipped in vitriol, inditing libels upon the great, good, and wise of the day? Wonder upon wonders, Grubstreet sits in a handsome study, listening to his wife laughing over her crochet work at Mr Polyphemus's last attack on him, and dandling a little child on his knee! . . .

Thus the beehive continued to hum, while Thackeray, as usual, assured his friends of his immunity to annoyance from "the little papers: I don't care as I never read one."

Immediately after the general meeting of the Garrick, he took his daughters off to the Continent for the customary summer tour. They were abroad for five weeks, chiefly in Heidelberg and Switzerland, but he returned without improvement in health or spirits. He described himself as "constantly unwell now—a fit of spasms—then get well in about five days; then five days grumbling and thinking of my work; then fourteen days work, and spasms *da capo*." He still insisted that *The Virginians* was "horribly stupid," and lamented that there was "no go left in this dreary old expiring carcass." Having taken a house in Brighton for August, he spent part of his time there, although he went back to town frequently to consult reference books; and that resort once more stimulated him to the extent of carrying

The Virginians forward for the first time a little way in advance of the publication date.

In September he went over to Paris and settled down in an hotel. His Baltimore friend, John Pendleton Kennedy, was in Paris at the time, and his diary records a remarkable episode. On September 26, "Thackeray calls to see me and sits an hour. He is not looking well. He tells me he has need of my assistance with his *Virginians*, and that Heaven has sent me to his aid. He wants to get his hero from Fort Duquesne, where he is confined a prisoner after Braddock's defeat, and to bring him to the coast to embark for England. 'Now you know all that ground,' he says to me, 'and I want you to write a chapter for me to describe how he got off and what travel he made.' He insists that I shall do it. I give him a doubtful promise to do it if I can find time in the thousand engagements that now press upon me." Four days later the diary says, "Thackeray calls. I tell him I am so much occupied with the engagements which press upon me that I can do no more than give him a few hints for the description he wishes. I do this in conversation, which he tells me is precisely what he wishes, and I promise him to repeat it in some notes which I shall prepare for him." On October 3, "I write nearly all the morning preparing notes for Thackeray—an outline of the chapter he wants—and in making a rough map of illustrations." The next day, "I send Thackeray the notes." Several years later, Kennedy stated that Thackeray "partially incorporated" his sketch in the book.

Yates, meanwhile, continued to clamor for war. Although he had demanded the general meeting of the Garrick, he refused to accept its verdict, and after a due interval his name was expunged from the roll of members. Still under guidance from Dickens, he sought legal advice, and prepared for a law suit by invading the Club premises, accompanied by his solicitor, and being formally ejected by the secretary. When he discovered, however, that the secretary was not liable, and that his only recourse would be an expensive Chancery case against the trustees of the Club property, he was somewhat sobered. Late in November Dickens accompanied him to interview the prominent counsel who had been retained. As a result of the visit, Dickens obtained the materials for his character of Mr Stryver in *A Tale of Two Cities*; but he also received the impression that the case had better not be prosecuted. He therefore attempted to do what he should have done to begin with: he appealed directly to Thackeray, begging for "some quiet accommodation of this deplorable matter, which will satisfy the feelings of all concerned." His proposal was that he should act as Yates' representative in conferring with some friend appointed by Thackeray (as he had once done in the quarrel with Forster), and he closed with the assurance that he was acting, "God knows in no hostile spirit towards anyone, least of all to you."

Although Dickens had requested that, if no mediation resulted, his letter should be burned, Thackeray was too deeply aggrieved to comply. He notified the Garrick Club committee of the terms of the proposal, and informed Dickens stiffly that he had done so, stating that from the moment he submitted the case to the Club he had ceased to take any personal part in it. His letter was couched in the most formal terms, ending with a frigid "Yours, &c."

The only positive outcome of the great "Yates affair" was then and there determined. Dickens felt humiliated, and his friends rubbed salt in the wound. "He be damned, with his 'yours, &c.'!" exploded Forster, on seeing the letter. The Garrick committee took no action on the appeal; the Yates lawsuit was silently dropped; but the twenty years' friendship of the two pre-eminent novelists was at an end.

JOHNSON AND GOLDSMITH

CHAPTER 22

A Princely Income

"AT FORTY-SEVEN Venus may rise from the sea, and I for one should hardly put on my spectacles to have a look," Thackeray declared to John Brown. This was early in November, while he was still in Paris. The spell of that city no longer stirred him: the weather was cold, and he sat in his expensive room at the Hôtel des Deux Mondes, trying vainly to keep warm, and thinking doleful thoughts. He told Brown that he could look forward to no greater pleasure in life than the beefsteak and claret on which he had just dined, and that even from them he could part without a very sore pang. "What *is* a greater pleasure? Gratified ambition, accumulation of money—what? Fruition of some sort of desire, perhaps? When one is twenty, yes . . ."

This mood of disenchantment pervaded *The Virginians* until his digressions became tedious in their cynicism. He was at last waking up to the book's lack of movement; while working on Number Fifteen he confessed that the story ought to have been at its present stage in the tenth number, had he not "dawdled fatally between five and ten." Through the first half of 1859 he plodded on with it, seldom more than a month in advance of publication. He finished the February number at 2:30 a.m. on January 26, and felt so energetic that he disappointed the girls by cutting short their "monthly lark" in order to write two pages of the March instalment before dinner. Annie tried to persuade herself that this proved "he was much better than he has been for a very long, weary time. Except a one-day attack on Xmas day he has not been ill for nearly six weeks."

In an effort to give the novel freshness, and to make the difficult transition from Harry Warrington to George as central hero, he cast some of the later chapters in the form of George's autobiography, thus reverting to the technique of *Esmond*; but the result was merely a confusion in style and point of view. His problem of keeping an equipoise between his two heroes had not been solved. By the time he came to the episodes of the American Revolution, having given up all hope of vividness, he offered little more than a summary.

His attention was being withdrawn from the story by new projects that were under discussion. His firmest friend in the publishing business, George Smith, was still determined to secure the privilege of issuing his work; but experience had convinced him of Thackeray's loyalty to Bradbury & Evans so long as the practice of publication in monthly parts was persisted in. The alternative of writing a whole novel, and bringing it out in volume form, though successful enough with *Esmond*, was alien to Thackeray's methods of work; he needed the stimulus of the monthly deadline, and he needed the steady income. Smith, to be sure, would have been happy to pay in advance, but that arrangement, during the gestation of *Esmond*, had caused Thackeray agonies of conscience.

In February, 1859, Smith proposed an ingenious substitute. He was planning to establish a magazine, and he would pay Thackeray a salary of £350 a month for the exclusive rights to serialize his future novels in it, to issue them thereafter in volume form, and to resell them for American editions and foreign translations. Of subsequent reprint editions, the profits would be shared equally between publisher and author. Thackeray was readily amenable to this relief from all the chaffering that lowered the dignity of the literary vocation.

The next few months were occupied with the search for an editor. Smith adhered to a theory accepted among London publishers—that the success of a popular magazine depended chiefly upon a famous literary personage in the editorial chair. The routine work could be done by subordinates, but a great name must decorate the title page. He offered the position to Thomas Hughes, who had just made his resounding success with *Tom Brown's School Days*; but Hughes had sold his services to another magazine. Not until August did Smith come to the conclusion that the best of all available celebrities was the one whose aid he had already secured. Although he had no confidence in Thackeray's practical abilities, he was aware that many of the prominent authors were still chary of letting their work appear in the vulgar pages of a magazine; Thackeray enjoyed "a great reputation with men of letters as well as with the public, and any writer would be proud to contribute to a periodical under his editorship." In order to "supplement any want of business qualifications" on Thackeray's part, Smith would himself secretly control the editorial policies.

In planning the arrangement, Smith overlooked the complications that might arise if Thackeray considered himself to be actually the responsible director. At intervals throughout his career, Thackeray had been tempted by the idea of editing a periodical. It was therefore not merely the proffered salary of £1000 a year which made him accept Smith's proposal with enthusiasm. The amount of work, indeed, gave him some qualms. He had been planning, as he explained in a letter to Longfellow, to revisit America as soon as he finished *The Virginians*. "I intended to shut up my desk for a year—not write a line—and go on my travels. But . . . I am pressed into the service of this Magazine, and engaged to write ever so much for the next three years. Then, if I last so long, I shall be free of books and publishers."

In August the end of *The Virginians* was in sight, still hampered by illness. Thackeray whiled away one spell in bed by reading the newly-published *Idylls of the King*, and wanted to write to Tennyson at once to thank him for the "splendour of happiness" that he felt; but he was deterred by his inability to write legibly while flat on his back. The girls had gone to the seaside at Folkestone, and he visited them occasionally while struggling with the last chapters. During one of these visits, stimulated by two bottles of the hotel's best claret, he set about his letter of gratitude to Tennyson, and waxed redundantly eloquent as he asserted that "I have had out of that dear book the greatest delight that has ever come to me since I was a young man." The letter was not posted, however, and for a characteristic reason. Just then his arrangements with Smith for the editorship were consummated, and he realized that Tennyson would be one of the first authors to be asked to contribute. Feeling that "to ask a man for a favour, and to praise and bow down before him in the same page, seemed to be like hypocrisy," he put the letter away.

The novel was ended at Folkestone on September 7. "I am surprised I have finished *The Virginians* so well," he told Smith, "and what a load off my mind!" He would have liked to rest and make plans for the magazine, but he knew that his daughters had been looking forward to the usual foreign tour, and he would not disappoint them. Traveling by way of Boulogne, Tours, and Toulouse, they reached the Mediterranean at Genoa, and went on to Milan. The Franco-Austrian war had just been terminated by Louis Napoleon's sudden compromise, and the traces of it were everywhere—wounded French soldiers crawling in the sun at Milan, bullet-scars on the house-fronts and lamp-posts at Magenta. Prices had doubled since the last time Thackeray had been there; but he was rather pleased than otherwise, for he enjoyed the sensation of not having to bother about the size of the bills.

At Como Annie began to show symptoms of illness, and after the next day's journey by coach through the Via Mala she was so unwell that a stop had to be made in the quaint old town of Chur. For the succeeding ten days, Minny devotedly nursed her sister, while their father sought vainly for pastimes in the drowsy little city. He tried to do some writing, but found that he "hadn't the heart." Fortunately the innkeeper subscribed to *The Times*, and Jane Austen's novels were available, which carried Thackeray away into the charming atmosphere of Bath. The unwonted leisure also prompted him to take stock of his worldly position. He calculated that during the past twenty years his total receipts had been thirty-two thousand pounds, of which *Vanity Fair* had provided only two thousand, *The Virginians* six thousand, the lectures nine thousand five hundred. As he had invested some thirteen thousand, he was gratified to realize that his expenditures for the two decades averaged only a thousand a year. "If I can work for three years now," he wrote to his mother, "I shall have put back my patrimony and a little over—after thirty years of ups and downs."

The plans for the magazine were maturing in his mind. His contributions were to include a series of essays, and in the low-beamed sitting-room of the inn he began to write the first one. A name for the magazine also had to be selected. By a coincidence, Chur was the burial place of St Lucius, supposedly a British king of the second century and founder of St Peter's Church, on Cornhill, a few yards from the office where the future magazine was to be published. By further coincidence, Thackeray's first successful book had been named *Cornhill to Cairo*. Out of these facts came the notion of "The Cornhill Magazine," which Thackeray recommended to Smith as having "a sound of jollity and abundance about it."

On returning to London, early in October, he plunged into the details of organization. For an effective cover he applied to his old friend Henry Cole, who was now fostering the South Kensington Art School. One of the students submitted a design, which Thackeray accepted with enthusiasm, impressing upon Smith the necessity of paying the young artist generously.

Then a prospectus had to be issued. One of Smith's innovations was the low price of the magazine—one shilling instead of the half-crown that was customary. Another publisher, as it happened, got hold of the same idea at the same time, and the first number of *Macmillan's Magazine*, also at a shilling, came out in November. Thackeray was rather glad to have the competitor appear first; but the danger that it might monopolize the best authors (as already had happened with regard to Hughes) made him hurry to send out a circular letter. This was carefully phrased to represent him as "Conductor of a Concert," who did not "ask or desire to shine especially myself." He made clear that the magazine was not to be confined to fiction: "we want as much reality as possible—discussion and narrative of events interesting to the public, personal adventure and observation, familiar reports of scientific discovery, descriptions of Social Institutions. . . . There is hardly any subject we *don't* want to hear about, from lettered and instructed men who are competent to speak on it." Thackeray then conveyed to potential contributors certain specific regulations. He wanted "pleasant and instructed gentlemen and ladies to tell what they know, pretty briefly and good-humouredly, and not in a manner obtrusively didactic." Above all, the editorial policy would shun controversy and maintain a high moral tone: "There are points upon which agreement is impossible, and on these we need not touch. . . We shall not set rival politicians by the ears." And "at our social table we shall suppose the ladies and children always present."

As well as this general announcement, Thackeray wrote personally to many friends who might be useful. Both sides of the ocean were put under requisition. Of Longfellow he demanded: "Has Hiawatha ever a spare shaft in his quiver, which he can shoot across the Atlantic?" Motley was also invited, but replied that he could offer "nothing in the light and airy line." Closer to home, Carlyle had an excuse in his labors on *Frederick the Great*: "I am so crushed to death amid Prussian rubbish these long years past, I have nearly lost the power of thinking in any form."

Tennyson, too, was a disappointment, as he had not acceded to Smith's request for a poem. On a visit to London, however, he delighted Thackeray and his daughters by reciting some of Thackeray's verses; and the latter now felt free to send him the withheld letter about the *Idylls*. In reply, Tennyson explained that the only poem he had recently written was already taken by *Macmillan's*. He added, "I am sorry that you have engaged for any quantity of money to let your brains be sucked periodically by Smith, Elder & Co.; not that I don't like Smith, but that so great an artist as you are should go to work after this fashion." Although he declared also that "I dislike publishing in magazines," he relented sufficiently to send his next poem, *Tithonus*, in time for the second number.

As well as the celebrities who would occasionally lend their prestige, Thackeray was aware that he must lean heavily upon the steady producers, the men who wrote for a living. In *Household Words* two years earlier his attention had been attracted by some sketches of London life which were written, as he learned through inquiries at the Garrick and elsewhere, by a young man named John Hollingshead; and when the *Cornhill* roster was being compiled, Hollingshead was remembered and included. A better-known author of the same type of material was G. A. Sala, whose articles in *Household Words* had also won Thackeray's praise. "That paper of his, *The Key of the Street*," he had remarked to Hodder, "is one of the best things I ever read. I couldn't have written it. I wish I could." In spite of Sala's intimacy with Yates, he had remained on good terms with Thackeray, and was asked to contribute.

Yates had recently renewed his offence by publishing (with the connivance of Dickens) a pamphlet containing the whole correspondence over the dispute, accompanied by his unstinted self-justification. The rumors, however, of the high prices to be paid to contributors to *The Cornhill* made him rue his malice. When prosecuting his campaign, he had had no inkling that Thackeray would so soon become a dispenser of handsome commissions. He had the effrontery to submit a poem for the opening number, hoping, as he says in his *Recollections*, that Thackeray "might possibly possess sufficient magnanimity to induce him to regard me with a little indulgence." The poem went back by return post, with a formal rejection written by a clerk.

Thackeray's own share was to include not only the series of essays, under the title of *The Roundabout Papers*, but also a serial. Obliged to begin writing it in the midst of the countless tasks of organization, he was in no mood for vigorous invention, and so he fell back on the plot of his comedy, *The Shorn Lamb*, which had been rejected (and with sufficient reason) by the manager of the Olympic Theater five years before. To make a good novel out of a mediocre play would be a test of any man's genius; and as Thackeray ground out the opening instalment of *Lovel the Widower*, with only the vaguest idea of what its subsequent development might be, he had no illusions about its merit. This fact, probably even more strongly than his announced intention not "to shine especially myself," induced him to bury it modestly in the middle of the magazine, and seek another serial to occupy the leading place.

Luckily a man was available who combined distinction in novel-writing with the dependability of the industrious hack. During the preceding five years Anthony Trollope had produced five novels (including the first three of the *Chronicles of Barset*) and was gaining attention as a sound realist. Thackeray, indeed, who almost always fell asleep over a novel when he tried to read one after dinner, had amazed his daughters the year before, when *The Three Clerks* was new, by coming downstairs wide awake in the middle of the evening and demanding the second volume. Still, he was not personally acquainted with Trollope, whose post-office inspectorship kept him isolated in Ireland, and he had not included him in the preliminary roster of contributors. On hearing of the projected magazine, however, Trollope wrote to offer some short stories, and promptly received a reply from Smith, asking if he would accept a thousand pounds for a serial to begin in the first number of the magazine.

Trollope was amazed at the amount offered—more than twice what he had received for any previous novel; and with his precise habits he was even more amazed at the cool request that the first instalment must be submitted within six weeks. He could not believe that so momentous a venture as the magazine was being organized at such short notice. Though he was in the midst of writing another novel, which was already contracted for, he could not reject the munificent offer.

Two days later it was followed by a personal letter from Thackeray, welcoming him as a contributor, and emphasizing again the intention to include much material that was not fiction. Already Thackeray's personal feelings can be seen influencing his editorial policy. His own boredom with novel-writing echoes in his explanations to Trollope: "You will see whether you can't help us in many ways besides tale-telling. . . You must have tossed a good deal about the world, and have countless sketches in your memory and your portfolio. Please to think if you can furbish up any of these besides a novel . . . one of our chief objects in this magazine is the getting out of novel-spinning, and back into the world. . ."

Trollope made a hasty trip over from Dublin, spent a day in London, and discussed the matter with Smith. Thackeray was not brought into the consultation, but Smith knew definitely what was wanted—a novel of the Barsetshire style, dealing with the clergy. On the journey back to Ireland Trollope made a good start on writing *Framley Parsonage*.

In his plan of encouraging amateurs to write about their special subjects, Thackeray encountered problems such as that recounted by his surgeon friend, Henry Thompson. "Before the *Cornhill* came out, [Thackeray] told me that he intended to develop a new principle—that he thought every man, whatever his profession, might be able to tell something about it which no one else could say. . . 'So,' said he, 'I want you to describe cutting off a leg as a surgical operation, and do it so that a ship's captain at sea, who had not a doctor on board, would be able to take a sailor's leg off by reading your description.' Having heard in a letter from [Thackeray], signed 'Yours in trouble,' that the article was lost, I was very glad to learn by an envelope addressed to me with the following words, 'The leg is found. W. M. T.' that the manuscript had come to light. The article finally appeared with a new title. When [Thackeray] had read it, it struck him that the paper he had asked for might be somewhat painful, so he wrapped it up in something sweet for the British public to take, and called it 'Under Chloroform.' "

To counterbalance his new recruits, Thackeray was happy to include in the first number an "Inauguration Ode" by the earliest and most loyal of his literary friends, Father Prout. From his Parisian attic the little priest sent over a poem full of his characteristic puns and fantastic rhymes. To Thackeray's embarrassment, however, it contained personal compliments to himself. In his opinion, too, some of the literary allusions were not plain enough for general readers. He therefore rewrote several of the stanzas; but with scrupulous honesty he had both versions set up in type and sent the proofs to Prout, with explanations of his changes. The padre then drastically revised the whole ode, keeping some of Thackeray's best lines intact and adapting others as he chose, so that the eventual poem was an amalgam of the work of the two friends.

In spite of countless unexpected difficulties, Thackeray got through the two months of preparation with surprising equanimity. He would pace interminably about his house, wander into a room, sit down for a minute, and then get up and hurry into his study to jot down some new idea. At the office in Cornhill, Smith and his staff were punctilious and thorough; sometimes several notes from them would arrive in one day, suggesting details or reporting fulfilment of the editor's requests.

The result of all the effort was a stupendous success. During the closing days of December, as the first copies were distributed, the orders exceeded all expectation. The printers and binders were kept at work day and night, and the circulation reached the unprecedented total of 120,000 copies. As messengers kept arriving at Onslow Square, with bulletins of the skyrocketing figures, Thackeray became half delirious with joy. Smith was equally delighted, and showed his gratitude for Thackeray's services by immediately doubling the editorial salary.

In spite of his modest disavowals, Thackeray must have been aware that the triumph was due in no small degree to the public trust in himself. He felt justified therefore in disregarding the conventional editorial aloofness and in taking his readers into his confidence. In his *Roundabout Papers*, he had found at last the medium that he enjoyed best—informal essays in which he could gossip about his own tastes and interests and prejudices, without the inconvenience of "plot-spinning." His affinity with Sterne was plainly revealed in the digressive, chatty papers, with their harmless cynicism and their unashamed bursts of sentiment.

The second one, written on January 9, gave him an opportunity to exemplify his theory of professional courtesy. Within the preceding six weeks two great literary figures had died—Washington Irving and Lord Macaulay. In an essay entitled "Nil Nisi Bonum" Thackeray paid high tribute to them, with emphasis upon the dignity that they had imparted to the literary calling. With regard to Macaulay, perhaps he had been moved by the information that when the historian was found dead in his chair, a copy of *The Cornhill* was in front of him, open at the first page of *Lovel the Widower*. Another implication of the essay, however, is suggested by his comment to his American friend, Sam Ward, who was visiting him the day it was written. "The idea and comfort," Thackeray exclaimed, "of having to write the obituary of two authors whom no hat was handed around to bury or to provide for their families!"

As a method of establishing the character of the new magazine, Thackeray and Smith adopted the *Punch* custom of assembling the contributing staff at dinners. The first one, given in January, brought to Smith's house chiefly the "rank and file" professionals who had already made their mark, such as Sala, Hollingshead, Robert Bell, William Howard Russell, George Henry Lewes, John Oxenford, and special friends of Thackeray's, including Sir Charles Taylor and "Jacob Omnium." As Thackeray entered the room he looked over the party with a quizzical eye. "I see," he remarked, "there are only a certain number of regular cabs on the stand, and whether they are bad or good, rickety or otherwise, we must make the best of them."

One unfamiliar face, however, was in the gathering. Anthony Trollope had persuaded the Post Office to transfer him to an English district, and he had taken a house near London, in order to enjoy fraternizing at last with his fellow authors. The *Cornhill* dinner was his first opportunity to see some of these future friends. Devoutly admiring Thackeray's novels, and encouraged by the cordiality of his letter, Trollope was especially eager to meet him; but when Smith performed the introduction Thackeray uttered a frigid "How do?" and turned on his heel. In angry humiliation, Trollope declared he would never speak to Thackeray again, but Smith succeeded in mollifying him by explaining—as Thackeray's friends now had to do so often—that when one of his spasms of pain occurred, he could not look pleasant or converse agreeably. With his high anticipations thus dashed, Trollope went home from the dinner disgruntled, and the next day he told one or two anecdotes about it to a friend, in the hearing of a third party. He was too new to literary society to realize the indiscretion of retailing private occurrences within reach of jealous ears. The bystander was Edmund Yates.

Thackeray, meanwhile, had discovered another of the drawbacks of editorship. Unsolicited manuscripts poured in upon him, and he felt a personal obligation toward all of them. They arrived not only at the publisher's office, but at the editor's house, "to which," as he lamented, "in spite of prayers, entreaties, commands and threats, authors, and ladies especially," addressed their communications. Even this he might have endured, but when they began to call at Onslow Square, asking questions about their manuscripts, and even requesting him to revise any passages he considered inferior, he had no recourse but to pack a portmanteau and flee to Paris. On the channel steamer he had a pleasant chat with Edward Lear, and proudly presented that laureate of nonsense with a copy of the magazine.

His Boston friend Fields, who happened to be sojourning in Paris, was summoned to his hotel, and found him "wild with exultation and full of enthusiasm for excellent George Smith." "London is not big enough to contain me now," he exclaimed, in that boyish style of burlesque that he always seemed to assume toward Fields; "I am obliged to add Paris to my residence. Great heavens!" he went on, throwing up his long arms, "where will this tremendous circulation stop? Who knows but that I shall have to add Vienna and Rome to my whereabouts? If the worst comes to the worst, New York also may fall into my clutches, and only the Rocky Mountains may be able to stop my progress!"

In mock fury he elaborated to Fields the persecution he had suffered from would-be contributors, particularly "the fair," as he called them. "The darlings demanded," he said, "that I should rewrite, if I couldn't understand their damned nonsense, and put their halting lines into proper form. I was so appalled, when they set upon me with their 'ipics and their ipecacs,' that you might have knocked me down with a feather, sir."

Fields describes these days in Paris as "simply tremendous. We dined at all possible and impossible places together. We walked round and round the glittering court of the Palais Royal, gazing in at the windows of the jewellers' shops, and all my efforts were necessary to restrain him from rushing in and ordering a pocketful of diamonds and 'other trifles,' as he called them; 'for,' said he, 'how can I spend the princely income which Smith allows me for editing the *Cornhill*, unless I begin instantly somewhere?' If he saw a group of three or four persons talking together in an excited way, he would whisper to me with immense gesticulation: 'There, there, you see the news has reached Paris, and perhaps the number has gone up since my last accounts from London.' His spirits during those few days were colossal, and he told me that he found it impossible to sleep, 'for counting up his subscribers.' "

This almost hysterical jubilation revealed much more than merely his satisfaction with an enlarged income. It marked the release from a deep inward shame that had gnawed him for twenty years. At last he had made a resounding success, and in the very same sphere in which he had lost the bulk of his patrimony. His other famous achievements during the twenty years, such as *Vanity Fair* and the lectures, had evolved slowly, and had been intermingled with disappointments and unhappiness; but the triumph of *The Cornhill* was immediate and unqualified—his vindication as a man of practical affairs. At a reception at Lord Palmerston's he announced to the Prime Minister, with mock solemnity, "My Lord, I too am now a power in the state."

His old friends, though happy in his success, were not carried away with admiration of the magazine. In February FitzGerald remarked: "Thackeray's first number was famous, I thought; his own little *Roundabout Paper* so pleasant; but the Second Number, I say, lets the Cockney in already: about Hogarth: Lewes is vulgar; and I don't think one can care much for Thackeray's Novel. He is always talking so of himself, too."

Aware of this sort of comment, Thackeray opened the third of the *Roundabout Papers* with a defense of his propensity:

Montaigne and "Howel's Letters" are my bedside books. If I wake at night, I have one or other of them to prattle me to sleep again. They talk about themselves for ever, and don't weary me . . . I read them in the dozy hours, and only half remember them . . . I hope I shall always like to hear men, in reason, talk about themselves. What subject does a man know better? . . .

And he went on to announce that the *Roundabout Papers* would continue to be openly egotistical. In *Lovel the Widower*, however, the digressiveness was already beginning to bore him: lacking an adequate plot, he had fallen back on his old device of a semi-fictitious narrator, who had but a small part in the action and yet kept himself interminably in the foreground.

The personal element in the magazine just then began to extend itself still further. Annie Thackeray, now almost twenty-three, was emboldened to revert to the literary ambitions of her childhood. On a subject suggested by her father, she wrote an essay to which he gave the title "Little Scholars," and which, he said, "moistened my paternal spectacles." He first thought of sending it to *Blackwood's Magazine*, but then began to ask himself, "Why should *Cornhill* lose such a sweet paper because it was my dear girl who wrote it?" His conscience warned him that he might not be an impartial judge; and so, after correcting the spelling and punctuation, he sent it to Smith with the request that he should accept or reject it. When it appeared in the May number, Thackeray was quite as overjoyed as his daughter.

The Carmichael-Smyths had once more been brought back from Paris and were established in Brompton Crescent, near enough for a daily visit from their son. More ambitious domestic schemes, however, were stirring in his mind, as he began to comprehend the vastitude of his new income. Ever since the *Esmond* days he had cherished his dream of owning one of the old houses in Kensington, and in March he bought one in Palace Green. His intention was to have it modernized to suit him, but after examining it the builders told him that it was in such a tumble-down condition that it could not stand any alteration. Regretfully he admitted that convenience was more important than tradition, and arrangements were made to have it demolished, with the stipulation that the new one must be in genuine Queen Anne style.

Activity and success had a good effect on both health and spirits. His letters became rhapsodic. "We've got two horses in our carriage now," he boasted to one old friend. "The Magazine goes on increasing, and how much do you think my next twelve months' earnings and receipts will be if I work? £10,000. Cockadoodle-oodloodle."

He could not expect, of course, to be wholly free of annoyances. In the June number his Roundabout Paper was a jubilant recital of the half-year's success; but the next month's was one entitled "Thorns in the Cushion," which revealed some of the woes of editorship.

Probably the fabulous success of *The Cornhill* and its lavish scale of payment had attracted more than the usual variety of would-be contributors; but a more experienced editor would have sent back the torrent of unsolicited manuscripts without a qualm. Thackeray, however, could not help imagining the feelings of the hopeful volunteers. He may not have read all the manuscripts very thoroughly, but he could not ignore the letters that came with them. Several still arrived every day at his private house, and when he got home at night he would feel so unequal to facing them that he would take them up to his room and open them the next morning. Some began with fulsome flattery of Thackeray's books, and these he consigned to the waste-paper basket. But many appealed to his sympathy with pitiful tales of poverty and disappointment, which would lead him to read the contribution "with the thousandth part of a faint hope that it may be suitable," always to find it utterly worthless. "Not a day passes," he declared, "but that argument *ad miseri-cordiam* is used. Day and night that sad voice is crying out for help. Thrice it appealed to me yesterday. Twice this morning it cried to me; and I have no doubt when I go to get my hat, I shall find it with its piteous face and its pale family about it, waiting for me in the hall." He did not mention in the essay the further fact that his rejection of such manuscripts was regularly softened by the enclosure of a banknote. As Smith remarked, "Thackeray was far too tender-hearted to be happy as an editor."

Another cause of discomfort was the fact that as editor he received the complaints about his own contributions. In the same essay he quoted two letters from actors in Dublin, violently attacking *Lovel the Widower* for libeling their profession by depicting a ballet dancer as a woman of easy virtue. Although he dismissed these with the obvious rebuttal that an individual character did not represent a group, his own dissatisfaction with the story had grown so strong that he brought it to an abupt end in the sixth instalment. To continue to fulfil his contract with Smith, he had to fall back on *The Four Georges*, which had not previously been printed in England.

Another petty vexation was aired in the next month's issue. An article on *The Cornhill* had been written by Yates for the American paper which had always been ill disposed toward Thackeray—the New York *Herald*. Yates asserted that the magazine "shows symptoms of being on the wane" in circulation, as he "should think forty thousand was now about the mark." He accused Thackeray of having touched up a contributor's article, and quoted him as saying to a writer who acknowledged the authorship of an anonymous contribution, "Ah, I thought I recognized your *hoof* in it." Proceeding to the dinners, he gave a malicious version of the unguarded remarks of Trollope. At the dinners, Yates declared, Thackeray "is the great gun, and comes out with all the geniality in his power," but nevertheless they were "tremendously heavy;" and to justify his description of Smith as "a very good man, but totally unread," he told an anecdote about his missing the point of a literary allusion in Thackeray's conversation.

This tissue of falsehoods being reprinted in the *Saturday Review*, Thackeray felt obliged to refute it. A Roundabout paper "On Screens in Dining-rooms" gave him some trouble; he lay awake most of a night before he found "a climax dignified and humorous enough" to make probable that "our friend won't sin again." Without naming Yates, the essay excoriated him with such quiet contempt that Thackeray was able to tell an American friend the next month that "in consequence of this last business even Dickens has cut him." In this opinion the wish was father to the thought: Dickens and Yates remained friends, but their intimacy was certainly not so close in later years as it had been. Trollope, meanwhile, having accused Yates of the treachery and obtained an apology, went to Thackeray and Smith with a confession of his own unwitting part in it, and was freely pardoned. But no more contributors' dinners were held.

For a summer holiday the Thackeray family went to Tunbridge Wells, where they took quarters in an old house—the grandparents on the ground floor and the others upstairs. Looking across the Common from his desk, or strolling to the Pantiles, Thackeray was reminded so vividly of his boyhood visits that he wrote two Roundabout papers of reminiscences of his schooldays. A little later, when he took his daughters on a jaunt to Belgium and Holland, he not only gloried in the fact that "nobody knows where we are, and we defy care and the postman," but also wove his fragmentary observations of Calais and Antwerp and Rotterdam and the Hague into a profitable essay for the series. Then after eight delightful days an urgent letter overtook him at Amsterdam with news that his stepfather had suffered a paralytic attack, and the tour was abruptly ended.

The routine of his task and the protests of troublesome contributors gradually exhausted the fund of enthusiasm that had been engendered in him by his new ca-reer and the magazine's triumph. By the autumn he was relapsing occasionally into a morbid mood, as a significant little occurrence shows.

A biography of Tom Hood had just been published by his son and daughter, a particularly feeble example of the filial memorial—badly written, inaccurate, and fulsomely sentimental. Recalling his own glimpses of the wry, valiant humorist, Thackeray read the book with growing disgust. He was lying on the truckle-bed in his study, and Annie was writing near the window, to catch the fading light of the autumn afternoon. It suddenly occurred to him that she would be subjected to tremendous pressure to be his biographer. With her literary skill, of course, she would do a much better job of it than most of the descendants who embalmed fa-mous men in print; but still she would be hampered by personal attitudes toward him, and by all sorts of considerations of friendship, discretion, and partiality. Turning on his side to gaze at her, he shut the book with a bang. Annie looked at him in surprise. He tapped the cover with his finger. "Let there be nothing of this when I am gone," he said, and dropped the volume scornfully on the floor.

CHAPTER 23

Thorns in the Cushion

THACKERAY'S GREATEST editorial worry was the realization that he was making enemies. He wrote courteous letters to unsuccessful contributors in the hope of softening the blow; but instead they were apt to blame him personally for their disappointment, rather than dissipating their grievance over the vague area of a nameless "editorial staff." In his annoyance over one incident, he poured out his complaint to his colleague, James Payn. A young man had submitted a long story, for which he begged for consideration from "the greatest of novelists," with the plea that he was the sole support of an invalid sister. Thackeray not only sent a donation from his own pocket, but wrote a letter of advice. "I feel for your position," he said, in effect, "and appreciate your motive for exertion; but I must tell you at once that you will never do anything in literature. Your contribution is worthless in every way, and it is the truest kindness, both to her for whom you are working and for yourself, to tell you so outright. Turn your mind at once to some other industry."

In reply came a letter of offensive abuse, informing Thackeray that though he had risen by good luck "to the top of the tree, he would one day find himself where he deserved to be, at the bottom of it." Payn, whose hide had been toughened by some years as editor of *Chambers' Journal*, could not repress a burst of laughter when he read it. "For my part," remarked Thackeray crossly, "I see little to laugh at. What a stupid, ungrateful beast the man must be! and if ever I waste another half hour again in writing to a creature of that sort, 'call me horse'—or worse."

Anecdotes of such mischances were circulated gleefully by his literary friends, whose sympathy was perhaps mingled with some degree of mischievous satisfaction. According to one tale, he earned the undying hatred of Alfred Austin by mistaking the egotistical young poet's letter about "unmerited neglect" for one of the usual appeals of indigence, and sending him half-a-crown. "Ah me!" sighed Thackeray, at the end of *Thorns in the Cushion*, "we wound where we never intended to strike; we create anger where we never meant harm. Out of mere malignity, I suppose, there is no man who would like to make enemies. But here, in this editorial business, you can't do otherwise."

The task of reading all the manuscripts was far beyond his power. Most of those that arrived at the publisher's office were accepted or rejected by Smith and his readers. The ones that reached Thackeray were apt to be handed on to his daughters or his rather muddle-headed amanuensis, Samuel Langley. Grateful for

Smith's generosity, Thackeray never disputed his decisions, and Smith for his part was punctilious in discussing all matters of policy. At Thackeray's suggestion, these consultations usually took the form of a dinner at Greenwich, with his Garrick Club crony, Sir Charles Taylor, often accompanying them, as a guarantee against too much dull shop talk.

His next serial story could not be too long delayed, and yet he still shrank from the ordeal of creating a new plot and group of characters, and planning a novel on the grand scale. He therefore fell back once more upon material that he had on hand. His first serious attempt at realistic fiction, exactly twenty years before, had been *A Shabby Genteel Story*, which was cut short after four instalments by his family catastrophe. When it was reprinted in the collected "Miscellanies," in 1857, he explained in a preface that "it was my intention to complete the little story," and he outlined in a few words how it was to develop to "a melancholy ending;" but he added that "the colours are long since dry. . . . It is best to leave the sketch, as it was when first designed."

Against this dismissal, however, his inner being rebelled. He retained a lingering fondness for the characters he had begun to create, and the wish to resume their history persisted in his mind with something of the same determination to vindicate himself that had driven him to restore the whole sum of his patrimony. Even the association of the story with his personal tragedy seemed to intensify its hold upon him. In November, therefore, he began to write *The Adventures of Philip on his Way Through the World*, bringing back to life Mr Brandon, his deserted wife, and her father, but adding new characters and more varied scenes, with Arthur Pendennis in the background, and an assortment of other incidental characters, revived not only from *Pendennis* but from *The Newcomes* and even from his early novelette, *The Ravenswing*. "I should like to make Mr Pendennis the author of my story," he remarked, "and let him walk through it. He can talk more freely than Mr Thackeray."

Not only in these affiliations was the book a retrospect of its author's career. Almost more intimately autobiographical than *Pendennis*, it followed the pattern of Thackeray's early life through Charterhouse, a lawyer's office, the inheritance and loss of a fortune. Philip turns to journalism, puts in a spell as Paris correspondent for a London newspaper, writes articles on foreign literature for the *European Review*, contributes a weekly letter to a snobbish New York journal and is not paid according to contract. His marriage exactly parallels Thackeray's, in its financial details, in the youthful devotion of the bride and the calculating schemes of her mother. "Philip is unfortunately going into Poverty and Struggle," the author explained to his publisher, "but this can't be helped, and as he will—*entre nous* —take pretty much the carreer of W. M. T. in the first years of his ruin and absurdly imprudent marriage, at least the portrait will be faithful."

The character of Philip, too, was essentially Thackeray's; the mask of fiction permitted a frankness of self-portraiture such as few autobiographies have contained:

> He had a childish sensibility for what was tender, helpless, pretty, or pathetic; and a mighty scorn of imposture, wherever he found it. He had many good purposes, which were often very vacillating, and were but seldom performed. He had a vast number of evil habits, whereof, you know, idleness is said to be the root. Many of these evil propensities he coaxed and cuddled with much care; and though he roared out *peccavi* most frankly when charged with his sins, this criminal would fall to peccation very soon after promising amendment. What he liked he would have. What he disliked he could with the greatest difficulty be forced to do. He liked good dinners, good wine, good horses, good clothes, and late hours; and in all these comforts of life (or any others which he fancied, or which were within his means) he indulged himself with perfect freedom. He hated hypocrisy on his own part, and hypocrites in general. He said everything that came into his mind about things and people; and, of course, was often wrong and often prejudiced, and often occasioned howls of indignation or malignant whispers of hatred by his free speaking.

The adherence to his own life story arose from two causes. As illness and boredom molded his current days more and more harshly into the shape of premature old age, his only real happiness lay in letting his memory linger with fond irony over the times when he was young and buoyant. And as his imagination balked from the task of creating plot, he fell back upon the one story which he knew in such profuse detail that repeated utilization had not yet quite exhausted it.

The faults of the novel arose from the same source. Its lack of integrated structure was disguised by a tissue of discursive comment. Repetition and trivial detail clogged its movement, with only an occasional dramatic scene to cut through the sluggish flow. Having found a congenial vehicle in the familiar essay that he wrote every month, Thackeray allowed the same techniques to control his work of fiction. In previous novels the author's musings had been kept subordinate to the narrative, but in *Philip* they too often seemed to be predominant.

Before the first instalment of *Philip* appeared in *The Cornhill*, the problem of illustrations recurred. Thackeray intended to make them himself, but his hand was losing the knack of drawing on wood, and so he sketched the first two or three on paper, leaving the reproduction to be done by some employee of the engraver. The results were not at all to his satisfaction, but neither he nor Smith could decide on an alternative. One day Smith happened to be passing through his outer office when the clerk was dismissing a shy-looking lad who had asked for an opportunity to draw for the magazine. On an impulse Smith inquired his name, which was Frederick Walker, and told him to bring some specimens of his work. These gave Smith the idea that the young fellow might be equal to the task of redrawing Thackeray's sketches. Walker, who was only twenty, was so terrified by the proposal that Smith could not make out whether he accepted or rejected it; but he reported the interview to Thackeray, who said breezily, "Bring him here, and we'll soon see whether he can draw."

In the cab, on the way to Onslow Square, Walker was so scared that he did not utter a word, and when they arrived Thackeray at once diagnosed his state of mind. He was never happier than when giving encouragement to young writers and artists. The memory of his own early rebuffs and exploitation made him understand their anxieties, and the pleasure of being able to dispense patronage emphasized his present prosperity. After a few kindly remarks, to set Walker at his ease, Thackeray asked, "Can you draw? Mr Smith says you can."

"Y-y-yes," stammered the artist, "I think so." It was obvious that in his state of agitation he could scarcely hold a pencil.

"Well, I'm going to shave. Would you mind drawing my back?" Thackeray turned to his toilet table and started to lather his face; Smith, taking the cue, strolled to the window and looked out into the square; and Walker was soon so absorbed in the work that he forgot his nervousness and produced a lively sketch. He was promptly engaged for the work of transferring Thackeray's drawings to the wood blocks, with such changes as he might deem necessary.

All through the year Thackeray had been looking forward to seeing the Baxters, who had announced their intention of visiting England; but the disturbed state of American politics interfered with their plans, and at Christmas came news of South Carolina's secession, and the immediate prospect of civil war. Sally Hampton, in Charleston, would be in the very center of the storm, and as Thackeray raised his eyes to a colored print of "The Belle of the West," which he had hung up in his room because it looked so like her, he could imagine her parents' distress.

During the Christmas holidays his house was full of children, and he took noisy parties of them to two pantomimes and to another favorite amusement of his—the Zoo. No matter how depressed he might feel, the strong surviving boyishness in his nature would always assume control of him when he visited these paradises of childhood.

His generosity to youngsters was notorious. He couldn't talk to a schoolboy without tipping him a sovereign, and his smaller change was constantly trickling away to poor children in the streets. Katie Dickens, always the favorite of the Thackerays among the Dickens brood, never forgot an afternoon when she watched him as he strolled along Portland Place, she being at a friend's drawing-room window. A group of ragamuffins were playing in the gutter. "Just watch," said Miss Dickens, "and see if he doesn't give them something." When he noticed the children he halted, put his fingers in his waistcoat pocket, stooped down to their level for a little conversation, and handed each a coin before walking on.

WALKER'S SKETCH OF THACKERAY'S BACK

With poor literary men he behaved similarly, but on a larger scale. London was full of anecdotes about the devices he invented for conveying ten-pound notes without humiliating the recipients. One much-quoted tale described him seeking out an old friend who had fallen upon hard times, climbing to his garret, administering a firm lecture on his past extravagances, and then hastening away. "I was very angry," the victim reported to his cronies, with tears in his eyes, "because he said I had been a reckless old goose—and then a hundred-pound note falls out of my writing book. I never saw him put it there. God bless him!"

In other respects, too, he had become a legendary figure among his colleagues. The Fleet Street journalists of the Sala school, glorying in their dissipations, adopted him as their patron saint, and colored their image of him with their own tints. John Cordy Jeaffreson, for instance, seems to have admired him chiefly for his indulgences in eating and drinking. One day he retailed to Thackeray an anecdote that he had heard from a barrister of Lincoln's Inn. This man, who knew Thackeray by sight, repeatedly met him walking eastward along Holborn, just at the hour when the lawyers were leaving the Inns of Court. At last the barrister became so curious that he followed Thackeray and saw him go into the Gray's Inn Coffee House, sit down at a table all alone, and order a dinner.

Thackeray chuckled on hearing the story. "Ah!" he said, "that was when I was drinking the last of that wonderful bin of port. It *was* rare wine! There were only two dozen bottles and a few bottles over, when I came upon the remains of that bin, and I forthwith bargained with mine host to keep them for me. I drank every bottle and every drop of that remainder by myself. I shared never a bottle with living man; and so long as the wine lasted, I slipped off to the Gray's Inn Coffee House with all possible secrecy short of disguise, whenever I thought a dinner and a bottle by myself would do me good."

The frequenters of the Reform Club loved to tell about the day when he dropped into the coffee-room and noticed that the evening's menu included "beans and bacon." He was engaged to dine at some great house, but he sent a note of regret to his host, explaining that he had just met an old friend whom he had not seen for years, and he could not tear himself away. Then he sought out a table in a quiet corner of the coffee-room and settled down to beans and bacon in blissful solitude.

His intemperance in diet was observed with some dismay by his American friend John Bigelow. Whenever Bigelow came over to London from his post in Paris as United States Consul, he enjoyed Thackeray's hospitality. In March, 1860, he was a guest at a large dinner party in Onslow Square. "Thackeray was suffering with chills and fever," he noted. "He drank a great deal, as it seemed to me, and garnished his food with red pepper and curry to excess, for the purpose, as he said, of staving off or drawing off the chills. He succeeded in bringing on a profuse perspiration about eleven o'clock."

In conversations with Jeaffreson he was frank about his weaknesses. "At a big dinner I behave like a child," he confessed, "like a schoolboy at a Christmas feast, eating everything that is offered to me, everything that comes in my way. The Season plays the devil with me, because I dine out a good deal, and I am in no sense my own master at any dinner table but my own, and even at my own table I can't control my wicked appetite when I am entertaining a lot of people. I can be admirably prudent so long as there is no need for prudence; but with the first glass of champagne away goes my prudence, and I must have something of whatever is going."

"You must have drunk a good deal in your time," Jeaffreson prompted.

"Enough to float a seventy-four gun ship," was the jovial reply. "Since I came out of my poverty, a bottle has been my daily minimum, and on three out of four days I have taken a second bottle. I may be called a two-bottle man; and that takes no account of the two or three glasses of wine at midday, nor of the punches and grogs in the hours about midnight."

The admiring Jeaffreson was careful to testify, however, that "though I have repeatedly seen him take in a few hours four and even six times as much alcohol as any one of his doctors would have authorized him to take in an entire day, I never saw him under the influence of the 'glass too much.' "

These gentry vied in circulating his gamy smoking-room anecdotes and probably attributed to him many more than he uttered. They voiced knowing innuendoes about sexual adventures, which they connected with the assertion that his consultations with Dr Thomson were not concerned with his acknowledged stomach-spasms but with a still more painful disease—stricture of the urethra. As Thackeray chatted with these colleagues at his clubs, and basked in the manifest adulation they displayed, he would have been infuriated if he could have overheard their gossip about him. Favorable though it was meant to be, it would have seared his reticent pride far more agonizingly than Yates's prattle that he had so savagely avenged.

During the early months of 1861 he plodded through *Philip* with all his customary discomfort. The characters of the story haunted his conscience. "They have interrupted my rest," he grumbled; "they have plagued me at all sorts of minutes; they have thrust themselves upon me when I was ill, or wished to be idle, and I have growled out a 'Be hanged to you, can't you leave me alone now?' Once or twice they have prevented my going out to dinner. Many and many a time they have prevented my coming home, because I knew they were there waiting in the study, and a plague take them, and I have left home and family, and gone to dine at the Club, and told nobody where I went."

Sometimes he sought stimulus by breaking his routine. His friend Elwin was astonished to hear him announce that he was going to "go over to Greenwich and write a bit of *Philip*." In explanation he added, "I can't write comfortably in my own room; I do most of my composition at hotels or at a club. There's an excitement at public places that sets my brains working."

Luckily the arrangement with Walker relieved him of anxiety about the illustrations; and before long the young artist plucked up courage to ask for greater freedom, suggesting that he might make better pictures if he could design them for himself. Thackeray willingly fell into the habit of merely suggesting the scenes to be depicted; and thereafter the traces of Thackeray's stiff, old-fashioned drawing gave place to a lighter touch that was Walker's own.

Editorial troubles continued. In his determination to keep the magazine in favor with refined Victorian households, he was constantly on guard against impropriety or vulgarity. His own relish for robust tales made him all the more particular in avoiding any possible shadow of offence. Though he had often protested sarcastically in his novels against the taboos of his era, he had no intention of endangering the sales of *The Cornhill* by using its pages for the campaign.

One of his most difficult problems occurred when Mrs Browning sent him her poem, *Lord Walter's Wife*. Not only were the Brownings his well-loved friends, but Mrs Browning was the favorite poet of that same genteel British public whose moral dogmas he was trying so hard to obey. And yet this poem contained "an account of unlawful passion felt by a man for a woman." After holding the poem for months, feeling—as he said—like a man who must have a tooth out but dreads to face the dentist, he sent it back to her with a long letter of apology, praising the poem for its "pure doctrine, and real modesty, and pure ethics," and praising its author as "one of the best wives, mothers, women in the world," but explaining that some of his "squeamish public" would be sure to "make an outcry" if it were published. Mrs Browning replied with a good-humored defence of her plain speaking, and sent him an irreproachable poem, *The North and the South*, inspired by a visit from Hans Christian Andersen.

For an identical reason he tried to reject a story by Trollope, not knowing that it had already been commissioned by Smith. Trollope charitably held the opinion that Thackeray had not read the manuscript and had been influenced by the report of "some moral deputy;" but as his attitude was exactly the same toward the poem by Mrs Browning, it must be recognized as his considered editorial policy. Trollope being by this time an intimate friend and devoted admirer, his account of the affair is revealing: "*Virginibus puerisque!* That was the gist of his objection. There was a project in a gentleman's mind—as told in my story—to run away with a married woman! Thackeray's letter was very kind, very regretful—full of apology for such treatment to such a contributor. But—*Virginibus puerisque! . . .* That Thackeray had suffered when he wrote it was plain to see, fearing that he was giving pain to one he would fain have pleased. I wrote him a long letter in return, as full of drollery as I knew how to make it. In four or five days there came a reply in the same spirit—boiling over with fun. He had kept my letter by him, not daring to open it. At last he had given it to one of his girls to examine—to see whether I had turned upon him with reproaches."

For a different reason he got into trouble over the series of essays called *Unto this Last*, in which John Ruskin began to set forth his revolutionary ideas of political science. The magazine had already published a harmless essay by Ruskin on Holbein and Reynolds, and so the new contribution was accepted without hesitation; but after three of the papers had appeared the editor wrote to say that such a furore of protest had been aroused that the series must be brought to an end in the next essay. It was the first time Ruskin had encountered defeat, and for many months he "sulked," as he called it, though he remained personally on good terms with Thackeray.

2 PALACE GREEN, KENSINGTON.
DRAWING BY EYRE CROWE

More satisfactory than either editing or novel-writing was the progress of the new house in Kensington Palace Green, which was growing into the mellow reconstruction of a Queen Anne mansion that he had planned. He did not stint expense, and some of his relations became disgusted with its pretentiousness. One of them, who had never been known to utter a joke, said to him grimly, "You ought to call it Vanity Fair." It had become for Thackeray not only a symbol of his long-delayed prosperity but a promise of the life of leisure when he would be released from grinding out novels and could devote himself to the history of the eighteenth century, which he had projected for so long. After the death of Macaulay, Smith had suggested his continuing that author's *History of England* through the reign of Queen Anne, on the same opulent scale. The proposal was exactly in accord with his own desires; but he knew he could not yet afford to give up the profits of fiction. Meanwhile, he seemed to have taken a positive step toward it by ignoring the drab pseudo-gothic architecture of the day and creating from glowing brick what he gleefully called "the reddest house in all the town."

He admitted that six thousand pounds was a heavy outlay, but justified himself by the fact that somebody had already offered to buy it for a thousand pounds more than he was spending. Besides, if the worst came to the worst, he could let the new house, and live on the income "almost without writing." But he was sure that once he was installed in the room with an arched window looking out on the noble elms of Kensington Gardens, he would write the life of Queen Anne and establish his true and proper niche in English literature.

Long before the house was finished, he was proudly displaying it to his friends. The Rev. Whitwell Elwin was invited to make a special trip from Norfolk to inspect it; and when John Blackwood was in London in June he reported that "it was pleasant to see old Thack, as delighted as a child, showing me all over it." Thackeray took him to dinner the next day at the Blue Posts, "where he seemed a sort of king, and we got a dinner and wines such as I never saw in the house before."

On September 9 Major Carmichael-Smyth died, at the age of eighty-one. His widow gave up the house in Brompton Crescent and nominally became once again a part of her son's household, though for many months she wandered back and forth between England and Paris, finding satisfaction nowhere.

No domestic changes had any effect upon the habits of living that had grown upon Thackeray for so long. More at his ease in clubs and taverns than anywhere else, he now became active in a congenial circle known as "Our Club", the last metamorphosis of a series of informal literary clubs that had revolved for years around Douglas Jerrold. As long as Jerrold lived, Thackeray had held aloof, knowing that their rather thorny friendship could best be maintained by not seeing too much of each other; but after Jerrold's death Thackeray drifted into Our Club and felt much at home there. Its dinners were held on an upper floor of Clunn's Hotel, in Covent Garden, next door to Evans's, his favorite haunt for so many years. The secretary of the Club was a grotesque character, Frederick William Hamstede, a hunchback dwarf who had retired from a city clerkship with a tiny pension and devoted his whole life to writing execrable poetry and managing the business affairs of Our Club. Attaching himself to Thackeray, Hamstede insisted on sending him reams of his verse, and Thackeray responded with an affection that astonished his friends. However gruff he might sometimes be when his spasms of pain were upon him, he was never anything but gentle and protective toward his "dear little Hamstede." At the Club dinners he was often bored by the speeches and would grumble that they were "insufferable," but Hamstede could always persuade him to come again.

He ended the year 1861 in gloomy spirits. From India came news of the death of Sir Richmond Shakespear, the cousin who had made the long voyage home with him when they were both six years old, and had shared the torments of the little school in Southampton. This led his mind to dwell upon the growing certainty of his own approaching end. It was a dozen years, now, since the first warning, and the symptoms were growing graver. John Skelton, a *Cornhill* contributor, urged him to consult James Syme, the great Scottish surgeon, who had perfected a new operation for stricture of the urethra. "I know Syme's method and high reputation," Thackeray replied, but he confessed that he shrank from the knife, however deftly handled. "We shall see," he temporized.

Another cause of concern was the war in America. The *Trent* incident in November, when the two Confederate commissioners were abducted from a British vessel, had convinced Thackeray that war between England and the Northern States was inevitable. English lads who were his friends were in the regiments hastily despatched to Canada. At a Christmas pantomime he found himself seated beside an American acquaintance, and the two agreed lugubriously that the Union government would not compromise on the *Trent* crisis. The American went on to mention that one of Thackeray's friends, his host on both of his visits, was a prisoner at Fort Warren, and in danger of execution. Thackeray sat through the pantomime with scarcely a notion of what was happening on the stage.

Early in January came news that Mason and Slidell had been freed, and Thackeray praised the Union government for "the most courageous act of the war." But at the same time he was infuriated by an editorial in the New York *Herald*, which declared:

> England cannot afford to go to war with us, for six hundred millions' worth of American stock is owned by British subjects, which, in event of hostilities, would be confiscated; and we now call upon the Companies not to take it off their hands on any terms. Let its forfeiture be held over England as a weapon *in terrorem* . . . Will England incur this tremendous loss for a mere abstraction?

Remembering his personal affronts from the *Herald*, and already disturbed because some of the railroads were omitting their dividends—that glittering eight per cent for which his American earnings had been invested—he wrote a bitter *Roundabout Paper* for the February magazine, "On Half a Loaf," defending the honor of his country against such a mercenary imputation. And to show that the protest was no mere gesture, he sold out his American stocks.

It was not long before he regretted his impetuosity. Three months later Bayard Taylor arrived in England and called on Thackeray in some trepidation, not sure whether an American would be welcomed. He was received with all the old affection, and Thackeray took the earliest opportunity of leading the conversation toward the controversial article.

"Why did you write it?" asked Taylor.

"I was unwell," was the answer. "You know what the moral effects of my attacks are, and I was indignant that such a shameful proposition should be made in your American newspapers, and not a single voice be raised to rebuke it."

"But you certainly know," protested Taylor, "that the *Herald* does not represent American opinion. I assure you that no honest, respectable man in the United States ever entertained the idea of cheating an English stockholder."

"I should hope so too," Thackeray replied; "but when I saw the same thing in the New York *Times*, which, you will admit, is a paper of character and influence, I lost all confidence. I know how impulsive and excitable your people are, and I really feared that some such measure might be madly advocated and carried into effect. I see now that I made a blunder, and I am already punished for it. I was getting eight per cent from my American investments, and now that I have the capital here it is lying idle. I'll probably not be able to invest it at a better rate than four per cent."

As a tacit admission of his repentance, he did not allow this essay to be included in a volume of the *Roundabout Papers* that was issued the next year.

That angry protest had been one of his last contributions to *The Cornhill* in the rôle of editor. Friends had been urging him to give up the irksome responsibility, but he had hesitated for several reasons—his sense of obligation to Smith, his pride in the success of the magazine, and not least the two thousand a year. When the new house was complete, however, he asked for his release, although it was still nine months short of the three years which he had originally stipulated as his servitude. His announcement of the resignation, which came out in the April number, reiterated his half-ludicrous despair over the contributors who had so pestered him. "I believe," he said, "my own special readers will agree that my books will not suffer when their author is released from the daily task of reading, accepting, refusing, losing and finding the works of other people. To say No has often cost me a morning's peace and a day's work. Oh, those hours of madness spent in searching for Louisa's lost lines to her dead Piping Bulfinch, for Nhoj Senoj's mislaid Essay!"

He explained his intention of remaining a regular contributor to the magazine: "Whilst the present tale of *Philip* is passing through the press I am preparing another, on which I have worked at intervals for many years past, and which I hope to introduce in the ensuing year; and I have stipulated for the liberty of continuing the little Essays which have amused the public and the writer."

To be his successor, Smith tried to obtain Robert Browning, who had recently returned to England, following the death of his wife, and was renewing his friendship with Thackeray at many dinners and soirées. When Browning declined, and no other "great name" was available, an editorial committee was formed, consisting of Smith and two rank-and-file journalists.

In the same month as his resignation, Thackeray moved into his "Vanity Fair

House" in Palace Green. In his diary on March 8 he wrote a solemn little prayer: "I pray Almighty God that the words I write in this house may be pure and honest; that they be dictated by no personal spite, unworthy motive, or unjust greed for gain; that they may tell the truth as far as I know it; and tend to promote love and peace among men, for the sake of Christ our Lord."

The spaciousness of the rooms, not yet crowded with furniture, tempted him and his daughters to give an entertainment more like those of Dickens than like the former unpretentious dinners in Onslow Square. Thackeray retained a fondness for his one experiment in drama, *The Wolves and the Lamb* (as he now called it), and so an amateur performance of it was undertaken, with relations and friends in the cast. The invitation cards included his favorite pun of the moment, bidding the guests to the "W. Empty House." Although he could not be persuaded to take a part in the play, the author consented to appear on the stage in the final tableau and drink a silent toast to the audience, while an epilogue, which he had written for the occasion, was recited by Horace Twiss, who had played the lead.

In the new library, a special bookcase was devoted to volumes dealing with the eighteenth century. "Here I am going to write my greatest work, a history of the reign of Queen Anne," he explained to a visitor.

"When do you expect to begin it?"

"Probably as soon as I am done with *Philip*; but I am not sure I may not have to write another novel first. But the History will mature all the better for the delay. I want to *absorb* the authorities gradually, so that when I come to write, I shall be filled with the subject, and can sit down to a continuous narrative, without jumping up every moment to consult somebody. The History has been a pet project of mine for some years past. I'm slowly working up to the level of it, and I know that when I once begin I shall do it well."

In a letter to Dr John Skelton, who was doing research in the same field, he explained, "Queen Anne has long been my ambition, but she will take many a long year's labour, and I can't ask any other writer to delay on my account. At the beginning of the year I had prepared an announcement stating that I was engaged on that history, but kept it back, as it was necessary that I should pursue my old trade of novelist for some time yet to come. Meanwhile her image stands before St Paul's, for all the world to look at; and who knows but some one else may be before hand with both of us, and sketch her off while we are only laying the palette."

The distractions of removal were just as bad for his writing as editorial duties had been, and he did not get the May instalment of *Philip* finished until April 18. Immediately afterwards he went to Paris, with anything but good results; he had "no pleasure except going to see my kind relations in grief," as he wryly remarked; he wrote nothing; and he went through four days of such acute illness that he consulted a doctor, who told him flatly that he had only a brief time to live. The doom was received stoically. "I wasn't very sorry," he said in a letter to Mrs Baxter. After he came back to London, his own physician contradicted the diagnosis; but he was not sure whether to be gratified by the reprieve, or even whether to believe it. His friend William Follett Synge was staying with him on the eve of going to an appointment in the Sandwich Islands. In the library one day Thackeray said, "I want to tell you that I shall never see you again. I know this will grieve you; but look in that book, and you will find something that I'm sure will please and comfort you." It was the prayer that he had written upon taking possession of the house.

For a while his health seemed so much better that he felt in a mood to break new ground with his summer travels, and made tentative plans for a trip to St Petersburg. "It will pay for itself," he argued, "in a couple of papers that will be as easy to write as letters and won't wear and tear the brains." Meanwhile there were pleasant doings of the sort he liked best—dinners at the "Star and Garter" with Trollope or Leech, and a supper party of all the closest family friends to celebrate the engagement of his daughters' companion, Amy Crowe, to their cousin, Edward Thackeray, who had won the Victoria Cross in the Indian Mutiny.

He wondered, sometimes, why no suitors were paying attentions to his daughters, and blamed himself for not introducing them to any men under fifty; but he was happy in their devotion to him, and proud that they showed no ambition to shine in society. No longer finding much enjoyment in aristocratic company, he went to no houses where the girls were not invited; and as they refused to be patronized by great ladies, he gave up many of his former friends, and admired his daughters for being less worldly than he.

Annie, moreover, was making great headway with her career. Her first novel, *The Story of Elizabeth*, was coming out anonymously in *The Cornhill* as a serial, and Smith was so rapturous in his praise that Thackeray began to realize that her work was really good, quite apart from his natural bias in her favor.

On July 2, with a jubilant flourish of the pen, he wrote "Finis" to *Philip*. Just as had been the case with *Pendennis*, he had intended to bring retribution upon the villain but relented at the last minute; and instead of depicting Dr Firmin as drowning in a gruesome shipwreck he allowed him a wealthy marriage and a peaceful deathbed, all in two or three sentences, while the main attention was focused upon sudden prosperity for the hero. "Rather a lame ending," he called it, and critics have condemned it as a melodramatic use of the *deus ex machina*; but as a matter of fact it was based on an occurrence in the Lowther family, which Thackeray had sometime jotted down in his notebook for future use.

When the last page of the manuscript had gone to the printer, he felt strangely lonely. He had been looking forward to this moment for months, as his final emancipation. He was convinced that "the novel-writing vein is used up." And yet, after living for twenty months with these beings who were more real and vivid to him than the people he saw every day, and in whose imagined reality were interwoven all sorts of remembered strands of his own earlier life, he had a sense of bereavement, as if loved friends had died.

The next evening he took his daughters to the *Barbiere di Siviglia*, and enjoyed a good sound nap in the back of the box. The day following he applied himself happily to drawing a picture, though aware that it was "very bad;" and in the afternoon he took the girls in their neat new carriage down to Twickenham for a gay garden party at Orléans House, where he looked with his usual ironic sympathy at the make-believe court surrounding the exiled Duc d'Aumale, and had a chat with his old friend Mrs Norton. On the third day of his liberation, he was ready to welcome the arrival of proofs to be corrected, and a reminder from Smith that the next *Roundabout* was overdue.

CHAPTER 24

All Dreams Fulfilled

AT THE AGE of fifty Thackeray had reached the fulfillment of all his dreams. The years of nomadic restlessness were at an end. Ever since he left India, when he was six, he had been essentially rootless—the various houses in London had been little more than caravanserais. Now he owned a home, built according to his demands and handsome enough to fulfill his ideas of luxury. Having earned the thirty thousand pounds to replace the inheritance he had squandered, he was able to give up the wearisome labor of editorship and to see some promise of escaping even from the creation of novels, which had always been an agonizing strain upon his nerves. The placid writing of history had beckoned to him for years as the future solace of his retirement. He was at last what he had always yearned to be—a gentleman of independent means and literary tastes, dwelling in the mellow atmosphere of the eighteenth century and preparing to apply himself to a suitably elegant hobby.

And yet the yoke could not be abruptly thrown off. In the announcement of his retirement from the editorship he had informed the public that he was already "preparing" the novel that would succeed *Philip*; and three or four days after writing the last lines of that story he committed himself again in a Roundabout Paper, *De Finibus*, by remarking that the only way he could reconcile himself to ending the existence of the characters in a story was to make an immediate start on the next.

The novel that he had so confidently described himself as "preparing" was none other than the historical romance of the fifteenth century, which he had started to write under the encouragement of Barham, twenty years before. It has always lingered in the back of his mind: in 1858 he had told Motley that it would be his masterpiece. To prepare for it, he had read intermittently in Froissart and Monstrelet and Brantôme, and sent the obedient Langley plodding through reference books to accumulate notes on armor and weapons and furniture. He hopefully looked forward to an episode (duly based on source evidence) wherein his hero should ride into the battle of Agincourt on a cow, owing to a shortage of horses; but that event would have to be late in the story.

Although comfortable in the new house, he was restless and did not sleep well. Sometimes in the summer dawns he would get up about four o'clock, tiptoe to the library, take a book from the shelves, and become so absorbed that when the girls came down to breakfast three or four hours later they would find him still standing there, beside the book-case. As the winter approached, the prospect of Amy Crowe's marriage disturbed him with its threat of disruption to the cozy family circle, and on the day of the ceremony he slipped away from home in misery to spend the afternoon at the studio of his young artist-friend Millais.

An intenser grief immediately followed. News came from America that Sally Hampton had died in Charleston, and that her family had not been able to obtain permission to enter the Confederate territory in time to see her alive. Thackeray's agony of spirit expressed itself in bitter denunciation of those who were conducting the war. The northern cause had grown more and more unpopular in England, with Lincoln caricatured and reviled as its arch-villain. In spite of a natural fondness for the easy-going hospitality of the South, Thackeray had tried to remain on good terms with all the Americans in London. He had paid his respects to the Minister, Charles Francis Adams, who was enduring many slights in his effort to keep England neutral, and had made friends with the minister's sardonic son, Henry, especially when he found that he, too, was a friend and admirer of Sally Hampton.

During this sad winter Henry Adams one evening went to a reception at Sir Henry Holland's. In the entrance hall a massive figure was struggling into an overcoat, chuckling because he had blundered into the wrong party. It was Thackeray, who had been invited to another house in the same square, and had not realized his mistake until he shook hands with Sir Henry and noticed that he was not the right host. When Thackeray saw Adams, the laughter faded from his face, and he poured out his grief and rage over the Baxters' tragedy. "In speaking of it," Adams records, "Thackeray's voice trembled and his eyes filled with tears." The coarse cruelty of Lincoln and his hirelings was notorious. He never doubted that the Federals made a business of harrowing the tenderest feelings of women—particularly of women—in order to punish their opponents. On quite insufficient evidence he burst into violent reproach. Had Adams carried in his pocket the proofs that the reproach was unjust, he would have gained nothing by showing them. By no means for the first time in Thackeray's life, all rational judgment had been swept away in a flood of personal emotion.

Nor was this his only contact with the ill effects of the War between the States. In November, when he was recovering from a sharp bout of illness, a clergyman of his neighborhood called upon him with the request that he be one of the speakers at a public meeting in Kensington to raise funds for the victims of the "cotton famine" —the depression that was ravaging Lancashire as a result of the blockade against the South. Thackeray declined on the grounds that he was not well enough even to attend the meeting, let alone speak.

The clergyman explained that he did not want a long address, as he had plenty of orators available. "In Kensington," he went on, "the great difficulty is to collect an audience. If you will only let me print your name in my handbills, I'll be sure of a large attendance, and I can depend on my orators to call forth contributions."

Amused at this candor, Thackeray replied, "Though I'm far from well, you may depend upon me. If I'm alive I shall be with you." He was greeted with loud applause by the large audience, made a brief but well-considered speech, and headed the subscription list with a donation of fifty pounds.

More and more his thoughts turned back to early associations. He made a point of going to Charterhouse for Founder's Day, in the course of which he entertained a knot of boys with a lively account of his great fight with Venables, and the "scrunch" of the blow that broke his nose. Later in the evening he dropped in at Evans's, and noticed two Cambridge undergraduates (one of them Richard Jebb) whom he recognized as having just seen at the Charterhouse dinner. At once he sat down at their table, chatted to them until their shyness wore off, and ended by asking them to dine at Palace Green the next day.

Another pleasant link with his schooldays was the fact that John Leech and his family now came to live in Kensington, not far away. The day they were moving into their house, Annie Thackeray happened to be walking home along the Kensington Road, and met her father carefully carrying two large blue china pots, which she recognized as being taken from his own study. "I'm going to see if they won't stand upon Leech's dining-room chimney-piece," he explained. The girls had never become reconciled to his habit of giving away the prettiest ornaments of the house, and so Annie followed him in the faint hope that they might not be suitable. Unconscious of the amused glances of passers-by, Thackeray carried the pots to Leech's house, marched up to the dining-room, and set them on the mantel-shelf. "I knew they would stand there," he announced.

He was invited by Monckton Milnes to spend the Easter holidays at Fryston. Their college companion Spedding was also there, and the three reveled in memories of happy old times. There was a violent gale one night, and the finest tree on the estate was blown down. When Thackeray went out with his friends the next morning to inspect the damage, he was overheard to mutter, with a gloomy shake of his head, "An omen, an omen!"

By this time he had given up hope of being able to handle the fifteenth-century romance, and in the early months of 1863 he began to think about a story of the period he knew better. He discussed it with his daughters as it took shape in his mind: it was to date from 1763, with a sailor for a hero, and a vigorous plot full of sea-warfare and highway robbery. Aware that *Philip* had been weakened by the slightness of its story, he was determined to make a success and restore his reputation. He forced himself to write at least a few lines every day, even if he was ill; he carried the first drafts about with him, and would pull them out of his pocket and pore over them at any spare minute. Even the names of the characters were mulled over; his heroine was first Agnes, and then Henriette or Blanche, and finally Agnes again. His hero began as Blaise Merian, and eventually became Denis Duval.

For the Duval family he used many traits of his own naval ancestors and those of his great-grandmother's various old neighbors in Fareham. In spite of having this traditional material, and his previous studies in the period, he soon found difficulties over questions of fact, owing to his ignorance of nautical matters. He sometimes wished that he could arrange to take a trip on a man-of-war to learn the technical terms, but he had to content himself with what he could find in books.

His daughter's novel had finished its serial publication, and in March was issued in book form. Thackeray's delight was so intense that it prevented him from reading the story. "I tried to," he told Smith, "but I broke down." Fanny Kemble sought to persuade him to make a fresh start on it, insisting that it would give him pleasure. "It would not," he replied. "It would tear my guts out!"

The book was reviewed harshly in *The Athenaeum* on April 25, with the accusation that it dealt with "a painful subject," and Thackeray went into one of his blind furies. He was to preside that night at the Shakespeare dinner of Our Club. Among the members of the club were the editor of *The Athenaeum*, Hepworth Dixon, and one of his chief assistants, Cordy Jeaffreson. Thackeray made a brief, constrained speech, announced that he was unwell, and gave up the chair early in the proceedings. When Jeaffreson spoke to him, an angry glare was the only response, and later it was reported that after leaving the hotel Thackeray spoke bitterly of Jeaffreson as "a man who, in order to give me pain, has slapped my daughter's face."

Jeaffreson, having regarded himself as rather a protégé of Thackeray, was hurt at being unjustly accused of writing the review, which was actually the work of Geraldine Jewsbury, the catty friend of Mrs Carlyle. But as the anonymity of reviewers had to be respected, the misunderstanding could not be easily repaired.

Within two months Thackeray had an opportunity of showing the bitterness of his wrath. Ambitious plans were on foot for a celebration of the tercentenary of Shakespeare. Hepworth Dixon was secretary of the committee, and various celebrities were invited to be vice-presidents, one of the four representatives of literature being Thackeray. To the invitation, which was signed by Dixon, Thackeray vouchsafed no reply. A second letter was sent, this time signed by the assistant secretary, who happened to be Jeaffreson. Again cold silence. After some time had elapsed, the matter was discussed at a meeting of the committee, and Henry Vizetelly proposed that a new invitation be extended. Dixon and Jeaffreson objected that the committee would lose face if it persisted after such discourteous treatment; and their faction, "composed of contributors to *The Athenaeum* and timid literary men who trembled for their next book," was strong enough to defeat the motion.

Thackeray, meanwhile, was making but feeble headway with the new novel. "For the last ten days I have been almost *non compos mentis*," he said in a letter written in May. "When I am in labour with a book I don't quite know what happens. I sit for hours before my paper, not doing my book, but incapable of doing anything else, and thinking upon that subject always, waking with it, walking about with it, and going to bed with it. Oh, the struggle and bothers—oh, the throes and pains about this trumpery!"

He went out of his way just then to pay a tribute to an old friend. George Cruikshank was aged and eccentric, out of fashion as an artist and laughed at by the public for his fanatical war against liquor. Very different had been the days when Thackeray had humbly sought him out for instructions in black-and-white caricaturing, and when they had foregathered in many a merry tavern dinner. Cruikshank was giving an exhibition of his cartoon, "Worship of Bacchus, or the Drinking Customs of Society," and the little gallery was usually pathetically empty. Thackeray dropped in one day, looked at the pictures with kindly gravity, and went home to write a review for *The Times*. He found difficulty in deciding what to say, and paced his library in impatience.

"If I were you, Papa," suggested Minny, "I'd write all round the subject and say as little as possible about it."

"Thank you, my dear," was the reply. And so the essay was chiefly devoted to reminiscences of older and happier days.

During the summer he was in fairly good health and spirits. On June 16 he dined at the Garrick with John Blackwood, Shirley Brooks, E. S. Dallas (a *Times* reviewer), and Charles Reade, and they had "capital fun." Although both were devoted members of the Garrick, Thackerary and Reade never became intimate. Being positive that he was the greatest living novelist, Reade considered Thackeray overrated; and being a blunt, contentious man, he suspected him of insincerity.

As some early scenes of *Denis Duval* were to be laid in Rye and Winchelsea, Thackeray made an expedition to those old towns, and came back with a sketch or two and his imagination stimulated by their picturesqueness.

The two young daughters of his cousin, William Ritchie, who had died the year before, spent the summer with the Thackerays, and one of them wrote her recollections. "Mr Thackeray was just then very happy, finding himself once more, after a long interval, in the full vein of historical romance. . . The atmosphere of *Denis Duval* permeated everything. . . I remember when the story of the poor Countess of Saverne absorbed him. 'The Countess is growing very mad,' he said one day; 'last night St Sebastian appeared to her stuck all over with arrows—looking like a *fricandeau*,' he added gravely, though with a mock shudder. . .

"The inspiration sometimes had to be waited for and caught at the flood. The carriage came to the door and waited, waited an hour, an hour and a half, two hours. Mr Thackeray wrote on. His daughters only said what a good thing it was that every ten minutes made a page of Papa's handwriting. At last he came, and got into the carriage with us, all in the best of spirits. As we drove towards Wimbleton or Richmond he would read *every* name on the small shops as we passed; he wanted Christian names for certain smugglers to come into the story. He commented on all the names."

In September Minny was in Scotland, and her father was lonely. "We three get on so comfortably together," he wrote to Dr Brown, "that the house is not the house when one is away . . . I have done no work for a whole year, and must now set to at this stale old desk, or there will be no beef and mutton. I have spent too much money on this fine house, besides gimcracks, furniture, china, plate, the deuce knows what . . . If I don't mistake there was a man who lived at Abbotsford over-housed himself. I am not in debt, thank my stars, but instead of writing to you why am I not writing the history of Denis Duval, Esq., Admiral of the White Squadron? Because I don't known anything about the sea and seamen, and get brought up by my ignorance every other page; above all, because I am lazy, so lazy that a couple of dozen would do me good."

Ever since the unpleasantness in April he had stayed away from Our Club, and when activities began in the autumn his friend Hamstede was determined to get him back again. Thackeray refused with the explanation that he had resolved never again to have friendly relations with the editor of *The Athenaeum*, and if he came to the club he might encounter him. Hamstede replied that he was certain a majority of the club would support a request to Dixon to resign; and that if Dixon refused, the majority would dissolve the club and reconstitute it without him. Thackeray's answer was that "he had already driven one man out of a club for a personal reason, and was not so satisfied with the consequences of the affair to be in a humor to repeat the operation for the discomfiture of Hepworth Dixon."

Henry Vizetelly had been so annoyed with the Shakespeare Tercentenary Committee for defeating his motion to resume relations with Thackeray that he published a report of the affair in the *Illustrated Times*. The dispute was thus thrown open to the public. Laurence Oliphant denounced the committee for ever putting the invitation in the hands of "the David and Jonathan of a literary organ whose columns had been disfigured by a virulent and indecent criticism, needlessly cruel, offensive, and unjust—on Miss Thackeray's charming novel." Shirley Brooks, one of Thackeray's favorites among the *Punch* staff and one of his staunchest adherents in the quarrel, wrote crossly to Dallas: "I wish . . . that Thackeray would leave off caring about the snarls of these little Bohemian curs. They know he writhes, and therefore snap whenever they can . . . Shakespeare be blowed. It's all cackle, but one daren't say so, except to the elect." Some of the "elect," under the leadership of Brooks and Theodore Martin, proceeded to protest so strongly that the eventual result was the collapse of the committee and all its plans.

At the beginning of November Thackeray was busy writing a poem. "I was in labour with some verses," he wrote to E. V. Kenealy; "and when I'm in that condition, and until my little bantling is born, I neglect my duties, my letters—even my invitations to dinner. My baby finally made its appearance last night."

He had been unwilling to undertake the serial publication of the new novel until he had adequate material in hand, but by this time he felt free to allow *The Cornhill* to announce in the December number that *Denis Duval* would begin in the next.

About this time he renewed memories of a chapter of his youth by spending an afternoon with his daughters at the Temple, attending service in the Temple church and wandering in the garden until twilight, after which they had tea at the chambers of a young friend, Herman Merivale. All who saw Thackeray during these days found him exceptionally mellow and genial. He was delighted to receive a message from the Benchers of the Middle Temple that they were about to elect him to their number—one of the few official honors ever offered to him. But he was equally touched by spontaneous recognitions. When he came home one afternoon he remarked that he could not get accustomed to the number of people whom he did not know but who seemed to know him in the street, and took off their hats as he passed.

His days were full of the usual amenities. Charles Mackay saw him one evening with Leech at Evans's Supper Rooms. "They both complained of illness, but neither of them looked ill enough to justify the belief that anything ailed them beyond a temporary indisposition. Leech was particularly despondent." Mackay, who was about to start on a tour of the United States, recommended six months across the Atlantic as a cure for his overwrought nerves. Leech protested that Bradbury & Evans would not like his leaving his duties with *Punch* for so long.

"Nonsense," said Thackeray. "B & E would highly approve, provided you sent them sketches. *I* think it a good idea, and you might put £5000 in your pocket by the trip. The Americans have never been truly portrayed, as you would portray them. The niggers alone would be a little fortune to you." But Leech only gloomily shook his head.

On December 12, as usual, Thackeray attended the Founder's Day at Charterhouse. After occupying his customary back seat in the old chapel, he listened to the oration in the Governor's room, and as he walked up to the orator with his contribution he was greeted with deafening applause. Afterwards at the banquet he sat beside Leech, and in a characteristic vein proposed the toast to the noble foundation. To one of the company, however, he confessed that he was "anticipating recourse to a small surgical operation."

Trollope had a pleasant chat with him a day or two later. "I sat with him for half an hour talking about himself," Trollope says. "I never knew him pleasanter or more at ease as to his bodily ailments." About the same time we hear of him being very cheerful at a dinner at the Garrick, "pretending to incite one old friend to give a party of an excessively gay description, in order, as he said, that we might fancy ourselves all young again."

One evening in the same week he and Annie dined with Dr Merriman, who had been one of his physicians at the time of his first severe illness, nearly fifteen years before. The doctor noticed at once that he was not looking well. "I would only have turned out," Thackeray said, "to come to you as an old friend." Among the guests there chanced to be two people he was eager to meet, Jean Ingelow and Lady Barrow (daughter of John Wilson Croker), and he soon became his usual cheerful self. "My friend stayed late," Merriman says, "his daughter going on to some other party, and I strolled up Young Street with him. We halted by Number 13, when he alluded to old times and happy days there; he told me *Vanity Fair* was his greatest work and *The Cane-bottomed Chair* his favorite ballad."

Denis Duval was beginning to take hold of his imagination with the same vivid sense of reality that he had felt with *Esmond.* His neighbor, Admiral FitzRoy, found data for him at the Admiralty about the fight between the *Bon Homme Richard* and the *Serapis*, and Thackeray was so carried away after a morning's study of it that he was not able to eat lunch, but described the engagement to his daughters with as much enthusiasm as if he had been an eye-witness.

His written account of it was interrupted midway. In a note to Smith he explained: "I was just going to be taken prisoner by Paul Jones when I had to come to bed. If I could get a month's ease I could finish the eight numbers handsomely with the marriage of Denis and Agnes, after the capture of Toulon by the English."

During the next week he seemed tired, and stayed at home more than usual, without carrying the story any further. When he took a friend upstairs to his room to see some book, the visitor was surprised to notice how he gasped for breath after climbing the easy staircase. To his daughters he seemed much the same as usual, but his mother became gravely alarmed.

On one of these days, as he was going into the Athenaeum Club, he met Dickens on the stairs. As usual, they gave no sign of recognition, but a moment later Thackeray turned back and hurried after Dickens with outstretched hand, saying that "he could no longer bear their being ill friends." They exchanged a warm handclasp and a few cordial remarks. "He told me that he had been in bed three days," Dickens recorded; "that after these attacks he was troubled with cold shiverings, 'which quite took the power of work out of him,' and that he had it in his mind to try a new remedy which he laughingly described. He was very cheerful and looked very bright."

Carlyle had a glimpse of him a day or two later. "I was riding in the dusk, heavy of heart, along by the Serpentine and Hyde Park, when some human brother from a chariot, with a young lady in it, threw me a shower of salutations. I looked up—it was Thackeray with his daughter."

On December 21 he attended the funeral of his cousin, Lady Rodd. The same day he was at the house of Mr and Mrs Charles Collins, "in famous spirits and full of fun," as Collins told his brother Wilkie. Mrs Charles Collins was Katie Dickens, and the young couple were among the closest friends of the Thackeray household.

As well as continuing to visit his clubs and the homes of his friends, Thackeray was as ready as ever to invite people to dine at his house. An article in the *Morning Star*, championing his side of the current controversy, pleased him so much that he made inquiries and learned that it was the work of a young Irish journalist, Justin McCarthy, who had been admiring him from a distance for some time. Thackeray sent him an invitation to dinner, with the promise that he would meet two or three other literary men.

On December 23 he felt ill and remained in bed. *The Times* was sent up to him, and later he had Annie in for instructions about writing some letters. During the day he worked on the proofs of the first instalment of *Denis Duval*.

When his servant came to wake him on the morning of Christmas eve, his dead body was stretched out, face upward, with his arms above his head and his hands grasping the bed-rail in a final paroxysm of pain.

x x x x x x x

The news cast gloom over the Christmas of all his friends. It was brought to a merry party of the *Punch* colleagues by one of his oldest comrades, "Ponny" Mayhew. They all remembered that it was twenty years that month since he had first joined the weekly conference around the editorial dinner-table. "I'll tell you what we'll do," said Mayhew; "we'll sing the dear old boy's *Mahogany Tree*. He'd like it." They all stood up while Mayhew sang in his clear tenor, and each one joined in with a breaking voice, whenever he happened to remember the words.

The tidings reached Gadshill when Dickens was preparing to receive guests for Christmas day. With a stricken face, he met two of them at the station. "What is it?" asked Marcus Stone.

"Thackeray is dead," he replied, with a choke in his voice.

"I know you must feel it very deeply," said Stone, "as you and he were not on friendly terms."

Dickens put his hand on his friend's arm. "Thank God, my boy," he answered, "we were." And he told of their handclasp at the foot of the Athenaeum stairs.

The Benchers of the Middle Temple, denied the privilege of electing him as they had planned, wished to bury him within their precincts, close to Goldsmith. The request was declined and the funeral was held at the vast Kensal Green cemetery, where his infant daughter had been buried a quarter-century before.

His friend Millais, the painter, complained that the ceremony was "badly managed. A crowd of women were there—from curiosity, I suppose,—dressed in all colours, and round the grave scarlet and blue feathers shone out prominently. Indeed, the true mourners and friends could not get near, and intimate friends who were present had to be hustled into their places during the ceremony of interment. . . There was a great lack of what is called 'high society,' which I was surprised at. None of that class, of whom he knew so many, were present. The painters were *nearly all* there—more even than the literary men."

William Howard Russell made an identical comment. "Such a gathering! Dickens, thin and worn, so rejoiced me by saying he had lately been speaking to Thackeray of familiar topics . . . The Garrick almost whipped of its cream, but not a swell, not one of the order. Little he cared!"

Dickens later remarked that when he looked at him as he lay in his coffin, "he wondered that the figure he had known in life as one of such noble presence could seem so shrunken and wasted."

The verdict of that "high society" which had ignored the funeral was uttered by one of its chosen spokesmen. The supercilious Henry Greville, mentioning the death in his diary, commented: "I believe he was a kind-hearted man, much beloved by his friends; but though at times entertaining, he was too restless and susceptible to be a very pleasant member of society in the long run."

A fairer judgment was that of Carlyle, who had spoken hard things of him in his time, and yet had become a firm friend with the passage of the years: "He had many fine qualities, no guile or malice against any mortal; a big mass of a soul, but not strong in proportion; a beautiful vein of genius lay struggling about in him."

x x x x x x x

There remained the family which he had loved so dearly and for which he had labored and worried so much. His mother survived him by fifty-one weeks, died suddenly at the age of seventy-two, and was laid in the same grave. His daughter Minny was married in 1867 to a rising young critic, Leslie Stephen, and died after eight years of happy married life. Annie Thackeray at the age of forty married her second cousin, Richmond Ritchie, who was seventeen years younger and had first proposed to her when he was a schoolboy at Eton. He rose to high office in the government service and became a Knight of the Bath. Lady Ritchie lived to be a matriarch of eighty-two, author of a score of books as gentle and wise as herself.

Newspaper readers were astonished, on January 11, 1894, to read a brief obituary notice of Isabella Getkin Thackeray, who had passed away at her place of retirement in Essex at the age of seventy-six. She had survived her husband by more than thirty years.

INDEX

INDEX

397